The Private Is Political

THE PRIVATE
IS POLITICAL

NETWORKED PRIVACY
AND SOCIAL MEDIA

• • •

ALICE E. MARWICK

Yale

UNIVERSITY PRESS

New Haven and London

Published with assistance from the foundation established in memory
of Amasa Stone Mather of the Class of 1907, Yale College.

Yale University Press books may be purchased in quantity for educational, business, or promotional use. For information, please e-mail
sales.press@yale.edu (U.S. office) or sales@yaleup.co.uk (U.K. office).

Set in Gotham and Adobe Garamond types by Newgen North America.
Printed in the United States of America.

Library of Congress Control Number: 2022944130
ISBN 978-0-300-22962-2 (hardcover : alk. paper)

A catalogue record for this book is available from the British Library.

This paper meets the requirements of
ANSI/NISO Z39.48-1992 (Permanence of Paper).

10 9 8 7 6 5 4 3 2 1

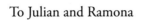To Julian and Ramona

Contents

1

The Private Is Political

Ravi and Diego, twenty-five and twenty-one years old, respectively, are men of color born and raised in New York City. They share a love of *Star Wars*, art, and video games. Diego is a technology enthusiast, but Ravi avoids all social media, calling it "poison." In a study that my colleagues and I conducted, he enrolled under a pseudonym and refused to give his exact age or race, telling Diego, "Let's face it, we're in a day where everyone can just spy on each other. There's such a thing as social media stalkers, and if they can't do it, they can always get a friend. You block one person; you can't block their whole friend network." The conversation continued:

DIEGO: Then they make a new account, or—
RAVI: Yeah, or if they're one of—you're connected to this person through a personal friend, there's no such thing as "this person is never going to find out." There's just absolutely no such thing. Let's say this person you can trust not to let them know. All right, fine. When this person leaves their phone on the table for two seconds to go to the bathroom, it takes two seconds for this person that you don't want them to know anything about you suddenly finding out everything you don't want them to know. It takes two seconds.
DIEGO: A lot of relationships have been ruined that way.
RAVI: Everything can fall apart in two seconds. That's it. You abstain, or you control.

Diego and Ravi recognize that it is impossible to strictly regulate how and where information travels. Ravi, despite staying off Facebook, YouTube,

Tumblr, Twitter, and LinkedIn, still imagines a scenario in which a friend's unsecured phone causes his life to "fall apart." The techno-optimist Diego deals with his anxieties around privacy by employing increasingly intense technical solutions such as carrying multiple phones, using the Dark Web, and installing virtual private networks to browse online.

Both men know that what other people share about them is outside their control. Ravi understands that information travels through social connections—that people talk about each other. To maintain a level of privacy he is comfortable with, he feels he must trust every person with whom he shares information, as well as their entire social network. He gloomily concludes that his only options are "abstain" or "control," saying, "the only thing you can ever actually control . . . is yourself, and you've got to control what you let out into the world." Knowing that anything he posts online can spread in unexpected ways, he abstains completely from social media. But as we will see, even this extreme solution is not enough. Ravi does not mention—and may not be aware of—compromising technologies such as "big data" assemblages that aggregate and combine data sources, often without the subject's knowledge.[1]

Growing up Dominican in a heavily policed neighborhood in New York City under the "stop-and-frisk" policy of the aughts, Diego experienced continual privacy violations. He deploys a creative variety of methods to achieve privacy, such as disabling his phone's SIM card so that he can move around the city undetected. Choosing to use social media's amplification to promote himself and his projects, Diego focuses on avoiding state surveillance and outwitting people and organizations that might want to learn things about him he does not want them to know. He needs technology to collaborate with other artists and raise his online profile but knows firsthand that his race and socioeconomic status make his privacy more precarious.

Ravi and Diego, like most of the other people I spoke with for this book, think of privacy as *the ability to control how information about them flows.* But it is not actually possible to do this. In explaining why, I make three claims in this book: first, privacy is networked; second, it is unequally distributed; and third, these concepts are connected. Thinking about privacy as *networked* exposes our powerlessness to command how our personal information spreads through networks that we can never fully control.

The term "network" can mean all sorts of things, but I use it here to describe three levels of connections, all insecure. There are the social connections made explicit by social technologies; the behavioral networks mapped and traced through consumer-level tracking and aggregation of big data; and perhaps most powerful and invisible, the deeply rooted and interconnected networks of surveillance by which the state controls its citizens through education, employment, social services, and criminal justice. As Ravi says, the agency to control the flow of information—to determine who receives it and in what context—is necessary to personal privacy, but when privacy is networked, this ability is always compromised. Networked privacy is enabled not only by social platforms and the actors behind them but by the very act of digitization. Digitization transforms ephemeral information like who your friends are or what you buy into something visible, traceable, and measurable. *Networked privacy* is a new framework for understanding privacy in a world saturated with social media, state and corporate surveillance, and big data technologies.

Because privacy is networked, individual control over information flows is impossible. Legal and technical protections are completely inadequate, sometimes intentionally so. In many cases, privacy loss has been weaponized. Being doxed, harassed, or called out are common online experiences, and these forms of digital abuse often involve public exposure of very personal thoughts and images. As technologies commingle, they require people to adopt more intense and strategic forms of silence and hiding. The tension between the desire to share and the desire to control that sharing—the back-and-forth between forced exposure and forced concealment—is at the heart of networked privacy. (As the privacy historian Sarah Igo points out, these dueling desires often coexist in the same person.)[2]

Thinking about privacy as networked also allows us to recognize that privacy and its inverse, publicity, are distributed unequally and always have been. While concerns over data breaches or hackers regularly make the news, public discussion often ignores power differentials in race, class, gender, and sexuality that affect how privacy is experienced and addressed. In the modern United States, some people benefit from being seen and some do not, and some are allowed to remain invisible while others are forced to reveal themselves.[3] The young Black woman courting viral fame on TikTok may be judged more harshly for it when she applies to college than her white classmate.[4] A schizophrenic man could be denied a disability claim on the basis of his Instagram photos, and his pregnant neighbor might be asked intrusive questions about her sex life while applying for Medicaid.[5] We often use "privacy" as shorthand for a wide variety of harmful power imbalances brought about by the spread of information. It is an umbrella term that people use to determine the limits of information collection. In this book, I explore how the intersections between social categorizations like class, gender, race, and sexuality affect both how society views privacy and publicity and how the harms of privacy violations affect people differently.

I encourage you to think of privacy as personal and political rather than an abstract concept. When we scroll through an article detailing the ever-more-granular information that social platforms collect about their users or receive an alert telling us to change our password because of a security breach, many of us do not know how to respond. We believe privacy is important, but we do not know how to protect ourselves from leaks of information that large, shadowy corporations have collected from us. Many people suspect that technological innovations like social media, digital assistants like Alexa and Siri, genetic ancestry testing, and GPS may compromise or diminish their privacy, but they do not know how it affects them directly. Others shrug it off. Nothing can be done, and I have nothing to hide, so why worry?

But privacy is intimate. It is about our bodies, our homes, our friends, and our family. It is related to where we feel safe walking at night, whether we censor ourselves online to avoid losing our job, and our vague sense of uneasiness when we give our credit card number online, if we can get a credit card at all. All these things depend on our ability to control the dissemination of information about ourselves. We feel angry or "creeped out" when people know things about us that we never told them, and we are not always sure how they got the information. We may have to endure privacy violations at school, at work, even in our own homes and intimate relationships. These harms are felt very differently based on who we are. To fully understand privacy, we must center the perspectives of the vulnerable rather than the concerns of technology companies, policy makers, or the state. This bottom-up approach starts with the people for whom privacy violations have a real material impact: those who must maintain their privacy to achieve their personal goals and avoid unwanted consequences.[6]

Privacy as Networked

The basic argument of this book is that it is difficult, if not impossible, to avoid privacy violations in a networked information landscape. The broad, connected audiences of social media and the aggregation common to big data challenge our previous ideas about privacy, which mostly revolve around the individual.

We are all part of networks. A circle of friends is a network; so is a family. These networks are part of larger systems of connections. A school is a network of students and teachers, each of whom constitutes what network scientists call a "node." The school is part of a district, another network. Each person in the school has a family, friends, and other connections that extend far beyond the schoolyard. The school might use Google Classrooms, individual students are on TikTok or Instagram, and their teachers may be on LinkedIn and Facebook. Everyone we connect with is the center of their own network, but we do not know who else is in it.[7] You tell a friend a secret, she tells someone else, and it could pass through nodes in a dozen networks.

The ability to create content on social media has given regular people access to potentially enormous audiences.[8] These audiences can be reached intentionally, as when a YouTuber or Instagram influencer works to increase their number of followers and views, or unintentionally, as when a tweet goes viral or a video taken by a cellphone spreads beyond its origins. In both cases, people must grapple with challenges of publicity that previously only celebrities and politicians dealt with. The people who view this content are also connected. Fans create Facebook groups to discuss podcasts or blogs, using the same tools for content creation and participation that creators do. This ability to talk back to creators may be tremendously fulfilling for audience members and artists alike, but it has drawbacks, as we will see when we discuss forced publicity and online harassment.[9]

Social media platforms differ from interpersonal communication media, like letters and landline phones, because they are designed to facilitate sharing. The same technologies that enable sharing enable leaking, the unintentional sharing of information. While interpersonal digital technologies like WhatsApp, Facebook Messenger, and text messaging seem to allow greater privacy than large platforms like YouTube or Twitter, the ability to screenshot, forward, and copy messages and distribute them at scale means that a message meant to remain between friends may easily find a large audience. And social media is by definition social. People talk about each other both online and offline: they gossip and spread rumors as they always have, and now they also tag people in photos and videos, "check in" with their friends, and post "Memories" and "throwback Thursday" pictures. Social media makes connections between individuals explicit. It maps out social groups, making entire networks visible and thus vulnerable to other actors. Even someone who has carefully chosen to avoid social media can have a presence on Facebook or Instagram.

These complex dynamics make it clear that privacy can no longer be thought of as individual and defensible; it is deeply social, contextual, and fragile.[10] Our networks are only as safe as our chattiest contact, and our cultures, social groups, and families of origin have norms around information sharing that may not match our own. "I come from a family of oversharers," said Paul, a focus-group participant. Even if he meticulously locked down his Facebook and Twitter profiles, he knew his mom and aunt would reveal information about him online without his consent.

The technical affordances of social media further complicate things. When Instagram or Telegram changes its privacy settings, we are reminded that networked technologies are, as the media theorist Wendy Chun argues, leaky by design. They connect disparate nodes.[11] But these leaky technologies do not mesh with the way we communicate. Our communication choices are affected by the media we use, the audiences we speak to, the discursive frameworks we have available, and the spaces in which we speak. We talk differently to our friends than to our family; we speak differently in church than in a bar; we write differently on Twitter than on LinkedIn. We use different words, different tones of voice, different emoji. Social media enables information to spread quickly and seamlessly among these contexts, while it obscures whom information is shared with. If a user cannot tell whom they are speaking to online, they cannot fully understand the context and cannot shape information in a way that maintains their desired level of privacy or that is appropriate for their audience. A white person comfortable making a racist remark to like-minded others may be dismayed to face larger consequences when their slurs are made public; the political viewpoints of a socialist TikTok creator might seem outrageous or strange when publicized in right-wing media.

We need a theory of privacy that is suitable for this landscape, not one formulated for an era of photography, newspapers, and telephones. Overwhelmingly, in the United States, online privacy is framed as a matter of *individual responsibility.*[12] We believe that if something posted on Twitter, Instagram, or even supposedly ephemeral platforms like Snapchat leaks beyond its intended context, it is the fault of the person who posted it—not the people who leaked it, the entities that used it, or the platforms designed to encourage such posting. Mothers are shamed for posting pictures of their children online when those images are used without consent by facial-recognition companies or stolen and placed on advertisements.[13] When hackers posted the phone numbers of half a billion Facebook users online, a Facebook spokesperson blamed users for failing to keep their privacy settings up-to-date.[14] When Representative Katie Hill was forced to resign after her ex-husband released nude photos of her, Nancy Pelosi said she should have been "careful" since "appearances on social media can come back to haunt you."[15] Both the legal system and the technological protections available to users are predicated on this model. Privacy in the United States is an individual right, and in social media, privacy settings are configurable at the individual user level.[16]

This book argues that despite this assignment of responsibility, most online privacy violations are virtually impossible for an individual to avoid. Social media software, large-scale government and corporate surveillance, and data-mining mechanisms regularly and systemically aggregate and spread personal information. Just as neoliberal philosophy blinds us to the structural underpinnings of poverty by putting the onus on the individual, making people accountable when their privacy is violated erases the structural underpinnings of those violations.[17] In this book, I highlight these structural underpinnings to offer an alternative framework to be used in technology development and information policy.

The theory of networked privacy maintains that information is revealed within a particular context—a group of friends at dinner, a platform like TikTok or WeChat, an online community—and flows from its origin through networked social groups and big data technologies to unforeseen contexts and audiences.[18] This flow through the network is often experienced as a privacy violation, as a loss of agency, or as something "creepy," a term people often use when they feel that a social norm has been breached.[19] Beyond mere feelings of creepiness, such privacy violations can create deep problems for people. They can cause interpersonal or romantic conflict, cost one's job or apartment, or even lead to arrest. These harms are often experienced most acutely by people at the margins in other aspects of life.[20] (Note, for instance, how wealth and privilege often protect people who have been "canceled.")

To prevent these consequences, people try to maintain their privacy boundaries by establishing norms and rules.[21] Knowing that technical mechanisms for privacy protection often fail—screenshots, for instance, circumvent most social platforms' privacy settings—they ask, "Please don't put this picture on Facebook" or "Don't tell anyone I'm thinking of getting divorced." But given big data technologies and the networked audience of social media, it is impossible to negotiate these rules with every member of the audience or even know who this audience is. Social obligations often do not extend beyond close friends and family members, and not everyone has the same ideals of information sharing. This lack of control can make people feel frustrated or resigned, aware of a privacy violation but feeling helpless to prevent it—a kind of resignation that is sometimes mistaken for apathy.

Privacy as Unequally Distributed

The second argument in this book is that while the individual model depends on all people possessing the same right to privacy, in practice, privacy is unequally distributed. To understand how and why, we must understand the origins of the right to privacy in the United States and its link to inequalities of gender, class, and race.

A Feminist History of Privacy

The US second-wave feminist slogan "The personal is political" emphasized that individual experiences of sexism were manifestations of cultural misogyny and systemic gender inequality. I argue that our experiences of privacy are similar. In the United States and many Western nations, privacy is bound up with power and politics and has historically been used to silence, surveil, and oppress marginalized groups, including people of color, white women, immigrants, people with marginalized sexualities and genders, and the poor.[22] I ground this book in feminist movements because privacy law in the United States is allied with gender ideology. Early legal rulings and theories on privacy depended on conventional models of gender difference and norms. They drew from a model of life that divided tasks and identities into two spheres: the public, the realm of paid employment, political discourse, and law; and the private, the domestic world of family, sexuality, and intimacy.[23] Decades later, feminists attempted to dismantle this dichotomy when they argued that matters that were considered private, like intimate partner violence and child abuse, should be pulled into public light.

The binary model of private and public spheres is rooted in the "cult of true womanhood," a value system prevalent in the middle and upper classes of the United States and United Kingdom in the eighteenth and nineteenth centuries.[24] It held that women belonged in the domestic sphere, the home, where they were responsible for upholding piety, purity, submission, and domesticity. This ideology served to circumscribe women's behavior and naturalize an array of cultural practices, including the gendered division of labor and the sexual double standard.[25] In this period, when the first privacy legislation was enacted and cultural concepts of privacy were developing in the United States, white women were often required to maintain silence under the guise of modesty. It was immodest to participate in public life, act politically, work outside the home, or report abuse. The idea of the home as a man's castle purported to protect women from unwanted eyes, but in fact it maintained the privacy rights of men at the expense of women, whose labor sustaining the castle was made invisible. Seclusion within the home often meant that women had very little privacy, very little right to their own ideas or space, and very little agency over how information was shared.[26] The ideals of "true womanhood" excluded Black women, immigrant women, and poor women, who often had to work outside the home.[27] For domestic laborers and housewives, the home was not a refuge but a workplace. For people—usually women and children—experiencing domestic violence, it was a place of abuse and surveillance.

"True womanhood" was promoted by a small number of white, Protestant New Englanders, but it had outsized influence because it was foundational to the distinction between public and private that still characterizes US society.[28] Scholars often date the legal beginnings of privacy in the United States to 1888, when "A Bill to Protect Ladies" was introduced into the House of Representatives by Congressman John Roberts of Illinois. Roberts wanted to protect women from their pictures being published without their consent, which he considered a violation of their modesty and virtue. He was apparently disgusted that companies were using portraits of the new, pretty First Lady, Frances Cleveland, to sell soap, cigarettes, pianos, and other wares.[29] These ideas of privacy and womanhood were enshrined in Samuel Warren and Louis Brandeis's "Right to Privacy" (1890), perhaps the most famous law review article of all time, which is situated precisely in the white, upper-class gender norms of the northeastern United States where true womanhood flourished.[30]

Warren and Brandeis were moneyed Harvard graduates horrified by two developments: the new communication media of telegraphy, telephony, and photography, and the bustling news media eager to mine those media for news and gossip.[31] The feminist legal scholar Anita Allen argues that Warren and Brandeis masterfully exploited the paternalistic framework of separate spheres throughout the article to vindicate the need for privacy. "The Right to Privacy" maintains that publicity enabled by media violates the rights of the individual, particularly women, who belonged in the private sphere of the home. Publicity threatened the seclusion and humility central to "true womanhood." Photographs would bring women out of the private, domestic sphere into the public sphere—an act that Warren and Brandeis framed as antithetical to women's desire to be sequestered. (They did not mention that visibility would also give women more access to power and independence.) While the article asserts that the right to privacy should accrue to everyone, "whatsoever their position or station," it is steeped in the sentimental norms of its authors' upper-class social milieu.[32] Those norms, they worried, could no longer protect the sacred private sphere from new technologies without the assistance of the law.

Several lawsuits strategically used the violation of women's modesty to argue for legal privacy protections. Warren and Brandeis approvingly cite the 1890 case of Marion Manola, a prima donna performing in a comic opera called *Castles in the Sky*. The manager of the theater, trying to boost flagging attendance by displaying racy publicity posters, hired a photographer to take Manola's picture during a performance. Manola obtained an injunction against the publication of the photograph, "owing to her modesty," because it showed her in tights—stage attire suitable for a performance but not acceptable outside that context.[33] Interestingly, Manola was already a public figure, one of many nineteenth-century women who led a life that subverted the ideals of true womanhood.[34] Alongside the cult of true womanhood, the Gilded Age also saw the emergence of the suffragette movement and the New Woman. In Manola's statement that she objected to the photo because she did not want her young daughter to see it, she leveraged the cause of female modesty to control the dissemination of her information, appealing to the gender norms of the time and widespread cultural anxieties around emerging technologies.

In a feminist analysis of the emergence of the right to privacy, Jessica Lake discusses a similar lawsuit, *Roberson v. Rochester Folding Box Company* (1900). Abigail Roberson, a "feisty" young orphan, paid a photographer to take her picture. The photographer then sold the photograph to the Franklin Mill Flour Company, which used it on posters and fliers promoting a boxed flour mix with the punny caption "Flour of the Family." Roberson sued the Rochester Folding Box Company, which manufactured the boxes for Franklin Mill that showed her image. She won in the lower court, but the decision was overturned by New York State Court of Appeals, which ruled that there was no precedent for a right to privacy. In response to an outraged New York populace, the state legislature passed the first law in the nation protecting privacy, in 1903.[35] In both cases, establishing a right to privacy was rooted in a binary, inherently unequal conception of gender and femininity.

Who Deserves Privacy?

Even in the earliest days of the legal protection of privacy, it applied only to white, middle- and upper-class men and women. The safeguarding of modesty and innocence was not extended to people of color. During the same period in which Abigail Roberson appealed to "true womanhood" to prevent her portrait being used to sell flour, other packaged goods frequently used racist imagery of Black Americans.[36] While legislatures self-righteously protected white women's privacy by drawing on an ideology that reproduced their subjugation, those same legislatures did not even acknowledge the possibility that people of color might have a right to privacy at all. Entire categories of people, including people of color, immigrants, indentured servants, criminals, orphans, the very poor, the mentally ill, and people with disabilities, were both barred from participating in the public sphere and allowed little or no privacy. Enslaved Africans, for instance, were surveilled, patrolled, and branded, viewed as property rather than autonomous individuals.[37] During the Progressive era, reformers undertook "sanitary surveillance" of groups they believed might threaten public health, regularly inspecting the tenements and homes of poor urban families and scrutinizing the habits of Black washerwomen in the South and Chinese laundry workers in San Francisco.[38] Governments developed new technologies like fingerprinting to use against threatening populations such as immigrants, anarchists, Native Americans, potential criminals, "degenerates," and union members.[39] The surveillance studies scholar Simone Browne considers surveillance "the fact of antiblackness" and argues that the systematic removal of privacy is a primary way in which racial borders are drawn and enforced.[40]

Surveillance is the systematic collection of personal information to manage a population, and it typically focuses on people who are considered dangerous, meaning that some groups are deemed to "deserve" privacy while others are deemed not to.[41] In *The Condemnation of Blackness*, the historian Khalil Gibran Muhammad traces the link between Blackness and criminality. He shows how census data, crime reports, and prison statistics were used to "prove" Black inferiority and justify discriminatory treatment, racist laws, and heavy surveillance of African American communities. Muhammad points out that as Irish and Italian immigrants were brought under the umbrella of whiteness, their criminal activities were framed as individual failings linked to structural poverty or the ills of industrialization. This sympathy, which required seeing criminals as individuals subject to social inequality, was not extended to African Americans.[42]

As Simone Browne argues in her groundbreaking work *Dark Matters*, many of today's modern surveillance practices are undergirded by techniques pioneered in the transatlantic slave trade and the plantation system of enslaved Africans.[43] Black organizing and activism, from Nat Turner's rebellion to the Black Panthers and Black Lives Matter (BLM), has been the subject of systematic and focused official surveillance for hundreds of years.[44] It is thus impossible to truly understand modern surveillance practices without addressing Blackness. Everyday privacy violations such as stop-and-frisk, omnipresent closed-circuit television (CCTV), and even widespread police surveillance of social media are all rooted in the presumption of Blackness as dangerous and alien to the norm of white innocence.[45] While excessive surveillance of Black people and communities continues today, states now also apply these racially rooted practices to other populations.

Surveillance of racial and ethnic minorities is even more normalized now in the United States than it was in the nineteenth century.[46] This is apparent not only in the criminalization of Black people but in the treatment of Arab American and Muslim men after 9/11. The US government rounded up and detained many of these men and placed hundreds more on no-fly lists, simply because of their looks or reports of suspicious activities. Out of more than a thousand detainees, not one was successfully linked to terrorism.[47] These detainments were followed by thousands of interviews and systematic surveillance of Arab American communities that continues today, including scrutinizing the emails, Facebook posts, and online purchases of Muslim Americans.[48] Under the Trump administration, Immigration and Customs Enforcement (ICE) escalated surveillance of suspected undocumented Latinx immigrants, using automated license-plate readers; Stingray devices, which track cellphone signals; and "ruses" in which ICE agents pretended to be local police officers or even potential employers.[49] These highly invasive practices, justified under the guise of preventing criminal behavior, are heavily targeted at Black, Latinx, and Arab American populations.

Meanwhile, white middle- and upper-class men and women continue to enjoy a presumption of innocence and so are deemed worthy of privacy. The post-9/11 frustration with intrusive airport practices like searches and body scanners demonstrates that racial and class privilege has generally protected middle-class white people from egregious privacy violations.[50] Consider the differing treatments of white and Black activists in the summer of 2020. White activists, many of them armed, protested state lockdowns aimed at slowing the spread of COVID-19 and staged counterprotests at Black Lives Matter rallies. After the 2020 election, supporters of the defeated President Trump held protests around the country, culminating in the violent insurrection on January 6, 2021, in which five people died and dozens more were injured. Under Trump, however, the FBI ignored the well-documented increase in far-right activism across the country and focused instead on surveilling antifascist and anarchist groups, leaving themselves unprepared for the January 6 attacks.[51] At the same time, a multiracial coalition of activists protesting police violence against Black people and racial injustice across the country came under heavy surveillance by state and local governments using technologies like drones, social media mining, and facial-recognition software.[52] Documents obtained by *BuzzFeed News* showed that federal law enforcement regularly used social media to catalog and identify attendees at BLM protests, while virtually ignoring far-right protests going on at the same time.[53]

Viewing privacy as networked helps us understand these inequalities. Contemporary privacy is situated within a context of large surveillance systems and widespread discrimination that makes these violations widespread, collective, and systematic. The older idea of privacy as individual allows us to ignore its unequal distribution along lines of race, gender, class, and sexuality.[54] A networked approach takes account of the systemic deployment of privacy as a form of political power—of how the surveillant gaze denies privacy to some while offering it to others. Second-wave feminists famously showed that the personal is political; I follow their lead when I say that *the private is political.*

Public and Private Feminisms

Feminism has always been intimately connected to the public/private debate. The first wave of feminism, in the late nineteenth and early twentieth centuries, attempted to dismantle the ideology of separate spheres promoted by the cult of true womanhood in order to let women appear in public and participate in work and political life. They did this partly by redefining what privacy meant and partly by leveraging old ideas of female domesticity to gain rights and agency. Women like Marion Manola and Abigail Roberson who sued to protect their images in the "ocularcentric" culture of the Gilded Age spurred public discussions about privacy. While their lawsuits relied on parochial concepts of female modesty and virtue, they established important precedents for privacy law. It was such women's objections to new technological and commercial developments that instigated the development of a legal right to privacy.[55] First-wave feminism tried to complicate the distinctions between private and public, redefine what it meant for women to have privacy and agency, and establish the right to exist in public without being harassed.

Both waves of feminist movements focused on structural rather than personal change in trying to address the inequities sustained by traditional notions of privacy. In the 1970s, radical women's groups like Redstockings and the Combahee River Collective held consciousness-raising groups in which women discussed how sexism affected their lives. They came to recognize that the problems caused by patriarchy were culturally ingrained and required equally collective solutions. Issues like reproductive rights, domestic labor, and sexual abuse were systemic and had to be understood as such to recognize patriarchy as institutionalized oppression. Groups of Black and Chicana women further recognized that structural racism made their experiences as women of color distinctly different from those of the mostly white women in radical second-wave feminism. By giving a vocabulary to shared experiences and linking them to structural inequality, women were able to view seemingly individual experiences as instances of large-scale power inequalities playing out in their daily lives.[56]

Second-wave feminists worked to dismantle not the distinct spheres of "true womanhood" but the separation of the personal, private, and individual from the structural, systemic, and political. Their translation of the personal to the political moved domestic assaults, rape, and abuse out of the dark privacy of the home and into the light of day, exposing the cost of viewing these problems as individual acts rather than expressions of larger forces.[57] If systemic issues are seen only as individual, then collective change becomes impossible to realize or even imagine, and responsibility is shifted to those who most suffered the harms of structural inequality. (We will see a similar deconstruction of the personal versus the structural when we get to stop-and-frisk, in chapter 5.) In other words, these feminists critiqued the very concept of privacy, which they believed served as a smoke screen for practices that oppressed women.[58] The privacy of "home" and "family," they argued, placed these realms outside of state regulation and provided legal justification for men to use violence to chastise their wives or children for behaving in ways they disapproved of.[59] This argument extended the first-wave feminist critique of privacy as infantilizing, limiting women's ability to participate in public life, be independent, and have their own agency. Feminist legal scholars argued that the false dichotomy between private and public allowed important issues to be excluded from public discussion and thus from accountability and prevented examination of how patriarchy functioned in daily life.[60] As the feminist linguist Susan Gal writes, "Far from being incompatible, the principles associated with public and private coexist in complex combinations in the ordinary routines of everyday life."[61]

To this end, feminists campaigned to recognize the harm of sexual violence and reframe the concerns of "battered women" from an individual, private concern to a public, and therefore legally actionable, issue.[62] Even today, the most common reason given for not reporting domestic violence is to maintain personal privacy and avoid state interference in one's home life.[63] Activists also pushed issues of reproductive rights, child abuse, LGBTQ+ rights, sexual harassment, rape, and sexual assault, all formerly private, into public, political discussion. Today, while we still lack solutions to structural problems like child care or inequity of housework, these are increasingly recognized as political issues rather than isolated household problems.[64] While court cases *Roe v. Wade*, *Griswold v. Connecticut*, and *Lawrence v. Texas* ruled that birth control, abortion, and consensual sexual intercourse are private matters and not subject to governmental regulation, this is likely to change given the Supreme Court's conservative majority.[65]

These changes show that the boundaries between what is considered private and what is public are not fixed. They shift constantly, and this is driven by the law, social norms, and technological innovations. The internet has also driven much of this change. It has facilitated consciousness-raising on a grand scale, popularizing new terms for common experiences such as "gaslighting" or "racial microaggressions," and encouraging people to view them not as individual incidents but as expressions of larger structural forces.[66] But the internet—and the large-scale privacy violations it enables, such as big data aggregation and increased state surveillance—has also foregrounded the traditional focus on privacy as a matter of individual responsibility.

I lean on these feminist engagements with the subject to discuss how we should conceptualize privacy, delineate a new relationship between private and public, and propose a new way of thinking about privacy as political. Privacy has always operated as a structural force to maintain and police existing power relations. Just as feminism focuses not on individual instances of sexism but on structural forces of patriarchy, we must think of privacy not as an individual right or responsibility but as a structural problem, created by political and institutional forces and addressable only by interventions at those levels. We experience privacy, however we define it, as *networked*, located in a society that is endlessly connected via the internet. Our public discourse, technical development, and legal regulations must take that into account.

Throughout this book, I apply this model of networked privacy to a range of examples to look at the harms in more detail and to tease out some recommendations to help counter its negative consequences.

Research Methods

My focus in this book is on the experiences of Americans, primarily those in their late teens through their forties—the generation we categorize as "millennials," although do not get me started on the empirical flimsiness of generational cohorts. To understand different perspectives within this very large group, I draw on long-form interviews and focus groups with four groups of people: college students, both undergrad and graduate; low-income people of color in New York City; LGBTQ+ individuals in North Carolina; and people who have experienced online harassment. These are, of course, very different demographics. I chose the people I spoke with based on the diversity of their experiences and identities, and their stories gave me a strong sense of the rich variety of ways in which people grapple with privacy, identity, and technology. Qualitative interviews tell us little about the statistical prevalence of different opinions, but they do illuminate the range of thoughts and opinions on a topic.[67] Thus, the book is a series of cases rather than a study of a statistically representative sample. The individual understandings of people experiencing different parts of a whole provide a well-rounded, if inevitably incomplete, picture of a particular phenomenon.[68] Overwhelmingly, my interviews supported the theory of networked privacy; I then focused on what I call *privacy work*—how people dealt with the networked information landscape—and the different impacts of privacy violations.

The data in this book comes from four qualitative studies, with a total of 128 participants, that took place between 2014 and 2019. In two of the studies, I was the sole investigator and conducted all interviews: one on online harassment (37 participants) and one on the privacy experiences of LGBTQ+ people (22 participants). The other two studies were done in collaboration with other researchers. The first, on low-socioeconomic-status young people in New York City, had 29 participants, and the second, which consisted of focus groups in a midwestern city, had 40. Overall, the four studies comprised eleven focus groups and eighty-eight qualitative interviews. For detailed information about each study, including recruitment and interview protocols, how I analyzed the data, and how I protected my subjects' privacy, please see the appendix.

A Note on Terminology

Throughout the book, I refer to my participants' race, gender, and sexual identity using their own terminology. For example, some of my participants described themselves as Black, some as African American, some as African, and some as biracial. I also use their provided pronouns, including nonbinary "they"/"them" when appropriate to reflect how the participants experience their gender. I identify my trans participants as "trans women" and "trans men" since our conversations were specifically about their experience as trans people, although in their everyday lives, most identify as women or men. Likewise, I use the participants' own descriptions of their sexual orientations. Some used "queer" to describe a sexual identity that is fluid or nonbinary, whereas for others, this term marks adherence to a radical political tradition. Because there is no collective, neutral term for people with diverse sexual and gender identities, I use the term "LGBTQ+" to encompass people who identify as lesbian, gay, bisexual, transgender, and queer, with the plus sign meant to include emergent sexualities such as pansexuality and asexuality and gender-nonconforming and nonbinary gender identities.[69] While my LGBTQ+ participants do not all describe themselves as queer, I use the term to denote "identities in tension with presumptions that individuals are heterosexual and cisgender."[70] (The trans studies scholar Susan Stryker notes that "queer" is often used synonymously with gay and lesbian sexual identities; she writes, "all too often transgender phenomena are misapprehended through a lens that privileges sexual orientation and sexual identity as the primary means of differing from heteronormativity."[71] I have tried not to fall into this pattern.)

Outline of the Book

The goals of this book are to offer a new model for understanding privacy as networked and explain that the term "privacy" delineates a variety of power imbalances brought on by information diffusion. When we talk about privacy, we often ignore the power differentials of race, class, gender, and sexuality that affect how it is experienced and addressed. Although early adopters of networked technologies are often the most privileged, we are past that phase. Social media and big data have spread to the point where people on the margins must also contend with their impact. The subjects of surveillance have always been the marginalized, but the typical subject of privacy research is male and middle class. Instead of this group,

I draw from stories about people in all areas of US society to understand how structural inequality plays into their vast array of experiences related to "privacy." Often, the harms of privacy violations are equally dependent on sexism, homophobia, racism, or classism. Our individual, cybernetic, liberal model of privacy gives us only limited language with which to explain these inequalities. Grounding them instead in feminist, queer, and critical race theory enables us to better understand how information diffusion, as we conceptualize it in our modern era, aids the establishment and maintenance of long-standing structural inequality.[72]

In chapter 2, I walk readers through the theory of networked privacy. There is a continuity between the audience, context, and discursive framework for which information is intended and those in which it is encountered. This continuity is violated when information leaks across contexts, goes viral, or is publicized, all of which are enabled and augmented by social media. I also trace how "big data" obscures the networked nature of privacy violations, enabling companies to push individual responsibility as the appropriate frame for privacy. To preserve privacy, we must understand that information is located within networks and relationships and is predisposed to spread beyond them. People create and enforce norms to manage not only their own information behavior but also that of their friends and family, but it is difficult or impossible to control leaks by these means. Individual actions cannot address other types of networks, such as the genetic networks mapped by ancestry companies, which often incorporate even very distant relatives. Networked privacy acknowledges that power differentials exist both on the individual and structural level and that privacy violations knit these levels together.

Chapter 3 focuses on privacy work: the variety of actions and decisions that people undertake to achieve their desired level of privacy. Many of these measures fall outside traditional privacy-protective behaviors, and they are often based on folk understandings of technology. My participants are unable to meaningfully decide which strategies to use and how to judge their effectiveness because making accurate decisions to solve these problems requires impossibly sophisticated risk assessment. I offer a feminist concept of privacy work that allows us to push back against the conventional norm that charges people with protecting their own privacy and blames them if they do not, one of the many ways in which privacy technologies and laws fail to take power into account. I thus locate privacy work within a feminist literature of invisible labor, such as Liz Kelly's concept of "safety work," the planning and strategizing that girls and women must undertake to avoid men's violence.[73] Such invisible labor is made strategically difficult to see by painting it as natural, essential, and inevitable. As a result, privacy work is endless and stressful, and it may not prevent any actual harms. We can assess its effectiveness only when it fails.

I propose a framework of *feminist privacy protection* that positions harm and vulnerability at its center, evaluating emerging technologies by focusing on their impact on marginalized people and minorities in the same way that cybersecurity focuses on collective threats and vulnerabilities. This approach also suggests that networked privacy is a set of structural challenges and lived experiences. As the cybersecurity activist Noah Kelley explains, "threats to digital autonomy are gendered, racialized, queerphobic, transphobic, ableist, and classist."[74] By centering harms like domestic violence, child abuse, or racist harassment, feminist privacy protection attends to the hidden vulnerabilities caused by information technologies. Situating privacy threats and harms at intersections of race, class, gender, sexuality, and ability leads us to ask, Who *gets* to have privacy, and who does not? Ultimately, it takes real work for anyone to maintain even a close approximation to their desired level of privacy, given the dominance of networked information technologies.

Chapter 4 explicates the linkages between privacy work and safety work by considering harassment in terms of privacy violations and furthering a concept of gendered privacy. I offer a taxonomy of harassment that includes *everyday harassment*, *dyadic harassment*, *networked harassment*, and actions that might be described as harassment but are not particularly clear-cut, showing how intersectional identities are affected by each. Harassment, a somewhat murky concept, is used to explore how forced publicness is used to bully, silence, and shame. In the second part of the chapter, I trace the connections between the individual model of responsibility for privacy and the "blame the victim" mentality that is endemic to violence against women. Women suffer twofold from the norm of personal responsibility: they are often blamed when they suffer sexual violence, and they are blamed for not protecting their privacy when networked technologies are used for similar forms of abuse. By centering a networked rather than individual model of privacy, this chapter shows how gender norms affect the way information circulates and imagines the possibilities of reform and redress within communities, collectives, and networks.

In chapter 5, I look at how the networking of privacy affects low-income Americans, examining the power of the state to violate privacy, surveil, and simply demand information. I draw from a study of millennials in New York City with low socioeconomic status, most of them people of color. I argue that low-income people face a dual dilemma: on the one hand, they are systematically denied privacy by institutions like the criminal justice system, social service agencies, and low-wage employers. In such cases, violating privacy is a disciplinary tactic for controlling and punishing the poor. On the other hand, low-income people must make themselves legible to receive needed assistance. The increasing incorporation of big data into regimes of social sorting—a form of networked privacy—disadvantages the poor, who may be denied educational or employment benefits because of such systems.[75] Furthermore, the impacts of privacy violations may be far greater for people who are on the margins of society and thus economically vulnerable. My participants deal with these challenges in several ways. Some try to protect themselves and their information no matter what or present a "vanilla" self to the world. Other young people with few economic opportunities try to leverage alternate forms of capital, such as their technical skills, to protect themselves. Many of these people have developed a sophisticated frame for understanding systemic police surveillance, such as stop-and-frisk, that places collective responsibility on the system rather than individuals. This provides a model for thinking about networked privacy as structural and how we might begin to change a discourse that blames individuals for privacy violations.

In chapter 6, I look at the lives of LGBTQ+ people in North Carolina to imagine alternate privacy models beyond the private/public binary. Asking how people with marginalized gender and sexual identities navigate networked privacy on social media, I discuss how the inevitability of information leakage complicates the idea of the "closet"—which in turn complicates the idea of a simple public/private binary. For my participants, the revealing and concealing of information in different contexts is an everyday concern that extends beyond their sexual and gender identity to many other types of information, such as their immigration status, religious beliefs, and romantic interests. These negotiations show how deeply contextual information is in a networked society: we reveal some piece of information to some audiences but not to others. Many of the people in this chapter claim a right to be both public and vulnerable, while others engage in strategic visibility, revealing information that a generation ago might have been deeply stigmatizing in a deliberate effort to disrupt existing epistemologies. These discussions also show how privacy and publicity can be leveraged for political purposes—not by others, as a form of harassment, but by the disclosers themselves. By exposing and amplifying their queer sexuality and nonbinary or trans identities, my participants hope to combat homophobia, transphobia, and heteronormativity. The binary of private and public is disrupted by the very existence of visible queer networks, which neutralize the threats of concealment and exposure that reinforce cis, hetero, and binary identifications. By highlighting how information is intrinsically neither public nor private, the queer network disturbs the entire dichotomy, providing a possible point of intervention by thinking of privacy as nonbinary.

Chapter 7 looks at how networked privacy might be used to reframe current assumptions about privacy. I dismantle a variety of myths about privacy, including the widely held beliefs that young people do not care about privacy, that people who use social media do not care about privacy, and that if you do not like privacy violations, you can just stop using social media. These discourses place responsibility on the victim and ignore the networked nature of information in the social media age. Those who speak throughout the book are deeply concerned with privacy but feel there is little they can do to protect themselves. I affirm this concern. I close chapter 7 with a brief discussion of how we might use the concept of networked privacy to better protect us all.

2

The Violation Machine

Networked Privacy in the Digital Age

Networked privacy is the desire to maintain agency over information within the social and technological networks in which information is disclosed, given meaning, and shared. This agency is continually compromised by aggregation, connection, and diffusion. Networked privacy can only be maintained by bounded audiences through shared discursive frameworks and contextual norms. Models of privacy that depend on individual agency over information are a fiction, but *networked* agency is removed by social media and big data technologies that work covertly to undermine norms and boundaries. Some people can maintain their desired control over information diffusion in some situations, while others cannot; but sustained networked privacy is only achieved, if ever, through collective efforts. Under networked privacy, information is not *public* or *private* but located somewhere on a spectrum of visibility.

This chapter describes networked privacy in detail. I begin by tracing the shift from individual to networked concepts of power. I then explain the theory's three presumptions: information is contextual, privacy is contextual, and privacy always involves power disparities. When I have asked study participants to define privacy, they have repeatedly told me that they want to maintain agency over how their information is disclosed. But this agency is continually removed, belying the myth of individual control over privacy.

While most people are more concerned with privacy violations caused by social media, big data violations are as, if not more, significant. Big data classifies people into groups based on enormous amounts of imperceptible information-gathering with enduring consequences, as we will see in chapter 5. Understanding this in terms of power, context, and agency requires conceptualizing privacy as networked.

From Individual to Networked Privacy

Since the nineteenth century, US legal models of privacy have depended on a notion of the individual as the liberal political subject: autonomous, rational, separate from their body, and nothing like an actual person.[1] In keeping with this notion, both US theories of privacy and the legal system define it as a right "possessed by individuals."[2] This is undergirded by a sense of privacy as property that can be stolen or given away, which must be guarded by the individual who "owns" it.[3]

Individuals are legally and socially responsible for protecting their privacy. For example, a person must bring their privacy claim to court themselves—you cannot file a claim on the behalf of another person—and they must name someone or something specific who injured them by violating their privacy. To be legally actionable, this violation must have resulted in concrete financial or reputational damage. This puts complainants at a disadvantage, because absent that concrete damage, privacy itself has no intrinsic monetary value under the law. This is why scholarship often frames privacy in the fuzzy language of morality or dignity rather than in clear legal terms. And it makes it difficult for someone to sue, say, Equifax or Facebook for leaking their personal information, since the consequences are very difficult to determine.

The Supreme Court's "reasonable expectation" test uses two criteria to determine whether a privacy violation has occurred. First, the person must subjectively believe that their privacy was violated. Second, they must have been in a place or situation where they reasonably expected to have privacy. But while courts have ruled that people can reasonably expect privacy in their home or car or in a telephone call or paper letter, legally there is no reasonable expectation of privacy in *any* internet communication, including email, GPS coordinates, or bank records.[4] This may explain why people in the United States overwhelmingly consider privacy an individual responsibility and believe that if someone's privacy is violated, it is their own fault.[5]

Tech companies have successfully promoted the neoliberal idea that it is the users of their products who are responsible for protecting their privacy. People are responsible for configuring their own privacy settings, even if these settings are confusing or change frequently. Facebook, for example, changed its privacy policy seventeen times between 2005 and 2015.[6] The settings are also difficult to use. In one study, not a single participant was able to correctly configure all their Facebook privacy settings, and most were sharing content that they did not intend to share.[7] On some sites, like Twitter or Instagram, the model of privacy is binary, meaning that the account is either public or private, with no option for further adjustment. (We will see in chapter 3 that people overcome this limitation by using multiple accounts, a risky strategy given that many platforms limit users to a single account.)[8]

The existence of privacy policies suggests that it is an individual's responsibility to determine whether to use a service, but we know that almost nobody reads them. They are written at the level of academic articles, whereas most American adults read at an eighth-grade level.[9] It would take most people twenty-five days every year to read the privacy policies of all the technologies they use.[10] If someone objects to a platform's terms of service, their only choice is to opt out completely, regardless of the costs of not participating.[11] In short, these policies are privacy theater. They educate no one, nor does reading them truly constitute consent. They are intended to be clicked through and ignored. But their existence allows platforms, when violations happen, to claim that they warned their customers.

This notion persists even though, as we will see, most technological privacy violations are structural and cannot be prevented by even the most careful individual. Technological platforms and interfaces like social media privacy settings presume that giving individuals control over how their data is displayed and shared is enough to protect their privacy. But this is untrue, and the presumption has very negative consequences. Technology companies, however, continue to insist that privacy is an individual responsibility.

Our modern suite of technologies, from social media to personal digital assistants to facial recognition to personalized advertising, were not designed to protect our privacy. If anything, they were designed to circumvent it. Individual solutions to these structural problems require technical expertise and are expensive, hard to use, and time-consuming. Rather than blaming individuals when their information leaks, we must look closely at the network itself.

The Theory of Networked Privacy

Networked structural threats make it impossible for any one person to protect their own privacy. The dynamics of social media and big data mean that digital networks spread information far beyond its original context, data is collected and aggregated to sort users into groups, and this aggregated data is used to make life-altering decisions about people's job applications, financial prospects, and potential criminality. These developments throw the inadequacy of individualized models of privacy into sharp relief. Threadbare notions formulated against a nineteenth-century bourgeois backdrop of photography and newspapers cannot help us deal with modern experiences of information sharing, grasp the harms of privacy violations, or know who should decide where and when a piece of information is shared. How can we think about privacy if the old-fashioned legal idea of individual right and responsibility no longer applies? I propose a new way of conceptualizing privacy that incorporates its intrinsic social and networked nature.

Thinking about privacy as networked requires the following assumptions. Information is not only shared but given meaning and formulated within behavioral and articulated networks and the relationships that constitute them. These networks overlap, connect, and leak to other networks, whose members may have different norms and discursive resources to interpret information. As information moves from network to network, it is recontextualized and reinterpreted. As it is combined with other pieces of information, it broadens and reveals even more. These information flows are subject to power differentials at both the micro and macro level. Power, like information, flows through networks and relationships. Whose information is shared, who is sanctioned for information sharing, and who feels the harms of privacy violations most deeply are all dependent on one's location within a network and social hierarchy of power.

Understanding Information as Contextual

While we take the word for granted, "information" is a relatively new idea that collapses all types of communication—thoughts, opinions, songs, novels, photographs, videos, memes, phone calls, conversations, text messages—into a single quantifiable category.[12] When I use the term "information," I do not mean the cybernetic model that addresses only the content but also the context—both that in which the information is shared and that in which it is created. By collapsing the technological medium and the human activity together, "information" strips away context, such as the setting, medium, audience, and social positions of the participants.[13] Contexts are cocreated by participants, and when we share information about ourselves or anyone else, we do it in ways particular to where and with whom we are sharing. As one of my study participants put it, "I like that idea of having almost different levels of privacy. Like this is what I would share with the whole world, and this is what I would tell people at my school, and this is what I would tell people on my floor, and people I'm close friends with, and my sister who's like my best friend. Just because certain things are kind of weighted differently in our lives. And so how we view them in relation to ourselves differs."

In some cases, there are enormous social and cultural differences between the contextual frame of the information sender and that of the recipient. Arya, a thirty-two-year-old medical student from a devout midwestern Muslim family, told me about an incident from her high school days. Her Facebook friends took a photo of themselves at a bar and tagged her in it. She was not shown in the picture and had never been in a bar. She was simply tagged in the picture by a friend. Her family, however, considered the association with alcohol so inappropriate for a Muslim woman that they forced her to change schools to get away from a bad influence—the person who tagged her. In this case, her secular friends' cultural norms conflicted with those of her religious parents. When information about Arya spread from her high school social network into her familial and religious networks, that audience received the tagged picture very differently from what her friends intended. To her friends, tagging Arya was no big deal; she was not in the picture. They did not share the norms that her parents did, nor did they understand how these norms might affect Arya. As we will see, this is an explicit example of the collapse of information's contextual integrity and the consequences of that.

Linguists, by contrast, recognize the importance of taking this full context into account in determining what a particular bit of information communicates. As the pioneering linguist Susan Ervin-Tripp explained in her studies of bilingual children, even very young children are aware of the "social and interactional" features of context, which they convey using their "choices of pronouns, person, aspect, modal auxiliaries, pitch, prosody, discourse markers, register and vocabulary choice." She provides an example of adult speech to illustrate the importance of context:

O: What's your name, boy?
P: Dr. Poussaint. I'm a physician.

O: What's your first name, boy?

P: Alvin.[14]

In a cybernetic model of communication, this conversation simply conveys the information of someone's first and last name. But the social and historical context reveals a much larger meaning. This interaction took place on a public street in 1967 between O, a white police officer, and P, a Black doctor. The officer's language conveys racial superiority and the threat of violence, as well as the general assumption that police officers can assert authority in public. "Boy" is a racist term historically used to denigrate Black men. The Black man, Dr. Poussaint, believes he is due respect due to his social status but also feels that, given the power imbalance, he must answer the question. Dr. Poussaint wrote in the *New York Times* that he felt "profound humiliation" after this encounter, and this was certainly the intention of the police officer, who used a racial slur, ignored Dr. Poussaint's perfectly acceptable answer, and repeated the slur in demanding his first name.[15] Imagine what would have been conveyed if the police officer had said, "Sir, can you give me your full name?" The full context not only shapes how the interaction is phrased but what is actually being communicated, which is not simply a name but an all-encompassing social order with a long history and intricate rules of behavior. When we think of privacy as solely about singular pieces of information moving from context to context, these subtleties are lost, along with much of the meaning.

Context also includes the media in which the communication occurs. As the anthropologist Ilana Gershon writes, we know that the medium shapes the message; *media ideologies* are our beliefs about how different media should "communicate and structure information."[16] How we understand a medium shapes what we use it for and how we communicate through it. For example, most people think of email as a more formal medium than text messages. There are reasons for this; traditionally, emails were written at desktop computers with keyboards, a setup that lends itself well to longer messages, while text messages were originally sent from mobile phones with alphanumeric keyboards, which most people found difficult to type on. And until the 1990s, email was used primarily in universities and offices, which generally adhere to more formal communication norms. But there is nothing intrinsically formal or informal about either email or text message. To discuss this concept in my undergraduate class, I use the example of an episode of *Sex and the City* in which the character Berger breaks up with the protagonist, Carrie, by writing, "I'm sorry. I can't. Don't hate me," on a Post-It. Carrie is furious that Berger used such an informal medium to break up with her. Would she have felt that way if he had written her a letter on nice stationery? Probably not. But the Carrie of the 2020s would be just as angry if he dumped her by text message.

Each social media platform structures communication in a different way, and users sometimes try to use these platforms to reestablish context stripped out by digital transmission. Most of my study participants were very careful on Instagram about which photos they posted to "the grid," or the main feed, which they used strategically to manage others' impressions of them. But Instagram stories, which expire after twenty-four hours and incorporate lots of filters, GIFs, and captions, were viewed as a more playful and private space where people could be goofy or emotional and post things that might be controversial or unflattering. Ava (eighteen, white) explained that she used Snapchat (which originated the expiring stories format that Meta then integrated into Instagram Stories) for "closer friends" and "sillier" content. She knew that "Facebook is more open to the public" and kept her content there "formal" so she would not "be caught in the turbulence of someone misreading something and then having that kind of create a bunch of drama." In text messages, people deploy emoji, slang, and punctuation to show emotion and convey how they wish their messages to be received. As Gershon writes, our media ideologies reveal our understanding that "communication is socially constructed and socially interpreted."[17]

This collapse of contexts is not limited to the digital world. Consider a funeral, where people from many areas of the deceased's life intermingle.[18]

Face-to-face, we can vary our self-presentation on the basis of whom we are speaking with and where we are, because our contexts are usually separate. Think of code-switching, the practice of alternating our speaking styles to fit the spaces we inhabit. This is especially true for people who speak multiple languages or have speech patterns that differ from the white American ideal.

Privacy as Contextual

Helen Nissenbaum's germinal work *Privacy in Context* examines what happens when information provided in one context, with one set of information norms, moves to a context with different norms.[19] She theorizes this in terms of "contextual integrity," arguing that people experience a privacy violation when their information is shared outside the context in which they imagined it would be shared. One example of contextual integrity is a doctor's office. People expect that when they share information in a doctor's office, it is governed by a particular set of norms. One of my study participants explained, "I mean, like, you go into the room, and you take off your clothes, and you put on a paper bag, and someone who you don't really know comes and looks at you and touches you and stuff like that. And that's just something that we give up our privacy because it's within the context of receiving medical care." Some of these norms have the force of law, such as the federal privacy law known as HIPAA. If a patient's information is then sold to a pharmaceutical company, which has a different and perhaps opaque set of norms around sharing information, contextual integrity has been broken, and the individual experiences a privacy violation. Nissenbaum's theory was formulated in response to theories of privacy that saw it as a property of information itself. Such theories of privacy are binary, regarding information as either private or not. Contextual integrity stresses that privacy is not an inherent property of a piece of information but of the context in which the information is shared.

Nissenbaum's theory is supported by the anthropologist Irwin Altman, who analyzed ethnographic accounts of many cultures to assess the differences and similarities in privacy attitudes and practices. He found that while every culture prizes privacy, it is maintained through culturally specific verbal, nonverbal, and environmental practices. For instance, in societies with limited physical privacy, where it is normal to see and hear your neighbors, people regulate information disclosure through elaborate systems of etiquette, hiding one's emotions, and taboos against direct questioning. In social contexts with extensive physical privacy, such as places with private homes, regulated roads, and strong norms against strangers entering houses, people may be more open and forthcoming about their emotional lives.[20] Privacy, in other words, is not just unequal but contextual.

The pioneering sociologists Robert Merton and Erving Goffman argued that people everywhere move across social contexts, but to do so successfully requires firewalls between different subgroups. Merton describes these contexts in terms of social status positions, or "status sets." Within each status position, an individual maintains different relationships with others. For instance, someone might be the Queen Bee in their social group but work in a low-status retail job.[21] Similarly, a medical student's status set might include the status of *student* with her teachers, *colleague* with her fellow students, *supervisor* with nurses, and *powerful expert* with patients.[22] These differing statuses are forms of context that affect how the student frames or disseminates information; she might be more likely to share personal information with her fellow students than with her teachers or patients. Several teachers I interviewed kept very strict boundaries between the social media that their students might encounter and the social media they maintained for friends and family, for these represent very different contexts: one personal and one professional, one collegial and the other dominant and powerful. Merton argues that to keep these contexts separate and keep information flowing appropriately within them, the frames must be separated—in other words, we depend on privacy to differ our social performances, which can only be maintained if information does not leak from one context to another.[23]

Goffman, whose work has been taken up by many internet research-ers, views different contexts as *social* rather than *status* performances and relationships. He wrote that people present themselves differently based on context and audience. The ability to vary one's self-presentation is abso-lutely necessary for people to maintain their dignity and social standing, so they must be able to control when information is revealed or concealed to perform appropriately in a social context. Goffman's famous example of performative self-presentation is the waiter who performs the role of cheer-ful server while on the restaurant floor but immediately drops his perky demeanor once he enters the kitchen or break room.[24] To Goffman, a cus-tomer eavesdropping on two waiters gossiping in the kitchen and then com-plaining to the manager about what they said would violate both social etiquette and the waiters' expectations of privacy. As the legal scholar Ari Waldman argues, Goffman defines privacy invasions as "socially inappro-priate behaviors that violate the trust and discretion we owe others."[25] To both Merton and Goffman, privacy is dependent not only on broad cultural contexts and norms but on the micro-norms and warrants that underpin each specific social context, or frame, that an individual inhabits at a given moment. We require privacy in order to shift between these frames. When someone moves from one context to another, whether physically or by ac-cessing information meant for a different audience and setting, that action collapses separate frames into one another. We experience this as a privacy violation.

Privacy is deeply contextual, although the law defines it as identical across situations.[26] Because what is considered private and what violates privacy is context dependent, uniform notions of private information, sit-uations, or spaces ignore this specificity. In the early 2010s, danah boyd and I interviewed teenagers around the country about privacy. She inter-viewed a young woman who, asked to name a space she considered pri-vate, named the back room of Panera Bread, where she worked. Once she was done with her shift, she took her iPod and her homework to the back room and sat, listened to music, and was not bothered by anybody.[27] We noted that for many teenagers, home was not automatically a private space, since they shared rooms with siblings, had nosy family members who read their instant messenger conversations over their shoulder, or had parents who searched their backpacks and dressers. Blake (nineteen, white, trans man) complained, "Well, I say my bedroom's private, but my stepdad, he'll just like—and then he'll just walk in, just like a very light knock. So when he comes in my room, that's when it's not private." This does not map to the traditional public/private dichotomy in which people expect that their homes will be private and their work public. Instead, home is just another context in which information should be shared appropriately according to its norms. Teenagers experience their parents' attempts to collapse the boundaries between home, where they hold authority, and the teenagers' social lives, where the parents have no authority, as invasions of privacy.

Social theories of privacy like those of Merton and Goffman see privacy not as a universal condition owned by an individual but as a set of frames that a person can inhabit. To act appropriately in each context, the person plays a specific role, speaks to a specific audience, and shares specific information. Privacy is what separates the contexts. Social theories of privacy thus see it as part of a network rather than a property of a single network node.

None of these contextual theories of privacy, however, tells us how contexts themselves interact. They do not explicitly engage the fact that information, particularly *digital* information, is intrinsically leaky and shared through networks and shared differently depending on who the audience is imagined to be. (We would describe our medical issues differently to our doctor than to our romantic partner or our parents.) To acknowledge this simultaneous separation and interconnection of frames, I borrow from critical discourse analysis the concept of a *discursive framework*, which describes how context affects the way information is shaped, expressed, and delivered. A discursive framework is at once a way of seeing the world and a vocabulary that expresses that worldview, which is shared with a group, or network, of people.[28] For example, President George W. Bush said in his 2002 State of the Union address, "there's power, wonder-working power, in the goodness and idealism and faith of the American people." While secular audiences did not find this particularly meaningful, evangelical Christians recognized "wonder-working power" as a phrase from the evangelical hymn "There Is Power in the Blood." Bush signaled his affiliation with born-again Christianity, giving evangelicals a powerful sign that he was in their corner.[29] He shared a discursive framework based on religious belief with his supporters that was imperceptible to others.

Discursive frameworks shape what is said and unsaid and, crucially, how information is interpreted by audiences that share the speaker's context. While discrete pieces of information like phone numbers are the same regardless of where or how they are shared, other information, such as political opinions, are framed very differently based on one's discursive framework. But just as people move between different social positions, they also have access to multiple discursive frameworks. A woman's evangelical roots might let her recognize Bush's coded appeal to his religious base, but she might also possess academic training that allows her to identify inaccuracies in a newspaper article covering a scientific finding.

Networked technologies like social platforms make it very difficult for people to determine whether they are speaking to the appropriate audience, as well as whether they are using a discursive framework that their audience understands.[30] Ava gives a light-hearted example:

> So, internet culture, you could totally tell when somebody has used the internet a lot because they'll get certain jokes and they'll have a certain sense of humor it seems like. Everybody just kind of understands it more, but if you talk to someone outside of the internet, if I were to talk about a meme around my grandma, she'd be like, "What the fuck are you talking about? Do you need help?" But if I were talking to one of my friends who I met through Twitter, then I'd be like, "Yo, here's this meme," and she would be like, "LMAO."

Information may take on a completely different meaning once it slips into a new context. Yet the ability to govern this is compromised by the intrinsically social nature of information and technologies that abet the collapsing of frames. We need a theory of privacy that describes the connected world in which we all live.

Power

Sociologists and anthropologists have chronicled the complex contextual ways in which people in different cultures think about, perform, and communicate secrecy, privacy, and disclosure. But few have examined the cultural specificity of marginalization and privacy: how people in different power positions and configurations, who are not the normative white male liberal political subject, experience, manage, and define privacy.[31] A key element of networked privacy is that, like everything else, it is subject to flows of power. Power is a crucial part of studying surveillance because surveillance assumes a power asymmetry between the watcher and the watched. But scholars, technologists, and policy makers rarely take power relationships into account when evaluating privacy. This is an immense shortcoming. Everyone does not have the same amount of privacy. Society makes judgments about who is and is not entitled to privacy, and these judgments are colored by interlocking systems of oppression with long histories. Recall the turn-of-the-century legal cases over the use of white women's images in advertising. Social norms positioned white women as bastions of morality who should be cosseted within the domestic sphere. They were thought to need privacy to preserve their modesty, even though they were given very little privacy. But there was no public or legal reaction to the use of Black women's imagery on consumer goods, because Black women were not thought to deserve privacy in the same way. These kinds of social determinations are expressed daily in micro-interactions and interpersonal relationships that reflect larger patterns and structures of power, just as privacy violations at the individual level mirror larger violations taking place through big data and social media. And these large structures also reflect inequalities and oppressions, such as predictive algorithms that are far more likely to see a threat in Black and Latinx individuals living in low-income neighborhoods.

Michel Foucault's concept of "capillary power" describes how power operates at the level of everyday social practice: it flows through networks. In Foucault's words, it is "deployed and exercised through a net-like organization."[32] Rather than being exerted from the top down, power circulates and is reproduced through micro-interactions between individuals. This is the difference between a mythical group of white men in a boardroom deciding how to oppress women and a man gaslighting his female partner about her experiences. The feminist philosopher Kate Manne makes a similar distinction between patriarchy and misogyny in her groundbreaking book *Down Girl*. Patriarchy, she writes, is an ordering system that subjects women and girls to different social norms than men and that disadvantages women or positions them in support roles, while misogyny is the "hostile or adverse consequences" visited on women who violate these norms.[33] In both cases, power differentials exist at all levels of relationships.

If we think of information sharing as, in Foucault's terms, a "micro-practice," we can connect it with these power differentials that, in aggregate, make up social life. Doing this allows us to connect network-level interactions with broader structural oppressions that are reinforced through individual- and group-level interactions. Both forms of power are crucial to understanding networked privacy. Someone installing "stalkerware" on their partner's phone without their consent is asserting power over them and committing technologically enabled violence. But understanding that, at the macro level, this is more *likely* to happen to women helps us to understand patterns of privacy violations that exist at the individual level.

Of course, we cannot reduce the complexity of human relationships to network ties or power relationships. We must examine them within their entire sociocultural context, of which power, structural oppression, and marginalization are only a part—even if a large part. We must acknowledge both individual-level and structural power differentials as we consider how information moves through and beyond networks and as we figure out how to live with the newly digital, more intensely networked nature of privacy.

Defining Privacy and Agency

What is privacy? A seemingly endless series of law review articles, scholarly monographs, and book chapters have taken up this question.[34] Legal and philosophical definitions of privacy often hinge on heady discussions of moral value, while sociological theories attempt to explain how people actually manage privacy, and anthropological discussions describe how privacy plays out in different cultures. Definitions of privacy are often strategically deployed to criticize some piece of technology for ruining privacy or to promote another for protecting it. As the feminist philosopher Susan Gal writes, "Public and private do not simply describe the social world in any direct way; they are rather tools for arguments about and in that world."[35]

Accounts shared by interview and focus-group participants reveal a slow shift of ideas about what privacy is, who is responsible for maintaining it, and who deserves it. Some participants struggled to distinguish the broader concept of *privacy* from information that is *private*, which they most often described as secret, unsaid, or available only to oneself. Others fixated on minute details of social technologies, while still others mentioned their cars and bedrooms as private spaces. But their definitions generally centered personal agency. Person after person argued that they should have the choice to determine how much access other people or institutions have to information about them. As a twenty-year-old Latina woman said in a focus group, "I think it's allowing other people to know as much or as little about your life as you want. I think the main focus is that what other people are viewing or able to know about you is controlled by you, that you're pulling on the reins of that, and that nobody else is interfering with that or sharing things that you wouldn't want to be shared." Broadly speaking, they agreed with the definition set forth by the pioneering privacy researcher Alan Westin in 1967: privacy is "the claim of individuals, groups, or institutions to determine for themselves when, how, and to what extent information is communicated to others."[36]

People disagreed on what was acceptable to share with others, on- and offline. They often judged what others posted, speaking disapprovingly of "too much information," "thirst traps" (sexy self-portraits posted to get attention from potential partners), and "depressing" narratives. But many participants pointed out that privacy was not about any one type of information but about boundaries. People wanted to decide for themselves what to share and when to share it, and when they set these boundaries, they wanted them to be respected. One young Asian American man said, "It's all about how much power you have. I mean, you can have a lot of privacy and still be sharing everything and standing on the street corner and yelling out your political beliefs, but you are the one *deciding* to yell those beliefs. That is what privacy is."

Another participant, Bonnie, a genteel, southern, trans woman in her forties, is happy to share intimate information about her transition, even with strangers who ask inappropriately personal questions. Her trans friends roll their eyes and tell her not to answer these questions, but she shares intimate information because she wants to educate cis people. She says, "I'm probably doing a disservice to some of the other trans community by explaining that stuff, but I want to help people understand better." While her friends deem this information private, Bonnie decides whether and when to share it. She has agency over sharing, so it does not feel like a violation.

Other people linked privacy violations to a lack of agency. Lauren (twenty-five, white) moved to North Carolina after graduating from an elite university and now teaches at a charter school. When I asked her to tell me about a time when her privacy was violated, she told me about writing a "really vulnerable, emotional college admissions essay" about her parents' divorce and her mother's subsequent remarriage. Lauren and her mother were very close, and she sent her mother the essay to get her mother's feedback and share her emotional growth around the divorce. Having intended the essay for her mother alone, Lauren was completely taken aback when her mother forwarded it to their extended family. She said, "I'm a very open person. I probably would've shared it eventually with any of the people she sent it to, but it was the act of her sending it without me knowing and then people receiving it without going through me as a filter. I didn't like the removal of my own context and my own explanation and my own agency in it." It was the infringement of her agency to share that Lauren experienced as violating, not the sharing itself. She wanted the ability to choose how and with whom she shared her essay. It was the removal of these choices that she experienced as a privacy violation.

My participants' emphasis on individual agency belies the fact that violations happen all the time in the digital age. From data breaches that reveal millions of personal records to social media settings that suddenly change, information we thought was inaccessible gets revealed. Privacy violations are not isolated experiences but structural. As the new media theorist Wendy Chun says, networks are designed to connect and leak.[37] These leaks are a normal part of life, and there are segments of US industry that could not operate without collecting and collating personal information without most people's knowledge, let alone permission. The overwhelming emphasis on the *individual* as the privacy subject does not consider that people are embedded within networks.[38]

Framing privacy as *networked* allows us to focus on the relationships among people who are situated in larger structures, both social contexts and technologically facilitated networks like social media and big data.[39] The natural sociability of information is brought to the surface by two emerging technologies: social media platforms like Facebook, YouTube, and Twitter, which digitize the cultural connections between people; and "big data" technologies like sorting algorithms and genomic ancestry testing.[40] Sorting algorithms aggregate data to make predictions about individuals, while genomic ancestry testing maps out biological relationships. These technologies are intertwined, as social platforms often rent their information to big data companies or even sell it to them outright.

Both social platforms and big data technologies enable data collection about people on a level far beyond what was previously thought possible. When the Detroit police asked wireless companies Sprint and MetroPCS to provide cellphone data about a suspect, for example, they received 127 days of information so detailed that, as the *New York Times* reported, they could tell "whether he had slept at home on given nights and whether he attended his usual church on Sunday mornings."[41] Such perfect surveillance poses deep challenges to legal and normative concepts of privacy that hinge on the individual. Social media and big data trace entire networks of people. They dredge up one person's data while unearthing another's, and they explicitly encourage people to share more about their friends and family. Our normal social connections make it impossible for technology to treat us as atomized subjects. Social and big data technologies exploit our connections for profit, and privacy violations are collateral damage.

Social Media

Social media is, of course, social. Its platforms and technologies subvert old models of privacy by connecting people and transmitting information through networks. In the famous article "The Strength of Weak Ties," which inspired the first generation of social platforms like Friendster and MySpace, Mark Granovetter argued that connecting formerly disparate networks would allow information to freely flow across them.[42] He did not anticipate that doing so might have disadvantages. While the idea of two separate spheres, "public" and "private," has never captured how humans actually behave and experience life, social platforms have broken down the physical and situational boundaries by which we kept things private. Digital social life is networked by design.

People use social media according to what they want to communicate, the social setting in which they believe they are acting, their audience, what the technology permits, and how they believe the platform should be used. They create, forward, and spread information for many reasons, some strategic and others oblivious. But social media is built for what Henry Jenkins, Sam Ford, and Joshua Green call "spreadable media."[43] It is built to leak, and it does.

Information Leaks across Contexts

In 2021, Senator Ted Cruz of Texas was intensely criticized for vacationing in Mexico while millions of his constituents were suffering through freezing, snowy weather without power or water. A day or two before, his wife had texted a neighborhood group chat asking if anyone wanted to join them at the Ritz Carlton in Cancún. Someone in the chat took a screenshot of the conversation and sent it to the *New York Times*, providing endless amusement for pundits and comedians.[44] What is notable is not simply that the fact of the vacation leaked but that the exact conversation was so easily recorded and transmitted. This would be almost impossible without cellphones and group text messaging. In 1997, the Pentagon civil servant Linda Tripp befriended Monica Lewinsky, a White House intern twenty-four years her junior. Lewinsky confided to Tripp that she was having an affair with President Clinton, and Tripp, hoping to write a book, began recording her phone calls with Lewinsky on the advice of a conservative literary agent. The recordings eventually became evidence in Clinton's impeachment trial.[45] They are almost painful to listen to: Lewinsky, completely trusting, is pouring her heart out to a friend. The *Washington Post* wrote in Tripp's obituary, "It's hard enough to know whom to trust in this most transactional of cities, but taping was next-level betrayal. The fact that, as a woman, Tripp had broken the confidence of a friend who had trusted her with the most intimate details of her life was beyond the pale."[46] As Tripp's betrayal shows, it is not that such intense privacy violations were unheard of before social media or that information never leaked from one context to another. It is that technology makes these betrayals so very easy. Lewinsky never imagined that Tripp might be recording their phone conversations, something that in 1997 was not only rare and technically difficult but also illegal in Maryland, where Tripp lived. Heidi Cruz's neighbors, on the other hand, just had to press a couple of buttons.

When most people's personal information leaks, it is not covered by the press. But it does happen. That is the unwritten purpose of social media, since people describe their lives and activities in ways that usually involve others. We post pictures that include our friends, tell stories about our partners and kids, and make videos that feature multiple subjects and sometimes random passersby. Social media posts can reveal lots of information about other people whether or not they have an account. Facebook-owned platforms even create "shadow profiles" for people who do not have accounts, gleaned from information provided by others. These profiles are generated from contact lists uploaded by users to "find friends" on the platform and from data collected every time a website is visited that includes one of Facebook's integrated ad trackers, an embedded "Like" button, or its advertising application programming interface (API).[47]

Usually, the information we share about others is harmless. But there is little you can do to control how other people talk about you on social media or what information they share. Often you do not even know about it.

Lindsay, thirty, is a vivacious young woman who loves watching makeup tutorials on YouTube and taking care of her dogs. She and her wife, who met in recovery, are raising Lindsay's kindergarten-aged daughter. Lindsay describes her daughter's biological father as "the sperm donor." A few years ago, she texted him a few school pictures of their daughter, telling him that she would consider supervised visitation on two conditions: that he get a job and that he stop using drugs. (It did not work. There was a warrant out for his arrest, and he was afraid the police would track him down if he agreed to visitation.) A few days later, Lindsay checked his social media. Although they were not friends on Instagram, his profile was open, and she saw that he had posted the pictures with the caption, "The mother of my child is keeping her from me." Lindsay told me, "I felt terrible because he was putting out this image to social media about me when that wasn't true; those weren't facts. Like, they [the audience] don't know the situation. They're gonna look at that and go on purely based on what that person says." She had sent the pictures in good faith, and her daughter's father had violated her privacy by using them to promote his own narrative about their relationship. His action changed the photos from private family information to a public post on an open Instagram profile, framed with a false narrative that made her the bad guy.

Of course, "talking trash" about other people is not new. Lindsay's ex certainly could have, and probably had, complained about Lindsay to his friends in person. But in-person complaints are ephemeral. Digital information persists and can reach a much larger audience. Anyone in the ex-husband's network—indeed, anyone at all—could come across his Instagram post. This is what happens when an intended recipient violates the original frame of a piece of information, either by publicizing it or by altering the context to appeal to their own needs and audience.

Information Is Publicized

While people had a "reasonable expectation of privacy" when using older technologies like letters and landline phones (Linda Tripp notwithstanding), the modern counterparts like email, text messages, and Facebook Messenger are built with the ability to screenshot, forward, and copy messages and distribute them at scale. Even technologies like Snapchat and the elite dating app Raya, which discourage such sharing, are easily circumvented by motivated users.[48] Social media makes it easy to strip information of its context, pull it from its discursive framework, and transmit it across relationships and networks. A message exchanged between friends can eventually reach a large audience of readers who do not understand the original contextual frame. Sometimes it even seems that social media is designed to enable such erasures. By articulating and connecting social groups, social media allows information to travel through multiple networks, which only need to touch at a single node to become part of the circuit of transmission.

When someone accidentally or intentionally reaches an enormous audience with a piece of information that was meant for a particular context, it is experienced as a massive violation of privacy. Unlike broadcast media such as newspapers or television, which were created by a small number of professionals, social media content can be created by anyone. "Regular person" and "unexpectedly enormous network of transmission" is a dangerous combination: a photo can rapidly become a meme, or an embarrassing cellphone video can spread far and wide. Huge audiences were once the realm only of the famous or powerful, who typically have systems in place to manage them; ordinary people rarely do, and the platforms do not offer any of these tools.[49]

Lindsey Stone worked as a caregiver to a group of high-functioning developmentally disabled adults. She and her friend and coworker Jamie took her clients on different activities—movie theaters, bowling—and in October 2012, Jamie, Lindsey, and her clients went on a field trip to Washington, DC. They visited the National Mall, the Smithsonian, the Holocaust Museum, and the US Mint. Jamie and Lindsey had a running joke in which they would take silly pictures in front of signs. They would hold a cigarette in front of a "No Smoking" sign or pretend to litter in front of a "No Littering" sign—the kind of inside joke that is only really funny if you are participating in it.[50] While at Arlington National Cemetery, Jamie took a picture of Lindsey posing in front of a "Silence and Respect" sign. In the picture, Lindsey is yelling and holding up a middle finger. After the trip, Jamie posted it to a Facebook album of pictures of their trip and tagged Lindsey. Neither of them thought much about it. Then the picture went viral.

Both women received thousands of Facebook messages, emails, and text messages like, "Lindsey Stone hates the military and hates soldiers who have died in foreign wars," "You should rot in hell," and "Just pure Evil." Thirty thousand people signed up for a Facebook group called "Fire Lindsey Stone," and three thousand signed a petition calling for the same thing.[51] She was fired.[52] Camera crews showed up outside her house. She received death and rape threats and barely left her house for a year. Lindsey's attackers weaponized the participatory potential of social media, perhaps motivated by partisan politics.

The picture was taken among friends in a particular interpretive context, and once detached from Lindsey and Jamie's social world, it was easily misconstrued. Part of the problem was that it was a photograph rather than a piece of text. Visual information is extremely easy to misinterpret when moved from one context to another. Simply removing the caption from a photograph can significantly change how it is interpreted.[53] Providing false context for a photograph, an act called "misappropriation" or "misrepresentation," is a primary way of spreading misinformation on social media.[54] This is why, unlike platforms like Tumblr and Twitter, which build in "retweeting" and "reblogging," Instagram has never allowed images posted by one account to be reposted by another. Instagram's original developers recognized that an image-based website was uniquely vulnerable to decontextualization.[55]

But Lindsey and Jamie's photograph was easily replicated and reposted. Like every other piece of digital content, it had an enormous potential audience. But that audience had no idea of the original context and latched onto a very different interpretation: that Lindsey believed veterans did not deserve "silence and respect." Without the original context, the recipients formed their own narrative.

Relational Context Changes

In other situations, the content remains the same, but the relationship between sender and recipient changes. When this happens, information given in a trusted context may take on new meanings. For example, Andre (nineteen, Black) told me about some "drama" that happened in his friend group:

> And two of my guy friends, they started talking. And they started messing around with each other. And they ended up breaking up. So my other friend took it on hisself to go on Instagram and post about how [the other guy] had an STD. And, yeah, it was like, everybody was in the business, and everybody was talking about him. And he had to delete his Instagram. . . . And he had a lot of followers, and he had a lot of—he'd built up his page and then he had to delete it because he got outed.

Andre's friend had revealed that he had a sexually transmitted disease in an appropriate context: a sexual relationship. When the relationship ended, the ex-boyfriend "put his business online," as Andre put it, and the information moved from an intimate context to a public one. But this movement happened because the social tie between Andre's friend and his partner changed. Andre was so disgusted with the ex-partner's action that he left the group of friends, but he said that he sees similar things online "all the time."

When we disclose private information to each other, it makes us vulnerable, and trust is central in the decision to share with others. It creates the expectation that the person or entity with which we share will respect our confidentiality and be discreet.[56] An alcoholic describing the consequences of her drinking to an Alcoholics Anonymous meeting trusts that the participants will keep her identity confidential.[57] Andre's friend trusted that his sexual partner would keep his confidence. When they broke up and that trust no longer existed, the partner broadcast a very private piece of information. Most activists object to the phrase "revenge porn," preferring "nonconsensual image sharing," but the slang term comes closer to the experience of Andre's friend: something was shared within a trusted context, but the context changed.[58] When nude images are exchanged between consenting adults, there is an element of trust that often vanishes when the two break up, especially if the breakup is acrimonious. As the digital media scholar Kath Albury and her colleagues write, "When images are shared without consent, it is a very significant breach of trust, and should be considered as a serious invasion of privacy rather than an inevitable outcome of recording a sexually suggestive image."[59] The person forwarding the image, or putting their ex "on blast," is in the wrong, not the person who shared it in the first place. (This is yet another instance of why making individuals solely responsible for their own privacy is a mistake.) Most nude images, in fact, are never shared outside their intended context.[60] Revenge porn is the nuclear option, an act of extreme betrayal.

"The Web Knows I'm Gay": Big Data Violations of Networked Privacy

Large-scale privacy violations—the collection, aggregation, use, and sale of "big data"—have much greater consequences than individual betrayals on social media, despite being far less visible. Big data is defined by the technology scholars danah boyd and Kate Crawford as "massive quantities of information produced by and about people, things, and their interactions."[61] This, of course, includes large amounts of social media data. Big data enables enormous leaks and illustrates why we must think about privacy as an element of a network rather than the property of a single individual or "node." An individual cannot even superficially address the protection of privacy in big data. It is only because people do not see the consequences of data aggregation, or even recognize the scale of its collection, that companies are able to claim that personal responsibility is the appropriate frame for privacy issues. While most big data violations of networked privacy were opaque, traces leaked into my interviews. Andre complained, "I hate going on YouTube and click on a random video about puppies or something, and YouTube will use their algorithms to play a PrEP commercial or an HIV ad.

I'm like, 'This video has nothing to do with that,' but it sees the video that I do watch, so automatically I have to have this STD or something. And I hate that." His concerns were echoed by a focus-group participant: "I think the web knows I'm gay. I don't know how, but I get gay dating sites, like all those ads and stuff, and I don't—I mean, I might have posted some gay-rights article or something, but I don't search things that are—I don't know. I don't know how they—I don't know how." Both men knew that they were being served ads for gay dating networks and HIV-prevention medication because they were gay. But neither understood why. The answer, of course, is big data. The profiles stored by online advertisers had categorized both men as gay. It is impossible to know whether this classification was made based on Andre's repeated viewing of Nicki Minaj videos, his visits to the Shade Room Instagram, the connections in his social network, or even his in-person location.[62] The opacity of such determinations is part of what makes them so insidious.

The aggregation of data reveals more than the sum of its parts. A person posting a picture of their biscuit-and-egg sandwich on Instagram may simply want to show off their tasty breakfast. If that same person posts pictures of high-calorie food every day, and if this is combined with fitness data such as the step counts automatically recorded by Apple iPhones, it may cause insurance companies, doctors, or personal trainers to make judgments about the person's potential health.[63] A person who sends a cheek swab to 23andMe might just be curious about their family history, but police can use the data to solve crimes, pharmaceutical companies can use it to develop new drugs, and insurance companies can use it to deny coverage for people with genetic risk factors for certain diseases.[64] Three examples of big data are worth discussing in depth: data brokers, who show how data aggregation enables new types of privacy violations; genomic data, which demonstrates how easily you can be implicated by other people sharing data about you; and predictive algorithms, which demonstrate how sorting people into categories can reveal very private information.

Data Brokers

Data brokers are companies that collect, combine, and sell people's data, a process called "data aggregation." The sources of this data include social media, location data from cellphones and mobile apps like Uber, credit reports, phone records, retail purchases, loyalty card information, warranties, student data, census records, voter registration data, motor vehicle registration and driving records, postal addresses, most wanted lists and terrorist watch lists, records of bankruptcies, professional and recreational licenses, tax records, mortgages, liens, deeds, foreclosures, court records, birth certificates, death certificates, marriage and divorce records, contributions to political campaigns, and gun ownership records.[65] That is a partial list. The biggest data broker, Acxiom, says it has three thousand pieces of information about every adult in the United States.[66] This information is used to create detailed customer profiles, which data brokers sell to a wide range of customers.

Acxiom claims that it sells data to most of the top US credit card issuers, retail banks, telecom and media companies, retailers, car manufacturers, brokerage firms, and insurance companies; investigative reporting shows that data brokers also sell to scam artists and governments, which in some cases are legally prevented from gathering this information themselves.[67] A Vietnamese identity thief bought two hundred million records from Experian.[68] According to the Federal Trade Commission (FTC), another data broker bought the financial information of "hundreds of thousands" of payday-loan applicants and sold it to "phony Internet merchants" who "raided the accounts for at least $7.1 million."[69] Both the Internal Revenue Service and the Department of Homeland Security have purchased detailed cellphone location data of millions of Americans, which is illegal to collect without a warrant.[70] A US military counterterrorism unit bought location data of millions of Muslim people from two different brokers.[71] ICE uses data brokers to buy cellphone records, health-care provider content, Department of Motor Vehicle records, and credit reports.[72]

Most of these small pieces of data do not reveal much by themselves. But when they are aggregated with hundreds of other pieces of data, they create a mosaic of a person that might be interpreted and used in ways its subject would never want. One data broker sells a list of men suffering from erectile dysfunction. The FTC criticized brokers for creating lists of "financially vulnerable" individuals, under names like "X-Tra Needy," "Hard Times," "Very Elderly," and "Very Spartan."[73] (Imagine who might buy such lists. One data broker marketed a list of gamblers over fifty-five, called "Oldies but Goodies," with the description, "These people are gullible. They want to believe that their luck can change." Criminals bought the list and used it to bilk elderly people of hundreds of thousands of dollars.)[74] Brokers have sold lists of rape victims, people with AIDS/HIV, and people with addictive behavior including alcoholism, drug use, and gambling problems.[75]

It is extremely difficult to avoid the privacy-violating collection of big data or remediate its effects once it is collected. This creates what the media studies scholar Mark Andrejevic calls a "privacy asymmetry" between regular people, who are subject to ever more extensive surveillance and monitoring, and those who monitor them, who are hidden and secretive.[76] There is an intrinsic power imbalance between a government or corporation and individual users, who have little chance of protecting their privacy against the violation machine that is the modern internet. Many people are only hazily aware that data brokers exist, and virtually no one has any idea what data these companies collect about them, where they get it, or whom they sell it to, let alone how to stop it. We cannot even correct inaccuracies in our own data once it has been collected by for-profit companies. This can cause immense problems when incorrect data is used to deny benefits or resources. In other words, data brokers prevent people from having agency over their own information.[77]

Personally Identifiable Information

Laws that protect the privacy of "personally identifiable information" (PII) cover "any information that can be used to distinguish or trace an individual's identity, such as name, social security number, date and place of birth, mother's maiden name, or biometric records."[78] Similar models of privacy protection exist in the Organisation for Economic Co-operation and Development's privacy guidelines and the General Data Protection Regulation, which define personal data as that which belongs to an identifiable individual.[79] But these legal protections do not apply to other types of data. When PII is stripped out, private data is considered "de-identified," and it becomes a commodity that can be bought, sold, and aggregated. Moreover, using PII as the gold standard for privacy protection ignores many other types of private information; as the privacy scholar Michael Zimmer notes, in many contexts, the contents of social media posts are *not* considered PII.[80]

And removing PII does not prevent re-identification by data triangulation. Researchers have been able to identify individuals in many anonymized data sets, including the browsing histories of three million users, the credit card transactions of 1.1 million people, the location data of more than a million people, and a billion mobile data points from taxi journeys in Shanghai and Shenzen.[81] Even though these data sets are "big" and do not include PII, they contain information that makes it easy to identify individuals. While twelve points of a fingerprint are required to positively identify someone, researchers were able to identify 95 percent of the million individuals in the location data set using only four data points. Consider that most people go to work and go home every day and that very few people live in the same place as the people they work with.[82] Re-identification casts doubt on whether any data set can be anonymized.[83] Given the networked nature of big data, protecting PII does nothing to protect privacy.

Shockingly, a similar process takes place with respect to the Health Insurance Portability and Accountability Act (HIPAA). While most people know that HIPAA protects the privacy of "individually identifiable health information," few know that the law allows companies to buy and sell personal information once your name and contact details—but not your age, gender, or partial zip code—have been removed.[84] Yet data aggregation and triangulation work just as well on health information as on consumer information. And certain data, such as genetic information, is innately identifi-able. PII cannot be stripped out. The privacy of this information is made even leakier by the intense networking of genetic data.

Genomics

A fundamental fact of genetics is that family members share DNA. Commercial DNA testing services promote the ability to flesh out the family tree, tell you your genetic propensity to disease, and find your distant rela-tives. The popularity of genomic testing services like 23andMe and Ancestry .com has heavily expanded the availability of genomic information. More than twenty-six million Americans have given their DNA to a consumer ge-netics company.[85] A study in *Science* reported that 60 percent of Americans with northern European ancestry can be identified by matching genealogi-cal data to a consumer genetic database, even if they have not added their own DNA. Scientists expect this to expand to 90 percent in the next few years.[86] Although genetic information uniquely identifies an individual, it is not analogous to a Social Security number or even a fingerprint.[87] Genetic data, by its very nature, implicates others. Even genetic material from your third cousin can be used to partially match DNA and identify your genome.

Perhaps a more immediate concern is the scenario in which a recre-ational DNA test calls family ties into question, revealing unexpected rela-tives and familial connections. Thousands of people have discovered through genetic ancestry testing that they had half brothers or sisters from a parent's extramarital affair. In this case, it is not simply one's own DNA but its loca-tion within a genetic network that reveals formerly secret information. The genealogist CeCe Moore told the *Atlantic*, "It's getting harder and harder to keep secrets in our society. If people haven't come to that realization, they probably should."[88] Leah Larkin, a biologist who consults with adoptees looking for their biological parents, tells clients to look for their second or third great-grandparents in commercial ancestry databases. She explains,

"From there, we work forward in time using genealogical tools, specialized databases, and strategic testing of other people to confirm your biological family."[89] Many people who are biologically related do not know about this familial connection, as there is a big difference between one's biological family and one's kinship network.

Commercial uses aside, police are learning to take advantage of the networked nature of privacy to breach social networks, arguing that genetic information should be a tool for criminal enforcement. State and local agencies purchase data from brokers, surveil social media, engage in contact tracing, and increasingly engage in genetic identification of criminals. The revival of cold cases using familial DNA searching (FDS) is seductive but raises questions that we lack the vocabulary or legal frameworks to answer.

Police use recreational and genealogical DNA databases to carry out FDS, which compares DNA recovered in a criminal case with matches found in a DNA database. After the database generates a list of partial matches, police ideally test the DNA of other relatives to isolate a particular individual.[90] The serial killer known as the "BTK killer" was famously caught in 2005 using his daughter's DNA. Wichita district attorney Nola Foulston had spent twenty years investigating the case and strongly suspected a man named Dennis Rader. Unable to obtain a DNA sample from him, she got a court order to test his daughter's DNA from a pap smear she had had five years previously.[91] Law enforcement has begun to partner with genealogists to use not only open databases like GEDMatch but those of private companies like FamilyTree.org.[92] These gigantic commercial databases dwarf the FBI's genetic database of more than eighteen million convicted offenders and defendants. But because familial searching often leads to false positives, FDS is banned in Maryland and the District of Columbia and heavily regulated in California, Colorado, Virginia, and Texas.[93]

Such cases raise tricky questions about who has the right to obtain or disclose genetic information. What privacy rights do biological relatives have over DNA databases? Can we guarantee anyone's genetic privacy?

Predictive Algorithms

Predictive algorithms use enormous amounts of data to match people with similar information and predict how they will behave based on the behavior of others. This sorting often reveals information that people never shared or that they might want to keep private.

Facebook's feature "People You May Know" (PYMK) is supposed to show users friends or acquaintances whom they might like to connect with on Facebook. But PYMK can also reveal concealed relationships, such as therapists, sperm donors, and estranged relatives—even, in some cases, linking stalkers with their victims.[94] These hidden networks are identified through contact tracing. Facebook Messenger encourages users to upload their entire mobile address book to "find friends," matching phone numbers to Facebook profiles. If one of your contacts does this—meaning anyone with your email or mobile number in their cellphone—Facebook now knows there is a connection between you, even if you are not Facebook friends. (This is the same process that enables Facebook to create "shadow profiles" of nonusers.) It aggregates this contact information with other information that users have provided, such as any interactions between them on Instagram, Facebook, or WhatsApp; tagged photos, which provide evidence that they have been in the same physical space; GPS information; mobile data; and each user's Facebook network. This lets Facebook determine who actually interacts with whom, on- and offline, giving the company a completely different layer of network information to add to the friends list. PYMK can divulge information that users had no idea Facebook had collected, the revelation of which may make them very unhappy. One former Facebook engineer said that the feature's golden rule was, "Don't suggest the mistress to the wife."[95] But to avoid this, Facebook must figure out who is the wife and who is the mistress. PYMK demonstrates that aggregated data can reveal information that people would prefer to keep secret.

More sinister and damaging predictive algorithms draw from data aggregated from many sites or even purchased from brokers. Such software is increasingly designed for much more consequential purposes than what movies you might like: how good a credit risk you are, how well you will perform in educational settings or at work, and whether you will obey the law.[96]

One such algorithm is built into applicant tracking systems, software used by large employers to assess job candidates. Algorithms sort through résumés and cover letters for keywords, as we might expect, but they also use data gathered from social media and dubious "personality tests" to ascertain personality type, "culture fit," and "social capital" within a particular field.[97] Even more devastating to people's lives and prospects are threat-scoring systems, which predict whether someone is likely to commit a crime on the basis of information available from commercial data brokers. Such tools often make incorrect forecasts and are notorious for their racial and class biases.[98]

Both applicant tracking systems and threat-scoring systems incorporate social media data, which they absorb without context and classify automatically. Jokes, performative utterances, satire, and braggadocio are often missed or falsely interpreted as violent or threatening speech. For example, two British twenty-somethings were interviewed for five hours at Los Angeles International Airport, detained overnight in holding cells, and flown back to the United Kingdom on the basis of two tweets, one that referred to "destroying America" ("destroy" is British slang for "party") and another that discussed "diggin' Marilyn Monroe up," referencing an episode of *Family Guy*.[99] Such nuances are even harder to discern in other linguistic and cultural contexts.[100]

These judgments of potential criminality do not only affect people whose jokes are misinterpreted. Such algorithms rely on intrinsically networked social media information, which implicates others once integrated into large data systems. In 2019, the US State Department began requiring visa applicants to list their social media accounts. The Department of Homeland Security (DHS) already collects social data on immigrants, naturalized citizens, and green-card holders, including "social media handles, aliases, associated identifiable information and search results" from "publicly available information obtained from the internet, public records, public institutions, interviewees, commercial data providers."[101] In other words, it combines social data with information purchased from data brokers. This DHS data is used by agencies like ICE to identify potentially undocumented immigrants and to justify the disproportionate denial of entry to Muslims and travelers from Latin America.[102] Such information obviously includes interactions with others. I am a naturalized citizen, so if you have ever corresponded with me or are part of my network on social media, congratulations—you are also caught up in this dragnet.

People whose social networks include members of groups the DHS considers suspect might find themselves under suspicion regardless of their own actions. This widespread social media surveillance may discourage Muslims, undocumented immigrants, and other vulnerable populations from participating online because they are afraid of government surveillance, regardless of whether they have done anything illegal.[103] Predictive threat assessments make users responsible not only for their behavior but for the behavior of others in their networks and of anyone they associate with.

Networked Technology, Networked Privacy

Big data and social media make it clear that understanding privacy as an individual concern is hopelessly outdated. Even modern academic understandings of privacy as social and contextual cannot tell us how we might imagine privacy in the face of networked media, which are designed to break down firewalls between people, information, and contexts. By design, internet networks reveal information by connecting nodes intended to be separate. This leakiness is not a bug in the system that can be fixed with elaborate privacy settings, although many social media companies frame it that way. Wendy Chun maintains that it is the very nature of the internet. The data aggregated through social media and big data analytics is transmitted through entire networks of people, meaning that even someone without a social media presence can experience privacy harms. "Regardless of your own individual actions," Chun says, "you are constantly betrayed by people 'like you' and who are algorithmically determined to be 'like you.'"[104] Even if you have the strictest possible privacy settings, you are only as secure as the leakiest person in your network.

The historian Sarah Igo argues that when the term "privacy" appears in public discourse, it serves to define where the citizen ends and the state begins.[105] Today we often use it to discuss the limits of social technologies and map the boundaries between information that is ours to control and that which is mined and monetized by surveillance capitalism. What parts of our personal lives should be off-limits to corporations and to the state? What should not be bought and sold? What should not be watched, photographed, listened to, or tracked? Privacy gives us a vocabulary with which to set limits on modern networked technologies, a way to talk about space and exclusion. In sketching a theory of networked privacy in this book, I am also attempting to create a vocabulary for talking not only about the limits of networked technologies but also about how privacy maintains or resists structural power and how it separates and connects us to larger forces. By integrating concepts of power that attend to differences of gender, race, class, and sexuality, privacy can be reframed from a personal issue to a political one.

How do people cope with the complexities of networked privacy in their daily lives? In chapter 3, I talk about *privacy work*: the activities, behaviors, and attitudes people employ to maintain the level of privacy they desire, in the face of widespread networked privacy violations. This work is invisible, unequally distributed, and often unsuccessful, but we all do it.

3

Privacy Work

How do people tackle the complex issues around the increasingly networked nature of privacy? There is a common belief that they do not, that people are generally fine with the erosion of privacy by networked technologies.[1] My research does not support this belief in the slightest.[2] People want agency over how their information flows, and they want to limit how far technology encroaches into their lives. They will often go to great lengths to achieve this, but their attempts to reclaim agency and maintain their boundaries often look quite different from the privacy-protective measures advocated by experts.

In this chapter, I describe these efforts as *privacy work*, the tasks, behaviors, and mental heuristics that people engage in to maintain personal privacy in the face of networked privacy violations. To discuss privacy work in any meaningful way, we must center inequity, since privacy work is unevenly distributed and privacy violations have greater consequences for marginalized people. I use feminist theories of power and inequality to describe privacy work and its uneven distribution and draw from feminist information security to propose a framework of *feminist privacy protection* that centers harm and vulnerability, auditing privacy by evaluating its impact on those who are the most marginalized. This places the burden on the institution—corporation or state—that benefits from unfair and unequal information collection.

TLDR: People Do Care about Privacy

Academics and journalists often discuss privacy attitudes with a sort of finger-wagging chastisement, an implied disappointment that people do not care as much as they should about their online privacy. Researchers describe people as "apathetic" or "uninterested" in privacy.[3] Other studies note that even when people claim to care about privacy, their practices show that they do not.[4] One frequently cited study found that 21.8 percent of people had traded their Social Security number for a small discount.[5] Journalists and pundits decry young people's use of social media and wonder why people repeatedly fail to use strong passwords or why they embrace fitness trackers and voice-activated digital assistants.[6] Someone *really* concerned with protecting their privacy—presumably the researcher or journalist—would never do such a thing. For years, tech luminaries like Mark Zuckerberg claimed that privacy was a disappearing social norm, a position he recanted in the wake of considerable outcry over Facebook's various data-breach scandals.[7]

In ten years of asking people about privacy, I have found little to support the idea that privacy is no longer a social norm or that people "don't care" about protecting their privacy. "But wait!" you say. "People post selfies! They sext! They include location data on Twitter! Someone who wanted to protect their privacy wouldn't do these things!" The idea that these actions are antithetical to protecting privacy is wrong (and I deconstruct it in detail in chapter 7). Selfies, sexts, and geotagged posts are types of information that people view as unimportant—or they feel that the benefits of sharing them outweigh the nebulous long-term risks. In other words, sharing information online does not mean that someone puts a low value on privacy. Rather, people want agency over how their information moves. Using social media is not antiprivacy; privacy violations take place when people do not get to choose when, what, or with whom they share.

Many people also feel, usually correctly, that their privacy will inevitably be violated and so are more or less resigned to the idea that despite their best efforts, they cannot completely protect it.[8] While much of the hand-wringing over privacy focuses on millennials and Gen Z, research has shown that young people are actually better at protecting their privacy than older people are.[9]

In my interviews with people across the social spectrum, I have found that many go to great lengths to protect their privacy online. Many of these measures, however, are not traditional privacy-protective behaviors:

> I am very careful where I take my pictures. I watch people around me, if they are taking pictures now to see if it's of me. And everything is password protected three different ways. I'm always worried about being hacked. It's really kind of sad. (Nicole, thirty, white)

> I have two Facebooks, two Twitters, two emails. All my online activity, I have doubles of everything. I have one under my real name for job, family, et cetera, and then I have one under my chosen name, real name. (Jazz, thirty-four, white)

People do care about privacy. They close the blinds at night, keep their credit card numbers close, protect their phone with a personal identification number (PIN), and discuss medical issues in low voices. They are angry when a friend shares their secret without permission. They are mortified when they are tagged in an old, unflattering picture. They are horrified when a parent or partner reads old text messages. These attitudes, consistent across ages, incomes, races, and genders, motivate a wide variety of behaviors intended to maintain privacy, whether online or off-, successful or unsuccessful.

I call these behaviors *privacy work*. Much privacy work has not been seen as part of privacy protection because the actions do not fit into the old ideas of privacy as individual and individually guarded. Under networked privacy, we must consider that privacy is not a noun—a static, individual right, something a person has or does not have—but a verb, a process that one engages in. Redefining it this way lets us recognize the efforts people make to maintain their online privacy. People do privacy work to retain agency over what, how, and with whom they share information.

A feminist concept of privacy work allows us to push back against the widespread belief that people are charged with protecting their own privacy and are to blame if they do not. This is not only wrong and unhelpful, since the great majority of privacy violations come from big structures and institutions; it also does not recognize that the weak privacy technologies and laws that do exist fail to take power into account at all. The structural forces that penetrate social networks and manipulate networked privacy unfairly target marginalized groups. When we rely on "notice and choice" regimes, presume that privacy is always about technology, or conflate "privacy" with "data protection," we ignore the social and unequal nature of both on- and offline privacy.

Feminist theories of power and inequality allow us to make privacy work visible and witness how it is distributed. The phrase "privacy work" echoes concepts in feminist sociology that surface the invisible labor that marginalized groups must do to protect themselves. The feminist sociologist Liz Kelly defines "safety work" as the planning and strategizing that girls and women undertake to avoid men's violence.[10] Women engage in wide-ranging behaviors to maintain their safety in public; in Kelly's words, safety work includes "thinking processes, decision-making, and embodied watchfulness."[11] Thinking of privacy maintenance as work thus situates it in a tradition of pioneering feminist scholars like Kelly, Arlene Kaplan Daniels, Arlie Hochschild, Judith Rollins, and Fiona Vera-Gray, all of whom described types of invisible work that are unevenly distributed by gender, race, and class.[12] This concept of privacy also makes us attuned to the intersectional, social, and unequal distribution of privacy, as well as the uses to which privacy violations can be put for the gain of unscrupulous actors.

We engage in privacy work preemptively, as we do safety work, to stave off the often-unpredictable harms of privacy violations.[13] Judging the effectiveness of these efforts requires an impossible level of risk assessment. As a result, privacy work is endless and stressful, and it is rarely clear whether it prevents any harms. We can assess its effectiveness only when it fails.

Privacy work is carried out both online and off. People seek to stop network leaks by managing passwords; configuring social media settings; using encryption, virtual private networks (VPNs), or ad blockers; setting information-sharing norms with friends and family; self-censoring; deciding whether to share information; using forms of "social steganography," which use vague or coded language to limit understanding;[14] strategically choosing usernames or avatars; obfuscating personal information, like using a fake email address when signing up for airport Wi-Fi; using different technologies to share different types of information with specific audiences; refusing to use certain technologies; disabling others; and leaving particular social media sites. Privacy work also includes efforts to control the spread of information by putting up curtains or blinds; wearing sunglasses or hats; installing tinted windows in your car; adding high fences or dense bushes around your home; lowering your voice to prevent eavesdropping; cutting up expired credit cards; shredding documents; covering your hand when entering your PIN at the automated teller machine (ATM); and hundreds of other actions we take every day. These strategies are unevenly distributed. The wealthy and tech savvy have more options, but marginalized people often need more protection. Someone who lives alone in a big house needs to do less privacy work than someone sharing a room with five people in an area heavy with police surveillance.

This chapter reframes privacy-protective practices and strategies as *privacy work* and describes how power and privilege affect the privacy work that we all do. While everyone does privacy work, both the level of effort and its success are unequally distributed. Marginalized populations are more likely to be subject to violations of their privacy, and those violations are far more likely to do long-term damage. Ultimately, we must acknowledge that it takes real work even to approach our desired level of privacy given the predominance of networked information technologies.

The Lived Experience of Privacy Work

How people experience and manage privacy work to retain a sense of agency depends on several factors: their reasons for being online in the first place, their comfort level with sharing information about themselves, the consequences they imagine might result from a release of sensitive information, their own identity and subject positions, and their level of marginalization. There is copious research on the different ways by which people protect their privacy online, but little of it shows how vast and contextual the spectrum of privacy work can be; nor does it consider many of the methods I describe here.[15] Some of these strategies are rarely spoken about, while others are widely encouraged and adopted; some are built into software, while others are improvised. People learn privacy "hacks" from friends and are lectured by educators, technologists, or parents on what they should do online.

Kien is an Asian American software engineer in his early twenties, the son of Vietnamese refugees. We met at Starbucks in an office park near his job at a tech start-up. Wearing black-rimmed glasses, a nondescript T-shirt and jeans, and a gold buddha on a chain around his neck, he described himself as "quite private online," which is an understatement. He has very high boundaries for what information feels safe to share. He guards his offline privacy in the same intense way, ensuring that there are no leaks from his network by limiting both his contacts and what he tells them: he is so private that when he moved to North Carolina from the Northeast, he told only a single professor and none of his friends. He shrugged. "They kind of know now, I think, for the most part, just because I haven't been there and they haven't seen me. So I'm pretty sure they figured that out." He has a Snapchat but never posts, preferring to watch his "louder" friends who post Snaps of their nights out. The privacy settings on his Facebook profile are so high that nobody besides himself can see anything but his picture and birthday. While he identifies as bisexual, he keeps that information firmly off the internet and recently deleted all his dating apps, deciding to focus on meeting people in person.

Kien worries that information he shares online might, in the future, cause problems with his family or employer. After he read a news story about how the comedian Kevin Hart's old tweets came back to haunt him, Kien deleted any information from the internet that he thought might portray him in a negative light. When I asked for an example, he told me about a goofy video of him riding a kid's bike around a toy store. "You know, obviously that's something innocent, something just kids do, but I was like, 'Well, what if twenty years down the road I'm running for an office or something, someone uses this against me, make me sound like an idiot,' or something like that." He does not seem to see this carefulness as unusual. He told me that he has always been private, but the Cambridge Analytica scandal has him increasingly worried.

Other people do privacy work not by keeping everything private but by stopping leaks before and after they happen. In New York City, I interviewed Diego, a twenty-one-year-old Dominican. Technologically elite but broke (he describes himself as "really poor, like super poor"), he is an autodidact who cultivates technical expertise to outwit authorities and protect himself and his family. He is not so concerned about privacy among his network of friends. In high school, Diego's friends would pay him to break into their girlfriends' emails and social networks. "It was mostly people dealing with jealousy and cheating; and then some people had some stuff stolen from them, and they wanted to see if another person had it." What he worries about is state intrusions on his privacy, the highest-level and most consequential type of privacy violation.

Diego has spent a lot of time learning how to manage his privacy at the source; his privacy work is elaborate and sophisticated. For example, he uses VPNs and proxy servers, keeps several SIM cards on him, uses iPhones because he can remotely erase them should they fall into the cops' hands, and even owns a shirt with a metal-lined pocket that prevents his phone from revealing location information to cellphone towers. (He enjoys "urban exploration"—breaking into forbidden, usually abandoned buildings and photographing their interiors.)

Diego is a hacker and proud of it. He fears state tracking because he believes the combination of his marginalized identity and his expertise makes him a threat: "I'm a minority from the hood who has a little bit of know-how." When I asked him if privacy differs depending on privilege, Diego was adamant. "It does. It absolutely does, 'cause it's like if you have money, if you have the means and you have power, if you see something you don't like on the internet, you can change it." (I am reminded of my experience attempting to scrub my home address from the internet, which was both expensive and annoying.) To ground his claim about money helping to guarantee privacy, he tells me about a teenage friend whose nudes appeared on a revenge-porn site. The friend asked Diego to help take the photos down, and after getting nowhere through legitimate means, he decided to hack the system. "It took me three days to get into that website and shut it down." From his perspective, if he had $50,000, he could have hired an expensive lawyer to force the site to take down the photos. But since he does not have access to wealth, he must leverage what he does have, technical skills.

Diego and Kien represent two extremes of how people manage privacy work online, but neither Diego's willingness to put in extensive time and effort to gain technical knowledge nor Kien's willingness to basically forgo online social connections to guard his privacy is particularly unusual. People employ a wide variety of privacy-protective mechanisms to maintain information boundaries in the face of networked digital technologies. In this section, I start with the types of privacy work that require technological know-how: manipulating technical mechanisms like privacy settings and dividing one's audience across platforms, which I call *social segmentation*. Then I talk about techniques to maintain agency over information, organized from sharing more to sharing less, beginning with security through obscurity, in which people hope that their relative unimportance will protect their information; social steganography; self-censoring or sharing less; and then the "nuclear" option: opting out. Finally, I discuss people's futile efforts to manage *other* people's privacy practices through setting norms. These examples reveal that average internet users take on significant responsibility to maintain their privacy, but their privacy work is rarely enough.

Technical Mechanisms

Perhaps the most familiar form of privacy work is configuring the settings on social media applications or, less commonly, using privacy-enhancing technologies such as VPNs or encrypted messaging. These are the privacy practices promoted by software companies and social platforms and the technologies most people know about. Most people I talked to had changed their Facebook settings to make them more private than the default. Many had turned off location settings. On Twitter, some people had changed their accounts from public to private after negative experiences, while others experimented with "closing" or "opening" their direct messages. Some used incognito browsing when looking at "sketchy sites" or pornography. And to manage their audience, one of the major challenges of networked privacy, most people blocked individual people or used filters that prevented some people from seeing their content or contacting them.[16] Those with the greatest potential impact of information leaking were often the most careful. Andre (nineteen, Black), for instance, a closeted gay man, told me he had blocked his entire family on Instagram so that he could be open about himself.

Using these technical mechanisms, however, is not so simple. Blocking people could have unknown consequences.[17] Fatima (twenty-one, Latina) is close to her young aunts and is worried they might inadvertently reveal something she does not want her strict mother to know. She cannot block them, however, unless she wants backlash from the rest of her family: "I feel like blocking, to me, should only be used when you feel threatened, not like, 'Oh my God, I don't want to talk to you anymore. Block.' I think that's very immature." Mike (twenty, African American) agreed. He feels that blocking lets people know that they have gotten to him: "I feel like me blocking you shows that I'm really worried about you." Instead of blocking people who irritate him, he tries to ignore them to maintain the upper hand.

More intense privacy-enhancing technologies are mostly used by people, like Diego, who are either highly technical, involved in activities that might subject them to surveillance (such as anti-ICE activism), or both. People use password managers, two-factor authentication, or apps like Signal, which offer messaging with end-to-end encryption. Carlos (twenty-eight, Latino), who is undocumented, is part of a WhatsApp group of people who notify each other of ICE raids in town. Andrea (twenty-nine, white), a trans woman, told me that she often edits the metadata in her photos to remove location information, a privacy breach that most of my participants were probably unaware of. The people who are most diligent about protecting their privacy by technical means are those who are marginalized in some way and have been subject to harassment.

But the technical ability to configure privacy settings is by no means universal. Researchers have documented that skills and capacities around internet and computer tasks vary widely, and this includes privacy work.[18] One study, for example, showed that whether people back up their data—considered a universal best practice—depends not on their income or education but on their overall skill at using the internet.[19] This is true of many people I interviewed; while all of them know that privacy settings exist, some feel incapable of setting them:

> Honestly, I haven't touched any of those [Facebook settings]. I just use whatever is default on it. I have not touched any of it at all so—it's something I need to actually look at. I actually don't know how. I will do that. Have to find out. (Ebo, twenty-three, Black)

> I know there's security settings and stuff [on Facebook]. I don't even know what mine are set at. I'm sure my wife did mine. I'm assuming all my friends can see anything I post. I don't think I have any kind of weird security thing. (Robin, forty-six, white)

Technical mechanisms are often inadequate for what people want them to do. In other cases, they change frequently, causing a great deal of frustration. Cimarron (forty, white) complained, "I mean, like Facebook changes how they publicize your stuff all the time. And for the longest time, I had it set so that I couldn't be found. And then I met a friend of mine in Vegas, and I was like, 'Oh, you probably won't be able to find me on Facebook,' and he found me right away. I'm like, 'How did you do that?' And he's like, 'Well, they changed their privacy settings again.'" Cimarron mistakenly believed their settings were configured in such a way to prevent people they do not know from finding them. Because such changes are frequently not publicized, people are wary of social media sites and are aware that information leaks. So they turn to other mechanisms.

In previous research, Eszter Hargittai and I found that even when people demonstrate better-than-average understanding of privacy, their knowledge is often spotty and incorrect.[20] This is partly because many of the issues around privacy remain opaque. For example, most of my participants, most college students I teach, and, it seems, most people overall believe that technology companies "listen" to them using phone microphones in order to accurately target advertising.[21] Every major technology company has formally denied doing this, but it shows how little faith people have in the willingness of technology companies to respect their privacy. For every person I interviewed who is as technologically savvy as Diego, I talked to someone who confessed that they store their passwords in a spreadsheet or share them with their partner.

The best practices of privacy protection most often recommended in online security guides are time-consuming and require a level of technical expertise far beyond average. Before I started publishing research on far-right groups, I bought a highly rated password manager, added two-factor authentication to every site that had it, and paid $100 to have my home address deleted from public databases. My research group started out by using email encrypted with the program Pretty Good Privacy (PGP) for everything and password protecting individual documents, but this quickly interfered with doing actual work. The knowledge, time, and resources needed to implement such measures are prohibitive. Justine (twenty-five, Korean American), who has been harassed for her writing, told me, "I think I spent, like, the last week just updating all my passwords and adding, like, two-step verification to everything. It was like you just have to leave an entire Sunday to do all of that."

Social Segmentation

Another common type of privacy work is social segmentation: controlling what information is shared with different audiences by using different sites, apps, and even accounts. Because we share information on the basis of context and audience, segmentation helps maintain contextual integrity, the social norms that govern how information flows in particular contexts. As discussed in chapter 2, the philosopher Helen Nissenbaum explains that social contexts like doctors' offices have specific norms around how information should be shared.[22] It is when information flows from one context to another—for instance, if a gossipy nurse tells his friends about a patient's strange condition—that people experience privacy violations.

Large sites like Facebook and Twitter often merge contexts with very different norms, making it difficult for users to strategically share information with some people and not others.[23] Those who use these sites employ strategies that include targeted friend lists and careful content separation to keep these audiences from intersecting.[24] But many of my participants reject broad sites like Facebook and Twitter in favor of online spaces with smaller, more focused audiences. They thus create separate social contexts with different informational norms.

Sometimes people make these choices on the basis of their perceptions of the site's norms. Different platforms have different implicit and explicit privacy expectations and are configured to share different types of information. On Reddit, for instance, most users go by a pseudonym, and many maintain multiple accounts; but both practices violate Facebook's terms of service. Sexually explicit talk is common on some dating sites but is considered "too much information" on others (and may be removed by the platform's moderation team). Andrea (twenty-nine, white) explained how segmenting her audience helps her decide how and when to share on the basis of site-specific norms:

> Like on Fetlife [a BDSM social network], it's perfectly fine to talk about fetishes I have and not so much appropriate at church. I think [social media] has made it easier because I have those distinct sites. I can be like, "Okay, I can share this kind of stuff here, but I won't share this kind of stuff there." Whereas if I didn't have that, it would be harder to tell where certain information or when certain information should be shared. Like on a dating website, I can share the fact that I'm trans immediately, and that's perfectly fine. But if I met somebody, like at a park, it's a little harder to tell when it would be a good time to share that information.

While she is committed to educating people about trans issues, Andrea does not feel the need to broadcast her trans identity to everyone she meets, "like, at GameStop." Her norms around privacy include sharing sensitive information only in places where others share similar information. She likes Reddit because she can swear, post risqué photos, and have frank discussions with other trans women, things she would not be comfortable doing on Facebook. She does not share her Reddit username with anyone and never posts her location or "real name."

Social segmentation was summarized by a twenty-two-year-old woman in a focus group, who explained that she segments her audiences by choosing particular apps for particular content types on the basis of the platforms' privacy norms: "The way I share content has become a lot more targeted. Instead of putting it on Facebook for a thousand people to see, I'll email pictures or something to a specific set of people, or I'll Snapchat it to a specific set of people. But it's just become, like, less—it has less of a reach now."

Snapchat appeals to many people because it claims to have strong privacy norms. Its early success was due to the ostensibly ephemeral nature of Snaps, which the app promised would be deleted in twenty-four hours. While it is less popular now, I talked to several young people who prefer it for interactions with intimate friends, especially those with whom they maintain lengthy "Snapstreaks." Snapchat is the place to share embarrassing selfies, banal daily updates, and private jokes, rather than the groomed self-presentation expected on Instagram.[25]

Other participants described more intense versions of audience segmenting. Fatima (nineteen, Latina) is majoring in Chinese and has become an enthusiastic user of WeChat, an immensely popular social network among Chinese-speaking diaspora communities, which she perceives as having better privacy features than US sites like Facebook. (This is a dubious claim, as Chinese social media apps have been accused of censoring content and passing information to the Chinese government.)[26] Fatima dislikes Facebook because it sells personal information, so she posts there only when explicitly trying to amplify a message, such as finding a home for an adoptable cat. By posting in Chinese on an app that is rarely used in the United States, she segments her audience with what feels to her like a nearly unbreachable firewall.

Justine is a passionate activist and a PhD student. She also segments her audiences by using applications with different norms. She uses Tumblr to talk about social justice and anti-rape activism, Snapchat to share lip-sync videos with her college friends, Twitter to connect to academics, and

Facebook to talk to people she knows in "real life." Her Tumblr account is completely separate from her other accounts. She described how she uses each platform:

> I don't really talk on Instagram. It's mostly just to post, and I'll do, like, the artsy-fartsy updates. But in terms of choosing what to share, I think I probably share the most on Tumblr. But that's because I've deleted my Tumblr account several times because of harassment, and now I'm at a point where I feel a little more confident in knowing that my Tumblr crowd will, like, never mesh with anything else. So in that way, it does give me a bit more liberty to share things in kind of abstract, vague, blogging format. Twitter, I've increasingly veered away from sharing anything personal on Twitter. I recently had a kind of harassment thing on Twitter in response to an article I wrote. So then I completely blocked it for a while, and I've just reopened it. Facebook, I'll do, like, updates, especially when I'm traveling to meet up with people. If there's an article that I felt was interesting, I'll share, but nothing too personal. Snapchat seems purely social to me.

The social segmentation strategy described by these participants is enabled by a complex social media ecosystem.[27] We use multiple channels to talk to people we are close with, including phone, text, email, postcard, or social media, choosing the appropriate medium on the basis of whom we are speaking with and the message we want to send.[28] My study participants similarly use different apps and platforms to speak to different people. Justine's Tumblr account feels safe precisely because her "Tumblr crowd" is completely separate from people who know her in other contexts; this allows her to share personal things, albeit in an "abstract, vague, blogging format."

Security through Obscurity

In contrast to the active strategies just described, some of my study participants passively depend on "security through obscurity." These people retain a sense of agency over what they share by telling themselves that only their very select audience is listening or that anonymity or pseudonymity will protect them from offline consequences. This is hardly unusual; obscurity is one of the main strategies that internet users rely on to protect their personal information and manage their online identities.[29] While many of my participants dutifully repeated that "everything you put on the internet is public," in practice, they often assume they are safe because nobody is paying attention. When you have only fifteen followers, none of whom know who you are in real life, it is much easier to avoid the exponential growth in shares that causes the ultimate context collapse and failure of audience segmentation: "going viral."

Obscurity *can* provide privacy protections when nobody is watching. As Camila (seventeen, Puerto Rican) said, "There may be a thousand people around you, but the question is how many of these thousand people are paying attention to you? And that's what determines whether or not it's private." This is true both on- and offline. Andrea, for instance, whom we heard from in the discussion of segmentation, told me that her obscurity protected her personal information: "I've got my phone on, it has GPS, et cetera, et cetera, et cetera. The information is there if somebody really wanted to get it. The only reason why people aren't trying to get it is because nobody knows who I am." Unlike high-profile people whose data is frequently hacked and exposed, Andrea believes her relative anonymity protects her.[30]

Most participants are most concerned that their friends, family members, coworkers, and ex-partners might access their online content. Their strategies for remaining obscure to these audiences take many different forms. Using pseudonyms, maintaining multiple profiles, or removing content from search engines lets people have the benefits of sharing information online without leaving everything they share open to curious family members or judgmental coworkers. Arya, the midwestern medical student who ran afoul of her conservative Muslim family after being tagged in a photograph, maintains her privacy by using a fake name on social media. This limits access to her content, as the only people who can find her online are those to whom she has given that name:

ARYA: So you know how I said I have a couple accounts?

ALICE: Mm-hmm.

ARYA: None of them have my real name on it.

ALICE: Interesting.

ARYA: So it's not easy for people to find me, my name, unless I go and *give* them my name and be like, "This is my name on Facebook." And it's something that's completely unrelated to who I really am. So personally, I have completely changed my identity. No one can find me on Facebook unless I go and add them, and no one can tag me because they don't know what my real name is. I used to add everyone on Facebook. I had friends of friends, I had friends of friends of friends, everyone, but now every single person who is on my account is a person I personally know or is one of the medical school students who has been cleared by the school.

Because she suffered significant repercussions as a teenager from her friends tagging her in photos, she makes it impossible for anyone she has not vetted to connect with her. She restricts her connections to people who presumably understand her concerns and share her norms. Her use of a false name ensures that if she is tagged, only her pseudonymous identity would be shared, not her real identity, which is connected to her parents' networks.

Arya's use of multiple accounts is common and was documented more than a decade ago by danah boyd in her study of "mirror profiles." boyd spoke to teenagers who maintained multiple MySpace profiles: one a squeaky-clean, parent-safe profile connected to their friends' similarly sanitized profiles and a parallel network of more frank profiles listed under nicknames or jokes.[31] This strategy continues today, as young people use false profiles to segment their content, curating the selves they show on each account. The "finsta," or fake Instagram, is perhaps the most common of these—perhaps because of Instagram's reputation as a place for only the most polished, curated images. (This is why participants in the previous section said they use Snapchat for more informal, sloppy posts where they are not performing their "edited self.") A finsta creates segmentation not by app but by profile. Finsta users typically maintain two Instagram accounts, one "real," which is carefully edited and curated, and the "fake" one, which is more humorous, "less edited," and "less filtered."[32] Gabriel (nineteen, Latino) described his finsta as including "usually bad hookups, weird Grindr conversations—those are always funny—some relationship stuff. . . . On my finsta, I'm like, 'This is me. I'm depressed, and I like to sleep around.'" Finstas are typically private, restricted to an intimate group of people, and use a fake name and profile picture.

These pseudonyms are often carefully chosen. Given the effectiveness of search engines, an unusual persistent pseudonym can leave an identifiable trail. Some users intentionally choose pseudonyms that will have few unique results to keep people from tracking them across sites and triangulating the segmented information shared on each one—breaking down the firewalls that make obscurity viable. For example, girl gamer Paige (nineteen, white) chose a Pokémon reference as her Reddit and Discord username because it is difficult to Google. (I tried; it had five million results.) Another participant, who had been stalked for years, legally dropped her middle name to make herself harder to find via search engines.

Others moderate the content they share to prevent this type of information triangulation. Constance (thirty-three, white), who was threatened over a difference of opinion in her fan fiction community, is careful not to post photos that could be identified by Google Street View. Danielle (twenty-seven, white), who does not want her abusive parents to track her down, told me, "I never talk about where I live. I don't talk about the weather. I don't talk about friends I'm visiting in different cities." She sometimes posts pictures on Twitter under a pseudonym but deletes them a week later so that they cannot be found by someone searching the site.

While obscurity is a common technique, it is very weak. Justine wrote an essay for a British feminist magazine to share her experiences with sexism and racism abroad. She explained,

I wrote about my experience working in Korea, about, like, Korea's military history and sex tourism and, like, white expats, because—and for me it was like a strategic choice, because I thought this is a small publication in London. It's going to be published on Sunday. It's for "International Women's Week" or whatever. Nobody's going to read it. If people do read it, it's going to be people who, like, share some kind of values, where I can, like, have some kind of decent engagement with it, if there's any engagement at all, because nobody's going to read it anyway.

She chose a niche feminist publication published in a different country because she felt it would be seen only by those who shared her activist values. She did not want broader publicity because she knew it might be controversial in some circles. Unfortunately, the essay was picked up by an expat subreddit, and she began getting nasty messages on Twitter—an entirely different platform—from a group of white men who took offense to her description of expat dating practices. Justine thought obscurity would protect her, but once the essay was no longer obscure, she had no privacy.

Steganography

Another type of privacy work segments the audience using language, making information widely visible but understandable only to a certain in-group. danah boyd calls this technique "social steganography"; my participants referred to it as "vaguebooking," "subtweeting," or "subliminals."[33] Social steganography involves posting about someone or something in a way that people "in the know" will get but that will be impenetrable to those who are not. As boyd describes it, this creates situations in which people have access to content but not to its meaning. Steganography involves stripping information of its context, resulting in deliberate vagueness, sometimes to sow doubt, as Camila explained:

Let's say I saw you walking with somebody else's boyfriend or, like, I saw you walking with my boyfriend, and I posted a status like, "Oh, females always trying to be with somebody else's man," and you saw it. You'd be like, "Okay. This might be about me." But I never directly said it's *you* with this person. So it was like—it could be about somebody else. Like, they could've seen you with somebody else, and then somebody could've seen me with somebody else, and then a third party posting this status, and then it could be about either one of us. No one really knows, because we don't know what they're talking about.

Camila *wants* uncertainty: she does not want to be accountable, but she wants the woman in question to wonder if she is being called out on her behavior.

This tactic is often used by teenagers, many of whom were exposed to intensive antibullying campaigns in school. Steganography allows the writer to bully others or stir up drama while maintaining plausible deniability. Moira (twenty-three, white) explained,

> The whole thing with the bullying that happened in my high school was you always had to have plausible deniability. Like, no matter what you did, you always had to be able to say, "No, I didn't mean it that way" or "It was an accident." We were taught to look out for people making Facebook groups called like "I Hate Amanda," and it was like, that's never going to happen because you can see who made that group and we *know* you can see who made that group. We're not going to be that stupid. We're going to send anonymous messages. We're going to talk shit in private messages or where we think people can't see us. Like, the stuff that's going to happen, we're not going to publicly attach our names to it because we're not stupid. We know we can get in trouble.

Social steganography allows people to bully others without facing the consequences. (Implicit in Moira's comment is that antibullying education rarely reflects the creative ways in which young people are mean to each other.) This is privacy work in that it allows people to control who sees their antipathy toward others; steganography shields users from the consequences of their online behavior, such as being confronted by someone they were gossiping about or facing punishment at school.

Others use social steganography to create online drama and watch what happens. When something is vague and untargeted, it is very easy for someone to interpret it as being about them and potentially strike back; then viewers can share the popcorn GIF, sit back, and enjoy the show. Having an audience is key. In previous research, danah boyd and I defined "drama" as interpersonal conflict that takes place in front of an audience.[34] It requires active, interested onlookers. Drama was often mentioned as a type of conflict that could be avoided through appropriate configuration of privacy settings. But some people do not want to avoid drama; indeed, they intentionally create it, trying to provoke people online, ranting, posting intimate information about their relationships, or posting "cries for attention." Gabriel (twenty-one, Latino) called such people "messy," which he defined as "creating really unnecessary drama for the sake of creating drama."

Participants were divided over drama. Some mentioned that they dislike seeing it on social media, while others, perhaps more honestly, said they find it entertaining. While my studies with danah focused on teenagers, I found that people of all ages engage in drama. While participants often dismissed it as silly, teenage, or feminine, they also related detailed examples of drama that took place between Wikipedia editors, open-source contributors, marketing consultants, and cybersecurity professionals. In all these cases, drama made conflicts public that many people believed should remain private.

Sharing Less: The Privacy Setting in Your Brain

Perhaps the most common type of privacy work is choosing not to disclose.[35] (Because this is so common, I discuss its implications in more depth in chapter 5.) But despite the stereotype of social media users who post every thought online, I found that people often spend quite a bit of time thinking over whether to post anything at all, and they usually err on the side of sharing less. One focus-group participant (woman, thirty-three, white) explained, "Yeah, because I think there's a privacy-setting issue in terms of managing, but there's also the human privacy setting, in the sense that you feel constrained to actually just not say stuff. . . . In addition to the privacy setting, there's always—there's also, at least for some people, some amount of inhibition about saying it publicly in the first place. There's kind of a computer privacy setting and also like a privacy setting in your brain." This self-editing demonstrates what the sociologist Bernie Hogan calls the "lowest common denominator" effect: people consider what the most sensitive person in their network might find offensive and share only what they think is acceptable to that person.[36] This is especially true of young people who are trying to establish themselves professionally, particularly those trying to raise their socioeconomic status. In my research with Mikaela Pitcan and danah boyd, we found that low-income participants who were focused on upward mobility considered it very important to maintain an online presence that would be acceptable to anyone they might need to impress, such as teachers or employers.[37] These participants censored themselves heavily, keeping opinions, viewpoints, and creative work far off the internet or making them viewable only to a small number of people. This frequently took a lot of time and effort.

Jorge (twenty-five), a Puerto Rican New Yorker who grew up in public housing, described his online presence as "neutral": "I carefully consider everything I say, put out there, and do. That's going to translate to the internet. If it's going on Twitter, if it's going on Facebook, if it's going on Instagram, I either try to make it as neutral as humanly possible or as PC as possible. I try hard to be a PC person in general. I don't want to offend or upset anyone, because why would you take part in trying to upset someone? It just—it really doesn't feel conducive to a good life." Interestingly, Jorge uses the term "PC" (politically correct) to describe his self-censorship. While "PC" is often used ironically to suggest an overreach of liberal norms, Jorge uses it without irony, as a synonym for "conventional."[38] Jorge wants to achieve success as an engineer, and he is wary of sharing anything even slightly unusual in case it compromises his future.

Other discussions of neutrality make it sound more like hiding. Andre, an African American teenager I met in North Carolina, discussed how he keeps discussions of his sexuality off the internet to keep those who disapprove from finding out and punishing him offline. Although he has blocked his entire family, who do not know his sexual orientation, from viewing his Instagram, he is still careful with what he shares; he wants to have control over when to share information he feels should be kept private, to ensure that people do not prejudge him for his sexuality:

ANDRE: Yeah, neutral, I like to stay neutral.
ALICE: Why do you like to stay neutral?
ANDRE: I don't really like to be the one that's out there, "Oh, I'm gay," or whatever.
ALICE: You don't want people to see . . . the first thing they see.
ANDRE: Yeah, it's like, "Oh, he's gay," or whatever. I like people to get to know me first, and then I open up to them more. Then they see that side.

Andre primarily uses his Instagram to catch up on celebrity gossip, post selfies, and share memes. He avoids topics he perceives as "feminine" or "gay," preferring topics that are "more masculine, when it comes to memes." (I do not know what he meant by masculine memes, and I failed to ask.) When his first boyfriend posted pictures of them on Instagram, Andre called him and asked him to take them down, afraid his family would see. He feels that there are very few places he can be himself, on- or offline. Andre engages in intense privacy work to maintain his safety. If his family finds out he is gay, he might be kicked out of the house, and he puts in effort online to try to prevent that from happening.

Opting Out

An extreme form of privacy work is for participants to delete their accounts entirely or delete or edit large swaths of content. Some people who have done this kind of privacy work simply wanted to "start over," to keep previous (perhaps embarrassing) selves from becoming public, just as an adult might lock up their middle-school diary. One focus-group participant, for example, deleted her Facebook account when she started college, wanting a clean slate. Keith, a thirty-five-year-old white graduate student, deleted all his old tweets to prevent curious onlookers from trolling through them to find something compromising.

This strategy is frequently used by participants who have experienced harassment, which I will take up in chapter 4. Jamie (twenty-eight, white) calls the deletion of old information or accounts "nerfing," a slang term that gamers use to describe when a game dynamic is dumbed down by the designers or reduced in effectiveness. She enjoyed posting selfies to subreddits about makeup, but they brought frequent sexual harassment, with strangers direct messaging her with creepy propositions. To stop this gendered violation of privacy, she would often scrub old content to keep people from searching back through it:

> I end up nerfing my Reddit account every couple of months at this point because of the online creepiness I usually experienced if I'd post any pictures or let it be known that I'm a woman on Reddit, especially on the Makeup Addiction subreddit. If you post selfies of yourself like, "Here's my face of the day" or "Here's my Coachella look" or what have you, dollars to donuts, within an hour you're going to have your inbox full of creepy messages from guys. . . . A friend of mine actually posted some makeup swatches, where it was just like the swatches of eyeshadow from her new palette, and she got three creepy messages by the end of the day in her Reddit account where somebody was hitting on her. And all that was in the picture were her wrists for her makeup swatches.

In addition to deleting old content, Jamie has frequently deleted her account and started a new one, losing her Reddit karma but keeping harassers from finding her.[39] Justine also deleted several Tumblr accounts because of harassment. While this is a "nuclear option," Justine, Keith, and Jamie feel that it is the most effective way to prevent information from disseminating against their will.

Setting Norms

Information flows through networks, both online, in our articulated networks, and in our offline lives. We tell our friends things, we gossip, and we tell stories and take pictures of other people. Our human connections naturally form networks, which is why sites like LinkedIn exist and why "networking" is considered the best way to find a job or apartment. But these same dynamics make it very easy for people to violate each other's privacy, even unintentionally.[40] This suggests that just as communication is a social process, so is maintaining privacy. It requires the collective (usually unsuccessful) effort of entire networks. Privacy is an active process of managing not only your information behaviors but those of your network. But as we will see throughout this book, managing other people's behaviors is very difficult. And even if an individual were able to command exactly how everyone in their family, group of friends, or workplace treated their personal information, there would be no way to prevent other types of privacy leaks and violations. When behavioral or genetic networks are surveilled, they violate privacy in ways that individual actions cannot address.

We frequently attempt to protect the privacy of our networks using social and behavioral norms.[41] Norms are beliefs about how people should behave. They govern everything from how we should stand in an elevator (facing the front, looking ahead or, more commonly now, at our phones) to who gets to speak in a meeting, to how many selfies we should post on Facebook (very few). Norms are often very strong, and people who violate them often face repercussions.[42] Some norms are explicit: I swear a friend to secrecy before telling her a juicy piece of gossip, or a Division 1 coach tells her athletes exactly what is and is not acceptable on Instagram.[43] But others are implicit and more difficult to ascertain.

Norms around information sharing and privacy are everywhere, both online and offline.[44] A coworker pretends he cannot hear his officemate fighting with her partner. A woman tells a new friend something personal and then worries that she has revealed "too much information." A job candidate is appalled when asked in a job interview whether she plans to become pregnant. A man decides not to tell his friend something personal because he knows the friend is a terrible gossip. The attendees at a baby shower stick to small talk that is appropriate for the mixed-age crowd and feminine formality of the event. At a work happy hour, colleagues speak more frankly than they would in the office. A man tells his friend something, knowing the friend will tell their husband. A woman is angry when she hears about a significant event in her sister's life secondhand, thinking she deserved to be told directly. A trans man speaks about his transition only to other trans friends. A graduate student hears a salacious piece of information about a professor and must decide whether to tell the rest of their cohort. A woman whispers to the other women in her office that a senior executive is a known lecher and warns against meeting with him alone. A Black man tells his friends to avoid a club with a racist dress code.

These practices suggest that we have clear ideas around what sorts of information are or are not our business and when it is appropriate to share something.[45] As Helen Nissenbaum writes, norms prescribe certain behaviors. People follow them not simply because the behaviors are common but because they feel they should and worry about the consequences if they do not.[46] Some norms are parts of larger systems, such as criminal codes or traffic rules. Some transcend cultures—murder, for instance, is universally abhorred—while others are specific to countries, subcultures, workplaces, or social groups. Some norms are explicitly written out, such as the rules of a subreddit telling users what content and behavior is appropriate and what will be removed by the moderators, while others are implicit, such as whether it is okay to use profanity in a class Slack.[47] The norms that people hold about appropriate information vary widely and are difficult to police;

they are much more effective in face-to-face communication or in small, tightly connected networks, where the social disapproval we get for violating them is a real deterrent.

The attempt to protect the privacy of others in one's network is apparent in the story of Andrew, a twenty-nine-year-old white freelance writer who moved back in with his parents before starting graduate school after a decade of living on his own. In Chicago, he had held a series of jobs in warehouse logistics while, on the side, pursuing his dream of being a sex columnist. The norms of the warehouse were quite different from those of the liberal, sex-positive online sphere where he wanted to make his name. To keep those two contexts from overlapping, he deliberately did not friend any of his coworkers on social media. Andrew takes consent and the protection of others' privacy very seriously, and so he is careful, when writing about sex and intimacy, that he does not implicate others in his work. When I asked him what kinds of things he is comfortable sharing on Facebook, he said,

> I feel like these days I'm pretty open about my identity. I feel like I still don't say a lot of details about my personal life, and I feel like that's a mix of once it involves other people, I'm not sure what they want said about them. . . . There was some article I was thinking about writing that would've been a more personal story, and then I realized it would say a lot about my girlfriend and that a lot of people would know who that was. And I was like, "I don't know if she'd feel comfortable with that," and I just forgot the idea.

Andrew has spent a lot of time thinking about issues of boundaries and consent. Because he writes about subjects that most people consider extremely personal, he draws strict boundaries between information he shares about himself (such as his bisexual identity) and information he shares about others in his networks (such as his sex life, which implicates his partner). In this case, his information norms respect the privacy of his partner.

Some groups of people already have norms in common: not sharing pictures of each other's children on social media or checking that friends deem a photo flattering before posting it to Instagram. But norms can be very different across different networks, and attempts to set them often fail. In a focus group in Chicago, a twenty-eight-year-old white woman said, "I think it really depends who your family and friends are [*sounds of amusement from group*]. I think some people would be responsive to you saying, 'Oh, please don't tag me,' and others would be like, 'I'll just tag you. You don't have to approve it.' Then it's kind of like, 'Well, it's available to all the people you know, but I can make sure that maybe five people don't see it.' But that's not really helpful." This quote shows how difficult it can be to set norms with others who may have different standards for what is appropriate or who see social media differently.

Sexual information often spreads quickly, as people find it juicy and interesting, and when people disapprove of some sexual behavior, they are less likely to keep it private. Ava, an eighteen-year-old white lesbian, told me, "I remember when I was thirteen or fourteen, I had been talking to this one guy, and he really wanted to take me out on a date. We were in Facebook Messenger, and I was like, 'Hey, I'm not interested in this. I'm talking to this girl. Obviously, nobody knows about my sexuality, so can you please just keep it hush?' I kind of soon after that tried to kill myself. While I was in the hospital, he had talked to another girl about it, and she had told the entire school that I was queer." Ava had tried to set an information norm—"please just keep it hush"—but the boy she told about her sexual identity told someone else. The technology scholars Solon Barocas and Karen Levy describe this as a "passthrough."[48] Information about Ava passed through her tie to a boy, then his tie to a girl, and then to "the entire school." Ava's norm was not respected, and very sensitive information became public.

Quinn (twenty-six, white, Jewish) is nonbinary and queer and must navigate different expectations on social media, such as their deadname and pronouns.[49] Quinn is fine with people knowing their identity, but they do not want to have awkward conversations about it. The norms they set are not around the information they share but around their willingness to discuss it. Their agency around their gender and sexual identity is focused on giving out information for their own purposes. Quinn explained, "I feel like I'm pretty down for most people in my life to know something about those parts of me. I just don't want to have the experience of telling them." They elaborated, "I grew up in a really small town, so they have heard through the grapevine. And I changed my name on Facebook and Instagram. 'Something's going on about that. Do you think that she's transgender?' I'm sure that question has been asked by some of my high school [friends], and I'm like, 'That's your confusion. I don't want to talk to you about it. I also don't really care about you that much.'" Quinn does not think their high school classmates are educated on gender and sexuality. They do not want the burden of educating people they have lost touch with on what it means to be nonbinary or teaching them about their pronouns. They would rather put the information out and let people grapple with it on their own terms. This is how they exert agency over their privacy.

Even in person, norms do not always work to enforce privacy boundaries. They are even less effective and more challenging to enforce online. When our social media connections run into the hundreds or even thousands, it is difficult or impossible to control how our friends and family share information. Someone might intentionally share information that another person wanted to keep private, either because they are not aware of its significance or because they are less invested in protecting the privacy of distant, weak ties. And there is no way to protect against accidental information sharing, as you cannot make everyone in a large, loose network change their privacy settings to protect you. As a thirty-four-year-old white woman said in a focus group, "I have friends who are not really paying attention to their privacy settings at all, which is totally up to them, but as soon as something gets shared from them or liked by them too, . . . I don't have any control over that. I'm not gonna contact each of my friends and be like, 'Fix your privacy settings!' You know, it's not my job, fortunately." When online privacy settings are inadequate, people frequently turn to norms to attempt to regulate information flow. Unfortunately, you cannot create new norms with networks of individuals. Norms are a crucial part of how information flow is regulated, but they fail in networked settings. This is one of the reasons why maintaining privacy often feels impossible.

Privacy as Work

Why should we think about protecting our privacy as work? The short answer is that it *is* work, and it is work that can feel both endless and pointless. Privacy work sits at two intersections. It is unpaid online work that people do that benefits corporations, and it is invisible labor that goes unrecognized and uncompensated. As Susan Leigh Star and Anselm Strauss write, "no work is inherently visible or invisible."[50] A similar battle, the feminist movement to define housework as work, was about making invisible labor visible, a first step in recognizing its value.

The literature of invisible work began with second-wave feminist activism and scholarship, which used the term to describe activities such as child care, meal planning, and housework, which took place in the domestic (or private) realm, were typically unpaid, and were undervalued and unrecognized as work precisely because they were domestic and unpaid.[51] According to Arlene Kaplan Daniels, such work was strategically rendered difficult to see through the idea that women would not want to be paid for this essential labor.[52] Much of the work that is typically coded "feminine," like running a household or maintaining social ties, is framed as part of women's biological nature rather than a set of learned skills that require effort.[53] The invisibilization of privacy work functions similarly: the corporations and governments that benefit from it want the labor of protecting privacy to be disregarded because they have shifted this responsibility to us. The less successful our privacy work, the more data is available for data brokers and the state and the more profit for social platforms. Not only do the platforms not want to pay for privacy work; they do not want it done at all—certainly not done well.

Thinking about privacy as work, and specifically as invisible work, helps us see how its unequal distribution serves existing power structures. While invisible work was first theorized in relation to gender, intersectional feminist scholars examining the interplay of social and political identity have shown how various types of work—both acknowledged and invisible—fall unequally on people who are already marginalized.[54] The sociologist Judith Rollins worked as a domestic for ten different white employers and found that they required her to ritually perform deference and inferiority, such as speaking in a soft voice, referring to her employer as "Ma'am," and exhibiting "an exaggeratedly subservient demeanor."[55] She concluded that the interpersonal rituals performed by white female employers and Black female domestic workers reinforced both white supremacy and economic inequality and functioned as a form of invisible labor done by domestic employees to maintain their employers' comfort levels and thus keep their jobs.[56] Black domestic workers were required to perform both racial and class inferiority, allowing the employers to justify paying them low wages for unpleasant work and strengthening the employers' sense of superiority. Such research shows how invisible labor is distributed unevenly along intersectional lines of power.

Understanding how a person's social position can affect the amount of invisible labor they must do on top of their paid, visible labor helps us see the same phenomenon in privacy work. People in precarious economic circumstances may heavily censor themselves online to avoid losing a job or educational opportunity. I talked with girl gamers who avoided voice chat when playing networked games because they were afraid of harassment and with a woman whose boyfriend installed "stalkerware" on her laptop, which required a lot of complicated information technology work to remove. These are all forms of privacy work that are unequally distributed; we will meet all these people later in the book.

From Feminist Infosec to Feminist Privacy Protection

Privacy does matter to people. It is a set of actions, a process, rather than a static state, and it can be protected through means that are often complex. Privacy work is a form of invisible work that benefits the corporations and entities that profit from our information, and it is unequally distributed depending on privilege. In other words, by identifying the ways that privacy *is* work and the kinds of work it entails, we can reveal the hidden costs of placing responsibility for protecting privacy on the individual.

As I talked with my study participants, it began to seem preposterous that we should each be solely responsible for protecting our own privacy— if such a thing is even possible in the current system. Imagine if we were told not to reveal personal information over the telephone, because if we did, the government would hear it, telecommunications companies would sell that information to dozens of other actors, and your friends or family might hear it even if they were not part of your original conversation. This would greatly decrease the utility of the telephone. A variety of court cases have established that eavesdropping on telephone conversations requires a warrant.[57] Yet we accept that any information revealed through social media platforms, which were created on the explicit premise to share personal information through social networks, may leak despite our best efforts. The internet, texting, and social media have become just as indispensable to modern life as the telephone. They are the central ways that we create and maintain social ties and interact with others—actions that almost inevitably involve sharing personal information. For most of us, opting out is not a choice, in the same way that few people in the 1970s or 1980s could have opted out of using a telephone.

Two enormous shifts help explain why we ignore the outrageous violations baked into today's internet. First, there is the widespread phenomenon of neoliberal *responsibilization*: in our modern neoliberal society, all kinds of risk have been shifted from large entities and institutions onto individuals.[58]

The individual, rather than the collective, is responsible for preventing poor outcomes and thus is to blame if they fail to do so. Neoliberal governments, for instance, have undermined the social safety net in part by asserting that individuals should be responsible for taking care of themselves; they frame unemployment, homelessness, or poor health as the consequences of a lack of individual responsibility and initiative, ignoring the structural forces that affect these things, such as a lack of decent jobs, affordable housing, or access to fresh food. Many companies now expect their employees to be responsible for training their coworkers, maintaining their skills, and managing their retirement plans. Some schoolteachers even have to buy their own work materials and supplies.[59] The second shift is the pervasive replacement of leisure time—time free of work that profits someone else—with the invisible work of digital labor, which benefits technology companies and social platforms financially yet is unpaid.

How do we address these problems? The short answer is that privacy work needs to be de-individualized. It should be treated like the field of information security, where much of the responsibility for information protection is put on structures rather than individuals. Information security, or "infosec," is the process of securing information from external threats to prevent unauthorized access to data or information. It creates *threat models*, using systematized processes for risk assessment, to determine what protections are needed to guard information from both external and internal threats. Once organizations have determined possible risks, they create processes to try to stop the leaks before the damage is done. Of course, there are obvious differences between privacy and security. Security has common objectives, what practitioners call "the CIA triad": confidentiality (information is protected from unauthorized views), integrity (data is protected from changes), and availability (authorized users can access the information they need).[60] Security practitioners evaluate their data's CIA against vulnerabilities and threats, implementing security controls to reduce risk when necessary.[61] Infosec is also an assemblage of standards, regulatory agencies, technologies, and firms, each playing a role in this system.

What privacy can take from information security is that security cannot be protected at the individual level: it happens at the institutional level and involves highly trained professionals.[62] The researcher Karen Renaud and her colleagues discuss how responsibility is assigned in relation to information security. They conclude that it is unreasonable to expect individuals to take responsibility for cybersecurity because securing one's device, operating system, or network requires a great deal of technical expertise, and the risks of failing to do it properly are calamitous.[63]

People's goals for their privacy differ, but we can assume that control over information flow is common to most. If we think of privacy work as similar to security work, we can recognize that it requires systemic measures and sophisticated tools. The individual is simply the wrong scale on which to address this problem. If we rethink networked privacy using the language of security—risk assessment, attack vectors, and threat models—we can place more of the burden for privacy protection on institutions like technology companies and governments. This requires employing what the Data & Society researchers Matt Goerzen, Elizabeth Anne Watkins, and Gabrielle Lim call "sociotechnical security." They write, "Any security framework that takes 'protection from harm' seriously must posit the individual and the community in which that individual is situated as the primary object of security. The task of sociotechnical security then is not only to edge out the vulnerabilities in code, but also the vulnerabilities in the social systems that design, inform, and use the code or its applications—with the pointed goal of securing individuals and communities, with regards to their situated evaluation of harms."[64] If social platforms and big data companies thought in terms of sociotechnical security, they would determine the success of their products on the basis of how well they minimize individual harms. A sociotechnical security audit of facial-recognition technologies would show that when only white faces are used in these algorithms' training, they fail to accurately recognize people of color.[65] It would also recognize the horrific potential for abuse and discrimination, such as software that distinguishes Uyghur people in China from those of Korean and Tibetan descent.[66] It might even note that facial-recognition data sets are often trained using images taken without the consent of those who are depicted.[67] Such an audit might conclude that in its current form, facial-recognition technology is unethical. What would an audit of privacy-related technologies reveal?

This approach to privacy protection, moreover, must be feminist. Feminist privacy protection would emphasize the structural nature of digital violations.[68] Rather than treat all individuals as if they were identical, it would acknowledge that specific attack vectors and vulnerabilities may differ greatly along lines of gender, race, sexuality, ability, and social class, requiring different strategies that account for various kinds of social inequality. By emphasizing these differences in vulnerability, we can ensure a more equitable level of privacy while making our technologies more resilient and flexible.[69]

Facebook, for instance, only allows users to go by names that correspond to formal identity documents such as passports, utility bills, or health insurance cards, which it frames as "authentic" identities.[70] Users cannot use adopted names, stage names, pseudonyms, or nicknames unless these are part of their "real name," such as "Jess" for Jessica.[71] This policy has led to repeated targeting and suspension of Native American and Tamil users, whose cultures often follow different naming practices from *first-name surname*, as well as speakers of Irish and Scottish Gaelic, whose names include characters and capitalization that Facebook does not recognize.[72] Most well-known is perhaps the case of drag queens and transgender or gender-nonconforming users who want to use names that do not correspond with state-issued identity documents.[73] As we have seen, using different usernames or obscuring one's gender is a common type of privacy work, particularly for those who are experiencing abuse or intimate partner violence.

After repeated protests, Facebook grudgingly acknowledged that some people *might* need to use identities that it terms "nonauthentic," but it required such users to disclose why they wanted to use such a name, a clear violation of privacy. Most recently, Facebook announced that it will require identity verification from "high reach" profiles with highly shared posts, to combat disinformation.[74] While these policies do not target transgender or Native American users, they directly and clearly affect those communities. Granted that Facebook's motivation for adopting the "real names" policy was entirely reasonable—it wanted to combat fake accounts or bots—the policy it came up with would not pass a feminist privacy audit. It is up to Facebook, not individual users, to do better by implementing a solution that works equally well for all users.

Securing privacy using a feminist frame—feminist privacy protection— threads through this book. Feminist infosec prioritizes threats that are often marginalized in information security overall, such as domestic violence, child abuse, or racist harassment.[75] Feminist information security might help someone experiencing intimate partner violence remove "stalkerware" from their device, advise a BLM protester how to protect themselves from police surveillance, or recognize the potential harm to children from abusive parents using GPS tracking.[76] Similarly, feminist privacy protection recognizes that some people are fundamentally denied privacy, that the harms of privacy violations are both contextual and differential, and that there are fundamental links between privacy and social inequality.

4

Gendered Privacy

Publicity, Harassment, and Abuse

Shana is a thirty-six-year-old nonbinary person of Middle Eastern descent who works in cybersecurity, a field that is 80 percent male.[1] Early in her career, she turned a blind eye to sexism, wanting to be considered a "cool girl" by her male coworkers. But she was continually confronted with gender inequality, such as when she found out she was getting paid 25 percent less than a male coworker with the same job. As she moved up in the field and began educating herself about diversity and inclusion, she became more vocal. Now she is known as an advocate for gender diversity and runs a Twitter account that highlights accomplished women in cybersecurity.

Through the account, Shana was offered the chance to give away three tickets to a well-known cybersecurity conference—let us call it "InfoCon." InfoCon was popular but had a much lower level of female attendance than similar conferences. Warnings spread through the whisper network. As Shana told me, "People know from experience and from being at the conference, there are stories of roofies being put into women's drinks. There's just too many men that are rowdy and they serve beer 24/7 at the conference. The environment just is not inviting."[2] She decided to offer the tickets anyway but noted on Twitter that the conference did not have a code of conduct.

As an academic, I did not know the relevance of this. Most academic conferences do not have codes of conduct either.[3] But they are a big thing in other communities, especially geeky communities. There has historically been so much sexist behavior at conferences and so many women have been harassed, that many conferences have adopted strict antiharassment policies that clearly spell out that sexual language and imagery is not acceptable.[4] InfoCon did not. Just suggesting that the conference might not be entirely safe for women opened Shana up to months of harassment on Twitter. Her accounts were flooded with negative comments and slurs. She blocked people left and right, but the harassment continued.

Shana then discovered that a prominent woman in security had an active restraining order against one of InfoCon's paid workshop organizers. The woman told the conference organizers, but instead of withdrawing his invitation, they showed her complaint to the abuser. Furious, Shana tweeted about it, prompting another flood of harassment. Shana's detractors sent so many emails to her boss that he set up a separate filter to deal with them. Someone dug up an old picture of Shana posing in lingerie and tweeted it. She reported this to Twitter, which claimed the harassing tweets did not violate its terms of service. Eventually, Shana discovered a private Facebook group where men (and a few women) coordinated harassment against her and prominent women in cybersecurity.[5] They discussed finding Shana at other conferences and punching her. She reported it to Facebook, which did nothing. Even though the harassers' names were clearly visible on both Facebook and Twitter, none of them lost their jobs or felt any repercussions. Shana no longer felt safe in her professional community.

Shana's story is one of harassment but also of publicity. The harassers broadcast information that was private, such as the accusation of domestic violence and the lingerie photos. They attempted to publicly humiliate Shana on Twitter in front of her followers and colleagues. They escalated the harassment to her boss, collapsing on- and offline contexts. Her story is not unusual. Just as social media has upended our sense of privacy, it has opened new possibilities for visibility and new forms of abuse.

As we have seen throughout this book, social media allows ordinary people to command the huge audiences once available only to the elite.[6]

This shift has amplified an array of social practices. The YouTuber or Instagram influencer uses social media to increase their audience for economic gain; the teenager or Silicon Valley entrepreneur does it for social status; and the troll or provocateur does it for entertainment.[7]

Many of these social practices center around voyeurism. Many people use social media primarily for surveillance, to "keep tabs" on peers and acquaintances, and the information they collect can be exposed to embarrass or injure another person.[8] This takes a variety of forms, such as social shaming and digital vigilantism, which aim to expose and punish an offender for alleged misdeeds; doxing, which is publicizing someone's "real" identity, address, or financial information; "revenge porn," in which explicit photos are spread without the subject's consent; and publicly displaying proof of someone's past misdeeds, often in the form of screenshots, colloquially called "receipts."

Such forced publicity can be an extremely effective way to hold public figures accountable. In 2012, Republican presidential candidate Mitt Romney gave a speech to a sympathetic audience of wealthy donors in which he described the 47 percent of the population who do not pay income taxes as lazy, entitled welfare recipients. A bartender at the event surreptitiously filmed the speech on his cellphone and gave it to the progressive news outlet *Mother Jones*, which disseminated it widely. The incident played into a public image of Romney as an out-of-touch multimillionaire and deeply damaged his campaign.[9] Other forms of forced publicity target powerful individuals, as when constituents search politicians' social media, public statements, and public records to unearth evidence of missteps, a practice Daniel Trottier calls "scandal mining."[10] (When political rivals do this, it is referred to as "oppo research.")

But forced publicity is often used against ordinary people. Sometimes this is done to enforce social norms, as people's actions are publicized to massive audiences in an attempt to humiliate or harm. In 2005, South Korea made an example of "dog poop girl," whose failure to clean up her pet's mess on public transit resulted in widespread humiliation.[11] Sometimes it takes place when information shaped in a context with one set of norms spreads to another. In the small town of Asheville, North Carolina, two coffeeshop owners found their reputations destroyed and business damaged when an anonymous user publicized their involvement in a pickup-artist blog on Facebook.[12] The sexist norms of the online pickup-artist community were starkly different from those of liberal, egalitarian Asheville. The men lived in two contexts, each of which endorsed sentiments that were anathema to the other. These people were in no way public figures, yet publicity was used to punish them for violating social norms, just as it was against Mitt Romney. Whether you think dog poop girl, the pickup artists, or Mitt Romney deserved the consequences of their actions will depend on your own sense of morality.

Forced publicity is not always taken seriously by those who propagate it, yet their targets can suffer ill effects far beyond the harms of their transgression. In this chapter, I use the concept of harassment to show how publicity, or publicness, can be used to bully, silence, and shame. Publicity is the flip side of privacy: when someone finds themselves dragged into the spotlight, it is often experienced as a traumatic invasion of privacy.

Most research on harassment has been done by feminist scholars who draw comparisons between online harassment and street harassment and investigate how emerging technologies enable new forms of stalking, abuse, and sexual violence.[13] Shana's case is a clear example of how gendered norms intersect with norms of privacy and publicity—the men who attacked her believed that amplifying the concerns of women who had been harassed at InfoCon was unnecessary "drama," harking back to ideas about the protected private sphere. But harassment as a privacy violation is not intrinsically gendered—anyone, of any identity, can be harassed. The twenty-eight people I interviewed who had experienced harassment included men, women, and nonbinary people of different political valences, sexual orientations, and ethnicities. I also interviewed nine people who work on social media platforms' trust and safety teams, charged with preventing, detecting, and disciplining harassment and other forms of online abuse. These interviews showed that networked harassment takes place across ideological boundaries and is used by members of left-leaning and nonpolitical networks as well as those on the right. Overall, however, people who challenge normative power structures (such as feminists, antiracist activists, and nonbinary and LGBTQ+ people) are more likely to be harassed by people who adhere to traditional social norms that privilege whiteness, heteronormativity, maleness, and so forth. And harassment, like revenge porn, often breaks down along intersectional lines of power and is intimately tied to structural inequality and sexual violence. It is not only that nonbinary folks, trans people, and women, especially those of color, report experiencing harassment at higher rates than others. Gender identity, sexual orientation, and race are well-known attack vectors for harassment.[14] An "attack vector," in cybersecurity parlance, is an exploitable vulnerability; in the context of harassment, it is a personal characteristic that opens the victim to identity-based attacks.[15]

Privacy, as we have seen, has always been gendered and raced. Recall that the legal concept of privacy developed out of court cases undertaken by young white women whose photographs were used without their permission to promote businesses and products.[16] They sued to protect their images and personal information from being disseminated, establishing a claim to individual privacy that persists to this day. But this claim applied unequally: the early cases were grounded in the widespread belief that women should not be visible in public. There is a long-standing, uneasy back-and-forth between traditional concepts of femininity that hide intimate and domestic life from the public eye and women's desire to participate in public life and bring formerly private matters into the political sphere.[17] Feminist legal theory, for instance, regards privacy with suspicion, often viewing the "private" realm as a masculinist space. As Catharine MacKinnon writes, "The law of privacy treats the private sphere as a sphere of personal freedom. For men, it is. For women, the private is the distinctive sphere of intimate violation and abuse, neither free nor particularly personal."[18]

This is even more fraught for Black women, indigenous women, and other women of color, who have traditionally been excluded from the public sphere because of both their race and their gender but who were never deemed worthy of protection by white society. Black women, for instance, have always been hypervisible to law enforcement.[19] Home can be a place of deep refuge from racism, yet such a "private space" is brutally violated by police violence, as in the case of Breonna Taylor, who was shot and killed inside her home by three white police officers.[20] They had a "no-knock" warrant, which allows law enforcement to enter a private residence without informing the occupants ahead of time. These warrants are a military strategy that was repurposed for federal and local police during the 1980s drug war, a set of policies justified by racist mythologies and disinformation.[21] These differences demonstrate how the "separate spheres" theory of privacy universalizes the experiences of white men and women. When we consider privacy, we need to consider the complex racial histories of the United States.

Harassment, as a concept to think with, illustrates many of these complexities. Privacy is gendered but also raced, and women of color bear the burden of multiple attack vectors. Although harassment is a tactic that can be used across the ideological spectrum, it must also be linked to structural systems of misogyny, racism, homophobia, and transphobia, which determine the primary standards and norms by which people speaking in public are judged. For example, whenever a nonbinary individual is harassed over comments about anything, their nonbinary status will frequently become an attack vector. In other words, they will be attacked for being nonbinary even if it has nothing to do with the matter at hand. Khalid, a twenty-three-year-old from the Middle East who identifies as nonbinary and Muslim, explained how harassment follows intersectional lines: "In my bio, I include my sexuality, my gender identity, but I also include my religion, and what I noticed is, generally when—my bio changes throughout and when I include my religion in that, there's more of a chance of people catching onto that detail and harassing me on that basis, rather than just, 'That's some guy on the internet. We really don't care.'" Khalid finds that when they explicitly define as Muslim, they are bombarded with Islamophobic statements. Similarly, being a woman opens one to gender-specific forms of violence, such as rape threats, pornographic imagery, gendered slurs, sexually explicit threats, and so forth, and being a woman of color adds racist slurs, stereotypes, and threats. Studies of harassment and misogyny, for instance, show that Black women experience harassment that is both racist *and* sexist and that the two cannot be disentangled.[22] Conversely, while I interviewed many men about their experiences, their gender status as men was not an attack vector. In other words, they were not subject to harassment based on their gender.

Thinking with harassment as a concept requires that we understand the cluster of practices and dynamics that make it up. My study participants described a wide variety of behaviors they experienced as harassment, including pejorative language and insults, doxing, "dogpiling" or "brigading" (coordinated attacks on particular people or targets), social shaming, and cyberstalking.[23] (Not all of these are privacy violations.) I have sorted these behaviors into several clusters reflecting common dynamics: *dyadic harassment*, in which one person harasses another; *networked harassment*, in which harassment is coordinated against a single target (like the brigading that Shana experienced, which was coordinated on Facebook); *normalized harassment*, in which harassment is constant and taken for granted but not necessarily serious (such as frequent sexual come-ons messaged to female Redditors); and interpersonal actions that participants experience as harassing but are better described as "drama" or "bullying."

The capaciousness of the term "harassment" allows it to be used in several ways. The word itself makes clear who is the good guy and who is bad; it imparts a moral judgment that can reduce complex issues of accountability to black and white. It is a cultural keyword, a hot-button issue for both progressive and far-right activists, both of whom automatically react to the concept while using it to mean quite different things. But like the more specific phrase "sexual harassment," "harassment" necessarily invokes a system of sexual violence in which seemingly small actions, such as telling women on the street to smile or asking women on forums to "prove" their gender, lie on a continuum of sexually violent behaviors—a pattern that has only been intensified by digital technologies.[24]

This taxonomy of harassment shows how gender intersects with forced publicity. The concept of *gendered privacy* helps us to understand that forced publicity is a form of privacy violation that is more likely to happen to someone, or harm someone, on the basis of their gender. In the second half of this chapter, I will show the commonality between the individual model of responsibility for privacy (outlined in chapter 1) and a widespread mentality that "blames the victim" for gendered privacy violations. Women suffer twofold from this discourse: they are frequently blamed when they experience sexual violence or abuse and then blamed again for not adequately protecting their privacy. A networked model of privacy illuminates how gender norms affect the way information spreads and flows and opens up possibilities for reform and redress that center communities and networks rather than individuals.

Taxonomy of Harassment

In this section, I expand on the brief taxonomy of harassment I introduced earlier—dyadic, networked, normalized, and what we might call "ambivalent" or "equivocal" harassment—by describing cases of each type. To avoid harassment, my study participants engage in intense privacy work. The examples show again that harassment is deeply tied to sexual inequality, suggesting that legal and technological solutions that focus solely on behavior are inadequate.

Normalized Harassment: Girl Gamers

Paige (nineteen, white) is a gamer girl from the South who loves playing *Overwatch*, a popular multiplayer first-person shooter. She describes herself as an introvert who loves cats and reading, but in our interview, she was chatty, even bubbly. A computer science major, she has made friends around the world through gaming and is extremely tech savvy. When I asked her about her experiences being harassed, she immediately sent me screenshots of a chat conversation, as well as a video she recorded in *Overwatch*. The video is from the perspective of Paige's character; you see her character blowing things up and shooting bad guys while she and her friends talk about the game over voice chat. Suddenly, a young-sounding American male voice, responding to one of Paige's comments, asks, "When was the last time you shaved your pussy?" cackling with glee at his wit. Paige tries to shut him down—"Why is that any business of yours?"—but he claims Paige would "suck [his] dick" in person. "Probably not," she says sarcastically, and he and his friend giggle with glee: "Dude, you got a 'probably'!" Paige blocked the offenders and posted the video to a forum for female gamers, whose participants commiserated with her. "I'm sorry that you had to babysit those infants without being paid to handle someone else's brat," wrote one commenter. "It's embarrassing that men are so childish," added another.

Paige has experienced only two instances of sexual harassment, a number that may seem low in a lifetime of gaming, considering gaming's reputation. (The other incident, a guy sending Paige sexual come-ons via in-game chat, included the priceless comment, "I've been e-pimping for over seven years. You need not tell me how to speak to a woman.") But Paige managed to avoid the volume of harassment experienced by most female gamers by masking her gender from other players. For example, she does not speak in voice chat unless it is absolutely necessary or when she is playing with a group of people she knows and trusts. Gender masking is not unusual among female gamers. In Paige's forum thread, several other women chimed in: "this is exactly why I don't use mic anymore," and "I got Overwatch for Christmas and I have yet to use comms because I am worried about this type of thing!" Every female gamer I interviewed told me she rarely uses voice chat for the same reason.

Another informant, Tamara (twenty-eight, white), a gamer girl ten years older than Paige but cut from the same cloth, told me, "I was joking the other day about how I was going to get a voice modulator to play *Overwatch* with Jessica, my roommate. Her screen name in *Overwatch* is Ginger Robot, and she's having to change that because she cannot use the microphone. When guys find out that she's a woman with the name Ginger Robot, it's just nothing but jokes about pubic hair, and it's disgusting." Tamara told me that she hates using games with microphones unless she is playing with friends; guys react badly when they hear she is a girl. If she plays better than they do, they get angry or accuse her of being a guy (because, of course, women cannot play games well), but if her team loses, they blame her for playing badly. Paige's and Tamara's attempts to keep their gender identities secret are a form of privacy work.

As these examples show, women are pervasively harassed online.[25] While there is plenty of research and popular commentary on sexism in online geek culture, this kind of privacy-invading harassment, with its implicit or explicit threats of coercion or retaliation, is also common offline and is by no means confined to nerdy communities.[26] It is not limited to gaming, digital culture, geekiness, or even the internet in general; in countries like the United States, Canada, and the United Kingdom, it is a near-universal experience for women.[27] But technology makes it easier. As the British sociologist Jessica Ringrose found in her studies of teenage sexting and mobile technology, privacy violations via sexual harassment are common in teenage peer networks; her participants described a hostile schoolyard culture in which sexualized insults, harassment, groping, and even assault were commonplace.[28] She also found that much sexting was coerced—an intense and obvious form of privacy violation, backed by threats. Coerced sexting is the ultimate stripping of people's agency about the information they reveal, dictating what, when, and to whom the victim must communicate information that she may feel should be private. As with most such violations, Ringrose found that the victims were considered responsible for the perpetrators' violation of their privacy. Girls disproportionately bore the blame for sexting when it was made public, even when they had been coerced. They were judged harshly for engaging in sexual behavior—for revealing information about themselves that others judged to be private—while boys were judged if they did not take part. The threat around sexting was enforced by social consequences, primarily from inside the peer network.[29]

The stories of gaming harassment fit this framework. Many of the young players are immersed in sexist peer cultures, and online gaming is dominated by male gamers and perspectives. This creates a self-reinforcing world where women conceal their gender to avoid harassment, so being *visibly* female is unusual, triggering more gatekeeping and harassment because the community looks even more predominantly male than it is. The communication scholar Adrienne Massanari identifies this dynamic as "geek masculinity," a white, middle-class form of masculinity that places great value on demonstrating technical skill and pop culture knowledge.[30] Because geeks may not have much physical or sexual prowess, their knowledge of tech and pop culture becomes an alternative form of masculine capital, and they reinforce this knowledge monopoly through overt verbal aggression and sexism.[31] Many women are wary of such communities. Breanna (twenty-two, white), another *Overwatch* player, said she rarely encounters another woman ("less than one in four matches") but pointed out that she might not recognize the real number of women because, like her, they engage in privacy work to protect themselves: "they probably also aren't using voice chat all the time."

For my study participants, concealing their gender was a necessary privacy-protective measure to avoid unwanted and unpleasant comments. Paige sounded apologetic when she explained that she prefers to play as a female character, perhaps because she feels that such an avatar invites sexual harassment. She sent me a screenshot showing her character's relatively modest costume so I would know that she is not deliberately soliciting men's attention. This suggests that she and other women online have internalized the idea that they are responsible for any privacy violations or harassment they might receive and are also responsible for avoiding them. Paige worries that anything that could be seen as publicizing her gender, such as playing a girl character, demonstrates a lack of interest in protecting her privacy and thus justifies harassment.

Girl gamers use other strategies to conceal their gender while gaming. In addition to playing male characters, they often choose gender-neutral nicknames. While Paige's username is the same on Reddit, Skype, Discord—a privacy risk because it could be tracked across platforms—she chose a Pokémon reference because it is hard to Google, as we saw in chapter 3. She and other women try to avoid voice chat when possible, but it is often necessary to coordinate with team members. Girls know that revealing their feminine voice makes them vulnerable, and my participants use strategies such as waiting to chat until the match really gets going, playing only with people they know, sticking to games they feel are female-friendly (*Overwatch*, with its diverse cast of heroes, was popular when I was doing my interviews), or using text chat instead despite the inconvenience. The privacy work of using text chat to avoid voice identification as a woman puts them at a disadvantage, but it is better than the distraction and humiliation of unwanted sexual comments.

These strategies also are both privacy work and, to use Liz Kelly's concept, *safety work*.[32] If we think of networked gaming as a public space, concealing one's gender is like avoiding walking home alone after dark; choosing a male character or a modest female costume is analogous to wearing bulky, unrevealing outfits to avoid "asking for it." While it is difficult to obscure one's gender in physical spaces, it is relatively easy online, especially in video gaming or forums like Reddit where nicknames and aliases are common. But women lose something when they must conceal their gender to protect their privacy: an agency over their revelations and online experiences. A qualitative study of female gamers found that while "actively hiding their identity and avoiding all forms of verbal communication with other players" was very common, it led to feelings of loneliness and isolation rather than belonging and camaraderie.[33] These women felt that withdrawing was a form of safety work, necessary to prevent online harassment.

These gamer girls withdrew from certain types of interactions and engaged in onerous privacy work because they wished to avoid forced publicity, which is closely connected to harassment, and to avoid being harassed, stalked, or doxed. They sought to avoid the forced publicity of public shaming, or "canceling," which can involve combing through past social media posts, unearthing public records, and examining the profiles of friends and relatives, in some cases surfacing statements made years ago or taken out of context to prove a point.[34] Recall chapter 2's discussion of the importance of context and the violation of privacy that frequently results when information is received without the accompanying knowledge and beliefs shared by the audience for whom it was originally embedded. Virtually every person who had been harassed, and many young people I interviewed who had not been, heavily self-censored or engaged in intense social segmentation, self-censoring, and even scrubbing past online histories to maintain as clean a public presence as possible.

Many sought to avoid notice by avoiding conflict that might draw attention and thus harassment. As Gisele (twenty-one, biracial Black American) said, "I make it a big point to not argue with people on the internet. I don't do it. Because you don't win. Nobody wins. It's a nightmare, and I value my sense of safety. And I'm very aware of Deep Net stuff, and one of my top fears is getting doxed and people coming after me." Gisele goes well past refraining from taking nude pictures or putting personal information on the internet; she avoids even mentioning controversial topics because she is afraid her personal information will be compromised if she angers the wrong person.

This is all normalized harassment—annoying, emotionally taxing, often carrying social consequences, and requiring significant work to avoid and therefore maintain one's privacy. But this type of harassment, as distressing as it is, is rarely physically dangerous. Other harassment is much more serious and requires more intensive privacy work to avoid or mitigate.

Dyadic Harassment: Stalkers and Stalkerware

My conversation with Kimberly, a successful tech executive, white and in her early fifties, illuminates many of this book's themes. Kimberly's very prominent online presence and networked social connections made it possible for a harasser to gain enough information about her to threaten her in real life. Just as the stories of everyday harassment showed the networked nature of privacy and the peculiar vulnerabilities of networked privacy online, Kimberly's story articulates the deepest principles of networked privacy: it is neither an individual right nor responsibility but is diffused through leaky networks that are only as strong as their weakest link; it is unequally distributed and less available to marginalized groups, including women; and while networked privacy is a structural problem, maintaining it requires individual work—sometimes intensive work both on- and offline.

Kimberly has a high-powered career as a senior engineer at a very successful Silicon Valley company. A lifelong tech enthusiast, she started volunteering for a popular open-source project fifteen years ago.[35] After several years of volunteer labor, she was promoted to the oversight committee, which dealt with safety and abuse. Part of her job was to remove open-source contributions that violated the project's safety guidelines. She told me, "Unfortunately, that kind of gets you in contact with a lot of malicious people, and that's where things started to go downhill." Like everyone on the oversight committee, Kimberly regularly receives death threats from angry contributors; she read one to me that was posted the previous day: "Tomorrow, at 8:00 PM, I will be paying your residence a visit. I already found out where that residence is. During my visit, I'm going to cut you up and gut you like a fish." While these threats are often hyperbolic, sometimes they are real, and victims do not know which ones are which.

Eventually Kimberly's work brought her into the orbit of a man I will call Jason, who had been removed from the project for harassing several prominent women in tech, including showing up at their homes, sending death threats, threatening their families, and doxing them. Kimberly worked with the victims to remove their personal information from the project after Jason's repeated doxing attempts. Eventually, Jason was convicted of misdemeanor stalking and spent several months in jail. While he was serving his sentence, another former contributor was systematically doxing people on the oversight team, including Kimberly. He later told Jason that it was Kimberly who had thwarted his efforts to dox his original victims, and Jason turned his attention to her. At the time of our interview, he had been stalking and harassing her for nine years. She has never responded.[36]

During that time, Jason has showed up to Kimberly's workplace, called and emailed her hundreds of times, sent letters and packages, made rambling YouTube videos about her, posted manifestos about her online, and threatened to kill her and her children. She has filed dozens of police reports; her company has given her a secure underground parking space, and campus security walks her to and from her car. Jason has been jailed multiple times for stalking and harassing various people, not only Kimberly but other high-profile Silicon Valley women and even the local police chief. At the time of our interview, he was in prison for felony stalking. But the maximum sentence for stalking in her state is five years, and he usually plea-bargains down to less time. Kimberly said that the only time she feels safe is when he is behind bars: "But when he's in jail, I go about my life. So I date guys, I look after my kids, I fix my car, and I do my day job. When he gets out, I go slightly vigilant. I check up online where I know where he hangs out. What's he doing? Where is he at? Is he harassing anybody? Is he after me? Da-da-da-da-da. One eye open. Every month or so, you know, I start to see he goes off his meds, and I'm like, 'Oh, shit. Here we go,' you know." As soon as Jason gets out of jail, he starts harassing her again. She said, "When he gets out in two to five and he goes on probation or whatever, I fully expect all this to start up again. I guarantee it. He will never stop, ever. He will never stop until he is drugged up to the eyeballs or dead. He will never, ever stop. And I am getting used to the fact." Kimberly thinks it is just a matter of time until he hurts somebody or someone shoots him—especially given his habit of targeting public officials.

To avoid Jason, Kimberly has had to engage in an incredibly intense and high-stakes version of privacy work. (The burden of protecting Kimberly's privacy and her safety falls squarely on her own shoulders, although she is the victim, not the perpetrator—a function of our notion of privacy as an individual responsibility.) She enrolled herself in her state's Safe at Home program, which allows victims of domestic abuse, sexual violence, human trafficking, and stalking to obscure their addresses on official government documents. Her mail goes to a post office box. Her employer has strict guidelines not to reveal her office information. Her children's schools know about Jason. She has manually removed her personal information from every search engine. She is in the process of legally changing her name to something difficult to Google. She never posts pictures online or stores her address on ecommerce websites.

An intelligent, driven, and deeply practical person, Kimberly keeps meticulous notes of Jason's attempts to contact her and works with law enforcement to protect herself and hold him accountable. This process has taken an enormous toll, both emotionally and in time, money, and effort. She said,

> I stonewalled this guy. He knows nothing. I never, ever contacted him in any way, shape, or form, only just connected with the phone. And when I talked to the police, I'm pretty hard-assed about it, you know, when I'm dealing with stuff. I get super pragmatic. And it got really bad. I didn't know how bad—I didn't know how much it was affecting me. I just need to work. I had to sit at my desk. I can't—I can't do anything. I just sit here. I can't do things. I can't deal. . . . I want to tell people this: It really damaged my life. I got dysfunctional. I got useless. I wake up at three in the morning checking my phone. Did he find me? Did he find me? What's he

doing now? Shit, will he answer? Does he know about me? Does he know where I live? Is he coming over here? Every day, I lost sleep. I was sick.

At this point in the interview, Kimberly, who had been reciting the facts in a very unemotional way, broke down and started to cry. She immediately apologized. But her words show the deep harm Jason has inflicted on her, which she believes is his goal; he wants to hurt her. He wants to scare her. It makes him feel powerful to violate her in this way, to know that he can threaten her no matter what she does—to show that she does not control her own privacy; he does.

Kimberly's story is a textbook case of dyadic harassment: it involves two people, the victim and the harasser, and is inextricably linked to stalking and sexual violence. This harassment is made possible by the networked nature of privacy and particularly the leakiness of digital systems and networks, such as databases generated from public records that publicize home addresses whether or not people consent to it. Kimberly was safely anonymous until a different disgruntled open-source participant doxed her. The online culture of harassment, of entitlement to women's information, the desire to remove their agency in order to intimidate them, is an intensified version of the everyday harassment culture described in the preceding section. Kimberly explained, "What happens with stalkers and people who harass women—and there are plenty of them—gets amplified online, because they find like-minded people. All you have to be able to [do] is go to Reddit or go over to Facebook, and then you find like-minded people who will encourage each other to harass, to dox." Not only does the internet enable the information gathering that makes stalking easier, but it helps stalkers find other people who will support and justify their efforts (like the Facebook group that Shana discovered was coordinating harassment against her).

Kimberly's story also shows that for women, privacy and control of information are always related to safety. Her efforts to protect herself from Jason involve concealing her personal information. Safe at Home is at heart a privacy-protective mechanism. For women, privacy work is always safety work. While it was Kimberly's participation in a male-dominated online community that enabled her harassment, not all harassment of women happens in male-dominated spaces.[37] Any woman is vulnerable to forced publicity and targeted online harassment for any reason.

Networked Harassment: Dogpiles and Brigades

Nicole (thirty, white) is a body-image advocate and blogger. She has written two books, gave a very popular TED Talk, and regularly speaks around the world about what she calls "body liberation." Her readers, primarily women in their twenties through forties, send her passionate messages about the difference she has made in their lives. By any metric, she is successful and happy. Yet her mere existence as a fat woman on the internet has led to a flood of harassment, often coordinated, targeted, and networked. Long before she was a professional blogger, she posted a photo of herself on Tumblr with the caption, "Don't Like It? Don't Look." The image was reblogged hundreds of times, mostly with vitriolic commentary from users angered by the very idea of a fat woman loving herself. She says, "I was shocked and surprised and horrified. This was my first experience where people were calling me a cow and being like—saying they hoped that I got run over because I was in an empty street holding up this sign. And I was so devastated. I think it devastated me for like a month, at least. . . . I look back now and I was like, 'Oh honey, that's not even close to what people get.'"

As Nicole's blogging career took off, she was subjected to hundreds of hateful, negative comments on every post or news story about her. It was extremely difficult; she felt alone and drained. She said, "For two years, it was a constant battle of seeing horrible shit about myself and then working through it and then seeing horrible shit about myself and then working through it." At the same time, her increased visibility led to a book deal and worldwide media coverage. The harassment got worse. It became net-worked and intentional, organized to punish the victim and drive her off the internet.

Nicole was working full-time, organizing a conference, and writing her book, and she was completely overwhelmed. A male friend of hers sug-gested she start a Patreon, a website that allows fans to financially support online creators like artists, writers, and activists. Money from a successful Patreon campaign might allow her to quit her day job and focus on blog-ging and advocacy full-time. But then a blog devoted to "fat hate" found her Patreon and began targeting her. What resulted blew up the harassment to enormous proportions, crossing platforms and making every space on the internet nearly unbearable for her:

> I was suicidal every fucking day for a month, two months maybe. It could have been three, at least solidly every single every day for at least a month and a half, and it was because I was bombarded in a way I never experi-enced before by hundreds and hundreds and hundreds and hundreds of people, I mean, on every single platform possible: all of my social media, my inbox, YouTube channels. I'm so accustomed to where I had settled on this online world that I didn't have all of my guards up. Like, nobody goes to my YouTube, but all of a sudden, people found my YouTube site. And I'd get the YouTube notifications in my inbox, and they would be hate messages, just overwhelming, to the point where I didn't think I was going to make it. It was really hard.

This is networked harassment, a coordinated effort within a network of peo-ple who encourage, promote, or instigate harassment against a particular target.[38] It does not fit the US legal definition of harassment or stalking, which presumes a dyadic model like Kimberly's situation, in which contact is repeated by a single person, whether in real life or online (although Kim-berly got little help from established laws around cyberstalking).[39] Each of Nicole's harassers may have sent only a single message, but it is the mass, targeted effort—the dogpile—that is so devastating, due to its sheer scope and scale.

This model is exemplified by Gamergate, the notorious backlash against diversity in gaming that its participants claimed was done to enforce "ethics in videogame journalism."[40] Empirical studies of Gamergate have found little evidence of any emphasis on ethics. Instead, there is considerable evidence that coordinated attacks on specific targets—almost all outspoken women—took place across multiple social media platforms.[41] The targets of networked harassment are disproportionately women and trans and nonbinary people, particularly activists and people of color, as well as women in male-dominated fields and the public eye, such as journalists, politicians, and so forth.[42]

In Nicole's case, the harassment originating from the "fat hate" blog intensified and reached a much larger network once it moved to fatphobic forums such as Reddit's infamous Fat People Hate community. One of these forums had countless topics devoted to Nicole, including a post from a woman who wrote about seeing her at the grocery store. Nicole described the post:

> She was directly behind me in line and documented everything about me: what I looked like, what energy I was giving off. I was fucking grocery shopping for my boyfriend, and I—people were like, "Did you cut her? Did you kill her while you were there because I would have loved to watch her blubber run out. And those people are so disgusting. And did she have diabetes?" And they started calling me "it" to dehumanize me. It just shocked my nervous system in a way that's never happened before because it was so close to home. They knew that my boyfriend lived around that part of town. And they also encouraged people to go find me there, like, "This is where she shops. Everyone go find her." "How are you going to handle her when you find her?" kind of thing.

Nicole was horrified by the online discussion about her daily movements—that the networked harassment had bled through to her offline life. This was an enormous privacy violation and a threat to her safety: her geographic location was publicized to a hostile audience, a clear form of forced publicity. The wide publication of this information might have caught the attention of someone like Kimberly's stalker, someone who would not restrict their threatening behavior to the online realm.

Like other violations of privacy, these "internet hate sites" often defend their targeting of individuals by claiming that their harassment is justified by the victim's bad behavior.[43] If she did not want to be harassed, this argument goes, she should not have posted information about herself online or shared messages the harasser disagreed with. Nicole's harassers claimed that she was spreading damaging messages about fat acceptance and obesity; they also argued that her Patreon was somehow conning people out of their money. (This has also been a criticism leveled at Anita Sarkeesian, one of the original women at the center of Gamergate, who is now a favorite target of male supremacist groups. To avoid accusations of sexism, her attackers instead frame her moral failings as "scamming" people through her successful Kickstarter or as promoting sexism against men.)[44] Nicole, who is articulate and thoughtful, believes that her very existence as a fat woman, and her visibility in her body online, threatens deeply held beliefs:

> In essence, [there is a social] promise that if we achieve a perfect body, we will become happy. And so there are these components of happiness, like success, worthiness, love. And so we invest everything we have in that industry, $60 billion a year. People spend their entire lives hating themselves in order to have this perfect body. And so, when somebody like me comes around, who doesn't have the perfect body, who also is not interested in working towards having a perfect body—there's compassion for fat people who are trying to lose weight; there's no compassion for fat people who don't want to lose weight—and they see I'm successful, I'm worthy, I have love, and I'm happy, they feel like they've been cut in front of in line. They feel like they've been ripped off and essentially everything they've invested in is like Monopoly money. And so, of course, they're really angry. I just

challenge everything that is valuable to them in their life. And so that's where I think a lot of the fat hatred comes from. It's complicated, obviously, but when it comes to people harassing fat women who are just saying positive messages, that's where I believe it stems.

Nicole's case shows how networked harassment is often morally motivated. Her harassers have constructed an elaborate justification for attacking her that they frame in moral terms—that she is dishonest, promoting unhealthy living, and somehow scamming her Patreon subscribers. This allows them to justify their behavior. Nicole, however, locates the harassment in fatphobia and misogyny, two manifestations of structural power inequalities that often go hand in hand.[45]

Morally Motivated Networked Harassment

What Nicole faced can be thought of as *morally motivated networked harassment* (MMNH).[46] Morally motivated networked harassment illuminates another set of potentially disastrous consequences that result when information moves beyond the context and audience for which it was intended and is made visible to people who interpret it completely differently. MMNH takes place when a member of an online community or network, such as the Fat People Hate subreddit, accuses someone of behavior that the community thinks is unacceptable. (Less commonly, this harassment falls on an organization or a brand.) Such accusations are often amplified by an influencer or micro-celebrity with a larger audience, whose members often share the same values. The accusation triggers what psychologists call "moral outrage," intense anger directed at someone who violates one's ideas of fairness or justice. Moral outrage spreads very quickly on the internet.[47] It feels good; it makes its perpetrators feel superior and shores up their sense of morality and identity. When it circulates throughout the network, it prompts members to send harassing messages to the target, messages that are often hateful, obscene, or profane. The person on the receiving end of this behavior experiences fear, depression, and anxiety and often pulls back from participating online to avoid future harassment.[48]

Morally motivated networked harassment reinforces the community's shared standards and signals that the people participating in the harassment share common values. Another woman I interviewed, Elise (twenty-eight), is an Asian American musician active on Twitter. One spring, her Twitter timeline was full of criticisms of a white-owned Chinese restaurant that promoted itself as a "clean" alternative to unhealthy, fatty Chinese food. Elise contributed to the critique by tweeting a thread about racist stereotypes of Chinese food and the history of Chinese American cuisine. It went viral. She received hundreds of attacks over the next few days, including angry tweets, furious emails, and hateful YouTube comments.[49] The harassing tweets frequently framed her as a racist. One tweet read, "Being a racist for the sake of being a racist is disgusting. These people are literally just trying to earn a living and you are single handedly trying to put them out of business, and for what. For what does this gain you? People eat better food, you get nothing in return." This tweet characterizes Elise as an antiwhite racist trying to put a hardworking restaurant owner out of business, rather than how she saw herself—an Asian American activist protesting a restaurant for its racism. The continued harassment showed that Elise's accusers successfully reframed her behavior as immoral and threatening, creating a justification for harassing her. In this case, the network reinforced the conservative belief that for people of color to call out white racism is worse than white racism itself. This reinforces the network's morality while shutting down behavior its members do not like.

This moral motivation explains several things. It explains why harassers feel that their actions are justified, how accusations spread so rapidly through networks, and why harassing behavior is so hateful: it is rooted in anger and outrage. This framing lets us think more precisely about the differences in norms and morals across social contexts and audiences. It also helps explain why harassment is more likely to happen to people who are marginalized in other ways. Misogyny, racism, fatphobia, and other prejudices can be justified through an elaborate scaffolding of violations of morality. Members of the Fat People Hate subreddit need to consider themselves good people, so rather than admit they harass people for being fat, they construct a moral justification for their hateful targeting of Nicole on the basis of health and financial integrity. The psychologists Zachary Rothschild and Lucas Keefer describe moral outrage as "a cleansing fire," concluding that it absolves people of guilt around their own moral failings and affirms their group and moral identity.[50]

People across the political spectrum suffer the consequences of networked harassment. In the preceding example, Elise's Twitter thread reflects her moral belief that the restaurant promoted racist stereotypes about Chinese American food, while the harassment she received reframed her criticism as antiwhite "reverse racism." This shows that no part of the ideological spectrum has a monopoly on harassment. Yet, as I discussed earlier, because traditional social norms privilege whiteness, maleness, and heteronormativity, people who are marginalized in other areas of their lives are more likely to face harassment.

Because harassment of all kinds often leads the accused to self-censorship, networked harassment is a regulating force for speech on social media. Nicole's privacy work is constant, intense, even radical. She uses a pseudonym online; she employs extremely secure passwords; she hired a moderator to deal with negative comments on her blog and across social media; and she carefully watches people she interacts with in public to ensure they are not taking pictures of her. She is so fed up with the harassment that she has basically stopped writing for the public. "It's just a choice I make to survive. I don't write anymore, to be honest. I don't write. I'm not vulnerable. I'm done being vulnerable at the expense of myself for others."

Virtually every harassment victim I interviewed for this project deeply self-censors themselves online, as do many who have not been harassed. Elise said, "I still feel like I'm still not completely myself on Twitter because now

I'm more careful about what topics I talk about. I don't really talk about racism and sexism so much anymore, or I don't really talk about politics. I am a lot more cautious now." By choosing not to participate in antiracist activism online to avoid harassment, Elise has changed her behavior to conform with the norms of her attackers. This is consistent with previous research. One study showed that more than half of women aged fifteen to twenty-nine censor themselves online to avoid harassment.[51] Other scholarship has found that female scholars, journalists, and politicians self-censor online due to both past harassment and the fear of more, culminating in what Candi Carter Olson and Victoria LaPoe call a "digital Spiral of Silence."[52] While this is understandable, it also means that harassment is systematically shutting down the voices of marginalized people, which is what the harassers intend.

There are no laws protecting people from the types of privacy violations that harassment often entails and very few technical protections. Most websites' terms of service adhere to US laws around harassment, which presume the dyadic model of one person repeatedly harassing another. This means that identifying networked harassment is very difficult. As Adrienne (thirty-two, white) said, "The Twitter staff might recognize it as harassment if one person sent you fifty messages telling you [that you] suck, but it's always the one person [who] posted one quote tweet saying that you suck, and then it's fifty of their followers who all independently sent you those messages, right?" Similarly, legal definitions of harassment presume ongoing harassment by the same person rather than a network. Justine (twenty-five, Korean American) said, "In terms of appealing to, like, a legal or policy definition, [my harassment experience] doesn't fit, because this one person shared, like, a selfie of me on the school gossip website, but there hasn't been a second offense, and it's unclear if it was a joke or not."

Social platforms must recognize the amplifying effect of highly followed networked nodes making accusations against other users. For better or worse, those with larger audiences bear a greater responsibility for their online

actions if they silence others. Given that the consequences of networked harassment can be the systemic suppression of marginalized voices, it is crucial
that platforms work diligently to prevent harassment's chilling effects.

When It Is Not Always So Clear

Some cases are not as clear as Kimberly's or Nicole's. For all harassment's strong moral valance, it has blurry boundaries. This blurriness allows
people to strategically leverage the term "harassment" to claim a moral high
ground in situations where they might otherwise be seen as contributing
to the problem. Moira (twenty-three, white) is a graduate student studying languages. She grew up in an isolated rural area with a tiny elementary
school; her class had only five students. In high school, she grew especially
close to one girl, Jiya. Jiya and Moira headed off to the same college and
decided to room together. Jiya's high school friend Emily became jealous of
their friendship. The way Moira tells it, Emily was offended one night when
Jiya abruptly ended a Skype call to go to dinner with Moira. The next day,
Emily blocked Jiya and Moira from social media and sent each of them a
long email message, saying she felt disrespected and neglected. A few days
later, she added them back.

At the time, all three women were very active on Tumblr. Moira and Jiya
were into *Supernatural* and *Harry Potter* and used Tumblr both for fandom
and as personal diaries. Few of their "real life" friends had Tumblr, so the
platform felt safe. The protection of obscurity gave them the feeling that
their posts would be read in the context and community for which they
were intended. Emily also used Tumblr. She wrote about fandom, her nursing studies, and what Moira called "really awful fiction about wanting to
sleep with her TA [teaching assistant]." All three women engaged in what
Moira called "vague-blogging," a form of steganography: "when you make
a blog post with no identifying information about whatever you're blog-
ging about." She gave the example of a post that would read, in its entirety,

"You're such an ungrateful spoiled little brat. You don't appreciate anything I do for you." After the dinner incident, a cycle began in which Emily would read a vague-blog from Moira or Jiya, believe it was about her (which, in many cases, it was), send them nasty anonymous Tumblr messages in response, and then apologize a few days later for the anonymous diatribe.

At the time, Tumblr limited users to 250 posts per day, which Emily, Moira, and Jiya all regularly hit. Moira and Jiya installed tracking software to see who was reading their Tumblrs and discovered that Emily was visiting them more than fifty times a day, reading every post. Emily's Tumblr was almost entirely about Moira and Jiya and their mutual high school friends. Moira framed this as harassment, but I was dubious, especially because Moira admitted that they would deliberately write vague-blogs to "bait" Emily and that she and Jiya had made Emily's terrible TA fanfic into one of their in-jokes. Moira explained,

> We would make a post that wasn't about her in a way, but we would word it in a way that it was so anonymous and so vague that she could interpret it was about her, because we knew that we would get this, like, massive reaction from her if we just posted basically nothing. Like absolutely anything, and she would blog it and bitch about it, and she would vague-blog about it, and she'd delete us, and she'd send us these messages, and she'd message all these people that we talk to about how awful we were, and then you could sort of afterwards be like, "Oh, no, that wasn't even about you! Oh, what?" and like feign innocence. But it was just—I mean, it was kind of entertaining in, like, a twisted way to sort of have that much power over her reactions to things, like, to be able to post something about, like—I mean, God, I remember one time I posted, "You're so vain. You probably think this post is about you."

In this case, Moira's frame of this situation as one in which Emily was "harassing" her allows her to avoid culpability for her own role, which might be better described as bullying Emily.

The incidents eventually petered out. Moira blocked Emily on Tumblr, stopped replying to her emails, and stopped reading her blog. But the conflict moved offline: back in their small town, Emily's grandmother got sick, and her doctor was Moira's father. Emily filed a complaint with the hospital, claiming he could not treat her grandmother fairly because of Emily and Moira's feud. (Moira's father did not know who Emily was, and the complaint was quickly dismissed.) Jiya publicized Emily's near-obsessive behavior, publicly posting a screenshot of Emily's visits to her blog, which had topped out at hundreds a day; Emily retaliated with a lengthy email listing the grievances she had with Jiya, at which point Jiya and Moira both blocked her email. While Moira says that Emily continued to talk behind their back, the mutual blocking had the desired effect.

This is not dyadic harassment. It is difficult to identify how the lines of power run or to determine who is the victim. If I interviewed Emily, I suspect I would hear a very different take. This seemed more like what danah boyd and I call *drama*: interpersonal conflict performed for an audience, usually involving social media.[53] Teenagers are much more likely to describe conflict as drama rather than as bullying, as bullying seems immature and requires the speaker to identify as either a bully or a victim. Yet when Moira described Emily's actions as harassment, she glossed over her own role in the situation. Interestingly, she used the word "drama" to describe Emily's motivations. When I asked her why she thought Emily had engaged in all this, she said, "I think she sort of wanted to create a more interesting life for herself in a way by involving herself in all of everybody's drama, like, in creating drama and having just something exciting going on." This use of "drama" puts the blame on Emily rather than acknowledging the participation of all three girls and certainly Moira's role in provoking Emily with cruel vague-blogs.

How does drama affect privacy and privacy work? If you need an audience, how do you work toward your desired level of privacy without giving up that audience? Moira did say that this incident affected how she thought of privacy online; she locked down her Facebook and stopped vague-blogging. However, she also admitted that this was not only a response to harassment; she "grew out" of Tumblr. (The three girls were only eighteen when these incidents took place.) As I discussed in chapter 3, vague-blogging is a type of privacy work, enabling people to talk honestly without revealing background information or experiencing consequences for the information they share. But, as in Moira's situation, it also provides plausible deniability if one is accused of bullying. Moira actually worked on a peer antibullying outreach program in high school, and she said that the types of bullying described by such campaigns did not look like the actual bullying that took place in school. Because of zero-tolerance policies in schools, much of today's bullying is not immediately visible. Bullying is social and often enabled by technology, which makes it invisible to adults in authority—especially when people have mirror profiles or finstas to keep secret accounts that adults cannot see. As Moira noted, online bullying had to be vague because "no matter what you did, you always had to be able to say, 'No, I didn't mean it that way' or 'It was an accident.'" In other words, bullies take advantage of social media's leakiness, which enables context to be stripped and a false context supplied so that posts are misunderstood.

Moira's privacy work was and is fairly low-key; she uses the same username for everything and said she is fairly easy to track down. This is probably because, unlike Kimberly and Nicole, she never actually felt threatened. She said, "I never at any point felt like [Emily] had any power in the situation. Like, it always felt like she was kind of being pathetic and that I always had the upper hand because I was able to make her react in the ways that she ended up reacting. And I knew her well enough that I know she would never actually follow through on, like, any serious threat or anything." Moira does not engage in safety work because she does not feel vulnerable. She feels that she always had more power than Emily. While she may label Emily's actions harassment, and they technically meet the definition of harassment as repeated and (according to Moira) unwanted contact, her situation is very different from that of Kimberly or Nicole, who fear for their safety and are forced to engage in deep privacy and safety work. This case shows that while harassment is very real, the label itself also carries power. Harassment, like privacy, is deeply contextual.

Gendered Privacy

Understanding harassment as a type of forced publicity helps us see how privacy violations can be gendered. Gendered privacy violations are those that are more likely to happen to or harm someone on the basis of their gender. Using this lens to analyze technologically mediated abuse, including harassment, stalking, and "revenge porn," makes two things clear. First, these forms of abuse are much more likely to happen to women, and second, they intrinsically involve privacy violations, forced publicity, or both. While anyone can have their nude photos leaked, it is *far* more likely to happen to women, who are also more likely to be coerced into sending nude photos in the first place.[54] "Stalkerware," software that covertly tracks everything done on a mobile phone and broadcasts it to someone else, is mostly used against women by current or former partners.[55] Intimate partner violence (IPV), which affects one in three women, is also increasingly tied up with digital technologies that facilitate violations of privacy.[56] The security researcher Diana Freed, drawing from the experiences of thirty-nine survivors and fifty professionals who help IPV victims, sorted attacks by abusers into four categories. Two of the categories involved privacy violations and included behaviors like controlling access to someone's phone, forcing a victim to reveal their passwords, installing spyware, and tracking the victim's location. The other two categories involved forced publicity such as threatening to reveal intimate images or posting content on social media to humiliate the victim.[57] The legal scholars Clare McGlynn, Erika Rackley, and Ruth Houghton argue that much sexual abuse involving digital images falls outside the common definition of "revenge porn"; it includes such things as voyeurism, so-called upskirt or jailbait photos, sexualized manipulation of images, and recordings of sexual assault.[58] All of these involve clear violations of privacy and are primarily experienced by women. Anyone who installs stalkerware on their partner's phone without their consent is committing technologically enabled violence, but this too is more likely to happen to women—and when it does, it exists on a continuum with other forms of gendered sexual violence, from street harassment to rape. These privacy violations are deeply gendered and tied to larger systems of gender inequality. This is why we need to integrate gender in our analyses of networked privacy violations.

The gendered nature of privacy violations, combined with the assumption that individuals are responsible for maintaining their own privacy, meant that throughout my interviews, blame for privacy violations fell on the victims. This also ties into gendered dynamics. Most of the people I spoke with who had experienced harassment had no doubt who was to blame: the perpetrators. But the belief that privacy violations are a woman's fault for "putting herself out there" in public harks back to the "separate spheres" theory of society, which relegates women to the home. This was clearest when interviewees discussed nude or sexually explicit image sharing.[59] Many of my younger participants, instead of criticizing those who circulated these photos, blamed the victims for sharing the pictures in the first place. They were very comfortable locating the problem with the subject of the photos for failing to guard her own privacy. Because women are more likely to be the subjects of revenge porn and more likely to report feeling coerced to share intimate images, this ties into deeper cultural narratives that blame women when they experience sexual violence.[60] As the communication scholar Amy Hasinoff writes in her excellent book *Sexting Panic*, "women, and in particular, racialized, lower-income, queer, and trans women, are often constructed as deviant risk-takers and thus held responsible for sexual assault."[61] While not all of my study participants placed blame this way, I heard it from young women who defined themselves as feminists, poor people who had experienced state and corporate networked violations of privacy, and people of color who knew that certain groups are unfairly targeted and blamed for privacy violations. While participants frequently saw their peers posting risqué images, many judged those who did so as lacking individual responsibility. The assignment of this blame lets abusive systems off the hook, just as placing the burden of privacy protection on individuals ignores the role of social platforms and big data aggregators.

Fatima (twenty-one, Latina) said, "I'm definitely not stupid enough to send anyone lewd pictures, because those don't end up where you want them to be. Don't trust anyone." Seeing the spread of nude photographs as inevitable, Fatima focuses on women who take or share nudes, rather than blaming male recipients for sharing them with others. She believes that once a woman makes the "stupid" decision to share a nude picture, there is nothing to be done, because "the interwebs can be a very savage place." For Fatima, the only agency available to a woman is to avoid sharing. Once she takes nude pictures, she has no recourse.

Shaka (twenty-three, African immigrant) and Jun (twenty-two, Chinese American) work together at a museum. They discussed what it is like to be a young woman online:

SHAKA: Yeah, and then just fucking random creepy-ass guys trying to talk to you and all that. So that's why I feel a little bad about females on social media, because any type of fucking rapist can talk to them. It's very scary in a way. You can't stop nobody to use social media, at the end of the day, but just be careful what you do on social media.

JUN: It's like what my aunt says: if you can't change someone, you gotta change yourself.

SHAKA: Exactly. Be careful what you put on social media and respect yourself, 'cause if people seeing that you don't respect yourself, they not gonna respect you. And they will talk shit about you, and they will fucking be creepy on you.

JUN: They begin to feel like they have the right to destroy you.

SHAKA: Exactly, because you destroying yourself, so they will help you to destroy you, of course. Nobody wanna see you taking care of yourself. That's why people talk bullshit about you.

Jun and Shaka are concerned by "rapists" and "random creepy-ass guys" on-line, but they also think women bear at least some responsibility for attracting negative attention. They conflate posting nude, revealing, or inappropriate pictures with self-destructive behavior or a lack of self-respect, arguing that negative consequences become the women's fault for disrespecting themselves. Similarly, Stacy (twenty-two, Latina) told Jun, "It boggles my mind how people can just put pictures of—provocative pictures of themselves on the internet or—and how that might suddenly lead to online harassment or some creep hacking into your device or finding your IP address, your address, your personal information. It's just—I don't know how people do it." To Stacy, while people who hack or harass others are "creeps," it is the individual woman's responsibility to make sure she does not put herself in a position to be victimized.

Others had more nuanced views. Malik (seventeen, African American) believes the responsibility lies squarely on the distributor of intimate photos. As a peer sexual health educator, he has spent more time considering the ethics of revenge porn than many of his peers. From his perspective, "the person felt comfortable enough with you to share that with you, and then after you stop dating them you share that. I think that shouldn't be the case. I think you should have enough respect for them, and if you really loved the person, you wouldn't have done that." Malik does not think people should be "sharing their sex life or stuff like that" or distributing "the nudes that some kids sext." He believes that "those images can affect human life" and "do harm to you," but he concludes that if sexual images are shared in the context of a consensual loving relationship, the logic of respect should prevail even if the relationship dissolves. This system of morality still places blame on people who share intimate images outside a monogamous relationship, reinforcing a conservative normative sexuality.

Camila (seventeen, Puerto Rican) is an active community and church member and participates in a variety of volunteer and after-school activities. She loves Instagram and is proud of her thirteen thousand followers but is careful to make sure her accounts are suitable for any audience, including her grandmother and her pastor. Camila also has a nuanced understanding of respect online. On the one hand, she believes that it is disrespectful to go digging for information about people or for young people to pass around nude pictures of others. On the other, she thinks that if you post inappropriate information online and people find it, it is your own fault. She takes a practical approach:

> If you're posting a picture where I can see 95 percent of your skin, and someone shows that around, if you posted that yourself, apparently that's something you want people to see. And I feel like it is wrong if someone goes and shows that to fifty thousand other people, but then if it's like if you didn't want or expect something like that to happen, knowing that teenagers do it a lot, then you shouldn't have posted it on there. Because at the end of the day, once you post something to the internet, no matter what you do, it's not coming off.

While Camila recognizes that it is wrong for people to distribute intimate images beyond their intended audience, she noted that this can be prevented by not taking the photos in the first place. She stated that once on a social platform, such photos are likely to spread and leak. But she is also very aware of the cultural forces that lead young women to link their self-esteem to their bodies:

> People who are posting these sexual things or all this different stuff aren't necessarily bad people. A lot of times, it's like they've had a poor experience or an experience that makes them—or what they've been shown—that makes them think things like this are okay. Like, I know a lot of teenagers that grow up with parents that are like, "Okay. I'm going to sleep with this man because he has money. And I just have to be pretty. I don't have to be smart. I don't have to think about anything. I can just be pretty, sleep with this man, get his money, and that's all I have to do."

While she recognizes that her peers may have formative experiences that lead them to post different types of content, Camila still believes that posting "inappropriate" content signals a lack of self-respect and dignity. But she is a pragmatist. While it is wrong to pass around naked selfies, teenagers are going to do it anyway, so the best way to keep it from happening is simply not to take them.

Two lines of thought intersect here: the idea that women are responsible for protecting themselves from harassment and abuse and the idea that people are responsible for protecting themselves from privacy violations. Revenge porn and harassment exist at a crossroads where women are blamed when others aggressively violate their privacy. This can be intensely humiliating. In my interviews, I heard stories of people switching schools, dropping out of college, leaving jobs, and otherwise trying to disappear to escape forced publicity. Responsibility is gendered.

Moving Forward

How do we combat online harassment? Some of my study participants had very clear ideas of how technologies should be modified to decrease the types of abuses described in this chapter. Jamie, who was repeatedly subjected to creepy sexual comments when she posted selfies on makeup-related subreddits, proposed that once Reddit has sanctioned people for antisocial behavior, it should make it more difficult for them to make alternate accounts. Paige suggested that *Overwatch* stop matching players with users they had previously blocked. Moira wants a more robust blocking system on Tumblr. Others are frustrated that reporting and flagging harassers or abusers does not result in any consequences, while still others bemoaned the downsides of privacy work. Justine, who was harassed for her work combating campus sexual violence, noted that when she password-protected her Tumblr blog, it no longer appeared on her followers' dashboards. This privacy measure slowed the harassment but cut her off from her community.

There are clearly many technical improvements that would lessen harassment, even if the underlying dynamics are structural.

For something so harmful, there are few effective legal protections against harassment, and many platforms are doing too little to govern behavior. It is telling that many participants mentioned individual solutions rather than collective, structural ones: protect yourself, reach out to friends, call your therapist. Even people who had been affected by harassment and understood the lack of systemic protection against it still think of privacy as an individual responsibility. Because of harassment's link to structural sexism and because it is facilitated by the nature of social media, an emphasis on individual solutions is unlikely to help change the problem. (When I asked Ava, a nineteen-year-old lesbian who constantly deals with homophobic comments on Twitter, what to do about harassment, she said, "Decrease the amount of men.")

By moving toward collective responses to harassment and violence more generally, we can imagine alternative paths to justice and accountability. Here I must note that reporting harassment to the state is dangerous for many people, especially BIPOC, undocumented people, and trans people. Many activists I spoke with told me about approaches to combating abuse that do not involve police. (This is particularly true given the ongoing discussion of police violations of privacy.) Anne (thirty-five, white), a feminist activist, said, "I'm an abolitionist, so I'm in favor of trying to work and create the structures of community accountability. That's just something that you can't have on Twitter. The way in which it's built, how do you have community accountability? What does that look like? It just was never thought about, never in that way. Humans weren't meant to all connect together at once without having some boundaries and structures. We can't do it offline. Why would we be able to do it online? At the same time, I love the internet, so . . ." Anne speaks to the futility of creating community-based responses to violence on spaces like Twitter, where communities have such different norms and values. She works in security and has been mulling over transformative justice as a framework for addressing online abuse. Transformative justice is a philosophy of conflict resolution that looks at the underlying conditions giving rise to violence and offers an alternative to punitive models of justice.[62] A transformative justice approach to sexual violence, for instance, centers the victims and ensures their safety while seeking acknowledgment and accountability from the person who created the harm.[63] At the same time, advocates of transformative justice engage in community work to change the social structures that facilitate abuse and harm in the first place. But as Anne points out, transformative justice generally assumes that the target and perpetrator of violence share a common community—which is far from the case with networked harassment. Still, transformative justice may provide a useful model to think with as we consider alternative approaches to combating networked harassment, given the limitations of carceral punishment systems.

The information studies scholar Sarita Schoenebeck and her research team have examined an alternative framework for dealing fairly with networked abuse, known as "restorative justice." The idea is to redress harm rather than punish a perpetrator. When a platform like Facebook sanctions a user for harassment, the target of the abuse is typically left out of the process and may not even be aware of any consequences after they report harassment. Restorative justice often uses mediation to resolve conflicts between a target, a perpetrator, and their community.[64] The perpetrator might be required to apologize, validate the experiences of the target, or facilitate a community conversation around the incident. Again, this is difficult to implement on enormous social platforms where communities embrace different or contradictory norms. These approaches may be more effective in small communities, such as subreddits or private Facebook groups.[65]

Another possible intervention is reminding users of platform norms that prohibit harassment. J. Nathan Matias's work with Reddit has shown that displaying community rules that reflect subreddit norms (removing abusive or off-topic comments, for example) made newcomer comments less likely to be removed and increased participation rates.[66] This would do little in communities where harassment is condoned, such as the Fat People Hate subreddit that harassed Nicole, but it suggests a possible source of friction for platforms like Twitter. Ultimately, moving from an individual to a networked model of privacy allows us to understand how privacy intersects with gender on a structural level and opens up solutions that focus on networks and communities rather than individuals.

Second-wave feminists were suspicious of privacy because they believed it allowed crimes against women that were committed in the home to be swept under the rug. Yet harassment, technologically enabled violence, and revenge porn show us that continued violations of women's privacy are a way to coerce, punish, exile, and control. Moving away from the binary model of privacy as separate spheres and toward a model of privacy as agency and control demonstrates that women's ability to maintain their privacy is key to self-determination and dignity. Unfortunately, it is not only malicious actors like harassers and abusers who compromise this ability. It is also platforms and data-driven technologies, as well as the state, showing once again how the private is political. The very foundation of social media—its purpose of allowing users to connect and share information as widely as possible—makes it easy to repurpose that information for abusive means. Social platforms make communities with different or conflicting norms visible to each other, enabling networked harassment that is morally motivated. In other cases, the way social technologies facilitate forced publicity allows them to be misappropriated for humiliation and social shaming. We must acknowledge that privacy violations are an integral part of abuse, that this is facilitated by technology, and that this is gendered.

My interview participants' diverse experiences also tell us that "one size fits all" solutions to harassment will not work. Women are not the only ones who experience forced publicity; men are frequently harassed on social media as well. But women are far more likely to experience unwanted monitoring and tracking, stalking, harassment over a long period of time, doxing, revenge porn, image-based sexual abuse, and sexual harassment.[67] The boundaries between harassment and sexual harassment and between privacy work and safety work are blurry. Integrating research on privacy with scholarship on harassment illustrates a central tenet of networked privacy: modern technologies enable networked privacy violations whose consequences fall disproportionately on marginalized people. Structural sexism facilitates harassment, and the burden of self-protective privacy work most often falls to those who are most vulnerable to harassment: white women and women of color, nonbinary folks, and LGTBQ+ individuals. The discourse of individual responsibility obscures this disproportionate impact.

5

Privacy on the Margins

Networked Privacy and Socioeconomic Status

Jorge is twenty-five and lives in public housing with his aunt, cousins, and brother in the Puerto Rican neighborhood of El Barrio in East Harlem.[1] Wearing a secondhand button-down shirt and running his hand through his curly brown hair, Jorge still looks a bit like a super-smart, geeky kid who does not fit in. His mom dropped him off at his aunt's house when he was five, and he did not see her for ten years: she was a drug addict and spent time in prison. Now she is sober and crashing on his aunt's couch while she waits for Section 8 housing to come through. Jorge is slowly working his way through community college, hoping to become an electrical engineer. He has tinkered with gadgets since he was a kid and loves fixing broken electronics he finds on the street. Eventually he wants to work for the Metropolitan Transit Authority (MTA) to help fix the beleaguered subway system; he spoke knowledgably about how signal malfunctions increase traffic delays.

Jorge grew up in the New York City housing projects, which he describes as places of constant surveillance, endless paperwork, and targeted enforcement. His neighborhood is full of CCTV cameras, and the police just installed floodlights outside his building that make it hard for him and his brother to sleep at night. He knows the beat cops by sight and what times they are on duty, and he tries to avoid them. Jorge grew up under stop-and-frisk, the New York Police Department (NYPD) policy that allowed police offers to stop, question, and search anyone they found suspicious; mostly their suspicion focused on young men of color living in low-income neighborhoods, the vast majority of whom had done nothing wrong.[2] Jorge has been stopped twice, once because he was carrying an umbrella and once because the police did not like the way he was riding his scooter. His brother and cousin have also been stopped. These experiences make him suspicious of the police. He said, "To avoid those kind of things, we keep our heads down. We keep our noses clean." In other words, Jorge and his family members try to make themselves less visible to the police, to avoid being punished for simply being a poor young man of color.

It is hard to maintain a low profile in that environment. The housing projects have a lot of strict rules, frequently broken but selectively enforced. Jorge explains that his family is not allowed to paint the walls or drill holes (although everyone does), that large dogs are not allowed (so people walk them at odd hours or far away from the building), and that his neighbors share keys because they worry that the hardware store might report them for making copies. While everyone violates these rules, they still exist and can be used as leverage or to punish people for something else. There is always the concern that your family will be the one that is evicted for having an extra person living in the apartment. Jorge, who is basically law-abiding, has adopted a lawyerly approach to rules:

> I want to get a bike because I don't like buses. Most people would just be like "Okay, you know, I'm going to go get a bike." But I've been learning the laws of cycling in New York, what I'm allowed and not allowed to do, 'cause I feel like that's an effect of the life I've led in housing projects and the lower-income areas I've lived in, is that, hey, if you don't know the rules, because I've seen cops around here, you're more likely to get targeted. Like, "Hey did you see that sign?" because I'm like, oh man, "You're not supposed to be riding in this direction. You're on the sidewalk. Where's your proper brakes?" Like, I know all this stuff because I'm afraid of riding a bike for ten minutes and being the one who's arrested for something dumb.

Like many of the young people my colleagues and I interviewed who live in precarious circumstances, Jorge is deeply aware of his vulnerability.

This constant low-level fear affects how he shares information and how he presents himself online. He has internalized his teachers' admonitions not to share anything online that might come back to haunt him. Thus, it is not enough simply to follow the rules; Jorge actively self-censors, keeping his online presence "neutral" and "vanilla." He stays away from politics and arguments on Twitter and Facebook, avoids swear words, and sticks to safe topics like Marvel movies. He says, "I feel it's logical to be paranoid, 'cause I've still done nothing wrong, but I still feel the eyes looking down my back." Jorge is primarily concerned with potential employers or schools seeing his online content, but his experiences with the dragnet of policing make him worry.

Poor people are under immense, disproportionate surveillance by state structures of policing, criminal justice, employment, education, and public assistance. These systems collect vast amounts of data, including networked data. It is fed through automated decision systems (ADS) that sort people into categories, allocate benefits, and determine risks or punishments.[3] Among the many examples of such systems are those that automate welfare eligibility processes using algorithms to determine who is entitled to benefits and to predict criminal behavior among potential recipients; alert child protective services to households at risk for child abuse or neglect; determine both K–12 and higher-education admissions; allocate neighborhood resources; surveil students, particularly those "at risk" (frequently those who are from low-income families or are otherwise known to the system); identify protestors, activists, or dissidents; monitor public health; and rank job seekers for open positions.[4] Such complex sociotechnical structures are based on vast quantities of data yet operate largely without accountability. The surveillant eye observes strategically, looking intensively at some people when it wants to control them but looking away when those same people need to be visible. The sociologist Virginia Eubanks, who studies the integration of ADS into public assistance, chronicles people's futile attempts to be seen accurately by unaccountable computer-driven formulas that repeatedly deny them benefits.[5] These technologies form assemblages within which people can have both too little and too much visibility, none of it decided by themselves.

Poor people are thus especially vulnerable to state violations of networked privacy. Elsewhere we have seen how this privacy can be violated by individuals, as with revenge porn on social media, or by large commercial entities that collect consumer data. Low-income people are of course subject to these too, but because they are more likely to apply for assistance, live in poor neighborhoods, and interact with other poor people, their information is also more likely to appear in state databases. These databases often connect to commercial databases, and they include extremely sensitive personal information such as credit history, salary, and past interactions with police or public assistance, all of which is analyzed by black-box algorithms that are difficult to identify, let alone protest. Networked privacy also presents another danger to low-income individuals because social media explicitly maps their networks and connections. These networks can be surveilled and mined to create profiles with harmful implications, as when police use social media to identify potential "criminal associates" or networks of activists and protestors. Finally, and perhaps most importantly, the harms of privacy violations are more difficult for poor people to weather. Having money stolen through identity theft or being fired due to information leaking on social media is never pleasant, but for people living in precarious circumstances, such difficulties have serious long-term consequences.

Low-income people thus face a dilemma: they are systematically denied privacy by a variety of institutions (such as criminal justice, social services, and low-wage employment) even as they struggle to make themselves legible to receive needed resources.[6] The incorporation of big data into increasingly sophisticated regimes of social sorting—a violation of networked privacy—disadvantages the poor, who may be denied educational or employment benefits by such systems. Furthermore, the impacts of networked privacy violations are far greater for people who are already on the margins. The harms of privacy violations are much more worrisome for people with little to fall back on than for people with security nets of education, employment, and strong family networks.

The surveillance of poor people, which today occurs heavily in the realms of social services, employment, education, and policing, influences how people growing up in these networks view themselves, their relationships, and their privacy. This chapter draws primarily from interviews with twenty-seven low-income millennial-aged New Yorkers, most of them immigrants and people of color. For many of the people we spoke with, especially those who were striving for economic security, the best way to deal with privacy violations was to protect themselves and their information no matter what. Many of these young people without many economic opportunities leveraged alternate forms of capital, such as their technical capabilities, to protect themselves. While this sense of individual responsibility for protecting one's privacy often resulted in harsh judgment of their peers who chose to engage online more openly, many of our study participants (who, like Jorge, had grown up under stop-and-frisk) had a sophisticated model of systemic police surveillance that placed collective responsibility on the system rather than on individuals. This provides a model for thinking about networked privacy as structural and how we might go about changing a discourse that blames individuals for privacy violations.

Surveilling the Poor

A few years ago, at an academic conference on privacy, I was struck by the number of papers on drones, the National Security Agency, and data breaches, while not a single paper talked about welfare or the criminal justice system. As we have seen throughout this book, although privacy affects different populations in disparate ways, privacy researchers often treat it as a single concept.[7] Mainstream privacy discourse typically reflects what is most germane to upper-middle-class people, such as credit card theft, airport security theater, or targeted advertising on Facebook.

Yet wealthier people are far less vulnerable to privacy breaches by the state. They do not bring themselves into the state's surveillance networks by applying for assistance; they seldom live in areas subject to intensive policing (and when they do, they are the ones being protected); they have greater choice about employment and can avoid suspicionless drug testing and invasive cameras in their workplaces; and their children are likely to go to better-funded schools with less aggressive school resource officers and more flexible policies that are not part of the school-to-prison pipeline.[8]

People of different social classes experience a very different level of privacy violations. Frequent travelers may be annoyed by airport body scanners; mothers seeking welfare are routinely asked for intimate details about their romantic relationships, sexual history, and parenting techniques.[9] White-collar workers worry about employers reading their email; low-wage workers often pass through fingerprint scanners to get to their jobs, where they work under the constant surveillance of CCTV cameras and devices that track their body movements and facial expressions.[10] People who live in neighborhoods with heavy police presence, or who are simply connected to other low-income people on social media, are often caught up in police dragnets and have their personal information gathered as part of investigations.[11] Young people in high-poverty, high-minority schools not only have fewer educational resources but deal with metal detectors, pat downs, and police surveillance on a daily basis; students in schools serving middle-class neighborhoods rarely confront these issues.[12] Monitoring and surveillance are embedded into the infrastructures people must navigate in order to access most state resources, and poor people who need those services cannot opt out. Privacy violations occur at several levels, from on-the-job physical surveillance to the aggregation of state-collected networked data about all aspects of a person's life. The anger that middle-class people may feel at airport pat downs or police searches at protests reflects a norm of bodily privacy that is not extended to those in less fortunate circumstances.

In chapter 1, I argued that US privacy law responded to middle-class concerns such as cosseting privileged white women within the private sphere of the home. A more contemporary concern, preventing information collected in one context to be misused, is also subtly classed, because it assumes that information is gathered in ways that are neutral or unobtrusive. This is deeply inaccurate for poor people, who are stigmatized even while information is being collected. The legal scholar Khiara Bridges documents a caseworker's onerous questioning of a woman seeking welfare; such interactions cost poor people dignity, respect, and a sense of autonomy. If someone needs such services, they have no agency over whether to share information that they might wish to keep private.[13]

Privacy frameworks that give people only the choice to opt in or opt out or that ignore the networked nature of privacy conflate privacy as a *right* with privacy as a *privilege*. If it is a right, privacy should be accorded equally to all people, but it is frequently treated as a privilege granted only to those who fit the mold of the law-abiding liberal subject. This implies that those who cannot afford to protect their privacy do not deserve to keep it. The legal scholar Michele Gilman argues that poor people, who are primarily female and racial minorities, experience privacy fundamentally differently from the middle class. The "right to be left alone" that is so valued by privacy scholars is not extended to the poor by either employers or the state. Instead, systematic surveillance, enabled by their low status, regularly undermines their dignity, respect, and trust. Gilman and other scholars trace this punitive approach to classist mistrust of the poor and an effort to contain, evaluate, and suppress low-income people's concerns.[14] Electronic ankle monitors, for instance, are worn by people on parole and probation, undocumented immigrants, people who have been convicted of minor offenses, and people awaiting trial who have not been convicted of anything.[15] Not only do ankle monitors enable constant surveillance, but they are highly stigmatized, signaling to everyone who sees them that the wearer is a criminal and possibly dangerous.[16] Anyone wearing an ankle monitor is therefore considered "undeserving" of personal privacy. Regardless of whether being convicted of, say, a minor drug offense justifies taking away someone's privacy so completely, these consequences are hardly distributed equally. The white and wealthy are *far* less likely to be convicted of a crime than those who are poor and people of color. Unfortunately, these inequalities persist throughout state policy.

Social Services

The US social services sector is a classic example of framing privacy as a privilege accorded only to those who "deserve" it. While the ideal welfare state protects every citizen's well-being, the United States distributes public benefits on the assumption that poor people are poor through their own character defects.[17] This narrative holds that anyone should be able to lift themselves out of poverty with hard work, that poor people are poor because of their own laziness, and that most who collect government benefits do not actually need them, implying they are deceitful as well as lazy. This widespread perception that the poor—especially poor women of color— are undeserving, lazy, and deceitful underpins a move toward an ever more punitive model of social service provision, in which the people who need these services the most are regulated and surveilled by the very systems purporting to serve them.

In *Automating Inequality*, on the integration of big data into the distribution of social services, Virginia Eubanks links what she calls the modern "digital poorhouse" to long-standing surveillance of poor people.[18] In the early nineteenth century, poor people in the United States were imprisoned in "poorhouses," which were modeled on those of Victorian Britain and which supposedly taught them to be thrifty and industrious. But the conditions in poorhouses were intentionally horrible to deter people from seeking social support. By the turn of the twentieth century, social concern for the poor was concentrated in the scientific charity movement and rooted in eugenics, which treated working-class neighborhoods as laboratories for inquiry. "Reformers," the precursors of today's social workers, tracked the hygiene and medical practices of immigrants and working-class African Americans, hoping to manage public health through surveillance.

Eubanks argues that since there was not enough public assistance to cover the need for it, data collection was used to separate the "deserving" poor from the "undeserving." Whether one was deserving, of course, depended on one's race and ethnicity. Immigrants were subject to harsh medical scrutiny because they were associated with disease and contamination, while African American poverty was mostly ignored in favor of "deserving" white people.[19] Sarah Igo writes that the same elites who wielded privacy as a tool to fight unwanted photography or press attention for white women "fell silent when it came to fingerprinting immigrants or common laborers" or invading immigrant women's homes to inspect them for hygiene.[20] As we saw in Jorge's case, this is still true today. Poor people are still subject to greater privacy violations.[21]

The scientific charity movement fell apart during the Great Depression and was replaced by the New Deal, which established Social Security and Aid to Dependent Children (ADC), which became Aid to Families with Dependent Children (AFDC), the program we usually think of when we imagine "welfare." These programs defined the deserving poor as white, able-bodied, working men and their wives and children, and the undeserving poor as part-time and precarious workers, African Americans, people with chronic illnesses and disabilities, the elderly, and single parents.[22] For the first thirty-five years of the existence of ADC/AFDC, from 1935 to 1970 or so, its recipients were overwhelmingly white widows, and payments were given to keep them at home with their children.[23] Caseworkers granted assistance only to women they considered of upright character, excluding people on the basis of their approach to child rearing and discipline and whether they were poor due to their own actions.[24] Women who were considered "sexually immoral"—including lesbians, divorced women, and never-married mothers—were excluded from benefits, while welfare recipients from eastern or southern Europe were required to "Americanize" in order to receive assistance.[25] Determining an applicant's suitability required a great deal of intrusive questioning, even for those who were deemed deserving of financial support. Caseworkers raided clients' homes, searched their personal belongings, examined them and their children for health concerns, and questioned them about their parenting, sexual relationships, and housekeeping practices.

After World War II, millions of Black Americans emigrated north in search of better lives for their families during the "Great Migration." However, new migrants faced housing and employment discrimination, leading many to seek public assistance. Narrowly defined, discriminatory state and city regulations often made it impossible for women of color who were eligible for welfare to claim benefits.[26] In the late 1950s and early 1960s, welfare recipients, mostly poor Black women, began organizing in their local communities, swapping strategies on how to handle their caseworkers and understand the complex regulations of government assistance.[27] These women eventually organized what came to be called the Welfare Rights Movement. They critiqued the model of welfare that required poor Black mothers to go to work yet rewarded white women for staying home with their children. They pushed back on intrusive information collection and advocated for a universal basic income. In the context of the War on Poverty in the 1960s, welfare regulations were liberalized.[28] While African Americans had historically been excluded from receiving state benefits at all, especially women with children out of wedlock, such reforms opened up public assistance to these groups. As we will see, this set the stage for public hostility and critiques.

Contemporary social service systems collect personal data both to coerce and to punish recipients.[29] Khiara Bridges argues that the intrusive questioning that poor mothers seeking benefits are forced to endure does not determine whether a woman can provide for her children but instead reinforces the moral construction of poverty, which holds that "people are poor because there is something *wrong* with them."[30] Asking in-depth, personal questions both allows the state apparatus to determine whether someone "deserves" assistance and punishes the poor for being poor. Depending on the jurisdiction, welfare recipients may also be subject to home searches, drug testing, fingerprinting, or even birth-control implantation; these privacy violations serve to deter people from applying for aid.[31] Consider the difference between applying for Medicare and Medicaid. Medicare, which provides health insurance for all Americans over sixty-five, requires simple online forms, whereas Medicaid, a supplementary insurance program specifically for poor mothers and children, requires intrusive face-to-face questioning.[32] The welfare state privileges a patriarchal model of the nuclear family, and who is judged deserving has more to do with their race, gender, and class than their actual circumstances or needs.[33] Government welfare thus has two tiers, with a "social safety net" of Social Security and Medicare extended to the deserving while the "undeserving" seek increasingly less-accessible public assistance. Rather than establish a universal benefits program, the New Deal justified continued investigation and policing of the poor.

It is not solely class that explains this difference. White Americans do not support antipoverty programs because they perceive them as primarily helping Black Americans, who are stereotyped as unreliable, immoral, and lazy.[34] As early as the 1960s, antifraud initiatives specifically targeted African American communities, making social services far more difficult to access and, in many cases, punishing those who sought them.[35] Campaigning for the Republican presidential nomination in 1976, Ronald Reagan described the "welfare queen," a Black woman in Chicago bilking the government of more than $150,000 a year by collecting "food stamps, Social Security, veteran's benefits for four nonexistent deceased veteran husbands as well as welfare."[36] This was a real person; her name was Linda Taylor, and she was a notorious con artist who, in addition to falsifying welfare benefits, was a thief, a pathological liar, a suspected kidnapper, a possible bigamist, and perhaps even a murderer.[37] (She also was not Black. She used her olive skin and dark hair to portray people of various races in her many grifting schemes.) Taylor was not representative of anything. She was an outrageous character and a criminal who conned virtually everyone she met, and welfare fraud was the least of her crimes. She was eventually convicted of defrauding the government and sentenced to eight years in prison.[38]

Taylor's trial was sensationalized in the *Chicago Tribune* and *Sun-Times* and sparked a wave of prosecutions for welfare fraud in Illinois. Once Reagan began using the term "welfare queen," coined by the Chicago newspapers to describe Taylor, it caught on instantly. It played into the racist and classist stereotype of the lazy Black matriarch who was utterly shameless about living in the lap of luxury while shirking all social and family responsibility. It also had enormous impact, as the belief that people receiving welfare were irresponsible and deceptive massively decreased public support for the program.[39] Between 1970 and 1979, investigations of welfare fraud increased 729 percent across the United States.[40] With this decrease in public support came highly expanded systems of surveillance and discipline of welfare recipients, often using technical and computational systems to determine access to benefits; this is what Virginia Eubanks calls the "digital poorhouse." These investigative actions and programs are built on two assumptions: first, that fraud is rampant—which is highly questionable—and, second, that most people who collect government benefits do not actually need them. Eubanks argues that these systems are working as planned: "They're designing the technologies to produce the results they want: less and less people getting the resources they need."[41]

To be clear, welfare fraud is not a real problem. Most accusations of fraud involve a poor mother receiving unreported income that is not used to calculate the benefits she receives, such as a student loan, an unexpected child-support payment, or a savings account for her children. Sometimes welfare laws change, and income that was previously allowable is disallowed; or a welfare worker has difficulty following complex regulations and gives their client inaccurate advice. In other situations, a woman's husband or boyfriend conceals income from her or tells her not to report it.[42] The harms of such "fraud" are infinitesimal compared to the very significant harms of poverty, such as housing and food insecurity, lack of affordable child care, and lack of access to needed medical services. As Janet Mosher and Joe Hermer write in their study of welfare policy in Ontario, Canada, welfare fraud is a "problem that has been constructed and deployed to disentitle and punish welfare recipients."[43]

But due to classist and racist beliefs about the poor, the specter of welfare fraud is used to justify grievous privacy violations and punitive policies. Recently the government has begun using "big data" to combat this nonexistent problem. The *New York Times* tech reporter Natasha Singer describes the case of Parvawattie Raghunandan, a Bronx resident who had received "$50,000 in health benefits over a decade" and whose fraud was detected by using a LexisNexis tool that searches property records, car-ownership databases, and business records to identify welfare fraud.[44] LexisNexis claims to use data from ten thousand sources and two billion records to save "billions in taxpayer dollars" and identify a laundry list of fraudulent activities, including "organized crime rings running complex schemes."[45] (I found no documentation of any "complex schemes" run by organized crime.)

In addition to violating people's privacy, these big data judgments are not even accurate. An investigative report from *The Markup* found that such reports are frequently sloppy and just plain wrong. They often conflate different people with similar names, even those living in different states with different races or birthdates. The Tennessee resident Davone Jackson was denied low-income housing on the basis of a screening report that claimed he appeared on the Wisconsin sex-offender registry and had been arrested in Kentucky for heroin trafficking. Those offenses were actually committed by men named Eric Jackson and James Jackson. As with many low-income people, being denied housing led to housing insecurity, and Davone and his daughter had to live in a motel for almost a year before they found a stable place to live.[46] Michigan implemented an unproven automated fraud-detection system that accused almost fifty thousand residents of fraudulently claiming unemployment benefits. The system required the accused to pay back the amount plus interest and penalties up to *four times* what they supposedly owed. This resulted in garnished wages, seized bank accounts, and withheld tax refunds, leading to evictions, homelessness, bankruptcy, and divorces. It later turned out that *93 percent* of the fraud accusations were wrong.[47] As bad as these systems are, they could be made worse. The latest antifraud mechanisms integrate facial recognition, which is not just frequently inaccurate but provably and significantly less accurate for people of color than for white people.[48]

Automated decision systems are also used to predict social difficulties before they happen—to precriminalize people. These judgments, too, are frequently wrong and always difficult to understand and appeal. For example, Pennsylvania's Allegheny County uses big data to predict which children are at risk of abuse and neglect. When a family is reported to the state's child abuse and neglect hotline, everyone in the household is run through an algorithm known as the Allegheny Family Screening Tool (AFST).[49]

Such an algorithm is intrinsically biased against the poor. Parents who use public services already have data in the county systems, while those who do not use public services have none. Allegheny County cannot access private insurance data or information from after-school programs, summer camps, nannies, babysitters, private therapists, or rehab clinics. People call the hotline about Black and biracial families disproportionately more often than they call about white families.[50] But more relevant to networked privacy, every member of a household is assessed by the AFST algorithm. Virginia Eubanks writes, "Under the new regime of prediction, you are impacted not only by your own actions, but by the actions of your lovers, housemates, relatives, and neighbors."[51]

This means that the networks in which poor people are embedded—their communities and sources of mutual aid and comfort—are used to paint them as fraudulent or unsuitable for social assistance. Of course, these strategies predate social media. Welfare-fraud workers regularly interview people who know their suspects personally, trying to learn whom they interact, live, or sleep with. Such informants have their own motivations for participating, including "bad blood," envy, or self-interest.[52] In an ethnography of poor Black people in Philadelphia, the sociologist Alice Goffman found that the police often pressured close friends, partners, and family to provide information about people wanted for various minor infractions, thus weakening these attachments.[53] The many advantages of strong social networks, which often provide a safety net for people in poverty, are diminished when those networks are exploited in bad faith.

Online platforms make it much easier to use social networks against their members. As social ties are comprehensively mapped and digitized online, entire communities are made vulnerable, including people whose information is revealed by others. Simply connecting to other low-income people on social media can open one up to accusations and scrutiny. Public Facebook data enables fraud investigators to use information posted for an imagined audience of friends and family. One such worker described using vacation photos to determine that a family was "intact" and "able to go on vacations every single year while receiving all types of different assistance," which she called an "egregious" violation.[54]

When poor people provide information to social services directly, it is not without risk, given the punitive emphasis and networked nature of state systems. Wendy Bach calls the intersection between systems like social welfare, child welfare, and criminal justice "regulatory intersectionality," "a set of mechanisms" that "intersect to share information and heighten the adverse consequences of what those systems deem to be unlawful or noncompliant conduct."[55] This is especially true for people who are poor, young, Black, and female. By seeking support, such individuals increase their risk of punishing consequences. For example, poor women are frequently drug tested while accessing prenatal care and are subject to criminal sanctions if they test positive. Data collected in one context (such as a prenatal visit) thus feeds into both the criminal justice system and child protective services. The state is empirically much harder on poor Black women who test positive for drugs than it is on, say, their wealthy white counterparts. The sociologist Sarah Brayne argues that surveillant institutions are bound up together: welfare and purported systems of "support" feed into and are compliant with the criminal justice system. As a result, poor people who wish to avoid the watchful eyes of the state may avoid government help to which they are entitled, even much-needed medical or support services.[56] One can imagine a woman avoiding prenatal care, for instance, if it may make her vulnerable to arrest.

Poor people have fought back against this surveillance in several ways, doing many kinds of privacy work to combat government scrutiny and overreach. Yet the public remains hostile to recipients of assistance, viewing them as lazy and undeserving. Today, movements like the Poor People's Campaign push back against such attitudes, arguing that increases in racism, poverty, and militarism are due to structural and systemic issues.[57]

Policing

Blaming the poor for their poverty and punishing them with intense surveillance is foundational to the US approach to crime. The expansion of police surveillance is central to the growth of privacy violations of low-income people. Just as the social services sector repeatedly and disproportionately violates poor people's privacy by framing poverty as a moral issue, criminal justice repeatedly and disproportionately violates poor people's privacy by framing it as a criminal issue.

Legally, the poor have fewer privacy rights than the rich do. The Fourth Amendment frames privacy as something that exists in particular spaces, like the home. But wealthy people—even middle-class people—have more access to such private spaces than their poor counterparts.[58] One's car is considered a private space, but poor people are far more likely to use public transportation, which not only is public but also frequently contains video cameras and other surveillance technologies. Poor people live in smaller homes than the rich and often use public spaces like stoops, the street, and common hallways to live and socialize. Rich people are more likely to have private offices, while poor people who work in kitchens, factories, or retail establishments do not. In other words, the laws that protect people from unreasonable search and seizure by the government primarily protect spaces frequented by the wealthy.[59]

While the Fourth Amendment protects people from unreasonable searches of their homes, this right is frequently violated by law enforcement. ICE, for instance, raids the homes of people suspected to be undocumented, without warrants and often with flimsy evidence.[60] "No-knock" warrants allow police to enter a private residence without announcing their presence. This tactic is not only intrusive, aggressive, and sometimes, as in the tragic case of Breonna Taylor, deadly; it is also a flagrant privacy violation.[61]

Moreover, poverty itself is often criminalized or subject to intense surveillance. People with homes, for example, rarely run afoul of laws that prohibit begging, loitering, or sleeping in public, behaviors that are often necessary to those experiencing homelessness.[62] Stop-and-frisk laws, which legalized street searches of individuals without probable cause, were mostly used against low-income Black and Latino men. State and local police have worked with ICE to coordinate with federal immigration enforcement, which primarily affects poor Latinx communities. Arizona's controversial SB 1070 law, for instance, required immigrants to carry proof of legal immigration at all times and allowed state and local police to stop and interrogate anyone they suspected was undocumented, leading to heavy racial profiling of Latinx people.[63] People can be arrested simply for walking through poor neighborhoods, which are far more heavily policed than their wealthier equivalents.[64] This constellation of practices means that low-income people, especially low-income people of color in urban environments, are much more likely to experience privacy violations from police than those in the middle class, regardless of their behavior.[65]

The consequences of these violations are also far heavier for the poor. Say a poor person of color is frisked on the street and arrested for possession of marijuana in a state where it is illegal. He probably cannot afford a lawyer who can get the charges dropped or reduced or negotiate a plea deal. He may be asked to pay a cash bail and be detained before trial if he cannot. (Some half a million people are in jail every day in the United States because they cannot pay their bail amounts yet are legally innocent.)[66] He may be charged a fine in lieu of being arrested, but if he cannot pay that fine, it will accrue late charges and eventually result in a suspended driver's license, making it impossible for our fictional subject to drive to work, perhaps costing him his job.[67] This vicious cycle can result in even more privacy violations—imprisonment, drug testing, home visits and regular searches by parole or probation officers, GPS monitoring, and even collection of DNA samples.[68]

Living with Stop-and-Frisk

Our study participants, who had grown up under New York's stop-and-frisk policy, knew well the problems of state overreach and the criminalization of poverty. They spoke with expertise about dealing with daily police surveillance, particularly those who were Black and Latino men. Ryan, who is twenty-six, Black, and from Queens, explained, "I've seen so many wrongful arrests go down. I've seen people attacked while in handcuffs. I've seen people not Mirandized. I've seen a lot of things. I've seen people falsely accused. The cops don't know how to proceed properly. They don't have [a] proper line of questioning. They may bash your friend's head into a car for no reason." These eyewitness accounts and embodied experiences were common and led to frustration and anger. As Shaka, whom we met in chapter 4, told his friend Jun, "I have experience myself about police following me—yeah, harassment, police harassment. There was plenty time that shit happen to me, and I'm not gonna let my guard down because of fucking police fucking around with me." Mike (twenty, African American) said he was at risk of being stopped and searched simply while walking home:

> I'm walking home. That block particularly, I guess, that if you're just around it, they're just going to suspect that you're from there or something. So I know a cop stopped me before asking me where I'm going, and I said, "Home." Asked me where I lived, and I said, "More down the street." They asked me why I'm where I'm at right now, and I'm walking over there. So, you know, they left me alone. . . . [But] I feel like some cops just do it for the fun of it. I've seen the bad things where cops will just stop others just for no reason. I've seen it before.

These young men see the pervasiveness of police surveillance in their neighborhoods. They also recognize that no matter what they do or how innocent they act, their gender, race, and neighborhood make it inevitable that they will be stopped. They share strategies with their friends on how to act around police, what to say if arrested, and how to act if questioned—all forms of privacy work.

While others have not had the same experiences—many white or white-passing interviewees had never been searched or stopped, though their friends of color had—they are largely suspicious of the police. They are fully aware that law enforcement rarely considers marginalized people worthy of privacy. Aviva, who is twenty-three, white, and Jewish, said, "I'm Caucasian. I'm female. . . . So personally I don't feel worried when I'm, like, out on the street and I see a police officer. If anything, I feel like they're more willing to protect me. That being said, I do have a lot of friends who aren't white, who aren't female, and they have been stopped by police or harassed. And it's mind-boggling to me." Aviva not only acknowledges racism but believes the police are particularly willing to protect her as a white woman. She thus echoes Simone Browne's insight that contemporary regimes of ubiquitous surveillance are part of a system for the protection of whiteness, specifically the ideal of white female purity.[69] As Isabella, who is twenty-one and described herself as "a white-passing Latina," explained, "There is a part of me that the Hispanic side kind of gets scared because you see what happens on social media with prominently—with just Black and Hispanic people, where it's always terrible. So sometimes I would change trains [if police get on the subway], because I do get scared, even though I don't necessarily fit the physical features of a Latina. But, you know, you get scared."

Predictive Policing and Networked Data

Our study participants spoke mostly about law enforcement invasion of privacy in physical spaces. But the criminal justice system also regularly violates digital privacy, to investigate and prosecute crimes by tracking social networks and surveilling online activity. All types of law enforcement use evidence from platforms like Facebook, Instagram, and YouTube to map out offline social connections, identify and locate suspects, and ask the public for help finding potential criminals or parole violators.[70] The ethnographer Fanny Ramirez found that a quarter of all the cases that passed through the Manhattan District Attorney's office included social media data, and 80 to 90 percent of criminal cases did.[71]

But as we have seen throughout the book, networked social data is unreliable. The communication scholars Jeffrey Lane, Fanny Ramirez, and Katy Pearce studied the use of social media evidence to identify suspected gang members and found that much of this content was expressive, meaning that young men used social media to brag about their exploits, toughness, and reputation. This type of braggadocio is very common and serves to increase social cohesion and reputation building among gang members. It is often heavily exaggerated or even entirely made up, given how contextual social media is, but such expressive communication was treated as fact by prosecutors. Simply connecting to suspected gang members on social media implied guilt—literally by association—although young people who live in gang-heavy areas are obviously likely to interact with gang members even if they are not in a gang.[72]

ICE uses aggregated social media data to track down people it suspects are undocumented, tracing networks under the assumption that undocumented people are connected to each other or live in the same communities. It exploits and invades familial and support networks to find and deport undocumented people, frequently dragging US citizens or documented immigrants into its net.[73] To do this, ICE uses an array of information: databases from state and local governments (like the Department of Motor Vehicles), data sources generated by private companies (such as CLEAR, the travel product aimed at frequent flyers), and bespoke data gathered by companies like Palantir and commercial data brokers. ICE heavily increased its domestic immigration raids during the Trump era, confronting suspected undocumented people at their workplaces, in their homes, and in their neighborhoods. These raids are highly militarized, often including battering rams or excessive force, and can endanger people's employment or living situations. They are primarily targeted at Latinx individuals and frequently result in "collateral detainment," in which undocumented people are arrested simply because they exist in a network with other undocumented migrants. These raids violate many of the privacy standards established by the Fourth Amendment, which the Supreme Court ruled in 1970 apply to noncitizens.[74]

It is clear that structures of policing, digital surveillance, data aggregation, criminalization, and confinement violate the privacy of marginalized groups much more than they do that of nonmarginalized groups. But perhaps even more disturbing is the use of networked data to *predict* criminal activity, identifying prospective perpetrators and victims and pinpointing "hot spots" where police should be deployed in advance of criminal activity.[75] These data-driven surveillance practices are an increasingly fundamental part of the criminal justice system, a response to the public focus on crime statistics and resulting pressure on police to show reductions in criminal activity.[76]

Predictive policing uses records of previous crimes combined with social network and social media data to create "precrime maps"—areas where crimes are likely to take place. These systems can suggest potential criminal actors and even possible victims. Civil rights activists and academics point out that such systems may further entrench the surveillance, oppression, and incarceration of low-income and racialized communities.[77] This is because anticipatory policing inevitably builds on data about race and socio-economic status, leading to unequal outcomes that further marginalize poor communities of color. One study of the Oakland Police Department in California showed that if information about drug crimes were used to predict future crimes, police would be deployed almost exclusively to low-income neighborhoods primarily housing people of color, even though drug use is widespread throughout the city.[78] (Note that the Oakland Police Department does not use predictive modeling, for fear of precisely that outcome.)

Police departments across the United States are sensitive to this criticism and typically defend predictive policing in two ways. First, they claim that it draws from reports of criminal activity rather than arrest records, so as to correct for any bias in policing practices. In theory, if officers arrest people more frequently in a poor or minority neighborhood, this should not influence predictive reporting (this of course does not account for bias in reporting crime). Second, they use "place-based models" to avoid using demographic data. In *The Rise of Big Data Policing*, Andrew Ferguson explains that police officers in Newark, New Jersey, created a "risk terrain" model to identify local areas where shootings were likely to take place. The model identified eleven factors, from the presence of liquor stores, bars, and takeout restaurants to increased foreclosures and abandoned buildings. The police concluded that these areas were where young men—the most likely to commit or suffer the consequences of gun violence—hung out while drinking. In other words, the police were able to isolate characteristics of these spaces that identified them as risk factors: "the physical, environmental reality" of the place, such as "abandoned buildings" that "could be used to sell drugs."[79] The objectivity of these physical criteria ostensibly explains away any appearance of race or class discrimination. Clearly, such factors are far more likely to exist in low-income neighborhoods than in wealthier ones. "Risk terrain" becomes a proxy for race and class even when race and class are explicitly excluded as criteria.

Once police identify potentially threatening places, people, or buildings, they deploy increased presence: increased patrols, traffic enforcement, property inspections, and license-plate-reader technology.[80] Of course, as the surveillance studies scholar Torin Monahan and others argue, the increased presence of police in surveillant capacities has frequently led to police killings of low-income and minoritized populations.[81] Moreover, since poor people are obviously likely to live in poor neighborhoods, they are more likely to get caught up in police dragnets or be categorized by algorithms as dangerous or problematic. A system called Beware, used in Fresno, California, assigned each person, house, street, and neighborhood a "threat score." Individual threat scores were based not only on criminal records but on credit reports, social media postings, and social network.[82] The Los Angeles Police Department uses a system developed by Palantir that identifies subjects for "secondary surveillance" on the basis of their connections to people of interest.[83] For poor people of color, simply living in a poor neighborhood or connecting to neighbors on social media makes it more likely that they will be classified as a threat, with potentially deadly consequences.

Much of the targeting of network data-based policing is structural, based on race and socioeconomic status. Marginalized people are already more likely to exist in state databases that track public housing and assistance. And because poor people of color are targeted and criminalized at higher rates, they are more likely to have arrest records, a history with the courts, or outstanding warrants or tickets that they have been unable to pay. And because they have low incomes, they are likely to live in areas that are already heavily targeted for police presence. As we saw in Jorge's case, it is virtually inevitable that poor people of color will directly encounter police surveillance, monitoring, and privacy violations, regardless of their individual actions.

Employment

The systematic denial of privacy to poor people is deeply linked to classist conceptions, pervasive among both social services and criminal justice, of the poor as undeserving, shifty, and potentially criminal. These stereotypes also contribute to the normalization of surveillance in low-wage employment, done to ensure that workers are not stealing inventory or slacking off on company time. Relatively low-wage forms of employment, such as retail work, warehouse jobs, long-haul truck driving, farm labor, nannying, babysitting, ride-share labor like driving for Uber, call-center work, grocery distribution, food service, and digital gig work, are all subject to privacy violations.[84]

Worker surveillance is nearly ubiquitous in low-wage jobs because it is predicated on the concept of the worker as suspect. The sociologist Madison Van Oort writes about biometric systems leveraged in fast-fashion environments. These systems attempt to prevent employees from clocking in incorrectly or doing so for their friends, but they often malfunction. These errors benefit employers, enabling them to engage in common forms of wage theft such as failing to compensate employees for hours worked.[85]

Most of our study participants had worked in retail environments where every employee was treated as a potential criminal. Angelina resents having her bag checked at work. She was especially angry when her employer accused her of stealing; she had purchased an item from work and put it in her purse. Jun, who works at a toy store, was upset when a colleague was unfairly fired for stealing. One of the store's CCTV cameras observed him picking up a toy and then moving to another area, where the camera was broken. Jun said, frustrated, "If that camera worked, it would've seen that he didn't steal it. But they accused him of that. I think those cameras really are just for show sometimes." She expected that the employers would use the camera to prove her colleague's innocence, but they used the system only to "confirm" guilt to protect themselves against worker theft. Jun also saw her manager set traps for employees: watching employees over the CCTV system, calling the phones at their registers, and checking whether they behaved correctly. Dealing with such persistent surveillance in retail environments is a form of emotional labor.[86] Workers fear that systems will glitch in their disfavor, causing them to lose a paycheck or even their job. Both Jun and Angelina consider worker surveillance deeply unfair and an infringement on their ability to work while retaining their dignity.

Participants also spoke of how disconcerting they find workplace surveillance of their movements. Beth (twenty-one, Black) said, "I think that in the physical world, it's more intrusive and violent to be surveilled. Like, you can see and feel the camera bearing down with its red dot of death." She believes online surveillance is less visible and less emotionally taxing. Other participants think the cameras in their workplaces were installed more to prevent employees from stealing than to prevent shoplifting or increase security. Biometric scanners, cashier metrics, and the integration of networked big data into systems that schedule employees reinforce their sense of precarity.[87]

Other types of surveillance focus on worker efficiency and labor cost savings—on avoiding what large companies consider "wage theft." These assume that the worker is lazy and will do as little work as they can get away with. Walmart, which uses video surveillance to prevent unionization and target potential organizers, deems employees chatting to each other "time theft."[88] The company collects daily statistics on each employee, ranking workers on metrics like customer satisfaction or number of scans per hour, and rewards them accordingly. While Walmart calls these practices "motivational," it constantly reminds employees that they are being watched, which dissuades solidarity and sociality between workers.

Or consider Amazon warehouses, where algorithms assign ideal timings to mundane tasks like unpacking, storing, sorting, picking, packing, and shipping goods. Such methods integrate nineteenth-century Taylorism, which breaks every action into small, simple segments that can be easily analyzed and taught, with twenty-first-century digital tracking and quantification, to optimize every bodily action to the employer's ideal. At Amazon, pickers scurry around the warehouses assembling boxes of disparate items to be mailed to customers, carrying hand-held devices that map their routes from one area of the warehouse to another, monitor their progress, and tell them whether they are walking too fast or too slow. They must continually improve or else face penalties; too many penalties and they are fired.[89] This goes far beyond the closed-circuit cameras typical of retail workplaces or the scanning of white-collar workers' email. And yet it is not enough. Amazon recently filed a patent for wristbands that would track the movement of employees' hands, with the idea of optimizing how they reach for packages on a shelf and giving "haptic feedback" if a worker does not move their body correctly.[90] The surveillance is so extreme that it foretells automation: Amazon treats workers like unruly versions of the robots that will no doubt replace them.

Amazon is famously anti-union and recruits vulnerable populations, such as retirees with insecure finances, for its warehouse work.[91] These people often have few other options for employment, even if they are unsuited for physical labor. The workers' experiences, revealed primarily by investigative journalists, are almost entirely terrible.[92] Rather than thinking of warehouse workers as humans deserving respect and dignity, Amazon sees them as nodes in the network, tracked and monitored at every point of their day, each action subject to punitive scrutiny. This extensive data collection deeply violates individual privacy and removes agency over decisions as small as how to walk through the warehouse or when to go to the bathroom. The networked data collected from each employee feeds further into the system, generating algorithmic recommendations on how long each box should take to pack and how many steps a worker should take to find a particular shelf.

Our study participants responded to such violations and assumptions about their work ethic with strategic privacy work. For example, several people mentioned the "blind spots" that exist in every retail environment, where cameras do not reach. Stacy's first job was working in a convenience store where her sister was the assistant manager. Her sister would tell her, "I'm not supposed to tell you this, but this is a blind spot over here." Stacy said, "There were certain blind spots that I would take advantage of, just so I could use my phone, but not for malicious purposes. It was just because I knew that under—like, I know that when they look at the camera, they are not getting the story. They're not going to ask me, 'What's that about?'" Eluding surveillance is a tactic to avoid the decontextualization that people working in low-privacy environments know is likely.

White-collar employees are also subject to surveillance, but it is usually less intense. Remote workers may be required to install keystroke monitoring software or keep their cameras on in Zoom meetings. Corporate computers, Slack chats, and email accounts are regularly monitored. But at many companies, white-collar employees are not drug tested, while people in lower-paid contractor jobs, such as janitorial or cafeteria staff, are subject to far-greater surveillance. At my previous employer, located in a low-income Black and Latinx neighborhood, the predominantly white faculty and administration were the only people on campus not subjected to drug testing.

White-collar workers also usually have more employment options. A worker without a college degree or high school diploma, with a criminal record, or living in a rural area with few employers has limited ability to job hop, and forgoing a paycheck or two may have disastrous consequences.

Without organized labor or alternative employment options, the privacy violations inherent in low-wage work have few consequences for employers.

Hiring

Employees' networked privacy is also violated in the hiring process. Both large and small employers frequently look at applicants' social media data before interviewing them, a practice known variously as "profiling," "screening," or "cybervetting." Most employers—90 percent in one survey—admit they look at the social media profiles of job candidates, while 79 percent say they have rejected an applicant on the basis of something they found on social media.[93] Of course, social media data can reveal far more than US employers are legally allowed to ask, including protected classes of information like marital status, religion, and age. This can have significant disadvantages for minority job applicants.[94] One experiment found that Muslim job applicants, whose religion did not appear on their résumés but was easily found on social media, were significantly less likely to be called for an interview in Republican counties.[95] A similar experiment undertaken in France found that employers responded far more negatively to candidates whose Facebook profiles revealed that they were North African immigrants than to those who were native-born and white.[96] A US study found that employers in highly partisan areas were far less likely to hire someone with oppositional political cues on their résumé; determining political orientation is often very easy on social media.[97] This kind of networked privacy violation is facilitated by social media's inherent leakiness, allowing employers to intrude into spaces that are not intended for their eyes. This form of context collapse can have severe consequences for marginalized applicants. Cybervetting often includes not just social media data posted by the candidate but information posted *about* them.[98] Recruiters also consider how "well connected" applicants are, suggesting once again that whom you connect with on social media is used to make inferences about the kind of person you are.

Social media and networked data is also incorporated into automated and predictive tools used by employers. Applicant tracking systems (ATS) collect and automatically review résumés, making it easier for employers to conduct job searches with hundreds or thousands of applicants. ATS are used by about half of all employers and almost 90 percent of large companies, including corporations like Walmart and Amazon, which hire many low-wage workers.[99] ATS are typically used to cut a gigantic pool of applicants down to a manageable number who can be evaluated by human recruiters.[100] Much ATS software integrates social media in questionable ways, from assessing someone's network connections in an attempt to determine their "social capital" to assigning them a personality type on the basis of Facebook "likes."[101]

Early screening processes also use predictive tools, like personality tests and algorithmic analysis of recorded video interviews. These tools supposedly determine a candidate's suitability for a job and are touted by their creators as more objective and less biased than traditional applicant screening. But automated video analysis is less reliable with nonwhite people. It has difficulty with cross-cultural emotion analysis and may discriminate against people with disabilities.[102] (Personality tests are generally hogwash.)[103]

The use of social media data in hiring algorithms and background checks has been heavily criticized for bias and inaccuracy. Social media content is decontextualized, and automated tools cannot detect humor, nuance, or speaker motivation.[104] Increasingly, social media background checks are subject to the Fair Credit Reporting Act (FCRA), state laws that prevent employers from asking recruits for social media information, and social platforms that cut off access to their data. As a result, the use of these systems will probably decrease.[105] To circumvent these obstacles, companies like Social Intel that run social media background checks now require clients to get consent from applicants. These companies claim that all their analysts are trained on the FCRA and that all "protected class information" is redacted from social media reports. Instead, they comb applicants' social media profiles to identify "racist, sexist, or discriminatory behavior," "sexually explicit material," "threats or acts of violence," and "potentially illegal activity," but they do not explain how they make these assessments.[106]

The more technical such screening tools are, the more they discriminate against people who may not have consistent internet access or who access the web primarily from a smartphone or tablet.[107] In addition to simple access issues, studies have shown differences in privacy skills between lower-income and higher-income people, with lower-income people (especially older ones) feeling less capable of configuring their privacy settings and having lower internet skills in general. Poor people may thus be more likely to lose employment opportunities due to problematic information found on social media.[108] Most concerning is the use of networked data in this context, as what friends and family do may require a great deal of privacy work to obscure. Low-income people are also more likely to have criminal records, which make steady employment difficult to find. Employers like Walmart or Amazon, which do hire people with criminal records, are able to push their employees beyond what may be reasonable, since these workers have few other options.[109]

Education

In neoliberal discourse, the education sector is a balm for low-income people, providing resources and stability to facilitate class mobility. Unfortunately, the education sector is increasingly responsible for significant privacy violations, using networked data to both surveil and regulate its subjects and to predict future behavior. This is important across the board, especially given that most students are minors, but these changes most crucially affect marginalized people.

School shootings and zero-tolerance disciplinary policies have brought intense surveillance and extension of police powers into public schooling. Metal detectors, suspicionless drug testing, locker searches, video

surveillance, and even armed police officers are now common in US public schools.[110] The distribution of these technologies and their harms is uneven, with more vulnerable students—including low-income students, students of color, students in foster care, children learning English, and young
people dealing with homelessness or disabilities—most likely to suffer the
consequences.[111] The school-to-prison pipeline, in which the juvenile courts
handle discipline for in-school offenses like suspension, systemically funnels
low-income Black, Latinx, and Native American students into the criminal
justice system at far higher rates than their white or Asian counterparts.[112]
As we saw during the COVID pandemic, remote learning efforts increased
student surveillance, from class requirements to keep webcams on to intrusive proctoring software that records students as they take tests.[113] This combination of surveillance and harsh discipline resulted in a Michigan judge
sentencing a fifteen-year-old Black girl named Grace to a juvenile detention
facility for "remote learning infractions."[114] Grace was on probation for stealing and fighting with her mother. In April 2020, her school switched to
remote learning, which Grace, who has attention deficit hyperactivity disor-
der (ADHD), found difficult to navigate. After she failed to turn in an assignment, she was incarcerated for seventy-eight days.[115] Her case pinpoints
the disparate impacts of both factors on low-income students of color, especially when these processes are exacerbated in a pandemic.

Educational surveillant practices integrate an array of student data, from
educational records to highly sensitive information like medical histories,
disability status, family relationships, and diet.[116] K–12 schools are rapidly
adopting "EdTech" like Google Classroom, Canvas, and Blackboard, pri-
vately owned software that promises personalized learning outcomes based
on the collection of personal and networked data.[117] Because these programs
are opaque, they present significant potential for discriminatory sorting of
students, but the companies behind them are tight-lipped about how this
information is used. Most of these technologies do not allow opting out.
They aggregate personal information in the service of ever-narrower sort-

ing, including grades, learning history, assessments, attention spans, and administrative data such as test scores and school lunch eligibility.[118] Like most big data systems, these products promise to de-identify their subjects and remove personally identifiable information, but re-identification is easy given just a few demographic variables.

While these systems ideally would help vulnerable students like homeless or LGBTQ+ youth, it is equally likely that increased surveillance will make them *more* vulnerable. Such software could generate information that would out closeted queer youth or reveal to police that a student is dealing with substance abuse.[119] On the basis of what I heard from our study participants, students concerned with such risks could decide not to seek support from educational environments to avoid being caught up in integrated databases.

Access to higher education, often seen as a path out of poverty, is also affected by networked data. A significant minority of college admissions officers (36 percent in a 2020 Kaplan survey) frequently check the social media profiles of potential applicants.[120] Given that much of social media self-presentation is performative or expressive, viewing these profiles out of context may lead to erroneous conclusions.

Moreover, higher-education institutions are increasingly using automated software to determine whether an applicant is suitable. As we have seen in the context of social services and employment, such predictions are heavily biased, prone to error, and almost impossible to appeal because they are opaque and proprietary. Because college rankings include metrics like graduation rates and "yield" (the percentage of accepted applicants who then enroll), schools want to admit applicants who will improve these numbers. Some schools use software that incorporates predictive modeling to determine whether an applicant or current student is likely to graduate.[121] Public concern over dropout rates and student retention levels led the US federal government and nonprofits like the Gates Foundation to heavily promote such software, with the Obama administration even considering creating a federal equivalent.[122] But predictive modeling, which is problematic enough just using educational data, also incorporates information gathered from social media, with some companies touting their integration of peer and family networked data.[123]

When students do enter college, many institutions monitor their success with learning analytics software that tracks their grades, attendance, and class performance. This is especially true of community colleges and other nonelite universities. Such software, as with its K–12 equivalents, incorporates an enormous amount of data, from students' social networks to their library records, ebook reading habits, course management system access, socioeconomic status, and financial aid packages. Learning analytics programs often sync with other university databases, such as ID card swipes and Wi-Fi logins, which reveal when students go to the library, the dining hall, the gym, and the dorm.[124] Students are generally entirely unaware of this data collection, which is funneled to advisors in the best case and third-party vendors in the worst.[125]

Learning analytics software is primarily used to identify certain students as "risks" and certain behaviors as "risky."[126] A news article on Georgia State University's (GSU's) use of learning analytics included the story of Keenan, a first-generation African American student who planned to major in nursing. Keenan earned a B average in his first year, which according to GSU's learning analytics programs meant he was unlikely to qualify for nursing. His advisor pushed him to respiratory therapy, a less lucrative career.[127] Perhaps this is a success story, but it is also a cautionary tale. Given the opaque nature of these systems, it is impossible for Keenan to know what kind of data led the system to this conclusion. Did the algorithm incorporate his race, first-generation status, or financial need? Would he have risen to the challenge of more difficult classes? Did Keenan benefit from the algorithm or from GSU hiring dozens of new advisors? Could he have been a successful nurse? These analytics serve the needs of the university; do they serve the needs of students equally well?

Our study participants were mostly unaware of these tracking systems, even though many of them had passed through local schools, like the City University of New York system, that use them. This is typical and perhaps intentional. Most universities are vague at best about their use of automated admissions products or learning analytics, usually mentioning them only in positive press releases. Students may be unaware that social media postings, or even their connections, could harm their college admissions chances. While our participants were extremely careful of what they put online, not all their peers were so cautious.

Navigating Networked Privacy

People navigate information issues differently with peers, with immediate authorities such as parents, teachers, and law enforcement, and with abstract entities like data brokers or the government. The greater the power differential, the harder it is for people to assert control over a social situation or even understand the context in which they are speaking. In networked privacy situations, where the leakiness of networks makes it impossible to concretely predict one's audience, these gaps are magnified. People of low status face different challenges from those who are more privileged and have different tactics for managing information in various encounters. These range from contact with social services to encounters with law enforcement to relationships with employers to educational experiences.

Low-status youth are constantly subject to the practices discussed in this chapter, and this culture of monitoring affects how they navigate information practices, including their social media engagement.[128] Low-income communities may have different frames for thinking about privacy, power, and resistance, whether that be systemically pushing back against purportedly well-meaning reformers, avoiding institutions that rapaciously gather information, or sharply criticizing interactions with police.[129] Most of our study participants were working hard to improve their circumstances, taking classes at City College or holding several retail jobs. They were constantly aware of the precarity of their lives and feared that networked privacy violations might knock them off their upward trajectory.

Habits of Hiding

One strategy for dealing with intrusive systems, used by many low-income populations, is to make oneself less visible. The term "habits of hiding" was coined by Lisa Dodson and Leah Schmalzbauer in their study of poor mothers, primarily women of color. Their participants knew that "staying quiet" in the face of denigration, going along with what authorities clearly wanted, playing into stereotypes, and keeping their real opinions to themselves often brought the much-needed social benefits they sought.[130] Judith Rollins's self-presentation work when employed undercover as a maid, as we saw in chapter 3, is an example of this strategy; she found that her employers expected an exaggeratedly deferential attitude. When participants could not avoid the authorities, they tried to act respectably to avoid any trouble. But in the end, they knew that their gender, race, networks, and geographical location made them vulnerable and that there was no foolproof way to avoid systemic surveillance.

Many Black and Latinx participants had complicated strategies for avoiding police surveillance. Some, like Jorge and Diego, mapped out local cops' beats and took circuitous pathways if necessary. Others, like Shaka, maintained a tough, "fuck the police" façade. A few were resigned to widespread surveillance. The primary method of avoiding harassment or arrest was to disappear or act as law-abiding as possible if police were nearby. But many participants recognized that regardless of the legality of their actions, they were still vulnerable:

> Like as soon as you see . . . [police], you know, we can be loud and joke, but as soon as we see like a uniform on the corner, it's just, "All right, like, get it together, get it together." Like, anything could happen. (Diego, twenty-one, Dominican)

But if you're in public, if a cop is watching me, I'm afraid. I am getting as far away from that cop as I can. They don't have to have a vocal threat. They don't have to do anything. It's just their existence . . . bothers me [*laughs*]. And so because I can see them, I'm wary. (Beth, twenty-one, Black)

Some of the white and white-passing participants admitted that while they were aware of the dangers of police brutality, they had never experienced it themselves. Others had police officers in their extended families and were more likely to identify police aggression as an individual failing rather than a systemic problem. Our interviews took place in 2015, during a high-water mark of the Black Lives Matter movement, when awareness of police racism, especially among young millennials of color, was at its apex. The topic was on everyone's mind.

Others had developed strategies if they were questioned, by police or anyone else in authority. Angelique (twenty-seven, biracial) explained how her mother coached her to respond to intrusive questioning by child protective services:

I was so young. They came to our house to ask if my mom was beating us and—oh, she was, she totally was—that's why they got called to begin with. But it was her or go elsewhere, and we didn't understand very much what was going on. So my mom coached us beforehand. "Okay, they're going to ask you these questions. Tell them 'blank.'" So we told them "blank." But she stopped. That was—once it was like "You could lose your children," the fear, she stopped. And they asked—oh God, honestly, I don't remember what they asked—I was so young. But they did ask a lot of questions about how we were living and what we had for dinner and what we were allowed to do and things that she did with us or to us, things like that.

Angelique's mother told her children to respond to such questions to position herself as a good mother rather than an abusive one. This strategy of hiding worked—Angelique and her siblings were not taken away—but the repressive and invasive tactics of social services backfired; the habit of hiding was so strong that the social workers missed the abuse. The children were left with their abusive mother, showing how such regimes often fail to protect the people they were designed to help.

Hiding can backfire in other ways. Virginia Eubanks argues that the "digital poorhouse" has a dual effect: some people are too visible to the state, but others need to make themselves *more* visible to collect benefits they are entitled to. The legal scholars Michele Gilman and Rebecca Green call this the "surveillance gap." Those who lack legal protections, social support, and economic opportunities because of state neglect, including the homeless, people with criminal records, the undocumented, and day laborers, are surveilled by the state but are not necessarily made legible by it.[131]

At the beginning of this chapter, we met Jorge, who engages in privacy work to avoid being stopped by the police or having his online content scrutinized. His mother also engages in privacy work to navigate complex systems, disclosing certain pieces of information while concealing others. She learned how to manage increasingly rigorous New York City regimes of paperwork, giving enough personal data to gain access to benefits but not enough to invite judgments and scrutiny. Jorge explained that his mom knows all the City Housing Authority rules by heart and has resigned herself to spending days filling out forms and standing in line when she needs something. Just as Jorge learned how to navigate his neighborhood, she learned how to navigate the social service bureaucracy. She uses this information to help her friends and family, sharing her experiences to cut down on other people's wait times. As a former addict and convicted felon, she is intimately familiar with jumping through administrative hoops. This privacy work undertaken to interface directly with government agencies resembles the work that some people do to protect themselves from networked privacy violations on social media: learning to be visible enough but not *too* visible.[132]

Vikram is a twenty-four-year-old immigrant from South America who lives in Brooklyn. When I asked what privacy means to him, he said, "the right to be left alone as long as you're not hurting anyone or breaking the law." He strives to seem normal online while concealing most of his life, which he believes might hurt his prospects. He moved to New York alone when he was nineteen—his family followed later—and worked extremely hard to graduate from a city college with a computer science degree. When I interviewed him, he had just landed his first "real job" as a database administrator, and he dreamt of working one day at Google. Vikram has a healthy awareness of privacy threats and is extremely careful about what he shares online, explaining that his computer science major taught him "the technical know-hows of how [his] privacy can be invaded." Vikram sees privacy as fundamentally incompatible with technologically dependent societies like the United States and thinks he would have more privacy amid the dense jungles and lax law enforcement of his country of origin than he does in New York City. To achieve privacy in the urban, securitized United States, he imagines that he would "have to move away from [his] daily routine": "like, not have my phone and go out on a rowboat on the middle of Central Park Lake." While he loves modern technology, he finds its potential for privacy violations horrifying.

Vikram is serious and determined, and each time I asked him a question, he paused before answering. When I asked him what he enjoyed most about college, he thought about it and solemnly answered, "the curriculum." Like many immigrants, he and his family moved to New York to improve their standard of living, and he is cautious of doing anything that might jeopardize that. But he knows he is not fully in control of privacy violations that could threaten his success, as data collection and the government often get things wrong. He offered an example of people being "falsely flagged with criminal records" and employers who "discriminate against hiring those people." He also told me about data brokers who make lists of people who have been prescribed arthritis drugs and sell them to insurance companies. "And in the process of doing that, some—there were some 'mix-ups.' Obviously, if you're dealing with information with tens of millions of people, there are going to be so many inaccuracies." The problem, he said, is that some people are illegitimately rejected for insurance because the data is wrong. His focus is on inaccuracy and the ability to meaningfully correct it, not on the unfairness of the insurance system. In other words, the problem is at the micro level—whether the data that is collected is correct— rather than in the ethics of data collection or its use in making life-altering decisions.

Vikram recognizes that there is a structural element to this problem, based in power disparities. For example, he described predatory lending and other discriminatory practices as "horror stories." For the most part, however, he buys into the individualized framing of privacy, believing he must take personal action to guard his own information. "It's very hard for me," he said, "to hit 'upload' on Facebook to put something up there, you know, because such information can really in the long term have some kind of negative impact on me."

Vikram heavily edits his social media presence. His LinkedIn profile lists only facts about employment and education, and although he has a Twitter account, he has never tweeted. While he enjoys professional wrestling and watching television shows about the outdoors, he never reveals these interests online because they are not "professional." He has a Facebook account because he needed it in college to connect to classmates, and he uses Facebook Messenger to talk to relatives back home; but his profile is empty. But knowing that potential employers use Facebook to screen applicants, he worries that an employer would think he is peculiar if they find an empty Facebook page. To resolve this conundrum, he uses a fake name and has never uploaded a photo or made a status update. His anxiety around employment leads him to censor and edit all but the most mundane details of his life. Vikram said he tries to be the same person at work, at home, and on the street: respectful, hardworking, and "putting his best foot forward." His sophisticated technical knowledge makes it difficult for him to use social media at all, knowing the possible consequences.

Our participants' awareness of how information leaks online, how it travels, and the near inevitability of context collapse makes them think about how to placate a broad audience beyond their small networks. Many of the people I spoke with completely avoided any controversy online, instead creating a "vanilla" or "neutral" persona that would placate the pickiest observer.

Beth (twenty-one, Black) sought to avoid scandalizing presumably white audiences. She compared her performative online persona to acting extra respectably in public: "So my performance Facebook self is kind of like the digital equivalent to wearing a suit, so Granny doesn't clutch her purse in the elevator." Her awareness of performing for the white gaze taps into a long history of respectability politics, a strategy developed by African American women to circumvent racist stereotypes of Black women as promiscuous or hostile.[133] Even someone like Angelique, who has very strong feminist views and pointedly critiqued structural racism in our focus group, avoids discussing these issues online. She explained, "For me on Facebook, it's like—for things that might be more polemical, like politics or whatever—I have very strong personal opinions about politics myself, but I don't post those because I would like to appeal to a broader audience, so to speak. So if I post something that I'm just like, 'This is really controversial, guys,' it'll be something stupid like, 'I don't like milkshakes that much.'"

Most of our participants' imagined audience consists of wealthy people or employers with enormous power over their lives. Jorge summed up, "Yeah, they kind of dictate what's good to say because we're trying to appeal to them. Because they're the ones who have the jobs and they're the ones who have the money to give us the jobs, so we don't want to say anything that would . . . I guess, make us seem lesser in their eyes. And that's kind of what I think Facebook is. It's the performance of, 'No, look, I'm viable for this. I'm viable for that. I'm vanilla enough so everyone enjoys me.'" To achieve upward mobility and to be *viable* to an employer, these participants believe that anything that could remotely challenge the status quo is not worth revealing. Instead, they stick to tried-and-true subjects on social media: superhero movies, television shows, food.

These two types of privacy work—that done by Jorge's mother in dealing with social services and by Vikram to make his social media presence palatable—are efforts to take the inevitability of privacy violations into account while making the self visible but not too visible. But the consequences are different, and they lend different types of urgency to the privacy work being done. The type of violation that Jorge's mother faces has immediate, palpable, and sometimes dangerous consequences if it is not managed; the type Vikram worries about, while also threatening long-term consequences, is often amorphous. Jorge described the difference this way:

> My cousin told me that—him and his friends, they don't do anything illegal. They're like the most straitlaced children I've ever seen. They were doing a science experiment, and one of them got a hold of a bit of dry ice. And he went to put it into a bottle to see it diffuse and expand and explode. They felt that because they live in NYCHA housing that they shouldn't do this. It's completely legal to do, but they're like, "No, it's going to explode. It's going to make a gunshot sound. We're going to get arrested for something." They walk around paranoid, not because of the people in the neighborhood but because of the officers. And I think that differs from social media, because there's an immediate and physical reaction to them doing something in the streets that, even if they're not doing anything, they think they can get in trouble for it—as opposed to just saying something online, where there's very little or a very slow reaction to it.

Jorge's cousin curtailed perfectly legal activities in his own home because of his awareness of police surveillance, just as the same awareness causes other informants to avoid certain routes or get off subway trains. He internalized the surveillant gaze to regulate his own behavior.[134]

Many participants, just like Jorge's cousin, avoid interacting with surveillant systems offline as much as possible. This is what the sociologist

Sarah Brayne calls "system avoidance": people with past contact with the criminal justice system avoid interaction with record-keeping institutions to avoid increased surveillance and the resulting privacy violations.[135] Many participants described using a form of system avoidance to manage their privacy in online spaces: they opt out altogether. Several low-income people I spoke with avoid systems like Facebook that they view as centers for employee, educational, and family surveillance. They believe that it is their responsibility to do so and that they are culpable if their information leaks.

This was visible in a discussion with Diego's friend Ravi (twenty-six), an assistant at City College, who calls social media a "major pitfall that has eaten so many people's lives." In his interview, conducted by Diego, Ravi spoke of keeping many people in his life on an information diet, acknowledging that even if you share information with someone you trust, it can and does leak. He tells very few people anything personal—he refused to fill out a demographic form for this project—and avoids social media entirely:

DIEGO: Well, talking about privacy, what do you feel would remedy this current privacy crisis that we're in, where everyone feels like everybody's watching everybody? Do you feel like we as a collective society need to be censored? Do we need something in place to watch us? Should we limit what we share? What do you feel like would be the solution to this?

RAVI: I think the solution to this is that we just don't do it.

DIEGO: Just abstain completely from social media?

RAVI: I completely abstain from social media. You can get in touch with me through your phone, and that's exactly what we do. You know, I don't have a Facebook account anymore. How else do you get through to me? We have cell phones; they can text. It really is that simple.

Ravi believes the only way he can protect his privacy is to opt out. He knows that the networked nature of social media blurs the boundaries between public and private, and he considers this inherently dangerous. Discussing the widespread belief that social media can be used to build a brand, he doubts there is any benefit to sharing professional ideas online; he maintains that ideas posted to Tumblr or Instagram are likely to be stolen. That he is fine with cellphones and texting suggests that he is less aware of the data collection tied to these technologies or perhaps that his privacy concerns have less to do with data aggregation than with leakage of his personal comments and life events.

Ravi advised Diego, "The more other people know about you, in the way that it matters, the more power you're giving to them to throw that back in your face and get in your way. . . . Control your information. They don't need to find out." Even a single mistake that leaks, he said, can be taken out of context, with far-reaching consequences: "There have been people coming into the city college system who later on will tell us that because of a video that was posted of them when they were drunk, and they didn't know, they were in college, that through background checks, an employer's Googling their names, so that ruined their job prospects. Like, they just could not get hired at one point if they had a record of them being a party person or if it's just the one night of mistakes." Ravi thinks this is a structural abuse of power. He thinks it should be illegal for employers to survey social media to keep tabs on their employees. But he knows that it happens, and until privacy is less networked and social media is safer, he advocates opting out entirely.

Judging Others

Jorge's mother and other people who navigate between too much and too little visibility seem extremely aware that the privacy violations they endure are enabled by larger social structures. Other participants, however, believe the opposite: that they can protect their online privacy with individual actions like self-censoring and behaving respectably. Most of them do not believe they can avoid the police or social services, regardless of what they do. (They also frequently blame people for having their privacy violated online, especially women whose risqué photographs leaked.) Participants like Ravi seek to manage these violations by opting out of online activities;

others, like Beth, Vikram, and Angelique, do intensive individual privacy work to ensure that any leaks are not damaging.

It seems odd that our participants' attitudes about police or physical surveillance do not carry over to their beliefs about online surveillance. This may be because data collection and aggregation on social media are mostly invisible to users, while the structural force backing the privacy violations of social services and police is very visible. The sheer frequency of the latter violations makes it impossible to individualize responsibility for them. Participants know from personal experience that there is nothing they could have done to avoid being frisked or surveilled by police, and they rarely blame the victims of these state-driven violations. But they do often judge the victims of privacy violations that are enabled by social media and corporate data scraping.

As we saw in chapter 1, the most common argument against strong privacy protections is that if you have nothing to hide, you do not need to worry about the police, the government, or Facebook looking at your personal information.[136] Several participants offered variations of this argument when asked about online privacy and surveillance.

> You should be worried if you were doing something bad, but I don't feel like I'm doing anything illegal or unlawful. So for the government, I'm a pretty open book. (Arvin, twenty-one, Filipino)

> Is what you're putting out really that, you know, is it so insidious for them to be watching what you're doing? Are you doing something that's insidious? What are you afraid of if you're nervous about that? (Jake, twenty-four, Asian American)

> I don't feel like I post stuff that I need to worry about. So it hasn't been a concern for me. Like, what's the issue? Most of the stuff that I post, I would want the public to know about. (Javier, twenty-four, Belizean)

Both Jake and Arvin assert that objecting to mass data collection suggests individual culpability. Jake is judgmental even of those who worry about negative repercussions: "I don't live my life on social media, so I wouldn't say that anything I put out there could come back and hurt me in ways that I wouldn't want." Javier uses social media for work, strategically sharing information for publicity. He does not post anything that he would "need to worry about" and so is not troubled about privacy. These attitudes reflect the overwhelming belief in individual responsibility for privacy violations. (The "nothing to hide" argument also fails to recognize that the further one's self-presentation falls from a white, middle-class ideal, the more likely it is to be judged negatively even if it contains nothing illegal or improper.)

Given participants' strong belief in being careful online, they often contrasted their own online presence with those of their peers, whom they judged reckless or unrespectable. Most of this judgment fell on young women who post "inappropriate" photos, the term used by virtually all our interviewees for sexy or nude selfies. Others were criticized for engaging in arguments online, posting photos of themselves partying or drunk, or sharing "too much information." Participants used these disreputable others to draw lines between acceptable and unacceptable online behavior.

Many participants conflated people who did not censor their online presence with those who did not care or did not share their goals. This exchange happened in our focus group:

INTERVIEWER: What makes the difference between that kind of person who's doing something that you would not see as appropriate versus how you kind of control what you do online?

JORGE: I think the people—and it's going to sound kind of messed up—the people who have less goals to accomplish, less things that they're trying to get done, are the people that are more likely to just be like, "Hey, screw it. I farted today," and just post that on the internet. . . . As opposed to people like us or people who are trying to get a job or are busy with school or trying to have a goal linked to the social media—they're more likely to really regulate what they do, how they do it, what is said, what's seen. As opposed to people who don't have a goal, don't have an intent with it, but they're just—usually in their tagline they're like, "Oh, I'm here to have fun."

Jorge distinguishes people like him and his friends, who are trying to better themselves, from people he presumably grew up with who are not. Notably, he conflates providing information online that he disapproves of with a lack of care or concern. (We will revisit this in chapter 7.)

Similarly, Ryan (twenty-six, multiethnic) belittled those who post material he finds inappropriate online. He said he does not use social media much, only keeping a Facebook account to avoid giving his phone number to family members, and he was judgmental of his peers who participate actively on social media, particularly those who do not adhere to the respectability politics described by Beth and Angelique. He feels that if people post evidence of their "ratchetry" online, potential employers could and should take this as indicating their lack of professionalism: "Some people have something called professionalism, where they can be absolute jackanapes when they're out with their friends, but they can conduct themselves in a very mature manner when they're at work. Though there are some people who just—you need to see ratchetry coming from a mile away. If you have way, way too many pictures of you or videos of you twerking anywhere on social media and getting drunk on a weekday, I'm pretty sure I don't wanna hire you for my nine-to-five. There's a huge chance you'll come in hammered." Ryan distinguishes himself from "jackanapes" who engage in "ratchetry" and "twerking"—coded language for "lower-class African Americans." Because he himself is careful not to post such things on social media, he judges those who do not share his sense of decorum. When he sees this type of content, he assumes that the creators have shirked their individual duty to guard their own privacy and are thus unsuited to white-collar work. He enacts the professional consequences and harms that people like Vikram fear.

Stacy (twenty-two, Latina) told her friend Jun (twenty-two, Chinese American) what content she feels is appropriate for different platforms. She tries to segment her audience by interest, avoiding posting "geeky" content on Facebook and using her pseudonymous Tumblr for more personal information. Both Stacy and Jun criticized those who post personal information on Facebook, which results in drama and subsequent messy behavior:

STACY: I think Facebook has become this platform of drama, where . . .

JUN: Yeah. And a lot of people do actually use Facebook for the opposite reason that we use it for.

STACY: Absolutely. People on Facebook just put all their baby-drama mama— [*laughs*] baby-mama drama. They put, you know, just very petty things. It's pretty much on the same—in my opinion, it's become the same platform of ridiculousness as WorldStar.

WorldStarHipHop is a video aggregation site that is notorious for posting fights, celebrity gossip, and music videos and affiliates itself primarily with African American culture. Stacy's use of the term "baby-mama drama" brings up stereotypes of lower-class Black and Latinx people. These participants expect their peers to maintain highly curated social media presences, while those who post activities associated with the lower class show their unsuitability for the working world. In other words, these participants blame people who do not share their norms about privacy for not caring enough to do the privacy work needed to protect their personal information.

Nothing to Hide, Something to Fear

While the people I spoke with often blamed the victims of certain types of networked privacy violations, especially if the leaked information had been shared voluntarily, they were more generous to those whose privacy was violated by the state. Given their sophisticated understandings of police, retail, and social service surveillance, many participants recognized that they could not avoid the watchful eyes of their superiors by acting respectably or by doing nothing wrong.

Jorge, for example, knows that the police will bother and even arrest people who are not doing anything illegal. He, his family, close friends, and neighbors have all suffered police harassment, so he is suspicious of the cops and avoids them whenever possible. "There's a lot of times," he said, "where it's just like [police] just seem like they're just preying on the fears of people who aren't doing anything. Like, [*police voice*] 'Hey, you better be in line'—Black dude that's just walking down the street, who I know from my building is, like, the sweetest dude ever and doesn't do anything. But they're, like, giving him a hard time just because he likes to wear big coats and baggy pants." Jorge has lived in public housing his whole life and knows his neighbors, but the cops in his neighborhood do not; and he believes their reliance on racial profiling and stereotypes leads them to harass innocent people. He is deeply skeptical of the rhetoric that one can avoid police harassment through personal action, saying, "You know, the whole 'Oh, I'm not doing anything wrong, so I have nothing to fear' thing. I believe that, but in another way, every time I'm on a train car and there's cops just on the train car, I'll feel intensely uncomfortable. Because it's like, 'Oh. They're going to find something wrong. They're going to make something up.' I just don't trust the honesty of a lot of cops, because I've seen them lie."

Jorge's experiences with structural racism refute the idea that one can avoid police harassment by following the law. He described the people in his neighborhood who usually hang out outside, listening to music, talking, and gossiping. When the police show up, they all disappear, not because they are doing anything illegal but because they know that the police can and will harass and arrest Brown people without cause. He said, "It's like, 'We're not doing anything wrong, but we're going to get busted for nothing.'" He repeated one of his brother's favorite sayings: "Nobody sees it, nobody gets mad." Like many of our participants, Jorge often tries to be invisible as a way to avoid negative attention, even when he knows it does not always work.

Other young people reported similar experiences. Mike (twenty, African American) recognizes that the police could stop him at any time: "Sometimes I feel like some cops just do it for the fun of it. I don't really think they just do it because they are—they care, because I've seen—I've seen the bad things where cops will just stop others just for no reason. I've seen it before." Mike knows that the police can spin innocent behavior into something suspicious, making him feel he lacks any control over how others interpret his actions.

Nowhere is this lack of control clearer than when youth talk about why "nothing to hide" rhetoric breaks down when policing is involved. Youth of color know that they are not targeted because of something they have done but because of who they are. They feel and witness the consequences of Black and Brown bodies gathering in public, and even when they believe problems emerge only because of individually racist police officers, they are acutely aware that personal responsibility is rarely enough. Their tendency to emphasize personal responsibility in social media while dismissing it when talking about policing and everyday surveillance reveals a crack in the normative logic of power and agency.

6

Beyond the Binary

How LGBTQ+ People Negotiate Networked Privacy

Carlos is a twenty-eight-year-old gay man whose family is from Colombia. He described for me the complex decisions people make about what to share with whom, the privacy work used to enforce those decisions, and the shifting nature of what people feel is private and what is public in different contexts. In this chapter, I draw from stories told to me by LGBTQ+ people in North Carolina. I wanted to understand their use of social media and how they negotiated privacy and publicity around marginalized sexual and gender identities. (I was also interested in whether queer people in the South navigated different challenges from those in more purportedly accepting areas; I found that, for the most part, they did not.) My participants spoke about how networked privacy, particularly on digital networks, blurs and reconfigures the binary of private and public that still governs the conventional concept of individual privacy. The intersectional nature of privacy means that LGBTQ+ people must consider many aspects of themselves in addition to their sexual and gender identities when considering when and where to share. As we will see, many of my participants take advantage of the leakiness of social media to make themselves strategically visible, whether to push back against retrograde political beliefs or to make their own disclosures easier to manage.

Carlos and I met at a Starbucks in a North Carolina college town. Slight, wearing black-rimmed glasses and hip sneakers, he told me over coffee that he loves making fancy cocktails, watching horror movies, and going to museums. Carlos is both gay and undocumented; he grew up in rural North Carolina, where he was open about his immigration status but kept his sexuality quiet. He did this both at school, where he witnessed a scandal that resulted when two boys held hands in the hallway, and at home, where he felt his traditional Catholic, Colombian family would disapprove. Since he was not dating anyone, why cause trouble for himself by coming out? However, Carlos's conscious decision to conceal his sexuality from his family and his school community was undercut when he turned eighteen and first visited a gay bar. A club promoter snapped a picture of him shirtless and drunk, posted it online, and tagged Carlos in it. His mother saw it and asked him about it. Carlos, not yet ready to come out at home, made up a story. He described this as being "outed" by Facebook.

As Carlos got older and more confident, he decided he no longer wanted to keep his sexuality private. As he saw it, anyone who was turned off by this key part of his identity was homophobic, and he did not want them in his life. Today he is open about his sexuality in every area of his life, with coworkers, family, and friends. His mother was originally unsupportive, and they had a tough time for a few years—she kicked him out of the house, and he had to live with a friend—but she has come around and now loves his husband. He works with lots of religious people in his job as a baker. While he thinks he "acts really gay" and that his mannerisms give him away most of the time, he does not simply leave people to draw their own conclusions about his sexuality; he is assertively out, and he intentionally discusses his husband at work.

Carlos has mostly stepped back from posting on social media. When he does post, he is strategically matter-of-fact and open about his gayness. On Facebook, he posts pictures at Pride events and gay clubs and talks about his husband to his family back in Colombia. His Instagram is private, and he consumes more content than he posts, mostly because he places a high value on aesthetics and feels his photography is not good enough for the grid. He follows mostly photographers, bartenders, friends and family, and chefs active in the local restaurant scene. He is also big into Tumblr, where he likes the mix of funny memes and edgy content like gore and nudity, but on that site he uses a pseudonym.[1]

Although Carlos is now fully open about his sexuality, he keeps his undocumented status under wraps. He sees his negotiation of privacy and publicity around his immigration status as another political act, like his openness about being gay. Under the Obama administration, Carlos was unlikely to be deported if he did not do anything illegal. He shared his undocumented status openly to increase the visibility of undocumented people, who live in every community, and to give them a face—to show that they are not dangerous others. Although he has DACA status and is a Dreamer, when I interviewed him during Trump's presidency, he was much less open about it.[2] Carlos "hates everything about" immigration law. He has joined a WhatsApp group of undocumented people who alert each other when there is a local raid, a network of people who share his privacy norms and goals around sharing immigration information.

Carlos's story illustrates many of the mechanisms through which networked privacy operates, and it shows the difficulty of drawing lines between public and private. Like many of my participants, he experiences privacy as intersectional: his sexuality and his undocumented status are both central to his life. While his privacy needs vary as the stigma attached to each identity waxes and wanes, he has to deal with both; they cannot be considered separately.[3] On Facebook, networked privacy took away his agency to come out to his mother, with important consequences: years of homelessness and estrangement from his family. Information he felt safe providing publicly in one context—his undocumented status during the Obama administration— was no longer safe under the Trump administration's aggressive immigration policies. Unfortunately, it is still out there. These days, far more than his sexuality, Carlos is concerned about the very real consequences of living without citizenship. He no longer feels he experiences homophobia in everyday life, and he uses the visibility and ability to share offered by social media to strategically normalize his life with his husband to his network, including his religious American coworkers and Colombian relatives.[4]

Many of the people I spoke with for this chapter face the same complex issues. Because networked information intrinsically leaks, my participants strategize how to manage disclosures that might be stigmatized in one context but not in others. They work to firewall what, how, and to whom they disclose, using some of the same kinds of privacy work strategies documented throughout this book. Unlike the women interviewed in chapter 4 and the low-income young people discussed in chapter 5, many of the LGBTQ+ interviewees maintain extremely strong boundaries between context frames and seek even more intently to prevent those boundaries from collapsing. They do not navigate the idea of private and public as a binary but as a spectrum, a web, or a network. Just as the experiences described in this chapter complicate the idea of a binary distinction between "public" or "private" information, they also complicate the notion of out/closeted, as well as the strict boundaries between gay/straight or man/woman. Instead, the ways people share information about stigmatized identities are deeply contextual and social—and frequently nonbinary.

The spaces where my participants feel comfortable sharing the stigmatized elements of their identities do not always track with our ideas about public spaces, where one would assume that most feel the need to perform socially for others, and private spaces, where we assume we can be ourselves. Often it is within personal, intimate spaces like the home that they most strongly experience the enormous social forces of stigma and marginalization. My participants' stories critique the idea that there is a realm of the personal—the domestic, the private—that exists outside of politics. What we consider private, and especially what cannot be spread online or discussed with others for fear of repercussions, loss of respectability, or loss of employment or education, is clearly a political project.

Stigma and Secrecy

Carlos's openness about his sexual orientation does not extend to sharing explicit information about his sexual practices. Many, if not most, people consider their sexual practices and desires to be private, in the sense that
they are intimate information that they choose to reveal only to trusted others. Michael Warner and Lauren Berlant argue in their foundational essay
"Sex in Public" that the public has been partially defined in opposition to
intimacy.[5] Intimacy and sexuality are both relegated to the personal realm,
appropriately shielded from public eyes. Public expression of sexuality is
heavily regulated, often met with hostility or "get a room!"

But some sex practices are seen as more private than others, because
they express desires that should remain out of view not just because they
are intimate but because they are stigmatized. As Warner and Berlant note,
the project of heterosexuality is not banished to the intimate but exists quite
flamboyantly in public. The couple holding hands, referring casually to their
husband or wife, or going to church together enforce heteronormativity:
heterosexuality does not stay out of view but leaks into the public world.
Queer worlds, however, frequently must stay in the shadows, lest they be accused of flaunting their existence. Warner explicitly links this regulation of
public and private behavior to that of normative gender and sexuality.[6] This
highlights the difference between something one *chooses* to keep private and
something that *must* be kept private for fear of retribution. Privacy implies
agency over what information is shared, when, how, and with whom. It is
different from secrecy, which implies an inability to reveal information for
fear of consequences. The liberal subject gets to have privacy, whereas the
deviant subject must have secrecy. Things that are not viewed as deviant do
not raise an eyebrow when publicized: nobody must "come out" as a barista
or a dog owner.[7]

The queer theorist Gayle Rubin discusses the relative acceptability of
different sexual practices in her classic essay "Thinking Sex."[8] She posits a

"charmed circle" of "good, normal, natural, and blessed" sexuality, which emphasizes procreative, monogamous sex within a (preferably) married heterosexual relationship. The "outer circle," meanwhile, contains "unnatural, damned sexuality" such as homosexuality, sadomasochism, and gender nonconformity. The more one's sexuality or gender identity falls into the outer circle, the more social pressure one will face to conceal that fact from others. Even given the vast social changes around the acceptability of homosexuality in the past two decades, tolerance is most often extended to those whose lives most closely hew to those within Rubin's "charmed circle."

"Deviance" is regulated and pushed underground by what the sociologist Erving Goffman famously theorized as "stigma."[9] Stigmatized characteristics are those that society views so negatively that, once revealed, they change how we see a person. People with visible stigmas historically kept them hidden. Public expressions of homosexual desire, for instance, were stigmatized and heavily regulated for most of the twentieth century. Stigma reinforces stigma by creating more secrecy around itself; because stigmas are so dangerous to reveal, they are rarely made public and thus not normalized by visibility. The relegation of homosexuality to the private realm as a response to stigma helped to create and reinforce that stigma.[10]

This stigma has produced what the historian Lisa Duggan calls "homonormativity," a depoliticized gay identity that does not disrupt "heteronormative assumptions and institutions."[11] Homonormativity connotes a respectability politic in which gay or lesbian people who adhere to "white, middle-class, monogamous, patriarchal, and domestic" norms are given the same level of respect as their heterosexual counterparts, but only if they keep other parts of their sexuality private.[12] In a study of gay hookup apps like Grindr, the communication scholar David Gudelunas found that many gay male participants considered practices like anonymous sex, nonmonogamous sex, and leather or kink quite normal but were careful not to discuss them outside gay male spaces to maintain mainstream acceptability.[13] (The tired debate about respectability politics gets dusted off and refought when-ever people argue over whether Pride parades should be family-friendly.)

While homonormative, married, and publicly monogamous gay couples may live openly in some—not all—parts of the United States, those who fall in the "outer circle" of the LGBTQ+ spectrum often encounter intense discrimination if they are open about who they are. The stigma attached to varying levels of sexual "deviance" means that many groups of queer people must hide their identities and try to fit in with straight society. In the eigh-teenth and nineteenth centuries, some Black Americans did something sim-ilar, trying to protect themselves from enslavement or capture by "passing," or hiding their racial identities.[14] When people with stigmatized attributes try to assimilate in this way, the queer legal theorist Kenji Yoshino calls it "covering": visibly assimilating marginalized identities to avoid discrimina-tion.[15] For example, an actor with a visibly ethnic name might anglicize it: Issur Danielovitch Demsky becomes Kirk Douglas, and Natalie Hershlag becomes Natalie Portman. A lesbian might avoid discussing her wife in her night classes. A Black woman might advise her colleague to avoid African American slang at the law firm where they both work.[16] Yoshino argues that contemporary models of discrimination require minorities to assimilate to white, straight norms.

It is not illegal to require that people "cover." American civil rights law protects gender, race, and sexuality, but it rarely protects the expression of those identities. The Black girl who is expelled for wearing her hair in dreadlocks, the butch lesbian who refuses to wear makeup, or the Muslim teenager who wears a headscarf all experience discrimination based on their refusal to assimilate. It is usually perfectly legal to force people to hide ele-ments of their identity. As Michael Warner says, for marginalized people, "being in public is a privilege that requires filtering or repressing something that is seen as private."[17] What does it mean when some fundamental part of people's identities is viewed not as public but as private? In France, for instance, the steady stream of legislation to ban women from wearing a hijab in various venues results in their exclusion from the traditional public sphere, as they cannot *cover* this visible symbol of their Muslimness without violating their religious beliefs.[18]

Transgender, genderqueer, and nonbinary people are seen by many Americans as deviant identities, and as we will see shortly, it can be dangerous to reveal transness in particular. Nonbinary and trans identities are so deeply stigmatized that openly expressing them is often considered aggressive. At the same time, failing to reveal intimate information may be viewed as deception.[19] Secrecy around nonbinary and trans identities is thus simultaneously enforced and punished. The notion that it is deceptive to keep a stigmatized identity private is, in fact, part of Goffman's definition of stigma. It includes the notion that stigmatized identities, when made public, reveal a negative discrepancy between who we think someone is and who they "actually" are.[20]

Trans people have a unique set of privacy issues, because information that may not be considered private in other contexts, such as one's legal name or the sound of one's voice, can be extremely revealing.[21] Bonnie (forty-one, white) told me that people sometimes ask her very mundane questions, such as what time it is, simply to hear her talk. They are trying to "clock" her, an old slang term resurrected by trans and drag culture that roughly means "to spot what one is trying to hide." In this context, it is specific to a gender reveal; trans people use it to describe instances in which someone recognizes them as trans when they are trying to blend in with cisgender people. Being clocked can be hurtful and destabilizing: it invalidates one's gender identity.[22]

Other people I spoke with pointed out the extreme nosiness of cis people about trans bodies. When trans people work to achieve privacy around their bodies or the sex they were assigned at birth, it is frequently seen by cisgender folks, when discovered, as an attempt to conceal a truth for nefarious purposes. As the gender studies scholar Toby Beauchamp writes, "surveillance of gender non-conforming people centers less on their identification as transgender per se than it does on the *perceived deception* underlying transgressive gender presentation."[23] In popular discourse around trans identity, such as that around the so-called North Carolina bathroom bill (HB2, which I discuss later), a trans person who successfully passes as cisgender is reframed as concealing the biological reality of their gender assigned at birth—a line of thought that fully delegitimizes trans identity.[24] But this creates a paradox: the "stealth" trans person who keeps their birth gender private is deceptive, but gender-nonconforming individuals are publicly flaunting information that should presumably be kept private.

Trans people interpret this reaction as a feeling among cis people that some bodies do not deserve privacy. When I interviewed Quinn (twenty-six, white, Jewish, nonbinary), who is highly educated and from an upper-middle-class background, they explained, "I think there's a lot of conversation in trans community around who has maybe the privilege of having control over sharing their trans identity, or being able to choose when that's safe or not, and other people who maybe don't have that privilege, but so much of the way that transphobia and transmisogyny manifests is in investigation of people's bodies and identities and needing a lot of clarity and a lot of categorizing." Jazz (thirty-four, white, genderqueer) works low-wage line-cook jobs where it feels untenable to ask coworkers to use "they"/"them" pronouns. To Jazz, the ability to request the correct pronouns goes along with economic privilege. Jazz says, "It sucks, 'cause I don't get to be me, but being in such a low-income situation, it's not financially prudent."

As Quinn noted, cisgender desires to know exactly what a trans person's body looks like or how far along they are with a "transition"—in other words, requests or demands to reveal information that may be private and intimate—are a way to police, regulate, other, and discriminate against trans bodies. Trans people often experience such questions as extremely intrusive, and the idea that something so private would be considered appropriate public conversation speaks to the discrimination that trans people face.

Andrea (twenty-nine, white), who transitioned after six years in the navy, explained, "There's the running joke that talking to cis people about gender, it's like going into a kindergarten and talking to people about it. And then talking to other trans people about gender, and it's like Greek philosophy."

Trans people, especially trans women, live with a risk of violence that many other people do not. This returns us to the idea that concealing something stigmatized, or *keeping this information private*, is often viewed as deception. According to this frame, revealing a stigma proves that the bearer was concealing it, thus demonstrating their inauthenticity (and thus moral transgression). Consider the tragic murder of Gwen Araujo, who was tortured and killed by four men at a party after they determined that she was assigned male at birth.[25] The murderers, two of whom had had sex with her, mounted a defense of "trans panic," claiming that the subsequent discovery that they had had sex with "a man" was so shocking that their violent reaction was understandable.[26] This is the flip side of passing, the fear of what might happen when an individual fails to pass and something considered private by its bearer is forcibly publicized. According to the "trans panic" narrative, the men forced Araujo to admit her "real" gender before killing her.[27]

Our norms around gender and sexuality thus deeply affect what information we deem private or public. Sharing too much information about one's sex life is considered inappropriate or even scandalous, particularly for people with unusual sexual practices. In other situations, any attempt to keep a stigmatized identity private is seen as deception. And juries have sometimes been persuaded by trans panic defenses. The public/private dichotomy does not map easily to trans existence and trans lives—a fact that calls into question not transness but our binary notions of public and private.[28]

Portraying trans people as deceptive for not instantly and fully disclosing their gender history to everyone they meet frames them in the public eye as immoral, contributing to transphobia but also blaming the victim of heteronormative violence.[29] The crude internet slang that refers to trans women who pass as cisgender as "traps" suggests that this deception is deliberate, that the feminine makeup and clothes are a sham to lure heterosexual men to reveal their penises. In this framing, it is not the trans person who is victimized by having private information revealed but the person who discovers their secret. This framing justifies not only publicizing the secret but retaliating against the trans person who kept it. Moya Lloyd refers to this violence as "heteronormativity," "the violence that constitutes and regulates bodies according to normative notions of sex, gender, and sexuality," which conceptualizes some bodies as so abhorrent that their very existence justifies violent recourse.[30]

When sex and sexuality are "merely personal" or when the gender that one is assigned at birth must be publicized to avoid violent consequences, it undermines the possibility of a public culture based on nonnormative sexuality or gender.[31] And when expressions of racial or ethnic identity are considered unacceptably visible, it undermines the possibility of a culture based on anything other than whiteness. Diversity must be visible if we are to fight against the stigma attached to marginalized identities and to normalize the existence and expression of these identities.

The Closet's Revolving Door

This question of visibility leads us to the "closet"—the place where stigmatized sexual and gender identities are hidden away and the foundational metaphor for the difficulties that "living life out loud" posed for queer people in the twentieth century.[32] The concept of coming out of the closet originated in the gay-liberation movements of the 1960s. The phrase mixes the campy metaphor of "coming out," drawn from debutante balls in which young women from wealthy families were introduced to polite society, with the "skeleton in the closet," something hidden due to social stigma.[33] By revealing the prevalence of homosexuality rather than allowing it to remain a dirty secret, advocates hoped to lessen the stigma of queer sexuality and queer identity. Contemporary rituals like National Coming Out Day encourage queer people to publicly identify as such precisely for this reason.

While TV shows like *Glee* and *Will and Grace* portray coming out as something that needs to happen only once, the overwhelming social presumption that everyone is heterosexual means that even the most "out" lesbian, bisexual, or gay person must repeatedly assert their sexuality when meeting new people or finding themselves in a new work situation or social context.[34] Recall that some of my study participants used social media platforms as a way to come out; the persistence and wide audience of sites like Facebook meant that many of their friends and acquaintances would see a single post, lessening the emotional work involved in repeatedly coming out or educating people about nonbinary or trans identity. As Andrew (twenty-nine, white, bisexual) explained, "When I was in high school, I used to think of coming out as, like, as if you do it once and you'd be done, like everyone would know and you'd never have to say it again. And obviously as an adult, it's much more like choosing when and where and who you say what exactly to."

Negotiating these choices about when to share information is a form of privacy work. Queer individuals engage in a variety of tactics, both in person and on social media, to manage their self-disclosure, and these strategies help us better understand what privacy work looks like when we conceive of privacy as networked rather than individual. Some undertake a complex calculus in every new situation: Is this person safe to come out to? Will I suffer backlash or discrimination? Is this a situation where my sexuality is relevant, or will mentioning it be inappropriate? These assessments must be made on the fly and can be incorrect depending on one's understanding of the situation, the risk, and the audience. My informants had differing levels of success in making these calculations and choosing the right privacy work strategies.

Very few of the LGBTQ+ people I interviewed for this chapter experience the closet as a binary, in which their sexuality is either fully private or fully public. Instead, they reveal or conceal information situationally based on complicated criteria, some entirely personal, some deeply political. Karla (twenty-four, white, lesbian) works as a teacher in a liberal school district. She lives with her long-term girlfriend, and they are raising her daughter together. She is not out at school, although she put up a rainbow "Ally" pin in her classroom to signal her openness to queer issues. She told me, "I'll be in a situation, like when I was in my orientation for new teachers, and I have to sit there and contemplate like, 'Do I want to say that? And how do I want to word it? Do I want them to know?' There is kind of a split-second decision sometimes where you think, 'Do I say it? How do I say it?' And that kind of thing. Or, 'Is it relevant?'"

As a teacher, Karla is subject to respectability standards that differ from those of many other professions, and she worries that mentioning her girlfriend at work might violate them. But she is out to her supportive family and is open about her girlfriend on Snapchat, on her private Instagram, and on her Facebook moms' group. She has never made a big online pronouncement about her sexuality. She said, "I know people probably have a lot of questions, like, 'Well, you have a daughter, and we've seen you post things with men before.' And so that's something that I haven't talked about openly." She does not feel the need to resolve any ambiguity online or to come out at work. As long as she is open about her relationship to the people who matter to her, she does not feel that anyone else needs to know.

This is complicated by Karla's need to "lock down" her social media to prevent any contact with her daughter's father, whom she wants to keep at arm's length. He has never given her a cent or even met her child, but he performs the "fake persona" of an "involved dad" on social media. To prevent leaks that might reach him through a broader network, she is very careful whom she friends and frequently culls her friends lists on Instagram and Facebook. This is a form of segmentation: she chooses what platforms to use on the basis of their privacy controls and is more comfortable with Snapchat, where her posts disappear.

Other people I spoke to are carefully processing their own identities and do not want to come out so publicly. Cimarron (forty-four, white) is a longtime science-fiction fan who has used an internet nickname as his given name for twenty years. In my questionnaire, he wrote, "man/woman" under "gender identity," and when I interviewed him, he was sometimes using "he"/"him" pronouns at home with his wife but not at work, with his extended family, or in the fandom in which he participates. Cimarron explained that he originally identified as a cis lesbian because when he came out in the 1980s, there was little awareness of trans identities. He told me, "So I just assumed that lesbian was the thing. So that's what I went with. . . . Nowadays I guess I'd be considered trans. I went with 'two-spirit' for a while in between the two."[35] He is comfortable with "they"/"them" and "he"/"him" pronouns but has not publicized this fact. He said, "People that I work with have sort of assumed that I have a very masculine identity. But I don't like—I mean, I don't tell them, you know, pronouns and whatnots, just the same way I don't tell them what—you know, that I don't drink coffee. It doesn't occur to me to tell anybody." I suspected there was more at stake in telling people his pronouns than in his beverage preferences. Like Karla, Cimarron is a teacher, and with some probing, he admitted that he worries that he might lose his job if he begins identifying publicly as a male or using male pronouns. In the time period when I interviewed him, he did not correct anyone who gendered him female, and most of Cimarron's friends and family still assumed he identified as a cisgender lesbian. A year later, he publicly tweeted that his pronouns were "he" or "them" and began an online journal chronicling his transition to male. Discussing the transition online was a necessary part of Cimarron's journey, but it did not feel appropriate to him at the time we met.

These stories show that there is no such thing as "in" or "out," for the same reason that separating the world into "public" and "private" does not map to people's experiences. Needs and desires around privacy change, as do people's awareness about and comfort with their own sexual and gender identities. None of this is binary, and while heterosexual norms may demand that LGBTQ+ people choose between making their identities "private" or "public," this is not possible. What makes information private or public is simply the person's level of desire to share it with others: their agency determines what information they share, knowing that it can leak across frames, contexts, and audiences at any time.

Some people deliberately refrain from making explicit claims to identity or sexuality for political or strategic reasons rather than concerns about stigma or secrecy. Quinn, whom we met earlier in this chapter, is a graduate student committed to activism and social justice. Quinn's coming out as nonbinary and queer has taken place over a long period, in incremental steps. Quinn is also very clear that it is not their job to educate everyone about nonbinary identities, and they use social media primarily to ensure that information about themselves and their gender identity moves through the network without requiring them to come out to people individually. Quinn uses the inherently leaky nature of social platforms to reduce the burden they feel to educate others or repeatedly "come out." They told me that coming to terms with their queer identity was a progression, part of which involved shaving their head and dressing more gender neutrally. Quinn sees these choices as a privacy issue, in that they make publicly readable something that might otherwise have remained hidden. This has had mixed results. Quinn said, "I was actually demanding other people see me more accurately, and that is definitely net positive. And there are moments where it creates less safety for me." Quinn feels that they must make a series of complicated assessments when choosing to share their gender identity with someone: "Am I exposing new ideas to them? Am I just putting words to something they already know and get? Am I sharing with them because they have been somebody I've shared personal information with, and despite this new information may be bringing discomfort, it's more uncomfortable for there all of a sudden to be something private in our relationship?" Visible markers of queerness make this simpler.

For Quinn, there is a dialectic between needing a private headspace to process their sexual and gender identity and using visibility not only to clarify their identity to themselves but also to signal it to others. When a person who was assigned female at birth shaves their head, it is often a potent symbol of queerness.[36] Quinn also used head shaving to, as they put it, divest themselves of the male gaze and opt out of heterosexual relational dynamics. On the other hand, Quinn is not that interested in educating people about the basics of queer gender identity. They are much more comfortable talking with a person who has a relatively sophisticated understanding of gender than with someone for whom the concept of nonbinary is new.

Quinn is aware that people from their hometown gossip about them on social media and wonder if they are transgender or lesbian, but they feel no need to resolve this conflict. Rather, they take an "ambient" approach, going by their preferred name and pronouns on Facebook and Instagram and posting pictures of themselves in gender-neutral outfits. This has the advantage of removing Quinn from emotional reactions or awkward discussions.

> Coming out via social media just by existing on those platforms has been an interesting tool because people have been able to have their reactions far away from me. By the time we talk about it, it's something they know and have processed. . . . A relative of mine who I don't see often, and I wouldn't talk to her about this privately, said to my brother, "I know your sister's gay." That's actually kind of great. . . . It's a weird thing that it's kind of unseen or un-talked-about explicitly, but it's kind of convenient for me.

The leakiness of networks means that Quinn's identity flows "ambiently" through relationships, sparing them an uncomfortable conversation.

Unlike many trans people, Quinn does not much care if people use their deadname or misgender them—something that is more likely if people do not know exactly how they identify or what pronouns to use. Quinn feels that their journey to identifying as nonbinary is not the "typical" trans story, and they are fine with uncertainty and confusion. (This was not true of most of the other trans and nonbinary participants I spoke with.) For Quinn, the choice to share information is a calculus based not solely on risk but on trust, comfort, and the emotional labor of educating someone. Social media is a means to their own end, rather than a space where they must worry about leaks and forced publicity; they are not in the closet about their gender or sexuality in any sense.

The Pragmatic Closet

Other participants lead more complicated lives, with more complex privacy needs and less ability to safely make stigmatized identities public. I met Jazz (thirty-four, white, genderqueer, pansexual) in a bustling Starbucks on a chilly November afternoon. Next to us, two well-dressed older women unpacked and examined a vintage sewing machine; across the table, a student typed on a MacBook covered with stickers from local stores. Jazz spread their tablet, cellphone, sketch pad, magic markers, and device chargers across the shared space, marking out their terrain and commenting that this Starbucks feels comfortable because it has trans employees. Jazz feels safe to be themselves there; with their curly hair and wide, eager eyes, clothed in jeans and a comfortable-looking sweatshirt, they are clearly a familiar presence to the young, hip baristas. At the time, Jazz was homeless and sleeping in their car.

Like many people living on the economic margins, Jazz lives a precarious, often chaotic life. Part of the chaos comes from their need to conceal their genderqueer identity and atheism from their conservative Southern Baptist family. Jazz's twelve-year-old autistic son lives with his aunt, Jazz's sister, and the family sometimes slips Jazz money or lets them sleep on a couch. Revealing themselves as either queer or nonbinary would cut off this infrequent but badly needed social support. The family's refusal to accept Jazz's atheism makes it clear that any public deviation from the family norms is punishable by shunning. Our interview took place only a few days after Thanksgiving, during which Jazz was kicked out of their grandmother's house for refusing to say a prayer with the rest of the family.

Jazz has taken deep precautions to firewall their real identity from their family. Online, they have two identities. They walked me through two Facebook profiles. One, which their family can access, uses their legal name and female pronouns; the other, under "Jazz," their preferred name, uses "they"/"them" pronouns and a profile picture of Captain Marvel. In addition to having two Facebook accounts, Jazz has two email addresses and two Twitter accounts. They are meticulous about segmenting information between the two identities; they will not add anyone to the real Facebook profile, which Jazz calls their "me page," unless they have known them for at least a year. (This "me page" is a form of the "mirror profiles" discussed in chapter 3.)

Jazz is keenly aware of the networked nature of modern privacy and of Facebook's desire to identify implicit or hidden connections. As a result, they will not even add potentially sympathetic family members. Jazz explained why: "Because say I had a friend who was on both of my friends lists. 'Mutual friend' would pop up. I have a cousin, Emily, who just friends people. She's like [enthused voice], 'Ooh, friends. People's friends list. Friends list.' When you friend-request somebody, you get to see more of their profile. So, if she friend-requested me not knowing it was me and then saw more of my profile, she might make the connection." As Jazz knows, Facebook uses "mutuals" (accounts that both people are friends with) to recommend users to each other. If Jazz's "me page" was friends with a relative connected to their cousin Emily, Facebook might surface the "me page" to Emily under the "People You May Know" feature, compromising Jazz's privacy.

Jazz's public account is full of dull updates and pictures of Jazz's son. It is a disguise, an attempt to conceal gender and sexuality that, behind a static cisgender, straight persona, is fluid and liminal. By contrast, Jazz's "me page" contains lots of liberal, activist, pro-trans, and anti-Trump posts and links to news stories on which they have commented in fiery rhetoric. Jazz explained why their "me page" is so intense: "Because sometimes you've got to let it out. When you have to keep everything locked in a little box, and then you need an outlet. Sometimes you get mean with it. I've been pretty mean with it on my 'me page,' but it's 'cause I need that release, because I don't get to be me in the wider sphere of the world."

Jazz is a line cook. They described kitchens as very sexist places and do not tell coworkers that they are nonbinary. It is bad enough dealing with harassment when Jazz is perceived as a woman; the discrimination would be unbearable should they come out as nonbinary. It is difficult enough to find work in their field as it is. They hope one day to have enough economic security to come out to their family or at least to stop living a double life online, but they do not feel like that will happen any time soon. They have tried getting social services, but in the South, many providers are affiliated with religious organizations, which Jazz, as an atheist, is not comfortable with. Their lack of privilege along many axes has forced them into a kind of pragmatic closet. They are kept in secrecy by financial and professional exigency, although they would like to share some information with others.

Jazz's on- and offline disguises upend traditional understandings of the closet and dichotomies of the public and private, which presume that the private sphere is where one can be authentic and intimate. Jazz is not closeted at Starbucks or walking around outside. They participate in public life both on- and offline as a genderqueer, pansexual atheist. But both in the private realm of the family and in the private sector of the workplace, Jazz performs as a woman to maintain cis privilege—or at least to avoid the stigma of being nonbinary. Moreover, as a homeless person, Jazz feels they have no privacy and nowhere even to go to the bathroom safely. This Starbucks and their "me page" on Facebook are among the few places where Jazz can be Jazz.

Jazz's story shows that networked privacy does not support the assumptions about "separate spheres" and binary thinking that underpin both the original legal definitions of privacy and the individual model of privacy that persists today. It starts from different premises. Under networked privacy, "the closet" is not a binary, because spaces are not inherently "private" or "public." They are contextual frames that give meaning to information. Recall the example of Dr. Alvin Poussaint, a Black doctor confronted on the street by a white police officer in 1967. The police officer asked him, "What's your name, boy?" To understand what this question *meant* requires understanding the context—the South under Jim Crow laws and the role of white police officers in upholding white supremacy. Without this context, the threat implicit in the question, and thus its meaning, is lost. While there are types of information, such as one's phone number, that do not change based on context, the extent to which I consider them "private" or "public" is entirely contextual. I am happy to provide my address when filling out a W-9 tax form, but I balk when I am asked for it as part of a transaction at Walgreens. If we must think of spaces as "private" or "public," there are private and public spaces everywhere, layered on top of each other, kept distinct only by contexts and discursive frames and strategically constructed firewalls between the different realms we all inhabit.

Like Jazz, Andre is deeply closeted at home. He is nineteen, gay, and Black. His family is Jamaican, a culture he describes as homophobic, and although he has known he is gay for most of his life, he has only recently felt comfortable admitting it. He carefully filters out his family from his Instagram, which he tells me is not *too* gay—he does not act feminine or anything like that. Still, he stans Nicki Minaj and appreciates modern fashion like H&M; he and his friends love to dress up and "flex."[37] When he was fourteen, his mother found his phone, read all his text messages—including those between him and his first boyfriend—and confronted him about his sexuality, which he denied. Since then, he has had to act butch at home. He cannot even have friends over. It is not that they are all gay, since lots of his friends are straight women; but his mother and sister would know in a second that those relationships were not romantic, and it would give him away. Like Jazz, he cannot be himself at home, but unlike Jazz, he is out at his job. There are always other gay and gay-friendly people in the minimum-wage retail jobs he works (at the time of our interview, a cellphone store), and he enjoys being able to be himself. (Jazz and Andre live in the same city, but Jazz works in restaurant kitchens, which are notoriously sexist, whereas Andre's workplaces are on the surface more liberal—the types of corporate retail where huge Pride displays go up every June.) Not until the end of the interview did Andre warm up to me and reveal glimpses of his flirty, fun personality. He hopes to save up enough money working in retail to move out of his house.

Like Jazz, Andre moves between contexts of work and home, performing a "gay" identity in some and a "straight" identity in others. Thinking about the closet as a dichotomous space does not describe either Jazz's or Andre's worlds; neither does the divide between public and private. Instead, they move through a world in which privacy is networked. Like many queer people, Jazz and Andre are not able to fully express nonheterosexual, non-gender-conforming identities in the traditionally private spheres of the home. Jazz can be themselves at Starbucks, a form of privatized public space, or on Facebook, a "networked public" run by a corporation.[38] Andre can be openly gay at the corporate leased and controlled cellphone store where he works and on Instagram, a subsidiary of Meta. But maintaining this selective openness requires a great deal of privacy work to prevent the contextual frames of home/work and family/friends from collapsing—to stopper the risk of nosy friends, coworkers, or relatives inadvertently or deliberately revealing information across contexts.

Jazz's and Andre's movement through the world further undermines the idea of a strong public/private binary, which they experience as blurry and liminal. Many of the spaces where they can openly express their identities—Starbucks, a store, social media—similarly blur the boundaries between public and private, commercial and connective.[39] To understand Jazz's and Andre's experiences through a lens of privacy, we must decouple notions of the public from heteronormativity and the private from secrecy. We must move beyond the epistemology of the closet.

Histories and Epistemologies of the Closet

How does Jazz's and Andre's ability to be public in some places and private in others fit with the idea of being "closeted"—of being either public or secretive about one's sexuality? The queer theorist Eve Sedgwick's concept of the "epistemology of the closet" maintains that the reinforcement of a dichotomy between valorized heterosexual and subordinate homosexual is the fundamental underpinning of twentieth-century Western knowledge and culture.[40] To Sedgwick, the duality of homo/hetero maps a fixity onto sexuality and gender: by admitting to same-sex desire or behavior, a person transforms into a homosexual, which is considered a fixed and permanent identity. In this process, the fluidity and instability inherent to sexuality and gender (dare I say a networked rather than binary nature) is made invisible and delegitimized. And because homosexuality is stigmatized, people conceal aspects of their identities in "the closet": a private space where the "love that dare not speak its name" resides. In the twentieth century, this forced secrecy was fundamental to understanding queer narratives and queer life in the United States and elsewhere. Just as the individualistic public/private binary breaks down in the face of networked privacy, gay/straight and male/female binaries break down when confronted with the fluid spectra of gender and sexuality. My participants' experiences with networked privacy explicitly connect these two histories.

Until very recently, to recognize oneself as queer required living a double life in all areas of behavior. This of course depends on time period and geography; by the 1920s, for instance, major US cities like New York, Chicago, and San Francisco had active gay and lesbian social scenes.[41] The historian George Chauncey writes beautifully about these urban subcultures, where the gay world was visible even to outsiders. New York City in the 1920s had three neighborhoods that were widely known to be gay and that hosted huge public events like drag balls. But to meet and connect with people outside those contexts, the gay men of this time created elaborate codes to signal their identities to others—red ties, dyed blond hair, and coded language: a form of social steganography.[42] Unlike race or visible disabilities, queerness could be concealed. But even to people living in the "gay world," the threat of exposure loomed large.

By midcentury, even this relative acceptance of homosexual behavior in large US cities had changed radically. The Hayes Code, instituted in 1930, stopped filmmakers from implying even heterosexual sexuality. In 1948, President Harry Truman signed the Miller Sexual Psychopath Law. Ostensibly put in place to guard against violent sex offenders, the law criminalized oral and anal sex and carried a twenty-year prison sentence and a fine of $1,000. Anyone convicted multiple times had to be evaluated by a psychiatrist and, if unrepentant, confined to a mental hospital.[43] While public discussion before the law's passage had focused on the danger to children from "psychopaths," it was immediately used to prosecute consensual relationships between adult homosexuals. Vice squads in major cities sent undercover police officers into gay bars and cruising areas; the federal government systematically purged homosexual employees from its rolls; and convicted homosexuals were stripped of their livelihoods and rejected by their families.

This criminalization of homosexuality in the United States went beyond any previous stigma, enforcing a repressive secrecy or closeting—an inability to be oneself in public lest one be jailed. This new mandatory secrecy played out in the daily practices of men and women who experienced same-sex desire. Given the social consequences of being outed, many queer people concealed their true sexuality from the world, even to the extent of marrying opposite-sex partners and having children. Others lived a double life, moving between, as Chauncey writes, "a straight world in which they were assumed to be straight, and a gay world in which they were known as gay."[44]

The latter was a world of closely guarded privacy norms and deep privacy work requirements, open only to other gay people who would face the same dire consequences if they were outed.

To understand the stakes involved in remaining closeted, we can revisit Laud Humphreys's remarkable ethnography *Tearoom Trade*, published in 1970.[45] Humphreys was a sociology graduate student who decided to study men who have sex with men in public restrooms. His work is now taught in ethics classes as a cautionary tale. Humphreys lurked in public bathrooms, posing as a voyeur so he could observe and take highly systematic field notes on the casual encounters that took place within. He found that within this subculture, the constant threat of discovery—of publicizing one's private activities—motivated every action.

Public restrooms were public enough to draw a variety of potential sexual partners but private enough for sexual encounters. As we saw with Jazz and Andre, these spaces are neither wholly public nor wholly private. The men Humphreys studied could reveal their secret desires in a public bathroom but not in ostensibly private spaces like the home. More than half of his participants were married to women, and only a small percentage lived semi-openly in the "gay world" that Chauncey described.[46] The bathrooms provided plausible deniability that did not exist if a man was caught entering an unquestionably gay space such as a bar or bathhouse.

Participants in the subculture undertook extensive privacy work. Lookouts were posted at windows in these bathrooms to watch out for unsuspecting straight men or, worse, police officers. To avoid revealing personal information, men never exchanged names and sometimes did not speak at all. At the time, homosexuality was so stigmatized that men who were known to have sex with men faced the threat of blackmail. While Humphreys's wealthier participants were able to pay off blackmailers, this was impossible for working-class men, who faced the threat of social ruination. The stigma and forced secrecy were even used by the federal government to justify its systematic purge of suspected homosexuals beginning in the 1950s, under the claim that "sexual deviants" posed a security risk because they were susceptible to blackmail by foreign agents.[47] Few in the straight world noted the irony that the government's criminalization of homosexuality was what made these men vulnerable to blackmail in the first place.

Tearoom Trade is a snapshot of a world structured entirely around the epistemology of the closet, yet it shows the same troubled boundaries between private and public that characterize networked privacy. The ethnography was written during an extraordinarily homophobic era, when people were deeply motivated to keep their homosexual activities or identities secret—including Humphreys himself, who was married to a woman but later came out as a gay man. His participants used public spaces to meet and have sex while avoiding traditionally private spaces like the home, all to conceal information they did not wish to share.

At the same time, Humphreys radically violated his subjects' privacy. He wrote, "I am convinced that there is only one way to watch highly discreditable behavior and that is to pretend to be in the same boat with those engaging in it."[48] Believing that anyone who chose to participate in a study would be nonrepresentative, he never revealed to his subjects that he was doing research. Even more violating, he wrote down the license-plate numbers of men who parked at the public restroom and then used a contact at the police department to obtain their names and addresses—intentionally collapsing physically removed contexts. Under the pretense of conducting a public-health study, he then visited these men at their homes and collected data about their marital status, profession, and income, meaning that he possessed information that could have literally ruined lives if it became public. Humphreys violated many of the core precepts of social science research, including obtaining informed consent from research participants and minimizing harm to human subjects. But he also deeply violated networked privacy. Just as doxing or data "onboarding" connects online and offline identities, his sneaky triangulation of data collection brought together anonymous, private, stigmatized sexual practices with the public, respectable faces his subjects presented to the world.

To think through the problems that privacy and publicity pose for the binary idea of the closet, the media theorist Wendy Chun offers a new concept: the "epistemology of outing."[49] Chun maintains that in a world saturated by social media, it is not the forced *keeping* of secrets but the forced *exposure* of them that is a central motivation. In other words, by inverting the famous "epistemology of the closet," Chun asks us to focus not on the individual and their responsibility to guard their own privacy—framing the closet as an extreme form of privacy work—but on the person who reveals information against the subject's wishes. It asks us to hold responsible the person who leaks the information, not the person whose information is leaked.

While Chun ties this idea specifically to social media, *Tearoom Trade* shows us that privacy has always been networked: the prevalence of media technologies only makes this more apparent. We need no longer think in terms of the closet—especially since, as we have seen, many LGBTQ+ people are no longer closeted in all areas of their lives. Instead, we should consider privacy and publicity in terms of forced publicity and context collapse, the revealing of information formulated within a particular context and audience. In other words, we should not start from the assumption that queerness is or should be secret or that leaks occur due to a lack of care or sufficient privacy work by those who are outed.

This element of networked privacy is visible even in *Tearoom Trade*. One's same-sex proclivities were not secret to one's sex partners or to other men in exclusively gay male spaces, even when the dangers of a leak were extremely high (including the danger posed by Humphreys himself, had he been known to be a researcher rather than a participant). But the idea of an epistemology of outing, grounded in a networked theory of privacy, is even more relevant today than it was in the 1960s. This is because, as we have seen, social media is intentionally designed to be leaky. The natural flow of information through social ties is amplified, and its harms are escalated, when those ties are instantiated into visible, persistent networks that then become available for surveillance and profit-driven extraction. As we see in the examples of Jazz and Andre, networked privacy facilitates and often amplifies such leaks.

The blaming and shaming of people whose personal information leaks is not only misplaced. It partakes of an imaginary public/private dichotomy that reinforces heteronormative, patriarchal understandings of behavior.[50] Consider, for instance, a young girl who shares an image of her naked body with a potential romantic interest, who then distributes it widely online. Under an epistemology of closeting, this single instance of exposure is the fault of the girl for sharing, and her lack of care for her own privacy justifies public attacks and social shaming for promiscuous behavior. Instead, Chun argues, "we need to fight for the right to be vulnerable—to be in public—and not attacked."[51]

How does social media fit within the notions of private/public? As we have seen, some people think of social media as binary, believing that anything posted online is always public. Others consider it private, as when speaking only to friends and followers and expecting them to hold information in confidence. This blurry patchwork is what we saw in Andre's and Jazz's stories: sometimes private, sometimes public, and as we saw in chapter 5, sometimes a venue for state surveillance. Social media is neither fish nor fowl. It is not simply a place for private disclosures among friends; or simply a public "third space," neither fully private nor fully public, designed to enable the sharing of information; or only a commercial space with responsibilities to advertisers, global standards of expression, and conflicting ideals of acceptable speech.[52] It is all of these at once. Like networked privacy, it is nonbinary.

Bonnie, whom we met earlier, touched on many of these complicated issues in our conversation. Over coffee (me) and tea (her), we discussed how social norms around queer issues have dramatically changed during our lifetimes; we are both in our forties and grew up in a time when overtly homophobic language was acceptable and commonplace.

Bonnie described herself as a "software developer, poet, writer, just creative person in general; queer, trans southern belle, so totally . . . a Virgo." Originally from southern Appalachia, she moved to the Research Triangle six years ago to transition in a more supportive setting. She has deeply enjoyed getting to know younger queer people and has become something of a social butterfly, interacting with three distinct groups of folks: queer and trans people, activist and political friends, and writers and poets. While the first two networks overlap a bit, the third mostly does not. Her queer activist friends might enjoy slam poetry or edgy spoken word, but Bonnie's work is more traditional. She is a member of the state poetry society and writer's guild and is often the only trans person her poetry friends know.

Like many people, Bonnie is highly aware that trans people, especially trans people of color, are the most vulnerable members of the queer community with regard to the discrimination and violence they face. In 2016, the North Carolina state legislature passed HB2, the "transgender bathroom bill," which overrode local antidiscrimination laws and prohibited anyone from using a public bathroom meant for a gender other than what they were assigned at birth. The bill was met with massive protests within North Carolina and throughout the country and was condemned by President Obama and the European Union. It also resulted in the defeat of the governor who signed it into law as well as the loss of an estimated $400 million in corporate investment before it was repealed in 2017. HB2 made North Carolina look extremely transphobic and out of touch with changing social norms, and many of my participants spoke bitterly about the period after its passage as a very difficult time for them.

Bonnie was one of the activists who organized against the bill. She is also older than many of my other participants and keenly aware of the threats not just to herself but to her larger community. Some of the younger trans people I interviewed seem less worried, perhaps because they have seldom personally encountered deep prejudice or violence. Bonnie, on the other hand, is concerned that trans people are a target for white supremacists and Neo-Nazis. (When we spoke, North Carolina was at the epicenter of struggles over Confederate monuments, with protests that often culminated in angry standoffs between antiracist and Black Lives Matter activists and white supremacist groups.) She employs careful privacy work to protect not just herself but the more vulnerable people in her network. For instance, she worries about friending people on Facebook who are liberal but have "tons of conservative friends" (not uncommon in North Carolina), because, she said, "If I friend them, then that's gonna open a lot of my friends up to potentially all these other conservative people." These networks might expose people in her network to white supremacist groups. She is careful whom she friends and keeps her Facebook fairly low-key, using her profile to promote community fund-raisers, local activism, and poets she likes. She stays away from fiery rhetoric online, preferring a more nuanced approach.

Bonnie is simultaneously aware of the threat to trans women and of the vulnerabilities put in place by networked privacy. She serves as a mentor of sorts to a group of closeted queer and trans people in her Appalachian hometown, who communicate only through secret Facebook groups. Because many of these folks are not open about their identities to everyone in their lives, Bonnie knows that even well-meaning people may not realize that they are putting others at risk when they share on social media; sites like Facebook and Instagram make it possible to spread someone's trans or queer identity beyond the group they feel comfortable with. For example, she has many young friends who are excited to be trans allies, "but they don't really realize tagging somebody on Facebook about a trans thing, if they're not out," puts them at risk.

Bonnie worries that trans allies do not understand the dangers of outing or transphobic violence. Part of this, she believes, is generational. She thinks older people who grew up with the epistemology of the closet find it easier to fall back on signals and subtlety when political shifts make openness and visibility dangerous again. "There's just a lot of people don't realize," she told me, "just how hard or dangerous it can be to be out and to be known. It's like a lot of them are just now starting to relearn all the code words and signals and signs that we used to use decades ago that—just to kind of identify each other because they're just starting to realize that it can be dangerous at times." She highlights the steganographic strategies that vulnerable communities adopt to prevent information leakage.

In addition to accidental leaks from allies or her queer community, Bonnie is concerned about state surveillance of the activist communities she frequents. Trans people undergo certain types of state-sponsored surveillance simply for being trans—bathroom bills, pat downs in airports, strict requirements for changing the gender on one's driver's license—but most of my participants spoke more immediately about interpersonal concerns like clocking or outing. Bonnie suspects that the Black Lives Matter, anti-ICE, and socialist groups and marches she attends are infiltrated by the FBI. To prevent such surveillance, members of these groups often use private Slack chats, encrypted messaging apps like Signal, and the anonymous web network Tor to protect their privacy. Because she works in information technology, she is careful about her security and makes sure her passwords are secure and her virus scanner and patches are up-to-date.

Quinn also participates in various forms of activism and is afraid of both white supremacists and government surveillance—the former more than the latter. At the time we spoke, some of Quinn's Antifa friends had been doxed the previous weekend by Neo-Nazis. Because neither activist nor trans communities can rely on the state to keep them safe, trans and nonbinary people like Bonnie and Quinn instead focus on community-run safety efforts to spread protective strategies through the network. These risk infiltration but are better than dealing with the police.

Given this intense vulnerability and the leakiness of networked privacy, the efforts of trans people and their allies to engage in strategic visibility, claim public space for themselves and their voices, and normalize these stigmatized identities are both brave and significant. While they face unique privacy challenges, trans and nonbinary folks call into question the social compulsion to conceal themselves, instead challenging both the stigma of trans identities and the impulse to relegate queer lives to the private sphere. Trans people's online practices illuminate the possibilities of visible queer networks to destabilize not just gender binaries but the larger binaries of public and private.

Outed by Facebook: Forced Exposure

Both Jazz and Andre craft their online presences to carefully manage the visibility of their queerness. But information leaks. This is the basis of Wendy Chun's reworking of the epistemology of the closet to focus on outing, which seems almost unavoidable given the networked nature of social media among different audiences and networks. Andre was originally outed when his mother read his text messages on his iPad. Renata (thirty-one, Latina, lesbian) dates a woman who is in the closet. Renata must constantly navigate what is appropriate to post on her Instagram stories; she knows better than to say anything about their relationship but wonders whether uploading a picture of them together is okay. The leaky nature of social media makes it difficult to protect her partner's privacy.

Gabriel (nineteen, Latino, gay) also faced outing via social media. Gabriel is an undergraduate engineering student with a busy social life who describes himself as "depressed and likes to sleep around." He told me a complicated, gossipy story that shows how information leaks through both social media and social networks. During his senior year of high school, Gabriel met a guy named Matt on the gay dating app Grindr and hooked up with him. It turned out that Matt was friends with another gay guy named Donovan, who happened to be best friends with Gabriel's sister, Ashley.[53] After Gabriel and Matt hooked up, Matt took screenshots of their text conversation, including nudes that Gabriel had sent him, and forwarded them to Donovan, writing, "Isn't this Ashley's little brother?" This, naturally, got back to Ashley. She had suspected that Gabriel was gay, but they had not discussed it. To prevent that from happening, Gabriel had blocked Donovan on Grindr, but he did not know that Matt knew Donovan—or Ashley.

This type of gossip happens regardless of social media; the high school rumor mill in small towns runs nonstop, and in-person networks are almost as leaky as those online. Ashley, Matt, and Donovan all worked at the local supermarket, forming a network that was not visible to Gabriel. At the same time, social media's structural enablement of information sharing helped collapse the context between Gabriel's family network and his Grindr network; social media and digital technologies reinforced and intensified the flow of information. Gabriel met Matt on Grindr, a social network explicitly for men seeking men. He took nudes with his phone and sent them to Matt via text message. Matt used his phone to take screenshots of their conversation and forward them to Donovan.

Actions like Matt's, where nude photos are forwarded beyond their intended audience, are widely viewed as an enormous privacy violation that most of my participants scorned as unethical and immoral. This violation was not caused by social media or mobile technology, but they made the entire exchange possible. Social media allowed Matt and Gabriel to meet without knowing that they had mutual friends (in network terms, "shared nodes") and without even being in the same physical space before they met to hook up. The phone's front-facing digital camera made it possible for Gabriel to take nudes; text messaging enabled him to send them instantly; Matt's phone made it possible for him to send a perfect copy of Gabriel's correspondence to Donovan.

Gabriel was devastated at the time, but he now says he is thankful for how it happened, because he was very shy and would have had a hard time coming out otherwise. Now he no longer bothers to conceal that he is gay from most people he meets, figuring that they will react however they will react, and he will deal with it. He is still careful about Facebook. His mom uses it to talk to his relatives in Ecuador, and while Gabriel is not close with any of them, he thinks they would not approve of him being bisexual. He mostly restricts his disclosure of more private topics—the guys he hooks up with and his mental health—to his finsta (discussed in chapter 3), keeping it separate from his public Facebook, which is accessible to his relatives.

Strategic Visibility

> I think there's a really amazing, powerful network of people who are super explicit about their experience of their identity on social media and giving a ton of permission to each other, giving a ton of information to each other, providing community to each other—lots of celebration and really beautiful abandonment of privacy as a way of being like, "Actually, we are all here, and we're great." (Quinn)

Unlike the people we have seen who were outed against their will, other participants discussed deliberate decisions, often politically motivated, to share information that is often considered private. I call this *strategic visibility*: intentionally making oneself seen in a desired way for personal or political ends. Many do so to remove the stigma around nonnormative identities by showing that there is nothing to be ashamed of. Several participants use strategic visibility to combat homophobia, transphobia, or heteronormativity or to educate people about queer issues. Social media allows them to reach a wider audience and creates a central location for questions and conversations about their identity, circumventing the need to repeatedly "come out of the closet" and facilitating a visible publicness that also normalizes their sexual and identity expression.

This visibility also destabilizes the traditional notions of private and public, which presume that queerness should be relegated to the intimate, secret, or personal. By using the network's leaky nature to create visible queer presences, LGBTQ+ people use networked privacy to their advantage.

The difference here is their agency; these participants disclose for their own reasons, rather than having publicity forced on them via a leak.

One strategy, a form of *publicity work*, is to use social media as a broadcast medium to come out to many people at once. (By "publicity work," I mean the actions and tactics people undertake to achieve their desired level of visibility.) Andrea, Bonnie, and Morgan (twenty-six, white) all came out as trans on Facebook; Connor (eighteen, Latino) came out as gay and Blake (nineteen, white) came out as trans on Instagram. Morgan posted a picture of the court order affirming her name change to Facebook. This had required an enormous amount of paperwork, and she wrote a paragraph explaining it underneath. She said, "I think I put more effort into that prose than I think I ever put into anything, like any project I wrote for college or anything."

Of course, coming out as gay, bisexual, or queer and coming out as trans are radically different experiences. A trans person typically takes a new name and visually presents differently, whereas cisgender queer folks usually do not. Bonnie explained, "I had a Facebook page for years under my old name, a profile before I transitioned. I created a second one for just me." Like Jazz, Bonnie had a "me page" that she kept private—from everyone but herself, as though she were using social media to work out her new self-presentation before she was ready to go public with it. She said, "When I was finally at a point of fully coming out, fully transitioned, everything, then I posted about it one time on my old Facebook page and then just shut it down, and so there was a different split." While Jazz agonized over their two pages, fearful that features like "people you may know" would leak information they were not comfortable sharing, Bonnie's strategy felt safe to her. She was able to present her real self in a semipublic, semiprivate space that felt comfortable before "fully coming out."

Other uses of strategic visibility involve explicit attempts to educate others about gender and sexuality. Blake is nineteen, an energetic and outgoing trans guy who brought his on-again, off-again girlfriend Hailey to our interview. Dressed in baggy skater clothes and walking with a cool slouch, he hardly drew a second look in the coffeeshop where we met. He is passionate about trans issues. As one of the few openly trans people in his small North Carolina hometown, he gets involved in any trans-related community event he comes across and even served on the advisory board of the local university's LGBTQ+ group. He strongly believes in serving as a resource for other trans or nonbinary people and told me, "Even if I see someone on social media that I don't know, I'm like, 'Hey, if you need something, you let me know—advice or anything. Please, it's okay. The way you're feeling is valid. Everything is valid. There's a reason why you're thinking this, I promise.'"

Like Bonnie and Quinn, Blake is open and public about his trans identity as a form of strategic visibility—a political decision taken not only to normalize one's sexuality and gender but also to connect with and support other people who are less far along in their journey to self-acceptance. Blake does recognize that he may not always feel this way. He told me why he decided against doing a YouTube video of his transition: "I didn't ever know if I was going to be at the point in my life where I didn't want people to know me as 'Blake the Trans Guy' or as just Blake." Because social media is so persistent, he focuses on community support and answering the questions of people in his network; he uses his visibility positively without creating a permanent online identity as a trans spokesperson. This is a careful negotiation, an openness that nevertheless will allow him to decrease his visibility if his circumstances change. Recall Carlos, who explained at the beginning of this chapter that he had been strategically visible about his DACA status under the Obama administration but regretted that decision during the Trump years. People with stigmatized identities are often aware that their social acceptability is tenuous and are ready, if necessary, to retreat underground to protect themselves.

Amberley (twenty-seven, white) is a lesbian whose partner is trans and uses "they"/"them" pronouns. She strategically uses disclosure and social media to educate people on what it means to be trans, undertaking the emotional work of education to protect her partner from that burden. Covered in tattoos and wearing a cute flowered dress, she met me at a crowded indie coffeeshop. Amberley loves food and wine and speaks fluent Russian. Although she is mostly "completely out," she still confronts homophobia every now and then—for example, she worked at a Victoria's Secret, where they did not approve of having a lesbian help women try on underwear. Like other participants, she has tired of telling people that she is gay and then having to have some big conversation about it; sometimes she does not have the energy.

Amberley came out as a teenager, went to an extremely liberal college, and has since surrounded herself with a strong queer and trans community. As a result, she feels very comfortable with issues of gender and sexuality and believes it is her ethical and political responsibility to educate people on such matters so that trans people, who may be more vulnerable, do not have to. She said, "With my sexuality, it's one thing, but with my partner's gender, I really try to push for it because if they [the audience] react badly, at least it's to me and not to a trans person that they might meet later in their life." She explained that she will take on the labor of educating someone on what "they"/"them" pronouns mean if she feels it is worthwhile—even if it is in person, like when someone misgenders her partner.

Amberley uses Facebook to talk to a particular network, her friends and family from the rural area where she grew up. She also sees herself as educating many of these people, who may not know as much as she does about trans and nonbinary issues. "I posted there [on Facebook] a couple times," she explained, "to talk about my life and specifically my partner's gender to try to make a more wide-reaching announcement and try to be like, 'Just so everyone knows, my partner is nonbinary, and this is what that means. And if you have any questions, you can contact me,' and just trying to have that communication with as many people as possible." Few took her up on the offer. She said, "People are scared to ask because they think something might be offensive. I would so much rather you just ask me; and then if there's something that's offensive, we can talk about that, and I can tell you how to process these things."

Amberley knows these issues are fraught, and she believes it is safer for her to be a "trans ambassador" than it might be for a trans person. But she is not sure how effective her strategy is, since people are often afraid to ask difficult questions even when she positions herself as a resource. But social media allows Amberley to fulfill this educational role at times and in spaces when and where it makes sense for her, rather than every time she mentions her partner to anyone. When you are just out for groceries, it is not worth making a big announcement about gender identity. At the same time, she is extremely private about things other than sexuality and gender, doing extensive privacy work to protect herself from online harassment. She works on a high-profile media project with an intense fan base, some of whom can be hostile. She must be careful about whom she tells about her involvement with this project, so she has three Twitter accounts. One is "public," which she uses to talk about politics and promote her work. One is "personal"— open only to friends—which she uses the most. And one is "private," a highly curated subgroup of friends she created when she was going through a terrible breakup and wanted a space to vent where her words (hopefully) would not get back to her ex. On this account, which has about two hundred followers, she is "reckless" with personal information. Like many of the people in this book, Amberley stresses the importance of agency over what, when, and to whom information is disclosed. She said, "I'm a really open person, but I like to have control over that openness, which is why I don't like to post things on a public forum. So I'll talk about a lot of really intimate and personal details about my life to my friends, but I want some control over where that information goes. I don't want to know that it's just out there and anyone can find it."

Amberley understands intuitively that information is contextual, and she wants to make sure that certain information does not move beyond her network of queer and queer-friendly fandom folks. She uses the privacy protections she has set up—her three Twitter accounts—to ensure that she speaks about the media project only to fans who share the same discursive framework as she does. Amberley said, "The idea that people that are out of my circle and also out of my social environment who would not be speaking the same language as me . . . You're in an internet circle. You have all the same reference points. You're riffing off the same themes. You have the same phrases that you use. And the idea of people that are not in that in-group looking at what I post and not understanding it is threatening to me. I don't like that." She would rather share with people who fully understand where she is coming from. She quit Tumblr, where a lot of fandom discussion takes place, because it did not have enough privacy protections; she feels comfortable with Twitter.[54] But despite these precautions, she is open about her sexuality and her partner on all three accounts. She does not consider that private information and does not wish to hide it from anyone.

Network science has repeatedly shown that information flows from one dense network to another through "weak ties"—people you are connected to but not close with.[55] Amberley and Blake represent a set of queer folks who intentionally use these weak ties on social media to spread information that both normalizes queer and trans subjectivities and teaches people outside the community best practices for interacting with minority sexual and gender identities, such as appropriate terminology and how to use nonbinary pronouns. For such people, information's ability to flow beyond its network and context of origin helps them promote broader acceptance of queer and trans lives and norms.

Queer in the Triangle

Whenever I told friends in San Francisco or New York that I was interviewing queer and trans people in North Carolina, they seemed shocked that trans people were comfortable living openly in such an oppressive area.

There is some evidence for this opinion. The Gay and Lesbian Alliance Against Defamation, for instance, notes that discomfort with LGBTQ+ people is highest in the South and that there are no statewide protections for LGBTQ+ people in any southern state.[56] Despite this, 35 percent of the LGBTQ+ population in the United States lives in the South, more than any other region, with 250,000 LGBTQ+ adults in North Carolina alone.[57]

Many authors have identified differences between the experiences of LGBTQ+ people in the South and those on the West Coast or in the Northeast.[58] Following the traditions of ethnographic and qualitative research on sexuality centered on particular geographical areas, I had planned this study to delve into regional specificity of queer privacy practices.

But many of my participants did not report practices that appeared to be specific to either region or urbanity. The stereotype that rural areas are more homophobic may not be accurate; in *Out in the Country*, Mary Gray's book on queer teenagers in Appalachia, the anthropologist deconstructs the linkage between modern queer identity and urbanity. The contemporary narrative of growing up queer is to move from a less accepting area to a larger and more cosmopolitan one. But Gray argues that moving to a city, specifically a coastal city, is hardly a universal desire; many of her participants were deeply rooted in Appalachia and did not want to disconnect from their families and local culture, did not have the money to move, or simply preferred rural life.[59]

This finding seems to be borne out by my participants' experiences. While many of my older participants talked about growing up in homophobic circumstances, an equal number did not, and very few of my youngest participants described much bullying or hostility even in more remote parts of the state. All the teachers I interviewed, for example, work in schools that have openly gay teachers and students, although many noted that they strategically sought employment in queer-friendly environments. Many participants are close with their families and see them regularly. Quite a few had moved to North Carolina for work, school, or its high quality of life.

Several identify strongly as southern, like Bonnie, who described herself as a "southern belle" and spoke with a beautiful drawling accent. No one I spoke with voiced a wish to live in California or New York, except for a few people whose economic circumstances confine them to the Triangle. There are thousands of out LGBTQ+ people in the South, including many who express their gender and sexuality in very nonnormative ways.

However, my main finding is that generalizing about what LGBTQ+ people do—online or off-, in the South or elsewhere, in the country or the city—is like generalizing about what heterosexual people do. I can say that everyone in my sample uses social media, because it was a condition of participating in the study. Otherwise, the people I spoke with have little in common except perhaps opposition to homophobia and transphobia, which aligns them with liberal political values. (I am sure there are conservative, Trump-supporting LGBTQ+ North Carolinians, but I did not meet any in my fieldwork.) My participants work in retail and restaurants, drive recycling trucks, code software, and teach at all levels, from elementary school to college. They are married with or without kids or single or in "complicated relationships." They bake, read fiction or sci-fi, knit, go to church, play sports or video games, watch Netflix, play with their pets, and go out with friends. Most use Instagram and Facebook, some use Twitter, and many of the younger people in my sample use Snapchat; but what they do with those tools depends on their personality, life stage, and degree of openness about their gender, politics, religious status, and sexuality.

My participants share an awareness that information intrinsically leaks, and they spoke of the many ways they manage information that is stigmatized in one context but not in others. Their experiences belie the concept that information itself may be either "public" or "private," instead reinforcing privacy as *nonbinary* and emphasizing its contextual and social nature.

Returning to Michael Warner and Lauren Berlant's critique of the idea that there is a realm of the personal that exists outside politics, we see from my participants' stories how the enormous forces of modern culture are at play within the micro-interactions of everyday life and within very personal, intimate spaces. The experiences of these LGBTQ+ people illustrate how our decisions about what information is private—in particular, what information we do not want spread online or talked about with others—are political decisions.

7

Public Myths, Private Networks

The Implications of Networked Privacy

Lena is twenty-five and lives in Berlin. She is a critical scholar of technology—we move in similar orbits—and she ekes out a living applying for grants, doing freelance writing, and running a research consultancy. Social media is a key part of how she builds an online brand and finds clients.[1] It is important to her career that people know who she is and what she does. Although she must share information about herself to advertise her services, Lena is very conscious of privacy. She has shifted most of her interpersonal communication to "privacy-enhancing technologies" like Signal, an encrypted messaging app, but she retains a public presence on several social media platforms, including Twitter, Facebook, Instagram, Slack, and Spotify. As we have seen, these sites offer much less intense privacy protections, and they constantly, inevitably, leak. Lena thus makes trade-offs all the time, engaging in a complicated calculus of what to share and where. She told me, "I'm always searching between putting up my position and being publicly visible while at the same time not showing my location or giving too much private information where I could be at. I'm at all the time trying to navigate where to go, what to post, what not to post. It's actually quite a lot of work that goes into it to really determine which information to share and not." Lena recognizes that this calculus is a form of labor, what I have called privacy work.

Lena's new determination to use tools like Signal was spurred by an abusive romantic partner. When they were together, she granted him administrator access to her devices so he could install Tor and what she describes as "hacker tools" under the guise of teaching her about privacy-enhancing technologies. Unbeknownst to Lena, he also installed a virtual private network on her laptop and her phone that enabled him to intercept all her internet activity. While she is not exactly sure what he did, she knows he was able to see her location and whom she was calling and texting. After consulting with a passel of security researchers, she wiped all her devices and started from scratch. But she worries that he still might have some unauthorized access.

Lena's experiences are not unique. As we have seen, networked and digital technologies are commonly used to extend intimate partner violence, sexual harassment, and sexual violence.[2] Many instances involve the type of privacy violations that Lena experienced—which are exceptionally dangerous in the hands of abusers who are also technologically savvy, as Lena's partner was. One recent study reported twenty-seven different types of attacks that victims suffer, including location tracking and doxing.[3] Lena was lucky that she was able to get help from security professionals. But in our conversations, she emphasized that it was only her privilege and tech savviness that enabled her to overcome the privacy violations her ex subjected her to. She said, "It took me so much energy and effort to look up these things, involve friends. I really don't want to know what other women in this situation do or people in this situation do, because it's really crazy that it took me a lot of energy and effort to actually really find help as well."

This story could have appeared in chapter 4, on gendered privacy, but I share it here to demonstrate how even people who are very vulnerable to privacy violations—people whose privacy has been violated repeatedly and who may have a great deal to lose—have logical reasons to use social media and other technologies. Lena used leaky digital technology for professional advancement and to maintain relationships with the friends who supported her as her relationship dissolved. Other people I spoke with had similar reasons for using social media despite past privacy violations and sophisticated knowledge of the risks: they wanted to keep in touch with friends, were required to do so for educational or employment purposes, or simply enjoyed sharing their lives with others. (My much-younger research assistant thought it was "wild" that I had to emphasize this point; from her perspective, opting out of social media could never be a choice.)

This chapter looks at some of the consequences and implications of reframing privacy from *individual* to *networked*. I begin by discussing how this shift might reframe some current misconceptions about privacy. I then put forth a positive concept of privacy as networked and conclude by calling for collective networked responses to privacy like the ones described in this book.

"Young People Don't Care about Privacy"

The myth that people who provide personal information in digital spaces do not care about their privacy is mulishly persistent. The "privacy paradox" is an academic theory maintaining that while people claim to care about privacy, their actions show that they do not. While academics debate its validity, this theory has quite a lot of currency outside the ivory tower.[4] This is unfortunate, because it is not true. There are many reasons people might behave in ways that privacy researchers interpret as not caring about privacy. Instead of thinking about privacy attitudes and practices as two separate things that are always logically aligned, we should understand both as *privacy work* and recognize that they are dependent on a variety of intersectional factors. This framing makes the privacy paradox disappear. In addition, I often hear three other claims that supposedly prove that people do not care about privacy: because there is a generational shift, because people share personally identifiable information like birthdates and photos online, and because people share information online despite knowing the risk.

None of these presumptions hold up to scrutiny. And none of them were represented in my data.

Many people claim that young people specifically are uninterested in privacy, an attitude that is seen to mark a generational difference between millennials and Gen Z and the generations that preceded them.[5] In study after study, researchers have found that people's attitudes actually differ very little by age. Americans overwhelmingly care about privacy and want stronger privacy protections, both online and in their relationships with big corporations and the state. Recall the public support for Edward Snowden after he exposed the extent to which Americans were being surveilled by the NSA.[6] A 2019 study by the Pew Research Center showed that 79 percent of Americans were concerned about online data collection and more than 80 percent felt they had little or no control over government or corporate collection of their personal data.[7] While there are some differences between age cohorts—older people, for example, are far more comfortable sharing data with law enforcement—there are no significant generational differences in how people assess the importance of privacy.

This book has documented a range of privacy attitudes among people: some are more cavalier than others about their personal information. But no one I spoke with said they do not care about privacy, even if some of their actions might suggest this. For example, in chapter 3, I quoted Robin (forty-six, white, lesbian), who told me that she does not understand how Facebook privacy settings work and is happy to have her wife maintain them. But during our interview, she confessed that she had caught her mother-in-law reading the couple's private text messages. (Her mother-in-law had referred to some things she could not possibly have known otherwise, and Robin got suspicious; she bought a ten-dollar spy camera and caught her mother-in-law on video sneaking into the bedroom to read her wife's iPad.) Robin was incensed about this and, at the time we spoke, was dealing with the emotional aftermath of what she felt was an egregious privacy violation in her own home. Robin would never say she does not care about privacy, even if her loose configuration of Facebook settings would suggest that to some researchers.

Moreover, Robin's ignorance about her Facebook settings may be partly by the company's design. The legal scholar Ari Ezra Waldman explains that the design of social platforms encourages people to share as much information as possible, strategically hiding the dangers of sharing while emphasizing "powerful social cues" that encourage it.[8] Facebook, like most social media sites, accompanies each News Feed post with the number of friends who have "liked" or commented on it, providing a "nudge" for the user to do likewise. The privacy theorist Woodrow Hartzog's book *Privacy's Blueprint* similarly argues that technological design is critical to privacy. From baby monitors that broadcast unencrypted streams of sleeping children to mobile games that encourage people to pester their friends for free lives, technologies are frequently designed to maximize data sharing or simply built without adequate protections—in other words, inherently leaky.[9] But this does not mean users do not care about this leakiness or about their privacy.

Privacy scholars and technology companies also tend to zero in on people's willingness to share discrete types of information: personally identifiable information (PII) such as Social Security numbers, which do not change regardless of how or where they are shared. Of course, my participants are very protective of things like Social Security numbers, health information, and location. But they are *more* concerned about protecting information that is deeply sensitive to context, such as mental health conditions, their feelings about structural racism, or their parenting preferences.[10] Researchers wring their hands over people providing their name, email, or birthdate to a website, but they often overlook the types of information that people actually consider private. (In 2021, newly vaccinated people were scolded for posting their vaccine cards on social media without blurring out their birthdates, even though it is easy to find out someone's birthday on Facebook.)

Most of my study participants classify information as more private or less so not based on how personally identifiable it is but on how emotionally revealing it might be. This was discussed by Angelique (twenty-seven, biracial Black) and Isabella (twenty-one, Latina):

ANGELIQUE: How much of yourself would you say you put out online?

ISABELLA: A lot.

ANGELIQUE: Yeah?

ISABELLA: Thinking back six years, I was in a relationship with somebody. And I feel like everything was on there.

ANGELIQUE: Really?

ISABELLA: There's about over a thousand and something photos of us together including tags.

ANGELIQUE: So, well, there's a lot of pictures, but how much personal information?

ISABELLA: Besides my name, that's basically it, I'd want to say, and maybe my birth year. That's pretty much it. I try to keep my cellphone and email to myself.

ANGELIQUE: But a lot, lot of pictures.

ISABELLA: Yeah.

Isabella does not consider her name or birth year very personal, but she sees the thousand photos of her and her ex-partner as deeply revealing. Her distinctions between personal and nonpersonal information do not map to any legal or scholarly framework.

The types of information my participants consider extremely private include romantic or sexual details, "inappropriate" or risqué photos, and discussions of negative emotional states and mental illness. In addition to widely recognized categories of private information like health records and financial information, people frequently mentioned political opinions, pictures of their children, selfies, and discussions of drugs and alcohol. Selfies or discussions of depression are considered inappropriate not only for privacy reasons but because participants worry they might cause harassment or be judged by others as "too much information." For instance, when I asked Malik, a seventeen-year-old African American, what he wanted to keep from social media, he replied, "I would say my—the obstacles I would be going through at the moment. I wouldn't want to put that all over Facebook and social media because then I know that they're not really helping me, 'cause the likes and the comments, it's not really helping me get over the obstacle at the end of the day. Yeah, I would say that's the most thing I would keep private." He feels that sharing negative experiences might bring more judgment than solace. Gabriel (nineteen, Latino) said, "I have atypical bipolar. So I'm not necessarily personal about that. I'm more so personal about how I deal with it, if that makes sense. Like, I don't usually tell people what I'm feeling. I'll just deal with it on my own. And then at a later day, be like, 'Oh yeah, I felt really shitty yesterday.' Or, 'I was in a really good mood yesterday, and that's because I was having a manic episode.'" Gabriel is okay with his friends knowing he is bipolar, but he does not want them to see him dealing with his illness on a daily basis. Renata (thirty-one, Latina), whose female partner is in the closet, is also extremely careful with information about her relationship and emotional states: "To me, like with my relationship, because, like I said, my partner is mostly in the closet, [I only disclose to] close friends and people that I know are going to be spending time with. I think what it's more about, 'Oh, I'm feeling anxious or depressed,' or whatever. Or like, 'I'm not feeling well.' It'll be very, very close friends, like maybe two people and my mom and of course my partner. So I guess it depends on how vulnerable it makes me feel, in a way." Renata has to monitor how and when she mentions her partner to help the partner stay closeted, but she also feels that sharing her emotional state makes her too vulnerable to others.

The consequences of broadcasting one's negative mental state on social media are often more immediate than the more impersonal consequences of providing an email address to receive a coupon or using a digital service. Ignoring this type of risk assessment obscures the reality of how information and privacy work in people's daily lives. When we assess people's privacy work, we must evaluate not only the context and audience in which information is provided but the type of information being shared and the extent to which the individual believes it makes them vulnerable.

What Counts as Risky?

A related assumption holds that it is so risky to provide information online that people who choose to use social media in spite of this must not care about their privacy. But it is impossible to make a rational risk/benefit assessment around what to share when one does not actually know the risks. As my participants pointed out, what is emotionally risky—what feels like the weightiest, scariest information to share—is not usually what institutions and laws view as high-risk disclosure. Privacy calculations are thus far different from what researchers might measure.

In 2014, my collaborator Eszter Hargittai held a series of focus groups of college-age young people to learn more about how they view privacy.[11] When we drilled down into risk, we found that people do not fully understand the trade-offs they are making when providing information online, primarily because they do not understand how networked technologies function. Often this information is deliberately concealed. Tech companies frequently downplay or obscure possible risks by making it difficult to opt out of third-party cookies, hiding privacy options deep in nested menus, obfuscating important privacy information in the legalese of licensing agreements, or disingenuously encouraging people to "connect with others" to "improve search results." Many participants thus inaccurately believe that the trade-off they are making is between information provision and some sort of institutional benefit. For instance, several people mentioned that they would rather provide information to receive online services for free than pay for them, but the examples of information they were willing to give were more trivial than the actual information that social platforms collect. When one 20-year-old woman was asked if she would be willing to pay for a service that would give her more control over her data, she replied, "I'd rather it still be free, and then some advertisement company can know that I'm prone to buy granola bars in bulk or something." Yet a site like Facebook knows far more than how you buy granola bars; it may have ascertained your sexual orientation, your closest friends and family, and your political leanings, to mention just a few sensitive topics.[12] This illustrates the deep information asymmetry between what the company knows and what our respondent *thinks* it knows. Similarly, when the group talked about whether to provide an email address, the only downside anyone mentioned was possible spam. Few respondents—indeed, few Americans—understood that an email address given to a company acts as a unique identifier that provides access to larger demographic and data profiles constructed by third parties.[13]

Very few of the people I spoke with for this book grasp the extent of the networks through which personal information circulates and leaks, particularly the role of data mining in aggregating this information. While there were a few outliers, those with high levels of technical skill, like the urban hacker Diego or the conscientious computer scientist Vikram, the great majority hold attitudes like the college students in our focus groups. They think discrete pieces of information like the type of granola bars they buy or even their email address are unimportant because they are disconnected. They are unfamiliar with concepts like third-party data collection, as are most Americans. For instance, a thirty-three-year-old woman said, "I think that it's possible that nobody is taking the data that you could find out about me because it just sort of exists, and it would take dedicated effort to put it all together into some kind of narrative that actually said something that I would care about people knowing about." (This is a version of the "obscurity" strategy discussed in chapter 2.) While it is true that only the most motivated doxers would make the effort to aggregate one person's data in this way, such dossiers are automatically generated by data-mining apparatuses and sold in bulk to corporations, governments, and law enforcement by data brokers.[14]

Assessing the Benefits

Critics of social media users often presume that anyone can make a fully informed decision between providing or not providing information. Not only does this presumption ignore the information asymmetry between tech companies, which know exactly what information is collected and how they use it, and individuals, who almost certainly do not, it also assumes that opting out is a viable choice. But the scales are usually heavily tipped in favor of providing information. (This criticism is also deeply rooted in the individual model of privacy, which, as we have seen, assumes an all-knowing liberal subject who maintains strict divisions between private and public, which bears little resemblance to actual people's lives.) More obviously, there are many positive aspects of information provision that privacy critics frequently ignore. If you *want* to use social media or if you *must* use it, there is no real choice to be made.

As many experimental studies have shown, people are more likely to share information if doing so benefits them.[15] For example, the ability to use social media to maintain relationships and present oneself in a desired light may outweigh privacy concerns.[16] As we saw in the introduction to this chapter, even people like Lena, with significant negative online experiences, can benefit from social media. In the current climate, in which tech companies are heavily criticized for their roles in supporting hate speech, political polarization, disinformation, and privacy violations, these benefits are often overlooked. But they are significant. My participants mentioned lots of positive aspects of social media, such as keeping up with friends, documenting their lives, and getting social support:

> I think the biggest thing for me [about Facebook] is just being able to share with people that I don't see every day or every week or on a consistent basis. A lot of my girlfriends live so far away that we might see each other once a year, once every couple of years. And so it's a great way for us to kind of keep up without having to text all the time or that kind of thing. And then same thing with my family, my extended family that don't get to see us all the time. (Karla, twenty-four, white)

> I post pictures of myself [on Instagram]. I posted pictures of my sister's graduation, because she was valedictorian. I will post my accomplishments on there; like, when I went for Thanksgiving, I helped feed over two

hundred homeless people, so I made a status about that, and not really to gloat, just to . . . you know, let people know that it's good to do things for other people and not just do things for yourself all the time, because that's really how I am sometimes. (Camila, seventeen, Puerto Rican)

Tumblr is where I put things that are personal to my life, like long journal texts where I'm talking about my life in depth. That's where I would talk about my feelings about something that someone said in class or my feelings about whatever current event is happening and whatever I'm thinking about. (Beth, twenty-one, Black)

One of the benefits of social media is its ubiquity; most of your social circle probably uses a platform that allows you to keep up with all of them in one place. But this is also a drawback, because it gives the platform a powerful monopoly that economists call the "network effect."[17] People cannot completely opt out. Those who choose not to use Facebook, for instance, may miss significant milestones in their loved ones' lives, because everyone is used to posting announcements in one or two locations rather than calling or emailing dozens of people. (Recall the LGBTQ+ participants in chapter 6 who came out on social media.)

People who mistrust Facebook and YouTube are often stuck using them for the social connections they provide. Although alternative platforms like Mastodon and Diaspora exist, most have not taken off because they lack the network effect of a critical mass of users. Students are often required for instance, to use Google Classroom or Slack to organize group projects, work on extracurricular activities, learn about assignments, and talk to people in their classes. Moms use Facebook to meet other parents and organize playgroups. Others use Facebook Marketplace as a "side hustle" to buy and sell goods, as they might previously have used Craigslist or eBay. Still others use WhatsApp (owned by Meta) to speak with extended family. For many, then, it is almost impossible to opt out of big social platforms.

It is equally difficult to opt out when social media offers professional benefits. Participants mentioned the importance to their careers of applications like Facebook, Twitter, and LinkedIn, all of which require users to fill out profiles and post content. Participants described these platforms as essential for job hunting, self-branding, and promotion.

In a focus group, a twenty-year-old woman explained, "I'm looking for a job in communication social media, so I see Twitter as more important to my future now; it's a little more career focused." Arvin, whom we met in chapter 5, believes that "every marketing professional should have a Twitter account." In a different focus group, a twenty-two-year-old woman elaborated, "Also, for me, now I think being completely invisible from the internet is not good, especially for—at least for college students and post-, because it's weird, like, if a professional—there's someone that claims to be a professional doesn't exist on Google in some way. And when people say, 'No, I don't have Facebook' or 'I deactivated from Facebook,' well, I just I start to wonder, 'Oh, what happened?' [*laughter from group*] 'Did you have a fight?' I don't know." This respondent believes that opting out of social media has both social and professional costs. She said, "My friend who graduated two years ago, she would jokingly say, 'If you're not LinkedIn, you're not in.' She jokingly said that, but now she has a really nice-looking profile. We all do." While her tone was humorous, her comments reveal the worries many younger people have about getting and keeping a job. Most people I spoke with consider it risky to opt out of sites that might help them find work. Even people like Vikram, who is extremely cautious about what he posts on social media, decided that a "blank" account or a limited profile on Facebook is better than no profile at all. He worries that having no profile would make it look like he does not understand technology or is a social outlier. The trope "if you don't like social media, just don't use it" ignores the increasing difficulty of opting out as networked services spread.

Besides social media platforms, other online services have become indispensable to modern life. Virtually every modern digital technology requires some level of data provision, so if people choose to prioritize strict privacy protections, they may forgo online shopping, online maps, and other useful types of internet engagement. The original alternatives to many modern tools have actually been pushed out by newer, digital, leakier versions. The costs of not using something like Google Maps may be extreme, as many of the preexisting structures that supported nondigital navigation, such as pay phones, maps at gas stations, and road atlases, have fallen out of use or are difficult to find. Someone who does not use Uber or Lyft may find that there are fewer taxicab services than there were before ride-sharing apps became popular. Someone without a cellphone may have difficulty making calls when out and about since pay phones have decreased 95 percent since 1999, and a fifth of those remaining are in New York City.[18] In other words, as networked technologies proliferate, their progenitors wither away. This makes the "alternatives" not only unpopular but in many cases nonexistent.

Focus-group participants mentioned several clear benefits to providing personal information in internet contexts other than social media. Participants talked about how they enjoy personalized recommendations, the convenience of storing passwords in their browsers, and having software sync across devices. While strict privacy advocates may be horrified by voice-activated personal assistants like the Amazon Echo or Google Home, many people enjoy having a smart speaker that can answer questions, play music, and connect with other smart devices.[19] (Connor, a college student, described Alexa as "my alarm clock and it saves my life"; he takes the device with him whenever he goes home for the weekend.) As these gadgets integrate into our daily routines, their immediate benefits may far outweigh a set of nebulous risks that are unclear and often unlikely. When we diminish the usefulness or significance of contemporary networked services, from Uber to TikTok, we ignore the roles technology plays in most people's lives. "I can't imagine a point at which I would be uncomfortable sharing my personal information as long as it improved life," one nineteen-year-old man commented.

Why Opting Out Is the Wrong Frame

The depth, scope, and interconnection of modern data collection mean that individual responses to systemic problems—such as opting out of a single platform—are inherently ineffective. As the computer scientist David Garcia wrote in his study of Facebook shadow profiles, "These results call for new privacy paradigms that take into account the fact that individual privacy decisions do not happen in isolation and are mediated by the decisions of others."[20]

Given the networked nature of privacy, opting out does not prevent one's data from being collected or the larger consequences of data collection. For example, while many of my study participants fear that something they post on Facebook might be spread without their consent, it is perhaps more sinister that Facebook, as we saw in chapter 2, constructs shadow profiles of people without accounts. It creates these profiles by combining user-uploaded contact lists and photos with browsing data collected through Facebook's tracking pixels or social APIs.[21] In other words, if you visit a webpage with a Facebook "Like" button, Facebook knows it, even if you do not have a Facebook account.[22] And if you do not have an account, you cannot delete any of your information.[23]

Most of the consequential, long-term, difficult-to-understand privacy leaks do not come from information that people share voluntarily on social media but from data scraping and aggregation. Clearview AI, for instance, builds facial-recognition software based on billions of images scraped without permission from social media, which it then sells to police departments with little or no oversight.[24] Even if you have never posted a photo online, if you are even in the background of a single photo that Clearview AI swept up as part of creating its database, you are now part of its system and can be identified or misidentified. This is the fundamental condition of networked privacy and perhaps its most often overlooked structural feature: all our privacy work cannot prevent even individual leaks, much less large structural leaks.

As in the Clearview example, even if you opt out, other people in your network may share data that fully implicates and affects you. Recall the discussion in chapter 2 of the privacy implications of genetic data. A family member, even a distant one, can upload a DNA sample to a consumer genetic-testing company site like 23andMe, which can be used to identify and implicate relatives. The Golden State Killer was identified by a DNA sample gathered from the equivalent of a third cousin, someone with whom you share one of sixteen great-great-grandparents.[25] These databases are already sold to pharmaceutical companies, and it is not too much of a stretch to imagine their use by other large actors such as insurance companies, which might deny coverage on the basis of genetic predispositions. Privacy work, even opting out, can never protect you from something like that. Catching serial killers is the fantasy used to justify widespread collection, but it is a short slippery slope to insurance denials and other harms that are no one's fault and take place opaquely.

Similarly, anyone's location can be tracked because that data is recorded in multiple ways. It is inherently networked and can be cross-referenced and triangulated to give a clear picture of a person's movements. This is almost impossible for an individual to prevent. Someone can carefully turn off location tracking on their phone, but their cell signal pings off various satellites and towers as they travel, giving a rough trajectory of their route. Automated license-plate readers installed around the United States constantly track the movements of automobiles, information that is collected and sold not only to police departments but to private companies.[26] Every driver is required to display a license plate. Yet it is almost impossible to live in the modern world and fully opt out of driving and having a cellphone. What kinds of privacy work could plug these types of leaks? How can an individual guard their privacy when the leaks are this big and this intentional?

Digital Resignation

This depressing landscape has given rise to a set of attitudes toward on-line privacy that some people describe as apathy.[27] The privacy scholars Nora Draper and Joseph Turow call it "digital resignation," "the condition produced when people desire to control the information digital entities have about them but feel unable to do so."[28] In my research with Eszter Hargittai, we argued that people feel powerless to avoid networked privacy violations because they believe that they are inevitable and unavoidable.[29] While some critics may ungenerously see these attitudes as evidence of young people's cynicism, they are quite logical. In an environment of widespread digital technology and networked privacy violations and little understanding of how to prevent information leakage, resignation is, as Draper and Turow explain, a "rational emotional response in the face of undesirable situations that individuals believe they cannot combat."[30]

In my research, I encountered this sense of resignation from many participants:

ANDREA (TWENTY-NINE, WHITE): With how integrated everything is these days, I don't really feel that I have any privacy to begin with. I'm just lucky I don't really have any shame over myself, either, so it doesn't bother me.

ALICE: When you say you feel that you have no privacy, what does that mean?

ANDREA: It means that I think that the information is out there for anybody that wants to find it, and the only real privacy I have is anonymity.

I feel like I don't really believe in privacy in the sense that I don't think that I have that choice. People sort of say, "You can do this, this, and this to make sure X person doesn't know Y," and I think my sense of my ability to actually manage that in the way that I think it's going to be managed—I don't think that I can. So I think if I have a web presence at all and am not living off the grid in the woods or something, I think that I might as well just accept the fact that I am there and exist for the government or whoever to see. (Jessica, thirty-three, white)

For me, surveillance really isn't an issue, because every day that I go into the—not a lot of people like it, but every day that I go out to school or if I'm at the train or if I'm at—we're already in a heavily surveillant society. So I'm not saying, "Get used to it," but it's just like, after a while, you kind of fall into the routine of, "I know I'm being watched. I know that there are people eyeing what I do with my credit card payments—if I paid this, that, or whatever. I'm pretty sure the police could tell who—could find out who I called in the last ten hours." It's just—it's inevitable. (Stacy, twenty-two, Latina)

The government will breach your privacy anytime. You don't really have privacy, and then you have people who can hack into your account. Some people can figure out your password—a cousin or a friend or a jealous ex or something, and they can access your information. Putting too much of yourself out there on the internet strips more and more of your freedoms and more and more of your privacy away because it's at the fingertips of everyone. It's not just at your fingertips anymore. (Ryan, twenty-six, Black/multiethnic)

Participants from many socioeconomic and educational backgrounds believe that surveillance and privacy violations are so pervasive that their ability to regulate them is heavily compromised. No matter how much privacy work they do, violations could still happen. The following exchange from a focus group is especially revealing:

INTERVIEWER: Okay. So, do you think it's possible to have privacy online? Like when using social media or shopping?
WOMAN 1 (twenty): No.
WOMAN 2 (twenty-one): No.
WOMAN 3 (twenty-two): No.

In many cases, people calculate whether they benefit from giving up information that is already out in the world and cannot be protected anyway. They do not measure their actions against an ideal world in which their privacy is perfectly protected and they have full control over how their information flows. Participants recognize that, in many cases, their information is already widely available to e-commerce sites, advertisers, and the US government, so privacy-protective measures are an attempt to close the barn door after the horse has bolted.

When researchers or journalists are dismayed that people will give up information in exchange for a Big Mac, they fail to consider the current information landscape. People may use multiple devices, struggle to remember dozens of passwords, and take heroic measures to protect information in the face of software defaults that encourage sharing. Modern technology affords fast-moving work practices and instantaneous social connections, which are compromised by opting out. As another focus-group participant (male, thirty-five) explained, "But it's getting more and more difficult to control my information. Because [cloud service companies] are actually kind of just making it more easy to upload those things on the website, compared to you not trying to do. [*Sounds of agreement from group*]. And you don't want to do that. And also every device and every program has a different kind of access and things. It's really hard to control everything because I need to remember every ID and password and every condition, which file should go where, which drive, iCloud, Dropbox, Google Drive." Given these conditions, it is unsurprising that users prefer browsers that remember their passwords, use Facebook to log into multiple sites, and patronize e-commerce sites like Amazon that let them order without repeatedly typing in credit card numbers. Millions of people use these technologies, including myself, and professing incredulity at their popularity ignores the reality of contemporary internet use.

Resignation is not illogical. As we have seen, it is virtually impossible to avoid having personal data tracked and mined if you live in contemporary

US society, even if you do extensive privacy work or opt out of most networked technologies. It is rational for people to make incorrect assessments of privacy risks because these risks are designed to be very difficult, if not impossible, to determine.[31] Privacy work is an enormous effort that is frequently ineffective and often not visible until it fails. Approaches that increase the privacy work on already-overwhelmed people, such as notice-and-choice regimes or increasingly granular privacy settings, only make them feel more helpless. Instead, we need comprehensive structural solutions to information leakage: platform regulation, limits on institutional data collection, and consequences for those who fail to obey data-protection laws.

Recommendations

How should we temper some of the worst harms chronicled in this book? There is no shortage of proposals to improve the privacy landscape in the United States. The concerns of stakeholders from impacted and marginalized communities should be central to any legislative or technological reform, following the frame of feminist privacy protection discussed in chapter 3. I build on Virginia Eubanks's guidance for people building tools targeted at poor populations to suggest that anyone attempting to address the problems of networked privacy ask two questions:

- Does this solution increase the agency of the people it is meant to help?
- Would the tool be tolerated if it were targeted at privileged communities?[32]

By centering those who are made vulnerable and by evaluating innovation through a sociotechnical security framework that systematically identifies vulnerabilities and exploits, we can determine the feasibility and limitations of any proposed solution.[33] Taking the responsibility from individuals, especially those in already difficult or precarious conditions, places the burden on more privileged stakeholders and toward more collective solutions to systemic issues. We might learn from community-based responses to privacy violations and harms, such as transformative justice, restorative justice, and collective ethics of care.

In addition to legislative, social, and technological reform, recognizing privacy as contextual and networked allows researchers and advocates to push back against harmful design choices that nudge people to share more than they intend; encourage social platforms to prioritize privacy over surveillance and data gathering; increase knowledge about data brokers, mass surveillance, and the implications of DNA databases (ideally leading to increased structural regulation); and design privacy-protective replacements for leaky technologies. A sophisticated structural critique of networked privacy violations might enable young people to recognize the inevitability of privacy violations. Accepting individual culpability for privacy violations diminishes our ability to change the practices of technology companies, government agencies, data brokers, and other institutions that make networked privacy violations so widespread and consequential.

Legislative

The United States has an uneasy patchwork of privacy laws in which certain types of information, such as video-store records, are highly protected, while others, such as email, have no protection at all. It seems clear that the United States needs comprehensive information privacy legislation rather than a patchwork of different rules for different data types. Because many social media platforms are headquartered in the United States, they often export these privacy norms along with their technologies, which means that changing US privacy law could have global impact. But legislation must go further than simply regulating data collection on social platforms, difficult as that is. We must place clear limits on the use of networked data and what an aggregator, marketer, or government can determine by using it. Ideally, such regulations would govern how information collected in one context (such as automated license-plate readers) may or may not be transferred to another (such as immigration enforcement). For example, given that social data is contextual and not self-evident, there should be heavy regulation of police surveillance on social media and exoneration of those who have been convicted based on social media monitoring. This approach is advocated by the SAFElab at Columbia University, a research lab that investigates how young people of color navigate on- and offline violence, which calls these practices "virtual stop and frisk."[34]

Social Reforms

One cannot simply wave a wand and order social change. Yet the United States has the capacity for remarkably swift attitude change; witness public attitudes toward gay marriage and police brutality in the past two decades. While the harms of privacy violations may be harder to express than those of structural racism or homophobia, my research suggests some ways in which privacy activists, journalists, and academics might push for attitude change. Ultimately, the goal should be to push the public to understand privacy violations as structural rather than individual. There are precedents. As we saw in chapter 5, Black Lives Matter protestors and activists have been extremely successful in framing police brutality as a structural problem rather than a matter of a "few bad apples." And as discussed in chapter 1, second-wave feminists fought to bring issues of domestic abuse into the public realm rather than relegated to the private. This book is one step in framing the private as political.

Technological

Technologists can implement many changes without having to wait for social attitudes to change or comprehensive legislation to pass. Even though protecting networked privacy looks different based on platform affordances, one option would be to improve data interoperability to diminish the network effect, enable social segmentation, and facilitate transfer to smaller, more privacy-protective platforms. Dependence on a few enormous platforms facilitates data leakiness. (And *please* stop saying that "people don't care about privacy.")

Rethinking Privacy

I have been working on this book for six years. In that time, privacy has become more networked and privacy violations more immediate. Multiple disciplines, law and computer science in particular, have taken up privacy as a central challenge, but their scholarship has had little impact on popular understandings of privacy or legislation about it. This is frustrating.

This book is my attempt to enter the public conversation by delineating the social, cultural, and political aspects of privacy in the United States today. It is clear to me that "privacy" goes beyond social platforms and the internet itself and has become a heuristic describing many harmful power imbalances brought about by the spread of information—an umbrella term used to indicate where information collection should stop. This is because the way information is collected and diffused today directly helps to maintain structural inequality in ways both big and small. The creative strategies used by the people in this book, from the elaborate types of privacy work discussed in chapter 3 to the avoidance of state surveillance we saw in chapter 5 to the strategic leveraging of visibility to break down binaries discussed in chapter 6, speak to the resilience and ingenuity of people in the face of widespread and mostly unacknowledged privacy violations. That these are often people who are marginalized in other areas of life is no coincidence.

We need to move away from the model of individual responsibility and toward a model of community and network care to protect people's privacy. Feminist privacy protection draws both from feminist ethics of care and from information security, asking institutions to assess new technologies by evaluating their impact on the privacy of marginalized and minoritized populations. For those who are harmed by existing technologies, models of restorative and transformative justice, which center both the needs of the person experiencing abuse or harassment and the structural inequalities that made these harms possible, may provide starting points for redress. To help people understand networked privacy as a model that does not place the burden of responsibility entirely on individuals, we can look to the similarities between surveillance and susceptibility to structural police violence, as I discussed in chapter 5. And to understand how the binary model of public/private ties into rigid concepts of gender, race, and sexuality, we can be inspired by the LGBTQ+ folks who use strategic visibility on social media to combat ignorance and oppression. The private is political, but it is not individual. It is part of our collective life, and it requires a collective responsibility.

Acknowledgments

I wrote a very long sentimental introduction to my first book. This time around I am trying to be more concise, although brevity is not my strong point.

I am indebted to two scholars who deeply influenced my thinking on privacy: Helen Nissenbaum and danah boyd. Helen's understanding of contextual integrity was foundational to my understanding of privacy, and networked privacy builds substantively on her work. She also sparked my interest in privacy as a graduate student, when I joined a very early instantiation of her Privacy Research Group at the NYU School of Law. danah and I have written six journal articles and countless conference papers together, and the original theories of context collapse and networked privacy are collaborative efforts. She is one of the most intellectually generous people I have ever met, and I would not be where I am without her. Thank you both.

Much of the fieldwork for this book was conducted during sabbaticals sponsored by the Data & Society Research Institute, the Department of Communication, and the Institute for the Arts and Humanities (IAH) at the University of North Carolina at Chapel Hill. Thank you especially to the Staton family for generously funding the faculty fellowship at the IAH. The Reframing Privacy study was funded by the Digital Trust Foundation. The focus-group study was funded by the Merck Foundation. Time and space to finish this book was provided by the Andrew Carnegie Fellows Program. I thank all the funders for supporting this research but note that the findings in this book were not influenced by the funders in any way.

Thank you to my collaborators on the privacy-related papers on which parts of this book draw: danah boyd, Claire Fontaine, Michele Gilman, Eszter Hargittai, Karen Levy, Mary Madden, and Mikaela Pitcan; and my research assistants Shanice Jones Cameron, Ben Clancy, Katie Furl, Will Partin, and Courtlyn Pippert. Special thanks to my editor, William Frucht; my first-draft editor, Heath Sledge; my copy editor, Andrew Katz; and my research assistant, Elaine Schnabel, who collectively whipped an unruly book into shape.

Portions of this book were presented at the Privacy Law Scholars Conference; the Yale Symposium on Platform Governance, sponsored by the Justice Collaboratory; the "My Mother Was a Computer: Legacies of Gender and Technology" symposium at William and Mary; the International Communication Association annual conference; various Association of Internet Researchers annual conferences; the Telecommunications Policy Research Conference; and the "Fracturing Democracy: The Erosion of Civil Society in a Shifting Communication Ecology Symposium" at the University of Wisconsin–Madison. I have presented the concept of "networked privacy" at Cornell, New York University, Northwestern University, the University of Michigan, the Rochester Institute of Technology, Queen's University, and the University of Southern California. Thank you everyone for the feedback and for listening to me when you were probably expecting the *Status Update* book talk—yes, that's how long I've been working on this project. Thank you also to attendees of the NetGain Dis/Mis-information, Dangerous Speech, and Democracy Meeting and the Workshop on High Impact Research on Online Harassment and Moderation at the MIT Media Lab for generative discussions that helped inform my research on privacy and harassment.

The discussion of networked harassment in chapter 4 was deeply influenced by Lindsay Blackwell, Amy Bruckman, Robyn Caplan, Danielle Citron, Molly Crockett, Kat Lo, Adrienne Massanari, and Nate Matias. Thank you to these scholars for inspiration, advice, guidance, and foundational work, without which this concept would not have come to pass.

Thank you to Anna Lauren Hoffmann and my co-faculty fellows at the IAH for feedback on chapter 6.

Thank you to my colleagues at the University of North Carolina at Chapel Hill in the Department of Communication, particularly Cori Dauber, China Medel, Torin Monahan, and Mike Palm, and at the Center for Information, Technology, and Public Life: Tressie McMillan Cottom, Deen Freelon, Daniel Kreiss, Rachel Kuo, Gary Marchionini, Shannon McGregor, Katy Peters, Meredith Pruden, and Francesca Tripodi.

Thank you to members of the Association of Internet Researchers, the Microsoft Research Social Media Collective, the NYU School of Law Privacy Research Group, and the Data & Society Research Institute, who form a strong and supportive extended network to think through issues of technology and society critically and with nuance.

Thank you to all the caregivers who took care of my children so I could work, especially Grace Martineck-Randall and Ziyanda Kenya. My mother, Ann Marwick, deserves special thanks for extensive emotional support and child care during the COVID-19 pandemic. Thanks to my family: Dad, Ilene, Gordon, Dave, Amie, Valerie, Tessa, Carol Ann, Andy, David, Leigh, Elle, and Brother Wesley. The most thanks, as always, go to my husband, Harry, who, given our many years together, knows more about academia than any nonacademic (let's just say he's skeptical of the whole endeavor) and is a constant and steady source of support. And while I'm not sure if they should be thanked, as their contributions to the book were minimal and in fact mostly not helpful, my children, Ramona and Julian, are the light of my life. This book is dedicated to them and to all parents trying to balance work and caregiving.

Most importantly, thank you to my participants for their willingness to share their stories with me.

Appendix: Research Methods

The data from this book comes from four separate qualitative studies, with a total of 127 participants. I personally conducted a study on online harassment (n = 37) and a study on queer privacy (n = 22) in which I was the sole investigator and conducted all interviews. The other two studies (n = 28) and (n = 40) were done in collaboration with other researchers. The quotations and material used in this book are used with permission. Some of the methodological information in this appendix is taken from previously published papers; thank you to all my collaborators for generously allowing me to use our data.

All participants who are quoted have been given false names, and identifying information such as the names of schools or employers has been removed or changed. In some cases, an individual's location or age has been obscured. Online information such as social media posts has sometimes been reworded to prevent identification through search engines. I used the racial and ethnic descriptions of the participants throughout the book (e.g., some Black participants identified as Black and some as African American).

I thank all the funders for supporting this research but note that they did not influence the findings in any way. The writing of this book was partially funded by an Andrew Carnegie Fellowship.

Reframing Privacy

This project was conducted with danah boyd and Claire Fontaine of the Data & Society Research Institute and supported by the Digital Trust

Foundation. The study had twenty-eight participants, low-socioeconomic-status young adults (ages seventeen to twenty-seven) living in the five boroughs of New York City. Participants were required to have a smartphone or similar device, such as an iPod Touch, and to use at least one social media platform regularly, such as Twitter or Instagram. Dr. Fontaine recruited our first group (eleven participants) by emailing instructors at New York City–area high schools and colleges. Our recruitment fliers read, "We seek participants from diverse backgrounds, especially first generation college students, people from single parent households, immigrants or children of immigrants, residents of NYCHA, and recipients of Section 8 housing vouchers." Dr. Fontaine screened prospective participants by phone. All participants gave written informed consent. This study was approved by the Chesapeake independent Institutional Review Board.

The primary goal of this project was to identify new frames for thinking about privacy. danah boyd and I individually conducted semistructured interviews with the eleven selected participants for sixty to ninety minutes. Our interview protocol covered general questions (What are you passionate about?), questions about social media use, information-sharing practices (What kinds of things might you share with some people but not with others?), policing, privacy, and surveillance. We strategically did not use the term "privacy" until the end of each interview to attempt to discover different frames informants use to understand information flow. We paid participants $25 for the initial interview. After each interview, danah and I wrote field notes to capture information that transcription might not preserve, such as setting and context.[1]

On the basis of our initial interviews, we selected seven interview participants to be participant researchers (PRs). This methodological decision was based on two factors. First, Dr. Fontaine was trained in participatory methodologies like participatory action research (PAR), which centers the knowledge and expertise of research subjects, ideally to produce knowledge that propels social change.[2] Second, we recognized that as three white women attempting to understand the standpoints of low-income young people of color, we were replicating racialized processes of data extraction. By involving participants in the process of data collection, we hoped to generate rich data, enhance the validity of our findings, and work more collaboratively. I must note, though, that PAR research is generally activist and requires substantive input from participants in designing research projects, which we did not do. Each participant researcher interviewed between two and six friends and family members, although two did not submit any interviews. We gave the PRs some direction, suggesting themes we thought each of them would be well suited to investigate, encouraging them to respond to issues that arose during the interviews, and recommending that they ask questions naturally. Dr. Fontaine taught each PR how to conduct basic interviews and use a recording device. We paid PRs $25 for the training. Participants emailed or uploaded the audio files to a shared file system after the interviews were completed. An outside transcription service transcribed the interviews. We paid participants $50 for their first set of interviews (two or three) and another $50 for a second, optional set of three interviews.

While listening to the audio recordings, each author read, proofed, and coded the transcripts. The transcripts were coded at three levels: content, or what the interviewees explicitly stated; assumptions and cultural discourses underlying the content; and dynamics of the interviewer-interviewee interaction.[3] On the basis of our coding, we identified and wrote memos on an initial set of themes. Following the development of our hypotheses, we conducted a focus group with five of the PRs, which served both as a member check (sharing our findings with the study participants to determine their accuracy) and a time for collaborative meaning-making.[4]

Our participants were very diverse, and many are multiethnic and/or recent immigrants and do not easily map to typical US racial categories. Races and ethnicities represented include, in our participants' words, unspecified Hispanic/Latino (n = 5), African American (n = 4), Puerto Rican (n = 3), white (n = 3), Asian Indian (n = 2), biracial (n = 2), unspecified Asian American (n = 2), Chinese (n = 1), Filipino (n = 1), Dominican (n = 1), Belizean (n = 1), Ghanaian (n = 1), and Malian (n = 1). One member of our sample declined to share information on his race or ethnicity. Two participants identify as middle class (though one's mother has only a high school education) and one as upper middle class. The rest of the participants identified themselves as of relatively low socioeconomic status, though they expressed this in various ways: "really low income" (Angelique), "really poor, like super poor" (Diego), and "not getting the government cheese or anything" but with a household income "probably between twenty-two and twenty-six thousand a year" (Ian). We note that it is important not to conflate race and class and equate "low socioeconomic status" with "urban minorities of color."[5] Most low-income Americans are white, although poverty rates are higher among African Americans, Latinos, and Asian Americans.[6] But given that we conducted our study in New York City, most of our participants are people of color.[7]

Six individuals in the sample identify as sexual minorities (homosexual, bisexual, pansexual, and asexual). Twelve identify as heterosexual, two as "mostly" heterosexual, and eight did not disclose their sexual orientations. Eighteen participants identify as male, nine as female, and one as a biological female with a nonbinary gender identification. A range of religions are represented, including Catholic and nonpracticing Catholic, Christian, Muslim, Jewish and nonpracticing Jewish, and many nonreligious/atheist/agnostic participants. Most individuals in the study did not specify a religious identification. Sixteen participants live with family members (including immediate, nuclear family, and extended family), two with a roommate, and two with a partner, although eight did not provide information about their living situations.

We have published two previous papers from this project that provide more methodological and participant information. Both are available on my website (http://www.tiara.org):

Pitcan, Mikaela, Alice E. Marwick, and danah boyd. "Performing a Vanilla Self: Respectability Politics, Social Class, and the Digital World." *Journal of Computer-Mediated Communication* 23, no. 3 (2018): 163–79.

Marwick, Alice E., Claire Fontaine, and danah boyd. "'Nobody Sees It, Nobody Gets Mad': Social Media, Privacy, and Personal Responsibility among Low-SES Youth." *Social Media & Society* 3, no. 2 (2017). http://journals.sagepub.com/doi/abs/10.1177/2056305117710455.

Focus Groups

This study was funded by the Merck Foundation. The focus groups for this project were conducted under the supervision of Eszter Hargittai. Research assistance was provided by Elizabeth Hensley and Northwestern University's Summer Research Opportunity Program, Devon Moore, Somi Hubbard, and Karina Sirota through Northwestern's Undergraduate Research Assistant Program. This team conducted ten in-person focus-group interviews (with an average focus-group size of four) which yielded forty young-adult participants, all of whom were enrolled in college or graduate school. Recruitment included Facebook ads, fliers posted on campus and nearby establishments like cafes, and emails sent to local colleagues and neighbors to help identify potential respondents. To avoid biasing respondents, the ads did not specify the focus of the study beyond general internet use. Sessions took place on a midwestern college campus for approximately one hour. Participants were paid $20 for the session. The study was approved by the Northwestern University Institutional Review Board for Human Subjects Research.

Participants first completed a brief survey on their demographics and internet experiences. By starting with a survey, we were able to collect information about the participants' online experiences without influence from the focus group. Next, we described how focus groups function and then asked all the participants the first question to ensure equal participation. We asked participants what privacy meant to them and how they would define it, rather than imposing a definition. We next asked how much control participants thought they had over their personal data in various circumstances and what types of technological or policy advances would make them feel more in control (after the majority acknowledged a lack of control).

Of participants, 77 percent were enrolled as undergraduate students from six different institutions, while the rest were pursuing graduate study at the institution; 50 percent of participants were nineteen to twenty-one years of age, 27 percent were twenty-two to twenty-four, 13 percent were twenty-five to thirty, and 10 percent were thirty-one to thirty-five. Participants' racial identifications included white (65.9 percent), Asian American (19.5 percent), African American (9.8 percent), and Hispanic or Latino (4.9 percent). The majority of participants grew up in a well-educated household, with more than two-thirds (68 percent) having at least one parent with a graduate degree, 22 percent having at least one parent with a college degree, and only 10 percent having parents who had not completed college. More than a third of interviewees were majoring in humanities subjects (35 percent), just under a third in the sciences (30 percent), and less than a fifth in social science subjects (18 percent) and journalism and communication (17 percent). While we found no gender differences among participants, we do give age, race, and gender when quoting them for context.

Almost everyone in the survey had constant internet connectivity, as only one person did not have internet access on their phone. To get a sense of the participants' social media experience, we asked if they had heard of and/or utilized certain popular sites. Every participant had heard of Facebook, Twitter, LinkedIn, Instagram, and Google Plus, and only one person had not heard of Snapchat, Tumblr, Pinterest, and Flickr. Everyone utilized at least one of these sites, and the majority used many.

We have published two previous papers from this study, which provide more information. Both are available on my website (http://www.tiara.org):

Marwick, Alice E., and Eszter Hargittai. "Nothing to Hide, Nothing to Lose? Incentives and Disincentives for Sharing Personal Information with Institutional Actors Online." *Information, Communication & Society* 22, no. 12 (2019): 1697–1713.

Eszter Hargittai and Alice E. Marwick. "'What Can I Really Do?': Explaining the Privacy Paradox with Online Apathy." *International Journal of Communication* 10 (2016): 3737–57.

Online Harassment

This study was funded by the University of North Carolina Department of Communication and the Data & Society Research Institute. It draws from a corpus of semistructured interviews that I conducted with people who had experienced online harassment (n = 28) and workers at trust and safety teams at various social media platforms (n = 9). I posted open calls on Twitter, Reddit, and Craigslist to find participants over eighteen who had experienced online harassment, defined in recruitment materials as "being called offensive names, having someone try to embarrass you on purpose, being physically threatened online, having sensitive personal information exposed or your privacy invaded, having rumors spread about you online, being sexually harassed or cyberstalked, or being harassed over a long period of time." I conducted all the interviews via phone or video chat (Zoom or Skype), depending on what the participant preferred; thus, some interviews were audio only, while some had audio and video. Interviews lasted between thirty and ninety minutes and followed a semistructured protocol in which participants were asked about their experiences with online harassment, its effects, and their thoughts on online harassment in general. Subjects received a $20 incentive for participation, although a significant minority asked for it to be donated to charity.

Trust and safety participants were recruited through email and LinkedIn, using my and others' industry contacts to identify potential participants. Each participant was asked about their company's procedures for dealing with unwanted user behavior and their experiences working in trust and safety. These subjects did not receive an incentive. These interviews were conducted via Zoom.

All interviews were audio-recorded and transcribed by an outside transcription company with a confidentiality agreement. Transcripts were imported into the qualitative data analysis software MaxQDA. I coded a subset of interviews (n = 5) to generate the initial codebook, which was developed iteratively through initial coding as coding continued.[8] Initial coding allows the researcher to closely examine the data and identify potential categories.[9] Coding was done at both the *content* level (explicit statements by the interviewee) and the level of *assumptions* and cultural discourses underlying the content.[10] The second phase of coding involved focused coding to highlight significant and frequent codes.[11]

Participants who had experienced online harassment ranged in age from eighteen to forty-nine, with an average age of thirty and a half. Eighteen identified as women, seven as men, and three as nonbinary. One person identified as trans. Twenty-one identified as white, three as Asian or Asian American, one as Black, and two as Middle Eastern. Thirteen identified as heterosexual, one as "mostly straight," eight as bisexual, three as queer, one as pansexual, one as lesbian, and one as gay. Participants were located primarily in the United States (seventeen), although others lived in the United Kingdom (four), Europe (four), Canada (three), and Africa (one). All participants spoke English. Of the trust and safety participants (n = 9), five identified as women and four as men. Trust and safety participants were not asked their age, race, or sexuality to maintain anonymity, given the small number of people working in the industry. All participants' names and potentially identifiable information have been pseudonymized. In some cases, the specifics of the harassment or platform features have been obscured to prevent possible identification. This study was approved by the University of North Carolina at Chapel Hill Institutional Review Board, IRB #18-1916.

I have published one previous paper from this study, which provides more information. It is available on my website (http://www.tiara.org):

Marwick, Alice E. (2021). "Morally Motivated Networked Harassment as Normative Reinforcement." *Social Media + Society* 7, no. 2 (2021). https://doi.org/10.1177/20563051211021378.

LGBTQ+ Privacy

This research was supported by the Institute for the Arts and Humanities at the University of North Carolina at Chapel Hill; thank you to the Staton family for funding my faculty fellowship. This project was conducted entirely by the author in 2018 and 2019 and consists of in-person interviews with twenty-two individuals. Recruitment took place using fliers posted in coffeeshops, libraries, bars, and public spaces throughout the North Carolina Research Triangle area; recruitment emails sent to local LGBTQ+ organizations; and recruitment text posted on local LGBTQ+ Facebook groups and Craigslist. Participants were required to identify as LGBTQ+ (specifically, gay, lesbian, bisexual, transgender, nonbinary, asexual, and/or queer), use at least one social media site at least twice a week, be over eighteen, and live in the greater Research Triangle area. All interviews were conducted in person, and most took about an hour. They were conducted in a space of the participants' choice, including coffeeshops, public library workrooms, school offices, and participants' homes. Participants were paid $20 in cash for the study, plus a drink if the interview took place in a coffeeshop. Interviews were recorded, transcribed by an outside transcription company, and proofed and anonymized by the author. Transcripts were imported into MaxQDA and coded using a system of emergent codes. The author also conducted brief fieldwork as a volunteer at a local LGBTQ+ support center to get a feel for the North Carolina Research Triangle queer community. A pilot sample was used to generate a codebook, which was iterated on throughout the coding process. This study was approved by the UNC Institutional Review Board, IRB #18-1916.

The research questions for this study included the following:

- How do queer individuals navigate privacy on social media?
- How do individuals who identify as part of a queer community navigate different expectations of disclosure and concealment on social media among their different social contexts?

- What harms exist for queer individuals whose privacy is violated on social media? Are there differences vis-à-vis race, gender, or identity?

The study yielded twenty-two participants, who ranged in age from nineteen to forty-six, with an average age of twenty-nine. Of the participants, 40 percent identified as cis women, 27 percent as cis men, 13 percent as gender-fluid or nonbinary (one person wrote "man/woman"), 13 percent as trans women, and 4 percent as trans men. Seven identified as lesbian, three as pansexual, seven as bisexual, five as gay, and four as queer (note that some people voiced multiple identities). Most participants identified as white (68 percent), several as Latinx (18 percent), and fewer as Native American (4 percent), Black (4 percent), and Asian (4 percent). All participants lived in North Carolina. The sample was diverse with regard to occupation and social class, ranging from a homeless cook to an upper-middle-class college professor. Not all participants chose to share their marital status, but of those who did, 27 percent were single, 22 percent were married to a trans or same-sex partner, 22 percent were in long-term relationships with a trans or same-sex partner, and 18 percent were in a short-term or "complicated" relationship. No participants reported being in a relationship with an opposite-sex or nonbinary partner. Most participants did not have children, although 27 percent did. All participants' names and potentially identifiable information have been pseudonymized.

Notes

1. The Private Is Political

1. "Big data" is an inadequate term but serves as shorthand for large-scale, networked data sets. As danah boyd and Kate Crawford noted in 2011, the value of big data "comes from the patterns that can be derived by making connections between pieces of data, about an individual, about individuals in relation to others, about groups of people, or simply about the structure of information itself." boyd and Crawford, "Six Provocations for Big Data," in *A Decade in Internet Time: Symposium on the Dynamics of the Internet and Society*, SSRN, September 21, 2011, http://papers.ssrn.com/sol3/papers.cfm?abstract_id=1926431.

2. Sarah E. Igo, *The Known Citizen: A History of Privacy in Modern America* (Cambridge, MA: Harvard University Press, 2018).

3. Georg Simmel, "The Sociology of Secrecy and of Secret Societies," *American Journal of Sociology* 11, no. 4 (1906): 441–98.

4. Scott Jaschik, "New Data on How College Admissions Officers View Social Media of Applicants," *Inside Higher Ed*, April 23, 2018, https://www.insidehighered.com/admissions/article/2018/04/23/new-data-how-college-admissions-officers-view-social-media-applicants.

5. Khiara M. Bridges, *The Poverty of Privacy Rights* (Palo Alto, CA: Stanford University Press, 2017); Sarah Min, "Social Security May Use Your Facebook and Instagram Photos to Nix Disability Claims," *CBS News*, March 21, 2019, https://www.cbsnews.com/news/social-security-disability-benefits-your-facebook-instagram-posts-could-affect-your-social-security-disability-claim/.

6. Jamila Michener, Mallory SoRelle, and Chloe Thurston, "From the Margins to the Center: A Bottom-Up Approach to Welfare State Scholarship," *Perspectives on Politics* 20, no. 1 (2022): 154–69. https://doi.org/10.1017/S153759272000359X.

7. The exception might be your closest friends and family, but even then, there are probably areas of their network you are not privy to. I know all my husband's relatives and most of his friends, but I do not know all his work colleagues, for example.

8. One of the original selling points of the internet was this democratization of content creation, which was touted as broadening the power that was then held mostly by a small number of media professionals in newspapers and television. See Alice E. Marwick, *Status Update: Celebrity, Publicity, and Branding in the Social Media Age* (New Haven, CT: Yale University Press, 2013).

9. This too was idealized as leveling and democratizing.

10. Irwin Altman, "Privacy Regulation: Culturally Universal or Culturally Specific?," *Journal of Social Issues* 33, no. 3 (1977): 66–84; Christena E. Nippert-Eng, *Islands of Privacy* (Chicago: University of Chicago Press, 2010).

11. Wendy Hui Kyong Chun, *Updating to Remain the Same: Habitual New Media* (Cambridge, MA: MIT Press, 2016).

12. Julie E. Cohen, *Configuring the Networked Self: Law, Code, and the Play of Everyday Practice* (New Haven, CT: Yale University Press, 2012); Eszter Hargittai and Alice E. Marwick, "'What Can I Really Do?': Explaining the Privacy Paradox with Online Apathy," *International Journal of Communication* 10 (2016): 3737–57.

13. Lindsey Barrett, "Our Collective Privacy Problem Is Not Your Fault," Fast Company, January 2, 2020, https://www.fastcompany.com/90447583/our-collective-privacy-problem-is-not-your-fault; Kashmir Hill and Aaron Krolik, "How Photos of Your Kids Are Powering Surveillance Technology," *New York Times*, October 11, 2019, sec. Technology, https://www.nytimes.com/interactive/2019/10/11/technology/flickr-facial-recognition.html; Jessica Baron, "Vulnerable Moms Engage In 'Sharenting' Even When They Know The Dangers," *Forbes*, June 29, 2019, https://www.forbes.com/sites/jessicabaron/2019/07/29/vulnerable-moms-engage-in-sharenting-even-when-they-know-the-dangers/.

14. David Gilbert, "Facebook Says It's Your Fault That Hackers Got Half a Billion User Phone Numbers," *Vice*, April 7, 2021, https://www.vice.com/en/article/88awzp/facebook-says-its-your-fault-that-hackers-got-half-a-billion-user-phone-numbers.

15. Addy Baird, "Nancy Pelosi Said Katie Hill's Resignation after Details of Her Sex Life Were Published without Her Consent Shows That Young People Need to 'Be Careful,'" *BuzzFeed News*, October 31, 2019, https://www.buzzfeednews.com/article/addybaird/nancy-pelosi-katie-hill-resignation-pictures.

16. Alice E. Marwick and danah boyd, "Networked Privacy: How Teenagers Negotiate Context in Social Media," *New Media & Society* 16, no. 7 (2014): 1051–67.

17. Jennifer M. Silva, *Coming Up Short: Working-Class Adulthood in an Age of Uncertainty* (New York: Oxford University Press, 2013).

18. Helen Fay Nissenbaum, *Privacy in Context: Technology, Policy, and the Integrity of Social Life* (Stanford, CA: Stanford University Press, 2010).

19. Nissenbaum; Omer Tene and Jules Polonetsky, "A Theory of Creepy: Technology, Privacy and Shifting Social Norms," *Yale Journal of Law & Technology* 16 (2013): 59–102.

20. Rachel E. Dubrofsky and Shoshana Amielle Magnet, *Feminist Surveillance Studies* (Durham, NC: Duke University Press, 2015).

21. Sandra Petronio, *Boundaries of Privacy: Dialectics of Disclosure* (Albany: SUNY Press, 2002).

22. While this book focuses on US privacy law and norms, it is notable that this conceptualization of privacy is frequently exported through US-based social technologies.

23. Anita L. Allen and Erin Mack, "How Privacy Got Its Gender," *Northern Illinois University Law Review* 10 (1989): 441–78; Jessica Lake, *The Face That Launched a Thousand Lawsuits: The American Women Who Forged a Right to Privacy* (New Haven, CT: Yale University Press, 2016).

24. Barbara Welter, "The Cult of True Womanhood: 1820–1860," *American Quarterly* 18, no. 2 (1966): 151–74.

25. Mary Louise Roberts, "True Womanhood Revisited," *Journal of Women's History* 14, no. 1 (2002): 150–55.

26. Allen and Mack, "How Privacy Got Its Gender."

27. In the antebellum period, most free Black women worked outside their homes as domestic laborers in white households, and Black leaders often encouraged Black women to pursue education and community activism to uplift the Black community. However, in white culture, Black women were portrayed as sexually loose temptresses, against which white womanhood was defined. This gave rise to respectability politics, a strategy that encouraged Black women to present themselves as highly dignified and moral to resist such stereotypes. By the end of the eighteenth century, within free Black communities, women had to contend with social pressure to be "self-sacrificing and dutiful." This is despite the fact that, as Linda M. Perkins writes, "The emphasis upon women's purity, submissiveness and natural fragility was the antithesis of the reality of most black women's lives during slavery and for many years thereafter." Perkins, "The Impact of the 'Cult of True Womanhood' on the Education of Black Women," *Journal of Social Issues* 39, no. 3 (1983): 18; Shirley J. Yee, "Black Women and the Cult of True Womanhood," in *Black Women Abolitionists: A Study in Activism, 1828–1860* (Knoxville: University of Tennessee Press, 1992); Laurie Kaiser, "The Black Madonna: Notions of True Womanhood from Jacobs to Hurston," *South Atlantic Review* 60, no. 1 (1995): 97–109, https://doi.org/10.2307/3200715.

28. Susan Hill Lindley, *"You Have Stept Out of Your Place": A History of Women and Religion in America* (Louisville, KY: Westminster John Knox Press, 1996), 71.

29. Lake, *Face That Launched a Thousand Lawsuits*, 45–46.

30. Eden Osucha, "The Whiteness of Privacy: Race, Media, Law," *Camera Obscura: Feminism, Culture, and Media Studies* 24, no. 1 (70) (May 1, 2009): 67–107, https://doi.org/10.1215/02705346-2008-015; Allen and Mack, "How Privacy Got Its Gender."

31. Igo, *Known Citizen*.

32. Samuel D. Warren and Louis D. Brandeis, "Right to Privacy," *Harvard Law Review* 4 (1890): 193–220; Allen and Mack, "How Privacy Got Its Gender."

33. Dorothy J. Glancy, "Privacy and the Other Miss M," *Northern Illinois University Law Review* 10 (1989): 401–40; Allen and Mack, "How Privacy Got Its Gender."

34. Lindley, *You Have Stept Out of Your Place*, 55–57.

35. Lake, *Face That Launched a Thousand Lawsuits.*

36. Eden Koren Osucha, "The Subject of Privacy: Race, Rights, and Intimate Personhood in Modern American Literature and Law" (Ph.D. diss., Duke University, 2007), https://search.proquest.com/docview/304863177/abstract/245E6F169324FB5PQ/1; Osucha, "Whiteness of Privacy."

37. Osucha, "Whiteness of Privacy"; Igo, *Known Citizen*; Simone Browne, *Dark Matters: On the Surveillance of Blackness* (Durham, NC: Duke University Press, 2015); Christian Parenti, *The Soft Cage: Surveillance in America from Slavery to the War on Terror* (New York: Basic Books, 2003).

38. Igo, *Known Citizen*; Amy L. Fairchild et al., *Searching Eyes: Privacy, the State, and Disease Surveillance in America* (Berkeley: University of California Press, 2007).

39. Igo, *Known Citizen*; Simon A. Cole, *Suspect Identities: A History of Fingerprinting and Criminal Identification* (Cambridge, MA: Harvard University Press, 2002); Parenti, *Soft Cage.*

40. Browne, *Dark Matters*, 10–16.

41. David Lyon, *Surveillance Studies: An Overview* (Cambridge, UK: Polity, 2007), 14.

42. Khalil Gibran Muhammad, *The Condemnation of Blackness* (Cambridge, MA: Harvard University Press, 2011).

43. Browne, *Dark Matters.*

44. Gino Canella, "Racialized Surveillance: Activist Media and the Policing of Black Bodies," *Communication, Culture and Critique* 11, no. 3 (2018): 378–98, https://doi.org/10.1093/ccc/tcy013; Ward Churchill and Jim Vander Wall, *Agents of Repression: The FBI's Secret Wars against the Black Panther Party and the American Indian Movement*, vol. 7 (Boston: South End, 2002); Mark Morales and Laura Ly, "Released NYPD Emails Show Extensive Surveillance of Black Lives Matter Protesters," CNN, January 18, 2019, https://www.cnn.com/2019/01/18/us/nypd-black-lives-matter-surveillance/index.html.

45. Alexandra Mateescu et al., "Social Media Surveillance and Law Enforcement," *Data and Civil Rights* 27 (2015): 2015–27.

46. Rachel Hall, *The Transparent Traveler: The Performance and Culture of Airport Security* (Durham, NC: Duke University Press, 2015).

47. Louis A. Cainkar, *Homeland Insecurity: The Arab American and Muslim American Experience after 9/11* (New York: Russell Sage Foundation, 2009).

48. Arjun Singh Sethi, "The FBI Needs to Stop Spying on Muslim-Americans," *Politico Magazine*, March 29, 2016, https://www.politico.com/magazine/story/2016/03/muslim -american-surveillance-fbi-spying-213773.

49. Robert Snell, "Feds Use Anti-Terror Tool to Hunt the Undocumented," *Detroit News*, May 18, 2017, https://www.detroitnews.com/story/news/local/detroit-city/2017/05/18/cell -snooping-fbi-immigrant/101859616/; Lily Hay Newman, "Internal Docs Show How ICE Gets Surveillance Help from Local Cops," *Wired*, March 13, 2019, https://www.wired.com/ story/ice-license-plate-surveillance-vigilant-solutions/; Nausicaa Renner, "As Immigrants Become More Aware of Their Rights, ICE Steps Up Ruses and Surveillance," *The Intercept* (blog), July 25, 2019, https://theintercept.com/2019/07/25/ice-surveillance-ruse-arrests -raids/.

50. Hall, *Transparent Traveler*.

51. Adam Goldman, Katie Benner, and Zolan Kanno-Youngs, "How Trump's Focus on Antifa Distracted Attention from the Far-Right Threat," *New York Times*, January 30, 2021, sec. U.S., https://www.nytimes.com/2021/01/30/us/politics/trump-right-wing-domestic -terrorism.html; Rachel Janik and Keegan Hankes, "The Year in Hate and Extremism 2020," Southern Poverty Law Center, February 1, 2021, https://www.splcenter.org/news/2021/02/01/ year-hate-2020.

52. Anjuli R. K. Shere and Jason Nurse, "Police Surveillance of Black Lives Matter Shows the Danger Technology Poses to Democracy," *The Conversation*, July 24, 2020, http://theconversation.com/police-surveillance-of-black-lives-matter-shows-the-danger -technology-poses-to-democracy-142194.

53. Albert Samaha, Jason Leopold, and Rosalind Adams, "Newly Released Documents Reveal How The Feds Were Monitoring BLM Protests," *BuzzFeed News*, August 13, 2020, https://www.buzzfeednews.com/article/albertsamaha/newly-released-documents-reveal-how -the-feds-were.

54. I am indebted to Daniel Trottier for his discussion of why "surveillance" is a more apt term than "privacy" when discussing the institutional nature of online privacy violations. Trottier, *Social Media as Surveillance: Rethinking Visibility in a Converging World* (Burlington, VT: Ashgate, 2012).

55. Lake, *Face That Launched a Thousand Lawsuits*.

56. Combahee River Collective, "A Black Feminist Statement," in *Capitalist Patriarchy and the Case for Socialist Feminism*, ed. Zillah Eisenstein (New York: Monthly Review Press, 1979), 264; Carol Hanisch, "The Personal Is Political," in *Notes from the Second Year: Women's Liberation*, ed. Shulamith Firestone and Anne Koedt (New York: New York Radical Women, 1970), 76–78; Kimberlé Crenshaw, "Mapping the Margins: Intersectionality, Identity Politics, and Violence against Women of Color," *Stanford Law Review* 43, no. 6 (1991): 1241–99.

57. Jeannie Suk, *At Home in the Law: How the Domestic Violence Revolution Is Transforming Privacy* (New Haven, CT: Yale University Press, 2009).

58. Patricia Boling, *Privacy and the Politics of Intimate Life* (Ithaca, NY: Cornell University Press, 1996).

59. Kristin Anne Kelly, *Domestic Violence and the Politics of Privacy* (Ithaca, NY: Cornell University Press, 2003), 61.

60. Carole Pateman, "Feminist Critiques of the Public/Private Dichotomy," in *Feminism and Equality*, ed. Anne Phillips (Oxford, UK: Basil Blackwell, 1987), 103–26; Frances Olsen, "Constitutional Law: Feminist Critiques of the Public/Private Distinction," *Constitutional Commentary* 10 (1993): 319–27.

61. Susan Gal, "A Semiotics of the Public/Private Distinction," *Differences: A Journal of Feminist Cultural Studies* 13, no. 1 (2002): 78.

62. Kristin Bumiller, *In an Abusive State: How Neoliberalism Appropriated the Feminist Movement against Sexual Violence* (Durham, NC: Duke University Press, 2008); Kelly, *Domestic Violence and the Politics of Privacy*, 68–69.

63. Brian A. Reaves, *Police Response to Domestic Violence, 2006–2015* (Washington, DC: US Department of Justice, Office of Justice Programs, Bureau of Justice Statistics, 2017).

64. That is not to say that there is any meaningful public effort to solve these problems on any level other than the individual. This is especially true given the negative impact of COVID-19 on women's participation in the workforce, particularly women of color, due to disproportionate parenting, caregiving, and housekeeping responsibilities.

65. While I was finishing this book in June 2022, the Supreme Court overturned *Roe v. Wade*. Suffice to say that if this had happened earlier, I would have had much more to say about it in this book. In addition to this ruling's impact on women's very lives and autonomy, the implications for privacy are disastrous, and the ability of networked information technologies to predict pregnancy are well documented. Attempts to regulate birth control persist in the United States despite the Supreme Court establishing a legal right to privacy vis-à-vis reproductive decision-making (albeit for heterosexual married couples) in *Griswold v. Connecticut* (1965). Gal, "Semiotics of the Public/Private Distinction," 78.

66. Both "gaslighting" and "microaggressions" originated in therapeutic practice but have moved into colloquial use. Gaslighting, taken from the 1938 play and subsequent film *Gas Light*, is a manipulative tactic in which an individual's memories or experiences are systematically denied, making the individual feel unstable or unable to trust themselves. Microaggressions are "brief, everyday exchanges that send denigrating messages to people of color because they belong to a racial minority group"; the term has been expanded to include homophobic microaggressions, sexist microaggressions, transphobic microaggressions, and the like. See

Kate Abramson, "Turning Up the Lights on Gaslighting," *Philosophical Perspectives* 28, no. 1 (2014): 1–30; Derald Wing Sue et al., "Racial Microaggressions in Everyday Life: Implications for Clinical Practice," *American Psychologist* 62, no. 4 (2007): 271–86.

67. Michelle O'Reilly and Nicola Parker, "'Unsatisfactory Saturation': A Critical Exploration of the Notion of Saturated Sample Sizes in Qualitative Research," *Qualitative Research* 13, no. 2 (2013): 190–97.

68. Mario Luis Small, "'How Many Cases Do I Need?': On Science and the Logic of Case Selection in Field-Based Research," *Ethnography* 10, no. 1 (2009): 5–38; Robert S. Weiss, *Learning from Strangers: The Art and Method of Qualitative Interview Studies* (New York: Simon and Schuster, 1995).

69. Stefanie Duguay, Jean Burgess, and Nicolas Suzor, "Queer Women's Experiences of Patchwork Platform Governance on Tinder, Instagram, and Vine," *Convergence* 26, no. 2 (2020): 237–52. https://doi.org/10.1177/1354856518781530.

70. Duguay, Burgess, and Suzor, 13.

71. Susan Stryker, "Transgender Studies: Queer Theory's Evil Twin," *GLQ: A Journal of Lesbian and Gay Studies* 10, no. 2 (2004): 214.

72. Thanks to Anna Lauren Hoffmann for conversations that led to this insight.

73. Liz Kelly, "The Continuum of Sexual Violence," in *Women, Violence and Social Control*, edited by Jalna Hamner and Mary Maynard (Cham, Switzerland: Springer, 1987), 46–60.

74. Noah Kelley, "DIY Feminist Cybersecurity," Hack*Blossom, 2016, https://hackblossom.org/cybersecurity/.

75. Mary Madden et al., "Privacy, Poverty, and Big Data: A Matrix of Vulnerabilities for Poor Americans," *Washington University Law Review* 95, no. 1 (2017): 53–125; Virginia Eubanks, *Automating Inequality: How High-Tech Tools Profile, Police, and Punish the Poor* (New York: St. Martin's, 2018).

2. The Violation Machine

1. Julie E. Cohen, *Configuring the Networked Self: Law, Code, and the Play of Everyday Practice* (New Haven, CT: Yale University Press, 2012); Priscilla M. Regan, *Legislating Privacy: Technology, Social Values, and Public Policy* (Chapel Hill: University of North Carolina Press, 1995). This model most closely resembles *homo economicus*, the prototypical subject of early economics, which modeled people as detached, self-interested actors concerned primarily with maximizing their personal benefits through rational choices, in a marketplace where everyone has equal information. Julie A. Nelson, "The Study of Choice or the Study of Provisioning? Gender and the Definition of Economics," in *Beyond Economic Man: Feminist*

Theory and Economics, ed. Marianne A. Ferber and Julie A. Nelson (Chicago: University Of Chicago Press, 1993), 23–36.

2. Daniel J. Solove, "The Meaning and Value of Privacy," in *Social Dimensions of Privacy: Interdisciplinary Perspectives*, edited by Beate Roessler and Dorota Mokrosinska (Cambridge: Cambridge University Press, 2015), 71–82; Karen Levy and danah boyd, "Networked Rights and Networked Harms" (paper presented at the Privacy Law Scholars Conference, Washington, DC, June 5–6, 2014).

3. Morgan Cloud, "Property Is Privacy: Locke and Brandeis in the Twenty-First Century," *Georgetown Law Review* 55, no. 1 (Winter 2018): 37–75.

4. Richard G. Wilkins, "Defining the Reasonable Expectation of Privacy: An Emerging Tripartite Analysis," *Vanderbilt Law Review* 40 (1987): 1077–1129; Neil M. Richards and Woodrow Hartzog, "Taking Trust Seriously in Privacy Law," SSRN, September 3, 2015, https://papers.ssrn.com/abstract=2655719.

5. Alice E. Marwick, "Scandal or Sex Crime? Gendered Privacy and the Celebrity Nude Photo Leaks," *Ethics and Information Technology* 19, no. 3 (2017): 177–91, https://doi.org/10 .1007/s10676-017-9431-7; Alice E. Marwick, Claire Fontaine, and danah boyd, "'Nobody Sees It, Nobody Gets Mad': Social Media, Privacy, and Personal Responsibility among Low-SES Youth," *Social Media & Society* 3, no. 2 (2017), http://journals.sagepub.com/doi/abs/10 .1177/2056305117710455; Eszter Hargittai and Alice E. Marwick, "'What Can I Really Do?': Explaining the Privacy Paradox with Online Apathy," *International Journal of Communication* 10 (2016): 3737–57.

6. Jennifer Shore and Jill Steinman, "Did You Really Agree to That? The Evolution of Facebook's Privacy Policy," *Journal of Technology Science*, August 11, 2015.

7. Michelle Madejski, Maritza Johnson, and Steven M. Bellovin, "A Study of Privacy Settings Errors in an Online Social Network," in *2012 IEEE International Conference on Pervasive Computing and Communications Workshops* (New York: IEEE, 2012), 340–45.

8. Jessa Lingel and Adam Golub, "In Face on Facebook: Brooklyn's Drag Community and Sociotechnical Practices of Online Communication," *Journal of Computer-Mediated Communication* 20, no. 5 (2015): 536–53.

9. Uri Benoliel and Shmuel I. Becher, "The Duty to Read the Unreadable," SSRN, January 11, 2019, https://papers.ssrn.com/abstract=3313837.

10. Aleecia M. McDonald and Lorrie Faith Cranor, "The Cost of Reading Privacy Policies," *I/S: A Journal of Law and Policy for the Information Society* 4, no. 3 (2008): 540–65.

11. Levy and boyd, "Networked Rights and Networked Harms."

12. James Gleick, *The Information: A History, a Theory, a Flood* (New York: Knopf Doubleday, 2011).

13. Davis Foulger, "Models of the Communication Process" (unpublished paper, 2004).

14. Susan Ervin-Tripp, "Context in Language," in *Social Interaction, Social Context, and Language: Essays in Honor of Susan Ervin-Tripp*, edited by Dan Isaac Slobin, Julie Gerhardt, Amy Kyratzis, and Jiansheng Guo (Mahwah, NJ: Lawrence Erlbaum, 1996), 23.

15. Peter Hartley, *Interpersonal Communication* (New York: Routledge, 2002); Alvin F. Poussaint, "A Negro Psychiatrist Explains the Negro Psyche; The Negro Psyche (Cont.): 'Uncle Tomism Actually Shows Inner Rage and Deep Hatred,'" *New York Times*, August 20, 1967, https://www.nytimes.com/1967/08/20/archives/a-negro-psychiatrist-explains-the-negro-psyche-the-negro-psyche.html.

16. Ilana Gershon, *The Breakup 2.0: Disconnecting Over New Media* (Ithaca, NY: Cornell University Press, 2010), 18.

17. Gershon, 18.

18. Daniel D. Martin, "Identity Management of the Dead: Contests in the Construction of Murdered Children," *Symbolic Interaction* 33, no. 1 (2010): 18–40; Alice E. Marwick and Nicole B. Ellison, "'There Isn't Wifi in Heaven!': Negotiating Visibility on Facebook Memorial Pages," *Journal of Broadcasting & Electronic Media* 56, no. 3 (2012): 378–400, https://doi.org/10.1080/08838151.2012.705197.

19. Helen Nissenbaum, *Privacy in Context: Technology, Policy, and the Integrity of Social Life* (Stanford, CA: Stanford University Press, 2010).

20. Irwin Altman, "Privacy Regulation: Culturally Universal or Culturally Specific?," *Journal of Social Issues* 33, no. 3 (1977): 66–84; Altman, *The Environment and Social Behavior: Privacy, Personal Space, Territory, and Crowding* (Monterey, CA: Brooks/Cole, 1975).

21. "Bitch you ain't no Barbie, I see you work at Arby's." Kreayshawn, "Gucci Gucci," 2011.

22. Robert K. Merton, *Social Theory and Social Structure*, enlarged ed. (New York: Free Press, 1968), 42.

23. Merton, 399–400; Ari Ezra Waldman, *Privacy as Trust: Information Privacy for an Information Age* (New York: Cambridge University Press, 2018).

24. Erving Goffman, *The Presentation of Self in Everyday Life* (New York: Doubleday, 1959).

25. Ari Ezra Waldman, "Privacy as Trust: Sharing Personal Information in a Networked World," *University of Miami Law Review* 69 (2014): 601.

26. Daniel J. Solove, *Understanding Privacy* (Cambridge, MA: Harvard University Press, 2008), 8.

27. danah boyd and Alice E. Marwick, "Social Privacy in Networked Publics: Teens' Attitudes, Practices, and Strategies" (paper presented at "A Decade in Internet Time: Symposium

on the Dynamics of the Internet and Society," Oxford, UK, September 2011), SSRN, September 22, 2011, http://papers.ssrn.com/sol3/papers.cfm?abstract_id=1925128.

28. Norman Fairclough and Ruth Wodak, "Critical Discourse Analysis," in *Discourse as Social Interaction*, ed. Teun A. Van Dijk (London: Sage, 1997), 258–84; Michel Foucault, *The Archaeology of Knowledge and the Discourse on Language* (New York: Vintage Books, 1970); Norman Fairclough, *Analysing Discourse: Textual Analysis for Social Research* (New York: Routledge, 2003).

29. Bethany L. Albertson, "Dog-Whistle Politics: Multivocal Communication and Religious Appeals," *Political Behavior* 37, no. 1 (2015): 3–26.

30. boyd and Marwick, "Social Privacy in Networked Publics"; danah boyd, "Networked Privacy," *Surveillance & Society* 10, nos. 3–4 (December 22, 2012): 348–50; Alice E. Marwick and danah boyd, "Networked Privacy: How Teenagers Negotiate Context in Social Media," *New Media & Society* 16, no. 7 (2014): 1051–67.

31. Lenore Manderson et al., "On Secrecy, Disclosure, the Public, and the Private in Anthropology," *Current Anthropology* 56, no. S12 (December 1, 2015): S183–90, https://doi.org/10.1086/683302; Barrington Moore Jr., *Privacy: Studies in Social and Cultural History* (New York: Routledge, 1984).

32. Michel Foucault, *Power/Knowledge: Selected Interviews and Other Writings, 1972–1977* (New York: Vintage, 1980), 98.

33. Kate Manne, *Down Girl: The Logic of Misogyny* (Oxford: Oxford University Press, 2017), 13.

34. An excellent overview of different theories of privacy appears in chapter 4 of Nissenbaum, *Privacy in Context*. See also Waldman, *Privacy as Trust*; Julie Cohen, *Configuring the Networked Self*; Ruth Gavison, "Privacy and the Limits of Law," *Yale Law Journal* 89 (1979): 421–71; Solove, *Understanding Privacy*.

35. Susan Gal, "A Semiotics of the Public/Private Distinction," *Differences: A Journal of Feminist Cultural Studies* 13, no. 1 (2002): 79.

36. Alan F. Westin, *Privacy and Freedom* (New York: Atheneum, 1967), 5.

37. Wendy Hui Kyong Chun, *Updating to Remain the Same: Habitual New Media* (Cambridge, MA: MIT Press, 2016).

38. Levy and boyd, "Networked Rights and Networked Harms."

39. Stanley Wasserman and Katherine Faust explain in their foundational work on social network analysis that thinking in terms of networks emphasizes connections and patterns. Network analysis assumes that the ways in which actors, or nodes, behave is dependent on their relationships (called "ties") and social patterns (or structures). For example, if scientists wanted to use social network analysis to study how two online friends interact, they would try to understand their ties to other network members and the social patterns of their larger

network. It is through social ties that people access resources like information, social capital, jobs, and apartments. Connections to other people are the structure of the network itself; they either create opportunities for people to act or constrain their actions. In other words, network analysis links individual relationships and behavior to larger structural patterns. As Wasserman and Faust put it, "network models conceptualize structure (social, economic, political, and so forth) as lasting patterns of relations among actors." Wasserman and Faust, *Social Network Analysis: Methods and Applications*. Structural Analysis in the Social Sciences (New York: Cambridge University Press, 1994), 4.

40. There are considerable debates in the social network analysis (SNA) literature about the roles of norms, culture, and history in human behavior. Although I use SNA in this section to elucidate the network in networked privacy, I do not believe that mapping relational or even behavioral networks can explain all human behavior. See Mustafa Emirbayer and Jeff Goodwin, "Network Analysis, Culture, and the Problem of Agency," *American Journal of Sociology* 99, no. 6 (1994): 1411–54, https://doi.org/10.1086/230450; Sourabh Singh, "How Should We Study Relational Structure? Critically Comparing the Epistemological Positions of Social Network Analysis and Field Theory," *Sociology* 53, no. 4 (2019): 762–78, https://doi.org/10.1177/0038038518821307.

41. Adam Liptak, "In Ruling on Cellphone Location Data, Supreme Court Makes Statement on Digital Privacy," *New York Times*, June 22, 2018, sec. U.S., https://www.nytimes.com/2018/06/22/us/politics/supreme-court-warrants-cell-phone-privacy.html.

42. Mark S. Granovetter, "The Strength of Weak Ties," *American Journal of Sociology* 78, no. 6 (1973): 1360–80.

43. Henry Jenkins, Sam Ford, and Joshua Green, *Spreadable Media: Creating Value and Meaning in a Networked Culture* (New York: New York University Press, 2013).

44. Shane Goldmacher and Nicholas Fandos, "Ted Cruz's Cancún Trip: Family Texts Detail His Political Blunder," *New York Times*, February 18, 2021, sec. U.S., https://www.nytimes.com/2021/02/18/us/politics/ted-cruz-storm-cancun.html.

45. Anita Gates and Katharine Q. Seelye, "Linda Tripp, Key Figure in Clinton Impeachment, Dies at 70," *New York Times*, April 8, 2020, sec. U.S., https://www.nytimes.com/2020/04/08/us/politics/linda-tripp-dead.html; Roxanne Roberts, "Linda Tripp Wanted to Make History. Instead, It Nearly Destroyed Her," *Washington Post*, April 9, 2020, https://www.washingtonpost.com/lifestyle/linda-tripp-clinton-lewinsky-scandal/2020/04/09/0c3b7d68-7a7b-11ea-a130-df573469f094_story.html.

46. Roberts, "Linda Tripp Wanted to Make History."

47. Kashmir Hill, "How Facebook Figures Out Everyone You've Ever Met," *Gizmodo Australia* (blog), November 11, 2017, https://www.gizmodo.com.au/2017/11/how-facebook-figures-out-everyone-youve-ever-met/; Kurt Wagner, "This Is How Facebook Collects Data

on You Even If You Don't Have an Account," *Vox*, April 20, 2018, https://www.vox.com/2018/4/20/17254312/facebook-shadow-profiles-data-collection-non-users-mark-zuckerberg.

48. Raya is a dating app for "elites" and celebrities. While the app supposedly prevents users from taking screenshots to protect the privacy of its members, profiles of celebrities are frequently leaked online.

49. Indeed, when celebrities *cannot* manage the systems of publicity, it often ends badly. Consider the relentlessness of the paparazzi and its impact on celebrities like Princess Diana and Britney Spears.

50. Pete D'Amato, "Woman Fired over Offensive Photo Says She Can Finally Google Herself," *Daily Mail*, February 23, 2015, https://www.dailymail.co.uk/news/article-2964489/I-really-obsessed-reading-Woman-fired-photo-giving-middle-finger-Arlington-National-Cemetery-says-finally-Google-without-fear.html; Jon Ronson, "'Overnight, Everything I Loved Was Gone': The Internet Shaming of Lindsey Stone," *Guardian*, February 21, 2015, sec. Technology, https://www.theguardian.com/technology/2015/feb/21/internet-shaming-lindsey-stone-jon-ronson.

51. Neetzan Zimmerman, "Happy Now? 'Good Employee' Lindsey Stone Fired over Facebook Photo," *Gawker*, November 22, 2012, http://gawker.com/5962796/happy-now-good-employee-lindsey-stone-fired-over-facebook-photo.

52. CBS Boston, "Women Fired after Facebook Photo at Tomb of Unknowns Goes Viral," November 21, 2012, https://boston.cbslocal.com/2012/11/21/women-fired-after-facebook-photo-at-tomb-of-unknowns-goes-viral/.

53. Linnea Laestadius, "Instagram," in *The SAGE Handbook of Social Media Research Methods*, ed. Luke Sloan and Anabel Quan-Haase (Thousand Oaks, CA: Sage, 2017), 581.

54. Laura Mallonee, "How Photos Fuel the Spread of Fake News," *Wired*, December 21, 2016, https://www.wired.com/2016/12/photos-fuel-spread-fake-news/.

55. Kim-Mai Cutler, "Early Instagram Folks Had Very Deliberate Discussions *not* to Have a Re-Share Feature *because* Images Could Become so Easily Decontextualized," Twitter, September 20, 2018, https://twitter.com/kimmaicutler/status/1042920045146337280.

56. Waldman, *Privacy as Trust*, 5–7.

57. The twelfth tradition of Alcoholics Anonymous is, "Anonymity is the spiritual foundation of all our traditions, ever reminding us to place principles before personalities."

58. Feminist activists and scholars argue that "revenge porn," by focusing on the paradigmatic case of a "vengeful ex-partner," overlooks many other forms of image-based sexual violence and technologically enabled sexual violence more broadly. It presumes that "revenge" is a sole motivator for sharing images nonconsensually, and it conflates taking nude or sexual pictures of oneself with "pornography," rather than a normal sexual experience. See Clare

McGlynn, Erika Rackley, and Ruth Houghton, "Beyond 'Revenge Porn': The Continuum of Image-Based Sexual Abuse," *Feminist Legal Studies* 25, no. 1 (2017): 25–46, https://doi.org/ 10.1007/s10691-017-9343-2; Mary Anne Franks, "Drafting an Effective 'Revenge Porn' Law: A Guide for Legislators," SSRN, August 17, 2015, https://papers.ssrn.com/sol3/papers.cfm ?abstract_id=2468823.

59. Kath Albury et al., *Young People and Sexting in Australia: Ethics, Representation and the Law* (Sydney: ARC Centre for Creative Industries and Innovation / Journalism and Media Research Centre, the University of New South Wales, Australia, 2013).

60. Amy Adele Hasinoff, *Sexting Panic: Rethinking Criminalization, Privacy, and Consent* (Urbana: University of Illinois Press, 2015); Amy Adele Hasinoff and Tamara Shepherd, "Sexting in Context: Privacy Norms and Expectations," *International Journal of Communication* 8 (2014): 2932–55.

61. danah boyd and Kate Crawford, "Critical Questions for Big Data," *Information, Communication & Society* 15, no. 5 (2012): 663, https://doi.org/10.1080/1369118X.2012.678878.

62. Keri L. Heitner, Eric E. Muenks, and Kenneth C. Sherman, "The Rhetoric of Gaydar Research: A Critical Discourse Analysis," *Journal of Psychological Issues in Organizational Culture* 6, no. 3 (2015): 60–69; Carter Jernigan and Behram F. T. Mistree, "Gaydar: Facebook Friendships Expose Sexual Orientation," *First Monday* 14, no. 10 (2009); Ben Light, Peta Mitchell, and Patrik Wikström, "Big Data, Method and the Ethics of Location: A Case Study of a Hookup App for Men Who Have Sex with Men," *Social Media + Society* 4, no. 2 (2018), https://doi.org/10.1177/2056305118768299.

63. Stunningly, Apple step data could be used in criminal cases "for investigative and evidential purposes." Jan Peter van Zandwijk and Abdul Boztas, "The iPhone Health App from a Forensic Perspective: Can Steps and Distances Registered during Walking and Running Be Used as Digital Evidence?," *Digital Investigation* 28 (April 1, 2019): S126–33, https://doi .org/10.1016/j.diin.2019.01.021. For the complications inherent in evaluating the relationship between quantified self-health data and the US insurance market, see Liz McFall, "Personalizing Solidarity? The Role of Self-Tracking in Health Insurance Pricing," *Economy and Society* 48, no. 1 (2019): 52–76.

64. 23andMe has a data-sharing agreement with GlaxoSmithKline. See Denise Roland, "How Drug Companies Are Using Your DNA to Make New Medicine," *Wall Street Journal*, July 22, 2019, sec. Business, https://www.wsj.com/articles/23andme-glaxo-mine-dna-data-in -hunt-for-new-drugs-11563879881.

65. Federal Trade Commission, *Data Brokers: A Call for Transparency and Accountability: A Report of the Federal Trade Commission* (Washington, DC: Federal Trade Commission, May 2014), http://www.ftc.gov/reports/data-brokers-call-transparency-accountability-report

-federal-trade-commission-may-2014; Gary Anthes, "Data Brokers Are Watching You," *Communications of the ACM* 58, no. 1 (2014): 28–30, https://doi.org/10.1145/2686740; Stephanie Clifford and Quentin Hardy, "Attention, Shoppers: Store Is Tracking Your Cell," *New York Times*, July 14, 2013, http://www.nytimes.com/2013/07/15/business/attention-shopper-stores-are-tracking-your-cell.html; Craig M. Dalton and Jim Thatcher, "Inflated Granularity: Spatial 'Big Data' and Geodemographics," *Big Data & Society* 2, no. 2 (2015), https://doi.org/10.1177/2053951715601144; N. Cameron Russell et al., "Transparency and the Marketplace for Student Data," *Virginia Journal of Law & Technology* 22, no. 3 (2019): 107–57.

66. Matthew Crain, "The Limits of Transparency: Data Brokers and Commodification," *New Media & Society*, 20, no. 1 (2018): 88–104. https://doi.org/10.1177/1461444816657096.

67. Crunchbase, "Acxiom," accessed October 27, 2013, http://www.crunchbase.com/company/acxiom#ixzz2iy4tNOK7; Yael Grauer, "What Are 'Data Brokers,' and Why Are They Scooping Up Information about You?," *Motherboard* (blog), *Vice*, March 27, 2018, https://www.vice.com/en/article/bjpx3w/what-are-data-brokers-and-how-to-stop-my-private-data-collection.

68. Kate Knibbs, "Data Brokers Accidentally Gave an Identity Thief Access to 200 Million Consumer Records," *Daily Dot*, March 11, 2014, http://www.dailydot.com/technology/experian-data-brokers-give-thief-data/.

69. Reuters, "Data Brokers Sold Payday Loan Applicants' Information to Scammers: FTC," *NBC News*, August 12, 2015, http://www.nbcnews.com/business/business-news/data-brokers-sold-payday-loan-applicants-information-scammers-ftc-n408606.

70. Lee Fang, "IRS, Department of Homeland Security Contracted Firm That Sells Location Data Harvested from Dating Apps," *The Intercept* (blog), February 18, 2022. https://theintercept.com/2022/02/18/location-data-tracking-irs-dhs-digital-envoy/.

71. Joseph Cox, "How the U.S. Military Buys Location Data from Ordinary Apps," *Vice*, November 16, 2020, https://www.vice.com/en/article/jgqm5x/us-military-location-data-xmode-locate-x.

72. Estefania McCarroll, "Weapons of Mass Deportation: Big Data and Automated Decision-Making Systems in Immigration Law," *Georgetown Immigration Law Journal* 34 (2019): 705–31.

73. Federal Trade Commission, *Data Brokers*.

74. Charles Duhigg, "Bilking the Elderly, With a Corporate Assist," *New York Times*, May 20, 2007, sec. Business, https://www.nytimes.com/2007/05/20/business/20tele.html.

75. Gregory Maus, "How Data Brokers Sell Your Life, and Why It Matters," *The Stack* (blog), August 24, 2015, https://thestack.com/security/2015/08/24/how-corporate-data-brokers-sell-your-life-and-why-you-should-be-concerned/.

76. Crain, "Limits of Transparency"; Mark Andrejevic, *ISpy: Surveillance and Power in the Interactive Era* (Lawrence: University Press of Kansas, 2007).

77. Daniel J. Solove, "Access and Aggregation: Privacy, Public Records, and the Constitution," SSRN, September 24, 2001, https://papers.ssrn.com/abstract=283924.

78. Erika McCallister, Timothy Grance, and Karen A. Scarfone, *Guide to Protecting the Confidentiality of Personally Identifiable Information (PII)*, special publication, Computer Security (Washington, DC: National Institute of Standards and Technology, April 2010), http://csrc.nist.gov/publications/nistpubs/800-122/sp800-122.pdf.

79. Linnet Taylor, Luciano Floridi, and Bart van der Sloot, "Introduction: A New Perspective on Privacy," in *Group Privacy: New Challenges of Data Technologies*, ed. Linnet Taylor, Luciano Floridi, and Bart van der Sloot, Philosophical Studies Series (Cham, Switzerland: Springer, 2017), 1–12, https://doi.org/10.1007/978-3-319-46608-8_1; European Union, Regulation (EU) 2016/679 of the European Parliament and of the Council of 27 April 2016 on the Protection of Natural Persons with Regard to the Processing of Personal Data and on the Free Movement of Such Data, and Repealing Directive 95/46/EC (General Data Protection Regulation), OJ 2016 L 119/1 § (2016).

80. Michael Zimmer, "Addressing Conceptual Gaps in Big Data Research Ethics: An Application of Contextual Integrity," *Social Media + Society* 4, no. 2 (2018), https://doi.org/10.1177/2056305118768300.

81. Alex Hern, "'Anonymous' Browsing Data Can Be Easily Exposed, Researchers Reveal," *Guardian*, August 1, 2017, sec. Technology, https://www.theguardian.com/technology/2017/aug/01/data-browsing-habits-brokers; Yves-Alexandre de Montjoye et al., "Unique in the Shopping Mall: On the Reidentifiability of Credit Card Metadata," *Science* 347, no. 6221 (January 30, 2015): 536–39, https://doi.org/10.1126/science.1256297; Zheng Xiao et al., "Unique on the Road: Re-identification of Vehicular Location-Based Metadata," in *Security and Privacy in Communication Networks: 12th International Conference, SecureComm 2016, Guangzhou, China, October 10–12, 2016, Proceedings*, edited by Robert Deng et al., Lecture Notes of the Institute for Computer Sciences, Social Informatics and Telecommunications Engineering (Cham, Switzerland: Springer, 2017), 496–513.

82. Pre-COVID, obviously. Montjoye et al., "Unique in the Shopping Mall."

83. Natasha Lomas, "Researchers Spotlight the Lie of 'Anonymous' Data," *TechCrunch* (blog), July 24, 2019, http://social.techcrunch.com/2019/07/24/researchers-spotlight-the-lie-of-anonymous-data/; Luc Rocher, Julien M. Hendrickx, and Yves-Alexandre de Montjoye, "Estimating the Success of Re-identifications in Incomplete Datasets Using Generative Models," *Nature Communications* 10, no. 1 (2019): 1–9, https://doi.org/10.1038/s41467-019-10933-3.

84. Adam Tanner, *Our Bodies, Our Data: How Companies Make Billions Selling Our Medical Records* (Boston: Beacon, 2017).

85. Antonio Regalado, "More than 26 Million People Have Taken an At-Home Ancestry Test," *MIT Technology Review*, February 11, 2019, https://www.technologyreview.com/s/612880/more-than-26-million-people-have-taken-an-at-home-ancestry-test/.

86. Heather Murphy, "Most White Americans' DNA Can Be Identified Through Genealogy Databases," *New York Times*, October 11, 2018, sec. Science, https://www.nytimes.com/2018/10/11/science/science-genetic-genealogy-study.html; Yaniv Erlich et al., "Identity Inference of Genomic Data Using Long-Range Familial Searches," *Science* 362, no. 6415 (November 9, 2018): 690–94, https://doi.org/10.1126/science.aau4832.

87. Levy and boyd, "Networked Rights and Networked Harms."

88. Sarah Zhang, "When a DNA Test Shatters Your Identity," *Atlantic*, July 17, 2018, https://www.theatlantic.com/science/archive/2018/07/dna-test-misattributed-paternity/562928/.

89. Leah Larkin, "Frequently Asked Questions (FAQ)," *The DNA Geek* (blog), November 11, 2016, https://thednageek.com/faq/.

90. Sara Debus-Sherrill and Michael B. Field, "Familial DNA Searching: An Emerging Forensic Investigative Tool," *Science & Justice* 59, no. 1 (2019): 20–28, https://doi.org/10.1016/j.scijus.2018.07.006.

91. Ari Shapiro, "Police Use DNA to Track Suspects through Family," *All Things Considered*, NPR, December 12, 2007, https://www.npr.org/templates/story/story.php?storyId=17130501.

92. As of August 2019, GEDMatch has required people to "opt in" to law enforcement searches. FamilyTree.org has come under intense criticism for allowing the FBI to use its databases and has adopted an "opt out" provision. Amy Dockser Marcus, "Customers Handed Over Their DNA. The Company Let the FBI Take a Look," *Wall Street Journal*, August 22, 2019, sec. US, https://www.wsj.com/articles/customers-handed-over-their-dna-the-company-let-the-fbi-take-a-look-11566491162.

93. Avi Selk, "The Ingenious and 'Dystopian' DNA Technique Police Used to Hunt the 'Golden State Killer' Suspect," *Washington Post*, April 28, 2018, sec. True Crime, https://www.washingtonpost.com/news/true-crime/wp/2018/04/27/golden-state-killer-dna-website-gedmatch-was-used-to-identify-joseph-deangelo-as-suspect-police-say/; Brendan I. Koerner, "Your Relative's DNA Could Turn You into a Suspect," *Wired*, October 13, 2015, https://www.wired.com/2015/10/familial-dna-evidence-turns-innocent-people-into-crime-suspects/.

94. Siva Vaidhyanathan, *Antisocial Media: How Facebook Disconnects Us and Undermines Democracy* (New York: Oxford University Press, 2018), 61.

95. Kashmir Hill, "'People You May Know': A Controversial Facebook Feature's 10-Year History," *Gizmodo*, August 8, 2018, https://gizmodo.com/people-you-may-know-a-controversial-facebook-features-1827981959.

96. Mary Madden et al., "Privacy, Poverty, and Big Data: A Matrix of Vulnerabilities for Poor Americans," *Washington University Law Review* 95, no. 1 (2017): 53–125.

97. Madden et al.; Cathy O'Neil, "How Algorithms Rule Our Working Lives," *Guardian*, September 1, 2016, sec. Science, https://www.theguardian.com/science/2016/sep/01/how-algorithms-rule-our-working-lives.

98. Bernard Harcourt, *Against Prediction* (Chicago: University of Chicago Press, 2007); Kate Crawford and Jason Schultz, "Big Data and Due Process: Toward a Framework to Redress Predictive Privacy Harms," *Boston College Law Review* 55 (2014): 93–128.

99. Richard Hartley-Parkinson, "'I'm Going to Destroy America and Dig Up Marilyn Monroe': British Pair Arrested in U.S. on Terror Charges over Twitter Jokes," *Mail Online*, January 30, 2012, https://www.dailymail.co.uk/news/article-2093796/Emily-Bunting-Leigh-Van-Bryan-UK-tourists-arrested-destroy-America-Twitter-jokes.html; J. David Goodman, "Travelers Say They Were Denied Entry to U.S. for Twitter Jokes," *The Lede* (blog), *New York Times*, January 30, 2012, https://thelede.blogs.nytimes.com/2012/01/30/travelers-say-they-were-denied-entry-to-u-s-for-twitter-jokes/.

100. Faiza Patel et al., *Social Media Monitoring: How the Department of Homeland Security Uses Digital Data in the Name of National Security* (New York: Brennan Center for Justice at New York University School of Law, May 22, 2019), https://www.brennancenter.org/sites/default/files/publications/2019_DHS-SocialMediaMonitoring_FINAL.pdf.

101. Ron Nixon, "U.S. to Collect Social Media Data on All Immigrants Entering Country," *New York Times*, September 28, 2017, sec. U.S., https://www.nytimes.com/2017/09/28/us/politics/immigrants-social-media-trump.html; Sandra E. Garcia, "U.S. Requiring Social Media Information from Visa Applicants," *New York Times*, June 2, 2019, sec. U.S., https://www.nytimes.com/2019/06/02/us/us-visa-application-social-media.html.

102. Rachel Levinson-Waldman, "How ICE and Other DHS Agencies Mine Social Media in the Name of National Security," *Brennan Center for Justice Blog*, June 3, 2019, https://www.brennancenter.org/blog/how-ice-and-other-dhs-agencies-mine-social-media-name-national-security.

103. Elizabeth Stoycheff et al., "Privacy and the Panopticon: Online Mass Surveillance's Deterrence and Chilling Effects," *New Media & Society* 21, no. 3 (2019): 602–19, https://doi.org/10.1177/1461444818801317.

104. Chun, *Updating to Remain the Same*, 104.

105. Sarah E. Igo, *The Known Citizen: A History of Privacy in Modern America* (Cambridge, MA: Harvard University Press, 2018), 8.

3. Privacy Work

1. For example, see Cory Doctorow, "Why Is It so Hard to Convince People to Care about Privacy?," *Guardian*, October 2, 2015, sec. Technology, https://www.theguardian.com/technology/2015/oct/02/why-is-it-so-hard-to-convince-people-to-care-about-privacy; Matthew Hennessey, "Why Millennials Will Learn Nothing from Facebook's Privacy Crisis," *New York Post*, April 7, 2018, https://nypost.com/2018/04/07/why-millennials-will-learn -nothing-from-facebooks-privacy-crisis/; Greg Satell, "Let's Face It, We Don't Really Care about Privacy," *Forbes*, December 1, 2014, https://www.forbes.com/sites/gregsatell/2014/12/ 01/lets-face-it-we-dont-really-care-about-privacy/.

2. Nor does that of a lot of other qualitative scholars cited in this chapter.

3. Alan F. Westin, *Privacy and Freedom* (New York: Atheneum, 1967). For an excellent critique of Westin's categories, see Nora A. Draper, "From Privacy Pragmatist to Privacy Resigned: Challenging Narratives of Rational Choice in Digital Privacy Debates," *Policy & Internet*, June 1, 2017, https://doi.org/10.1002/poi3.142.

4. Nina Gerber, Paul Gerber, and Melanie Volkamer, "Explaining the Privacy Paradox: A Systematic Review of Literature Investigating Privacy Attitude and Behavior," *Computers & Security* 77 (August 1, 2018): 226–61, https://doi.org/10.1016/j.cose.2018.04.002; Spyros Kokolakis, "Privacy Attitudes and Privacy Behaviour: A Review of Current Research on the Privacy Paradox Phenomenon," *Computers & Security* 64 (January 1, 2017): 122–34, https:// doi.org/10.1016/j.cose.2015.07.002.

5. Alessandro Acquisti and Jens Grossklags, "Privacy and Rationality in Individual Decision Making," *IEEE Security & Privacy* 3, no. 1 (2005): 26–33.

6. Rani Molla, "People Say They Care about Privacy but They Continue to Buy Devices That Can Spy on Them," *Vox*, May 13, 2019, https://www.vox.com/recode/2019/5/ 13/18547235/trust-smart-devices-privacy-security; Claire Cain Miller, "Americans Say They Want Privacy, but Act as If They Don't," *The Upshot* (blog), *New York Times*, November 12, 2014, https://www.nytimes.com/2014/11/13/upshot/americans-say-they-want-privacy-but-act -as-if-they-dont.html.

7. Antonio Casilli, "Four Theses on Digital Mass Surveillance and the Negotiation of Privacy" (paper presented at the eighth annual Privacy Law Scholars Conference, Berkeley Center for Law & Technology, Berkeley, CA, June 4–5, 2015), https://halshs.archives-ouvertes.fr/ halshs-01147832; Anna Lauren Hoffmann, "Reckoning with a Decade of Breaking Things," *Model View Culture*, July 30, 2014, https://modelviewculture.com/pieces/reckoning-with-a -decade-of-breaking-things.

8. Joseph Turow, Michael Hennessy, and Nora Draper, *The Tradeoff Fallacy: How Marketers Are Misrepresenting American Consumers and Opening Them Up to Exploitation* (Philadelphia: Annenberg School for Communication, University of Pennsylvania, 2015), https://www.asc.upenn.edu/sites/default/files/TradeoffFallacy_1.pdf; Eszter Hargittai and Alice E. Marwick, "'What Can I Really Do?': Explaining the Privacy Paradox with Online Apathy," *International Journal of Communication* 10 (2016): 3737–57.

9. Evert Van den Broeck, Karolien Poels, and Michel Walrave, "Older and Wiser? Facebook Use, Privacy Concern, and Privacy Protection in the Life Stages of Emerging, Young, and Middle Adulthood," *Social Media + Society* 1, no. 2 (2015), https://doi.org/10.1177/2056305115616149.

10. Liz Kelly, "The Continuum of Sexual Violence," in *Women, Violence and Social Control*, edited by Jalna Hamner and Mary Maynard (Cham, Switzerland: Springer, 1987), 46–60.

11. Liz Kelly, foreword to *Men's Intrusion, Women's Embodiment: A Critical Analysis of Street Harassment*, by Fiona Vera-Gray (London: Routledge, 2016), xi.

12. For the purposes of this book, I choose to use "work" to situate myself within a critical tradition of feminist sociology. There is a great deal of scholarship about the difference between "work" and "labor." These terms imply different things in fields as disparate as sociology, economics, computer-supported cooperative work, social movement organizing, and Marxist theory. Of course, this distinction is not present in many non-English languages. I am not invested in the theoretical similarities or differences between "work" and "labor" given how many people use the terms interchangeably. Arlie Russell Hochschild, "Emotion Work, Feeling Rules, and Social Structure," *American Journal of Sociology* 85, no. 3 (1979): 551–75; Hochschild, *The Managed Heart* (Berkeley: University of California Press, 1983); Arlene Kaplan Daniels, "Invisible Work," *Social Problems* 34, no. 5 (1987): 403–15; Judith Rollins, *Between Women: Domestics and Their Employers* (Philadelphia: Temple University Press, 1985).

13. Fiona Vera-Gray, *Men's Intrusion, Women's Embodiment: A Critical Analysis of Street Harassment* (New York: Routledge, 2016); Gray, *The Right Amount of Panic: How Women Trade Freedom for Safety* (Bristol, UK: Policy, 2018).

14. danah boyd, *It's Complicated: The Social Lives of Networked Teens* (New Haven, CT: Yale University Press, 2014).

15. Exceptions include boyd, *It's Complicated*; Jacqueline Ryan Vickery, *Worried about the Wrong Things: Youth, Risk, and Opportunity in the Digital World*, John D. and Catherine T. MacArthur Foundation Series on Digital Media and Learning (Cambridge, MA: MIT Press, 2018); Niki Fritz and Amy Gonzales, "Not the Normal Trans Story: Negotiating Trans Narratives While Crowdfunding at the Margins," *International Journal of Communication* 12 (2018): 1189–1208; Janaki Srinivasan et al., "Privacy at the Margins | The Poverty of Privacy:

Understanding Privacy Trade-Offs from Identity Infrastructure Users in India," *International Journal of Communication* 12 (2018): 1228–47; Alyson Leigh Young and Anabel Quan-Haase, "Privacy Protection Strategies on Facebook," *Information, Communication & Society* 16, no. 4 (2013): 479–500, https://doi.org/10.1080/1369118X.2013.777757; Stefanie Duguay, "'He Has a Way Gayer Facebook than I Do': Investigating Sexual Identity Disclosure and Context Collapse on a Social Networking Site," *New Media & Society* 18, no. 6 (2016): 891–907, https://doi.org/10.1177/1461444814549930.

16. Eden Litt, "Knock, Knock. Who's There? The Imagined Audience," *Journal of Broadcasting & Electronic Media* 56, no. 3 (2012): 330–45; Jessica Vitak, "The Impact of Context Collapse and Privacy on Social Network Site Disclosures," *Journal of Broadcasting & Electronic Media* 56, no. 4 (2012): 451–70; Airi Lampinen et al., "We're in It Together: Interpersonal Management of Disclosure in Social Network Services," in *Proceedings of the SIGCHI Conference on Human Factors in Computing Systems* (New York: ACM, 2011), 3217–26, http://dl.acm.org/citation.cfm?id=1979420.

17. This is consistent with other research that finds that people will work around defriending or blocking, as it is seen as a nuclear option with potentially damaging social consequences. Jessica Vitak and Jinyoung Kim, "'You Can't Block People Offline': Examining How Facebook's Affordances Shape the Disclosure Process," in *Proceedings of the 17th ACM Conference on Computer Supported Cooperative Work & Social Computing* (New York: ACM, 2014), 461–74, https://doi.org/10.1145/2531602.2531672; David Fono and Kate Raynes-Goldie, "Hyperfriendship and Beyond: Friendship and Social Norms on LiveJournal," in *Internet Research Annual: Selected Papers from the Association of Internet Researchers Conference*, vol. 4, edited by Mia Consalvo and Caroline Haythornthwaite (New York: Peter Lang, 2005), 91–104.

18. Eszter Hargittai, "Digital Na(t)ives? Variation in Internet Skills and Uses among Members of the 'Net Generation,'" *Sociological Inquiry* 80, no. 1 (2010): 92–113; Eszter Hargittai, Anne Marie Piper, and Meredith Ringel Morris, "From Internet Access to Internet Skills: Digital Inequality among Older Adults," *Universal Access in the Information Society* 18 (2019): 881–90. https://doi.org/10.1007/s10209-018-0617-5.

19. Elissa M. Redmiles and Eszter Hargittai, "New Phone, Who Dis? Modeling Millennials' Backup Behavior," *ACM Transactions on the Web* 13, no. 1 (2018): article 4, https://doi.org/10.1145/3208105.

20. Hargittai and Marwick, "'What Can I Really Do?'"

21. Sam Nichols, "Your Phone Is Listening and It's Not Paranoia," *Vice*, June 4, 2018, https://www.vice.com/en_uk/article/wjbzzy/your-phone-is-listening-and-its-not-paranoia; Kaitlyn Tiffany, "The Perennial Debate about Whether Your Phone Is Secretly Listening

to You, Explained," *Vox*, December 28, 2018, https://www.vox.com/the-goods/2018/12/28/18158968/facebook-microphone-tapping-recording-instagram-ads.

22. Helen Nissenbaum, *Privacy in Context: Technology, Policy, and the Integrity of Social Life* (Stanford, CA: Stanford University Press, 2010).

23. Alice E. Marwick and danah boyd, "I Tweet Honestly, I Tweet Passionately: Twitter Users, Context Collapse, and the Imagined Audience," *New Media & Society* 13, no. 1 (2011): 114–33; Vitak, "Impact of Context Collapse and Privacy."

24. Woodrow Hartzog and Frederic Stutzman, "Obscurity by Design," *Washington Law Review* 88 (2013): 385–418; Vitak, "Impact of Context Collapse and Privacy"; Litt, "Knock, Knock. Who's There?"

25. Lukasz Piwek and Adam Joinson, "'What Do They Snapchat About?': Patterns of Use in Time-Limited Instant Messaging Service," *Computers in Human Behavior* 54 (January 1, 2016): 358–67, https://doi.org/10.1016/j.chb.2015.08.026; Saleem Alhabash and Mengyan Ma, "A Tale of Four Platforms: Motivations and Uses of Facebook, Twitter, Instagram, and Snapchat among College Students?," *Social Media + Society* 3, no. 1 (2017), https://doi.org/10.1177/2056305117691544.

26. Ana Swanson, Mike Isaac, and Paul Mozur, "Trump Targets WeChat and TikTok, in Sharp Escalation with China," *New York Times*, August 7, 2020, sec. Technology, https://www.nytimes.com/2020/08/06/technology/trump-wechat-tiktok-china.html.

27. Caroline Haythornthwaite, "Exploring Multiplexity: Social Network Structures in a Computer-Supported Distance Learning Class," *The Information Society* 17, no. 3 (2001): 211–26.

28. Ilana Gershon, *The Breakup 2.0: Disconnecting Over New Media* (Ithaca, NY: Cornell University Press, 2010).

29. Hartzog and Stutzman, "Obscurity by Design"; Woodrow Hartzog and Frederic D. Stutzman, "The Case for Online Obscurity," SSRN, February 23, 2012, https://papers.ssrn.com/abstract=1597745.

30. Alice E. Marwick, "Scandal or Sex Crime? Gendered Privacy and the Celebrity Nude Photo Leaks," *Ethics and Information Technology* 19, no. 3 (2017): 177–91, https://doi.org/10.1007/s10676-017-9431-7.

31. danah boyd, "Why Youth ♥ Social Network Sites: The Role of Networked Publics," in *Youth, Identity and Digital Media*, ed. David Buckingham (Cambridge, MA: MIT Press, 2007), 119–42.

32. Sofia Dewar et al., "Finsta: Creating 'Fake' Spaces for Authentic Performance," in *Extended Abstracts of the 2019 CHI Conference on Human Factors in Computing Systems* (New York: ACM, 2019), LBW1214.

33. Egle Oolo and Andraa Siibak, "Performing for One's Imagined Audience: Social Steganography and Other Privacy Strategies of Estonian Teens on Networked Publics," *Cyberpsychology: Journal of Psychosocial Research on Cyberspace* 7, no. 1 (2013): article 7; boyd, *It's Complicated*; danah boyd and Alice E. Marwick, "Social Privacy in Networked Publics: Teens' Attitudes, Practices, and Strategies" (paper presented at "A Decade in Internet Time: Symposium on the Dynamics of the Internet and Society," Oxford, UK, September 2011), SSRN, September 22, 2011, http://papers.ssrn.com/sol3/papers.cfm?abstract _id=1925128.

34. Alice E. Marwick and danah boyd, "'It's Just Drama': Teen Perspectives on Conflict and Aggression in a Networked Era," *Journal of Youth Studies* 17, no. 9 (2014): 1187–1204, https://doi.org/10.1080/13676261.2014.901493.

35. Sauvik Das and Adam Kramer, "Self-Censorship on Facebook," in *Proceedings of the Seventh International AAAI Conference on Weblogs and Social Media* (Cambridge, MA: AAAI Press, 2013), 120–27, https://ojs.aaai.org/index.php/ICWSM/article/view/14412/14261; Manya Sleeper et al., "The Post That Wasn't: Exploring Self-Censorship on Facebook," in *Proceedings of the 2013 Conference on Computer Supported Cooperative Work* (New York: ACM, 2013), 793–802; Kjerstin Thorson, "Facing an Uncertain Reception: Young Citizens and Political Interaction on Facebook," *Information, Communication & Society* 17, no. 2 (2014): 203–16.

36. Bernie Hogan, "The Presentation of Self in the Age of Social Media: Distinguishing Performances and Exhibitions Online," *Bulletin of Science, Technology & Society* 30, no. 6 (2010): 377–86.

37. Mikaela Pitcan, Alice E. Marwick, and danah boyd, "Performing a Vanilla Self: Respectability Politics, Social Class, and the Digital World," *Journal of Computer-Mediated Communication* 23, no. 3 (2018): 163–79.

38. John K. Wilson, *The Myth of Political Correctness: The Conservative Attack on Higher Education* (Durham, NC: Duke University Press, 1995); Norman Fairclough, "'Political Correctness': The Politics of Culture and Language," *Discourse & Society* 14, no. 1 (2003): 17–28, https://doi.org/10.1177/0957926503014001927.

39. "Karma" refers to Reddit's reputation system. A high karma score is required by some subreddits to post.

40. Hargittai and Marwick, "'What Can I Really Do?'"

41. Sandra Petronio, *Boundaries of Privacy: Dialectics of Disclosure* (Albany: SUNY Press, 2002).

42. Jonathan Bendor and Piotr Swistak, "The Evolution of Norms," *American Journal of Sociology* 106, no. 6 (2001): 1493–1545.

43. I have had many conversations with University of North Carolina student athletes about this. They are required to friend their coaches on social media and are even told they will be kicked off the team if they are found to have a finsta. Athletes are explicitly told to take down any pictures that the coaches think are inappropriate. These include outfits that are deemed too risqué (typically swimwear for women or shirts with a logo of a beer company), holding cups (even if they are twenty-one or if the cup has a nonalcoholic beverage in it), etc. At the beginning of the school year, many teams hold a meeting where they dig up embarrassing social media posts from first-year students and display them to the entire team, showing them how easy it is to be judged based on past posts. I could write an entire paper on the treatment of Division 1 athletes by their schools, but suffice to say that they are *not* given privacy on social media.

44. boyd and Marwick, "Social Privacy in Networked Publics."

45. Patricia Boling, *Privacy and the Politics of Intimate Life* (Ithaca, NY: Cornell University Press, 1996).

46. Nissenbaum, *Privacy in Context*, 138–39.

47. Anna Kasunic and Geoff Kaufman, "'At Least the Pizzas You Make Are Hot': Norms, Values, and Abrasive Humor on the Subreddit r/RoastMe," in *Twelfth International AAAI Conference on Web and Social Media* (Palo Alto, CA: AAAI Press, 2018), 161–70.

48. Solon Barocas and Karen Levy, "Privacy Dependencies," SSRN, September 3, 2019, https://papers.ssrn.com/abstract=3447384.

49. A "deadname" is the name a trans person was assigned at birth. Many trans people do not disclose this name to others and find the use of it to be hurtful. See Oliver L. Haimson et al., "Digital Footprints and Changing Networks during Online Identity Transitions," in *Proceedings of the 2016 CHI Conference on Human Factors in Computing Systems* (New York: ACM, 2016), 2895–2907, https://doi.org/10.1145/2858036.2858136.

50. Susan Leigh Star and Anselm Strauss, "Layers of Silence, Arenas of Voice: The Ecology of Visible and Invisible Work," *Computer Supported Cooperative Work (CSCW)* 8, no. 1 (1999): 9–30, https://doi.org/10.1023/A:1008651105359.

51. Marjorie L. DeVault, "Mapping Invisible Work: Conceptual Tools for Social Justice Projects," *Sociological Forum* 29, no. 4 (2014): 775–90, https://doi.org/10.1111/socf.12119.

52. Daniels, "Invisible Work."

53. Sustaining relationships with friends and family, for example, involves mundane activities like sending thank-you notes, attending birthday parties, "liking" social media posts, and checking up on people via phone or text. Managing a household requires keeping track of dozens of subtasks and appointments. These types of work, which are almost exclusively done by women, are framed in the popular imagination not as labor but as something en-

tirely outside the realm of money and commerce. They are seen as outgrowths of women's inherently caretaking nature. Lana F. Rakow, *Gender on the Line: Women, the Telephone, and Community Life* (Urbana: University of Illinois Press, 1992); André J. Szameitat et al., "'Women Are Better than Men'—Public Beliefs on Gender Differences and Other Aspects in Multitasking," *PloS One* 10, no. 10 (2015): e0140371.

54. The term "intersectionality" was coined by the Black feminist legal theorist Kimberlé Crenshaw, who developed it in the context of an employment discrimination case in which an employer claimed that it did not discriminate against Black women because it hired both Black men and white women. See Kimberlé Crenshaw, "Demarginalizing the Intersection of Race and Sex: A Black Feminist Critique of Antidiscrimination Doctrine, Feminist Theory and Antiracist Politics," *University of Chicago Legal Forum* 1989, no. 1 (1989): 139–67. For intersectional approaches to invisible labor, see Urvashi Soni-Sinha and Charlotte A. B. Yates, "'Dirty Work?': Gender, Race and the Union in Industrial Cleaning," *Gender, Work & Organization* 20, no. 6 (2013): 737–51, https://doi.org/10.1111/gwao.12006; Courtney L. McCluney and Verónica Caridad Rabelo, "Conditions of Visibility: An Intersectional Examination of Black Women's Belongingness and Distinctiveness at Work," in "Managing Visibility and Invisibility in the Workplace," special issue, *Journal of Vocational Behavior* 113 (August 1, 2019): 143–52, https://doi.org/10.1016/j.jvb.2018.09.008.

55. Rollins, *Between Women*, 162.

56. I was fortunate enough to study under Dr. Rollins at Wellesley College, where she is Professor Emeritus.

57. Susan Freiwald, "First Principles of Communications Privacy," *Stanford Technology Law Review* 2007 (2007): 3–20.

58. Alison Wakefield and Jenny Fleming, "Responsibilization," in *The Sage Dictionary of Policing*, edited by Alison Wakefield and Jenny Fleming (London: Sage, 2009), 277–78, https://doi.org/10.4135/9781446269053.

59. Karen Renaud et al., "Is the Responsibilization of the Cyber Security Risk Reasonable and Judicious?," *Computers & Security* 78 (September 1, 2018): 198–211, https://doi.org/10.1016/j.cose.2018.06.006; Ronen Shamir, "The Age of Responsibilization: On Market-Embedded Morality," *Economy and Society* 37, no. 1 (2008): 1–19, https://doi.org/10.1080/03085140701760833.

60. Thank you to Scott Shapiro at the 2020 Privacy Law Scholars Conference for this helpful frame.

61. Debbie Walkowski, "What Is the CIA Triad?," F5 Labs, July 9, 2019, https://www.f5.com/labs/articles/education/what-is-the-cia-triad.

62. James G. March and Zur Shapira, "Managerial Perspectives on Risk and Risk Taking," *Management Science* 33, no. 11 (1987): 1404–18.

63. Renaud et al., "Is the Responsibilization of the Cyber Security Risk Reasonable and Judicious?"

64. Matt Goerzen, Elizabeth Anne Watkins, and Gabrielle Lim, "Entanglements and Exploits: Sociotechnical Security as an Analytic Framework," in *9th USENIX Workshop on Free and Open Communications on the Internet (FOCI 19)* (Santa Clara, CA: USENIX Association, 2019), 6–7, https://www.usenix.org/conference/foci19/presentation/goerzen.

65. Joy Buolamwini and Timnit Gebru, "Gender Shades: Intersectional Accuracy Disparities in Commercial Gender Classification," in *PLMR: Conference on Fairness, Accountability and Transparency* 81 (2018): 77–91; Ruha Benjamin, *Race after Technology: Abolitionist Tools for the New Jim Code* (New York: Wiley, 2019).

66. Richard Van Noorden, "The Ethical Questions That Haunt Facial-Recognition Research," *Nature* 587, no. 7834 (November 18, 2020): 354–58, https://doi.org/10.1038/d41586-020-03187-3.

67. Inioluwa Deborah Raji and Genevieve Fried, "About Face: A Survey of Facial Recognition Evaluation" (paper presented at AAAI 2020 Workshop on AI Evaluation, February 1, 2021), http://arxiv.org/abs/2102.00813.

68. Noah Kelley, "DIY Feminist Cybersecurity," Hack*Blossom, 2016, https://hackblossom.org/cybersecurity/.

69. Anique Hommels, Jessica Mesman, and Wiebe E. Bijker, "Studying Vulnerability in Technological Cultures," in *Vulnerability in Technological Cultures: New Directions in Research and Governance*, edited by Anique Hommels, Jessica Mesman, and Wiebe E. Bijker (Cambridge, MA: The MIT Press, 2014), 1–25, https://catalog.lib.unc.edu/catalog/UNCb7846772.

70. Oliver L. Haimson and Anna Lauren Hoffmann, "Constructing and Enforcing 'Authentic' Identity Online: Facebook, Real Names, and Non-normative Identities," *First Monday*, June 10, 2016, https://doi.org/10.5210/fm.v21i6.6791.

71. Facebook, "What Types of ID Does Facebook Accept?," Facebook Help Center, 2021, https://www.facebook.com/help/159096464162185?helpref=faq_content.

72. Amanda Holpuch, "Facebook Still Suspending Native Americans over 'Real Name' Policy," *Guardian*, February 16, 2015, http://www.theguardian.com/technology/2015/feb/16/facebook-real-name-policy-suspends-native-americans; "Man Wins Facebook Battle over 'Fake' Gaelic Name," *Scotsman*, February 15, 2015, https://www.scotsman.com/news/man-wins-facebook-battle-over-fake-gaelic-name-1511563.

73. Haimson and Hoffmann, "Constructing and Enforcing 'Authentic' Identity Online"; Jessa Lingel and Adam Golub, "In Face on Facebook: Brooklyn's Drag Community and Sociotechnical Practices of Online Communication," *Journal of Computer-Mediated Communication* 20, no. 5 (2015): 536–53.

74. Taylor Lyles, "Facebook Will Start Verifying the Identities of Accounts That Keep Going Viral," *The Verge*, May 28, 2020, https://www.theverge.com/2020/5/28/21273784/facebook-id-verification-suspicious-accounts-viral-misinformation.

75. I was 80 percent finished with this chapter when I found a paper by Julia Slupska, who argues for a feminist approach to cybersecurity that centers harms to *people* and further that cybersecurity ignores threat models that disproportionately affect women, such as intimate partner violence. Slupska, "Safe at Home: Towards a Feminist Critique of Cybersecurity," SSRN, May 1, 2019, https://papers.ssrn.com/abstract=3429851.

76. Andy Greenberg, "Hacker Eva Galperin Has a Plan to Eradicate Stalkerware," *Wired*, March 4, 2019, https://www.wired.com/story/eva-galperin-stalkerware-kaspersky-antivirus/.

4. Gendered Privacy

1. Shana identifies as nonbinary but uses she/her pronouns.

2. "Roofies" are a slang term for "Rohypnol," a benzodiazepine often associated with drug-facilitated sexual assault. If taken with alcohol, Rohypnol induces amnesia and decreases inhibition.

3. This is changing for the better, but it is still not something most people think much about. And it differs a lot by discipline.

4. This is the code of conduct template, based on those created by the Ada Initiative and JSConf 2012: "Our conference is dedicated to providing a harassment-free conference experience for everyone, regardless of gender, gender identity and expression, age, sexual orientation, disability, physical appearance, body size, race, ethnicity, religion (or lack thereof), or technology choices. We do not tolerate harassment of conference participants in any form. Sexual language and imagery is not appropriate for any conference venue, including talks, workshops, parties, Twitter and other online media. Conference participants violating these rules may be sanctioned or expelled from the conference without a refund at the discretion of the conference organisers."

5. She showed me screenshots. Sample comment: "retarded e girls bitching about illwill again. They belong in the kitchen, not at an infosec conference."

6. Of course, attracting and maintaining such an audience is unlikely, and the ability to do so is a rarified skill.

7. Whitney Phillips, *This Is Why We Can't Have Nice Things: Mapping the Relationship between Online Trolling and Mainstream Culture* (Cambridge, MA: MIT Press, 2015); Crystal Abidin, "Visibility Labour: Engaging with Influencers' Fashion Brands and #OOTD Advertorial Campaigns on Instagram," *Media International Australia* 161, no. 1 (2016): 86–100;

Alice E. Marwick, *Status Update: Celebrity, Publicity, and Branding in the Social Media Age* (New Haven, CT: Yale University Press, 2013).

8. Alice E. Marwick, "The Public Domain: Social Surveillance in Everyday Life," *Surveillance & Society* 9, no. 4 (2012), http://library.queensu.ca/ojs/index.php/surveillance-and -society/article/view/pub_dom.

9. This is also a good example of context collapse and of how privacy is networked, given that information spread from Romney to the bartender to *Mother Jones*. See Chris Cillizza, "Why Mitt Romney's '47 Percent' Comment Was So Bad," *Washington Post*, March 4, 2013, https://www.washingtonpost.com/news/the-fix/wp/2013/03/04/why-mitt-romneys-47 -percent-comment-was-so-bad/; Steve Mullis, "Leaked Video Shows Romney Discussing 'Dependent' Voters," *NPR.org*, September 17, 2012, https://www.npr.org/sections/itsallpolitics/ 2012/09/17/161313644/leaked-video-purports-to-show-romney-discuss-dependent-voters.

10. Daniel Trottier, "Scandal Mining: Political Nobodies and Remediated Visibility," *Media, Culture & Society* 40, no. 6 (2018): 893–908, https://doi.org/10.1177/0163443717734408.

11. Samantha Henig, "The Tale of Dog Poop Girl Is Not So Funny After All," *Columbia Journalism Review*, July 7, 2005, https://www.cjr.org/behind_the_news/the_tale_of_dog _poop_girl_is_n.php.

12. Rachel Monroe, "From Pickup Artist to Pariah," *The Cut*, January 20, 2016, http:// www.thecut.com/2016/01/jared-rutledge-pickup-artist-c-v-r.html.

13. Sarah Banet-Weiser and Kate M. Miltner, "#MasculinitySoFragile: Culture, Structure, and Networked Misogyny," *Feminist Media Studies* 16, no. 1 (2016): 171–74; Danielle Citron, *Hate Crimes in Cyberspace* (Cambridge, MA: Harvard University Press, 2014); Emilee Eikren and Mary Ingram-Waters, "Dismantling 'You Get What You Deserve': Toward a Feminist Sociology of Revenge Porn," *Ada: A Journal of Gender, New Media, and Technology*, no. 10 (2016), http://adanewmedia.org/2016/10/issue10-eikren-ingramwaters/; Nicola Henry and Anastasia Powell, "Embodied Harms: Gender, Shame, and Technology-Facilitated Sexual Violence," *Violence against Women* 21, no. 6 (2015): 758–79, https://doi.org/10.1177/ 1077801215576581; Emma A. Jane, "'Your a Ugly, Whorish, Slut' Understanding E-Bile," *Feminist Media Studies* 14, no. 4 (2014): 531–46; Karla Mantilla, "Gendertrolling: Misogyny Adapts to New Media," *Feminist Studies* 39, no. 2 (2013): 563–70, https://doi.org/10.2307/ 23719068; Clare McGlynn, Erika Rackley, and Ruth Houghton, "Beyond 'Revenge Porn': The Continuum of Image-Based Sexual Abuse," *Feminist Legal Studies* 25, no. 1 (2017): 25–46, https://doi.org/10.1007/s10691-017-9343-2.

14. Amanda Lenhart et al., *Online Harassment, Digital Abuse, and Cyberstalking in America* (New York: Data & Society Research Institute, November 21, 2016); Alana Barton and Hannah Storm, *Violence and Harassment against Women in the News Media: A Global Picture*

(Washington, DC: International Women's Media Foundation, 2014), http://www.iwmf.org/ our-research/journalist-safety/violence-and-harassment-against-women-in-the-news-media -a-global-picture/; Mona Lena Krook, "Violence against Women in Politics," *Journal of Democracy* 28, no. 1 (2017): 74–88; Sarah Sobieraj, *Credible Threat: Attacks against Women Online and the Future of Democracy* (New York: Oxford University Press, 2020); Jessica Vitak et al., "Identifying Women's Experiences with and Strategies for Mitigating Negative Effects of Online Harassment," in *Proceedings of the 20th ACM Conference on Computer Supported Cooperative Work and Social Computing* (New York: ACM, 2017), 1231–45, https://vitak.files .wordpress.com/2009/02/vitak_etal-2017-cscw-online-harassment.pdf.

15. Alice E. Marwick, "Morally Motivated Networked Harassment as Normative Reinforcement," *Social Media + Society* 7, no. 2 (2021), https://doi.org/10.1177/20563051211021378.

16. Jessica Lake, *The Face That Launched a Thousand Lawsuits: The American Women Who Forged a Right to Privacy* (New Haven, CT: Yale University Press, 2016).

17. Carole Pateman, "Feminist Critiques of the Public/Private Dichotomy," in *Public and Private in Social Life*, ed. Stanley I. Benn and G. F. Gaus (London: St. Martin's and Croom Helm, 1983), 118–40.

18. Catharine A. MacKinnon, *Toward a Feminist Theory of the State* (Cambridge, MA: Harvard University Press, 1989), 168; Jennifer C. Nash, "From Lavender to Purple: Privacy, Black Women, and Feminist Legal Theory," *Cardozo Women's Law Journal* 11 (2004): 303–30.

19. Nash, "From Lavender to Purple"; Simone Browne, *Dark Matters: On the Surveillance of Blackness* (Durham, NC: Duke University Press, 2015).

20. Christen A. Smith, "Impossible Privacy: Black Women and Police Terror," *Black Scholar* 51, no. 1 (2021): 20–29.

21. Craig Reinarman and Harry G. Levine, "Crack in the Rearview Mirror: Deconstructing Drug War Mythology," *Social Justice* 31, nos. 1–2 (95–96) (2004): 182–99.

22. Lucy Hackworth, "Limitations of 'Just Gender': The Need for an Intersectional Reframing of Online Harassment Discourse and Research," in *Mediating Misogyny: Gender, Technology, and Harassment*, edited by Jacqueline Ryan Vickery and Tracy Everbach (Cham, Switzerland: Springer, 2018), 51–70; Caitlin E. Lawson, "Platform Vulnerabilities: Harassment and Misogynoir in the Digital Attack on Leslie Jones," *Information, Communication & Society* 21, no. 6 (2018): 818–33; Stephanie Madden et al., "Mediated Misogynoir: Intersecting Race and Gender in Online Harassment," in *Mediating Misogyny: Gender, Technology, and Harassment*, ed. Jacqueline Ryan Vickery and Tracy Everbach (London: Palgrave Macmillan, 2018), 71–90.

23. Lenhart et al., *Online Harassment, Digital Abuse, and Cyberstalking in America*.

24. Liz Kelly, *Surviving Sexual Violence* (Cambridge, UK: Polity, 1988); McGlynn, Rackley, and Houghton, "Beyond 'Revenge Porn'"; Fiona Vera-Gray and Bianca Fileborn, "Recognition and the Harms of 'Cheer Up,'" *Philosophical Journal of Conflict and Violence* 2,

no. 1 (2018), https://trivent-publishing.eu/triventvechi/journals/pjcv2-1/06.%20Fiona%20Vera-Gray,%20Bianca%20Fileborn.pdf.

25. Lenhart et al., *Online Harassment, Digital Abuse, and Cyberstalking in America*; Vitak et al., "Identifying Women's Experiences with and Strategies for Mitigating Negative Effects of Online Harassment."

26. Megan Condis, *Gaming Masculinity: Trolls, Fake Geeks, and the Gendered Battle for Online Culture* (Iowa City: University of Iowa Press, 2018); Adrienne Massanari, "#Gamergate and The Fappening: How Reddit's Algorithm, Governance, and Culture Support Toxic Technocultures," *New Media & Society* 19, no. 3 (2015): 329–46, https://doi.org/10.1177/1461444815608807; Anastasia Salter and Bridget Blodgett, *Toxic Geek Masculinity in Media: Sexism, Trolling, and Identity Policing* (Cham, Switzerland: Springer, 2017).

27. Fiona Vera-Gray, *Men's Intrusion, Women's Embodiment: A Critical Analysis of Street Harassment* (London: Routledge, 2016).

28. Jessica Ringrose et al., *A Qualitative Study of Children, Young People and "Sexting": A Report Prepared for the NSPCC* (London: National Society for the Prevention of Cruelty to Children, 2012), http://eprints.lse.ac.uk/44216.

29. June Larkin, "Walking through Walls: The Sexual Harassment of High School Girls," *Gender and Education* 6, no. 3 (1994): 263–80; Faye Mishna et al., "Gendered and Sexualized Bullying and Cyber Bullying: Spotlighting Girls and Making Boys Invisible," *Youth & Society* 52, no. 3 (2020): 403–26, https://doi.org/10.1177/0044118X18757150; Rosalyn Shute, Larry Owens, and Phillip Slee, "High School Girls' Experience of Victimization by Boys: Where Sexual Harassment Meets Aggression," *Journal of Aggression, Maltreatment & Trauma* 25, no. 3 (2016): 269–85; Nicole E. Conroy, "Rethinking Adolescent Peer Sexual Harassment: Contributions of Feminist Theory," *Journal of School Violence* 12, no. 4 (2013): 340–56, https://doi.org/10.1080/15388220.2013.813391; Amy Adele Hasinoff, *Sexting Panic: Rethinking Criminalization, Privacy, and Consent* (Urbana: University of Illinois Press, 2015).

30. Massanari, "#Gamergate and The Fappening."

31. Melanie Kohnen, "'The Power of Geek': Fandom as Gendered Commodity at Comic-Con," *Creative Industries Journal* 7, no. 1 (2014): 75–78, https://doi.org/10.1080/17510694.2014.892295; Anastasia Salter and Bridget Blodgett, "Hypermasculinity & Dickwolves: The Contentious Role of Women in the New Gaming Public," *Journal of Broadcasting & Electronic Media* 56, no. 3 (2012): 401–16, https://doi.org/10.1080/08838151.2012.705199; Eva Zekany, "The Gendered Geek: Performing Masculinities in Cyberspace" (master's thesis, Central European University, Budapest, 2011), http://www.etd.ceu.hu/2011/zekany_eva.pdf.

32. Kelly, *Surviving Sexual Violence*; Fiona Vera-Gray, *The Right Amount of Panic: How Women Trade Freedom for Safety* (Bristol, UK: Policy, 2018).

33. Lavinia McLean and Mark D. Griffiths, "Female Gamers' Experience of Online Harassment and Social Support in Online Gaming: A Qualitative Study," *International Journal of Mental Health and Addiction* 17 (2019): 970–94.

34. Meredith D. Clark, "Drag Them: A Brief Etymology of So-Called 'Cancel Culture,'" *Communication and the Public* 5, nos. 3–4 (September 1, 2020): 88–92, https://doi.org/10 .1177/2057047320961562.

35. For Kimberly's privacy, I am not mentioning the name or genre of her open-source project.

36. Even if she had responded, Jason's actions are completely unjustified and reprehensible. It is notable that is it so easy to blame the victim that I feel that I must emphasize the fact that Kimberly was not escalating the harassment and did not instigate it in any way. This, however, plays into a respectability politics that differentiates between "good" and "bad" victims.

37. Sobieraj, *Credible Threat.*

38. Alice E. Marwick and Robyn Caplan, "Drinking Male Tears: Language, the Manosphere, and Networked Harassment," *Feminist Media Studies* 18, no. 4 (2018): 543–59; Rebecca Lewis, Alice Marwick, and William Partin, "'We Dissect Stupidity and Respond to It': Response Videos and Networked Harassment on YouTube," *American Behavioral Scientist* 65, no. 5 (2021): 735–56; Marwick, "Morally Motivated Networked Harassment as Normative Reinforcement."

39. Citron, *Hate Crimes in Cyberspace.*

40. Andrea Braithwaite, "It's about Ethics in Games Journalism? Gamergaters and Geek Masculinity," *Social Media + Society* 2, no. 4 (2016), https://doi.org/10.1177/2056305116672484; Massanari, "#Gamergate and The Fappening."

41. Jean Burgess and Ariadna Matamoros-Fernández, "Mapping Sociocultural Controversies across Digital Media Platforms: One Week of #Gamergate on Twitter, YouTube, and Tumblr," *Communication Research and Practice* 2, no. 1 (2016): 79–96; Melinda C. R. Burgess et al., "Online Misogyny Targeting Feminist Activism: Anita Sarkeesian and Gamergate," in *The Wiley Handbook of Violence and Aggression*, ed. Peter Sturmey (Hoboken, NJ: Wiley, 2017), 1–13.

42. Gina Masullo Chen et al., "'You Really Have to Have a Thick Skin': A Cross-Cultural Perspective on How Online Harassment Influences Female Journalists," *Journalism* 21, no. 7 (2020): 877–95, https://doi.org/10.1177/1464884918768500; Madden et al., "Mediated Misogynoir"; Sarah Sobieraj, "Bitch, Slut, Skank, Cunt: Patterned Resistance to Women's Visibility in Digital Publics," *Information, Communication & Society* 21, no. 11 (2018): 1700–1714; Lenhart et al., *Online Harassment, Digital Abuse, and Cyberstalking in America*; Vitak et al.,

"Identifying Women's Experiences with and Strategies for Mitigating Negative Effects of Online Harassment."

43. Lindsay Blackwell et al., "When Online Harassment Is Perceived as Justified," in *Proceedings of the 12th International Conference on Web and Social Media* (Stanford, CA: AAAI, 2018), 22–31; Tamara Shepherd et al., "Histories of Hating," *Social Media + Society* 1, no. 2 (2015), https://doi.org/10.1177/2056305115603997.

44. XOXO Festival, "Anita Sarkeesian, Feminist Frequency—XOXO Festival (2014)," YouTube, October 7, 2014, https://www.youtube.com/watch?v=ah8mhDW6Shs&t=35s.

45. Wen-ying Sylvia Chou, Abby Prestin, and Stephen Kunath, "Obesity in Social Media: A Mixed Methods Analysis," *Translational Behavioral Medicine* 4, no. 3 (2014): 314–23, https://doi.org/10.1007/s13142-014-0256-1.

46. Marwick, "Morally Motivated Networked Harassment as Normative Reinforcement."

47. Zachary K. Rothschild and Lucas A. Keefer, "A Cleansing Fire: Moral Outrage Alleviates Guilt and Buffers Threats to One's Moral Identity," *Motivation and Emotion* 41, no. 2 (2017): 209–29, https://doi.org/10.1007/s11031-017-9601-2; William J. Brady, Molly Crockett, and Jay Joseph Van Bavel, "The MAD Model of Moral Contagion: The Role of Motivation, Attention and Design in the Spread of Moralized Content Online," *Perspectives on Psychological Science* 15, no. 4 (2020): 978–1010, https://doi.org/10.1177/1745691620917336.

48. Sobieraj, *Credible Threat.*

49. While Elise does not know who amplified her tweet, she believes it was a conservative account, given that most of the profiles of people who harassed her included content that marked them as American conservatives (e.g., support for President Trump, MAGA, etc.).

50. Rothschild and Keefer, "Cleansing Fire."

51. George Veletsianos et al., "Women Scholars' Experiences with Online Harassment and Abuse: Self-Protection, Resistance, Acceptance, and Self-Blame," *New Media & Society*, June 22, 2018, https://doi.org/10.1177/1461444818781324.

52. Amy Binns, "Fair Game? Journalists' Experiences of Online Abuse," *Journal of Applied Journalism & Media Studies* 6, no. 2 (2017): 183–206, https://doi.org/10.1386/ajms.6.2.183_1; Chen et al., "You Really Have to Have a Thick Skin"; Sarah Sobieraj et al., "Politicians, Social Media, and Digital Publics: Old Rights, New Terrain," *American Behavioral Scientist* 64, no. 11 (2020): 1646–69, https://doi.org/10.1177/0002764220945357; Candi Carter Olson and Victoria LaPoe, "Combating the Digital Spiral of Silence: Academic Activists versus Social Media Trolls," in *Mediating Misogyny: Gender, Technology, and Harassment*, ed. Jacqueline Ryan Vickery and Tracy Everbach (Cham, Switzerland: Springer, 2018), 271–91, https://doi.org/10.1007/978-3-319-72917-6_14.

53. Alice E. Marwick and danah boyd, "'It's Just Drama': Teen Perspectives on Conflict and Aggression in a Networked Era," *Journal of Youth Studies* 17, no. 9 (2014): 1187–1204, https://doi.org/10.1080/13676261.2014.901493.

54. Kathryn Branch et al., "Revenge Porn Victimization of College Students in the United States: An Exploratory Analysis," *International Journal of Cyber Criminology* 11, no. 1 (2017): 128–42; McGlynn, Rackley, and Houghton, "Beyond 'Revenge Porn.'"

55. Cynthia Khoo, Kate Robertson, and Ronald Deibert, *Installing Fear: A Canadian Legal and Policy Analysis of Using, Developing, and Selling Smartphone Spyware and Stalkerware Applications* (Toronto: Citizen Lab, 2019), https://www.citizenlab.ca/docs/stalkerware-legal .pdf; Stephanie Chan, "Hidden but Deadly: Stalkerware Usage in Intimate Partner Stalking," in *Introduction to Cyber Forensic Psychology: Understanding the Mind of the Cyber Deviant Perpetrators*, ed. Majeed Khader, Loo Seng Neo, and Whistine Xiau Ting Chai (Singapore: World Scientific, 2021), 45–65.

56. Diana Freed et al., "'A Stalker's Paradise': How Intimate Partner Abusers Exploit Technology," in *Proceedings of the 2018 CHI Conference on Human Factors in Computing Systems* (New York: ACM, 2018), 1–13.

57. Freed et al.

58. McGlynn, Rackley, and Houghton, "Beyond 'Revenge Porn.'"

59. Activists, advocates, and scholars prefer the term "nonconsensual intimate images" over "revenge porn." People may distribute such images for many reasons—money, entertainment, clout—not just personal vengeance. Second, pictures of nudity or sexual activity are not inherently pornographic. See People v. Austin, 2019 IL 123910, Illinois Official Reports 29 (Illinois Supreme Court 2019).

60. Elizabeth Englander, "Coerced Sexting and Revenge Porn among Teens," *Bullying, Teen Aggression & Social Media* 1, no. 2 (2015): 19–21; Danielle Citron and Mary Anne Franks, "Criminalizing Revenge Porn," *Wake Forest Law Review* 49 (2014): 345–91; Branch et al., "Revenge Porn Victimization of College Students in the United States."

61. Hasinoff, *Sexting Panic*, 3.

62. Mia Mingus, "The Practice in the Service of Longing: Everyday Transformative Justice" (keynote, Social Justice Summit, Humboldt State University, Arcata, CA, March 6, 2020), https://scholarworks.calstate.edu/concern/publications/7s75df87v?locale=en; Anthony J. Nocella III, "An Overview of the History and Theory of Transformative Justice," *Peace & Conflict Review* 6, no. 1 (2011): 1–10.

63. Judith Armatta, "Ending Sexual Violence through Transformative Justice," *Interdisciplinary Journal of Partnership Studies* 5, no. 1 (2018): article 4.

64. Sarita Schoenebeck, Oliver L Haimson, and Lisa Nakamura, "Drawing from Justice Theories to Support Targets of Online Harassment," *New Media & Society* 23, no. 5 (2021): 1278–1300, https://doi.org/10.1177/1461444820913122.

65. Amy Adele Hasinoff, Anna D. Gibson, and Niloufar Salekhi, "The Promise of Restorative Justice in Addressing Online Harm," *Tech Stream* (blog), Brookings, July 27, 2020, https://www.brookings.edu/techstream/the-promise-of-restorative-justice-in-addressing-online-harm/; J. Nathan Matias, "Preventing Harassment and Increasing Group Participation through Social Norms in 2,190 Online Science Discussions," *Proceedings of the National Academy of Sciences* 116, no. 20 (2019): 9785–89, https://doi.org/10.1073/pnas.1813486116.

66. Matias, "Preventing Harassment and Increasing Group Participation."

67. Lenhart et al., *Online Harassment, Digital Abuse, and Cyberstalking in America.*

5. Privacy on the Margins

1. This chapter builds on two coauthored articles. I am indebted to my collaborators danah boyd, Claire Fontaine, and Mikaela Pitcan for their work on the Reframing Privacy project, which was funded by the Digital Trust Foundation. Claire Fontaine recruited our participants, taught them how to interview, and organized all of our interviews, in addition to coding transcripts and coauthoring. Some of the quotes and analysis in this chapter appear in our two previous papers, which contain detailed information on methodology: Alice E. Marwick, Claire Fontaine, and danah boyd, "'Nobody Sees It, Nobody Gets Mad': Social Media, Privacy, and Personal Responsibility among Low-SES Youth," *Social Media & Society* 3, no. 2 (2017), http://journals.sagepub.com/doi/abs/10.1177/2056305117710455; Mikaela Pitcan, Alice E. Marwick, and danah boyd, "Performing a Vanilla Self: Respectability Politics, Social Class, and the Digital World," *Journal of Computer-Mediated Communication* 23, no. 3 (2018): 163–79.

2. Data collected by the DeBlasio administration overwhelmingly indicated that stop-and-frisk functioned as racial profiling, as 85 percent of those who were stopped were Black or Latino, most between the ages of fourteen and twenty-four; DeBlasio curtailed the practice on the basis of these findings but did not eliminate it. See Michael D. White and Henry F. Fradella, *Stop and Frisk: The Use and Abuse of a Controversial Policing Tactic* (New York: New York University Press, 2019).

3. AI Now, *Algorithmic Accountability Policy Toolkit* (New York: AI Now Institute at New York University, October 2018), https://ainowinstitute.org/aap-toolkit.pdf; Virginia Eubanks, *Automating Inequality: How High-Tech Tools Profile, Police, and Punish the Poor* (New York: St. Martin's, 2018).

4. Diana Budds, "One of New York City's Most Urgent Design Challenges Is Invisible," *Curbed NY*, August 24, 2018, https://ny.curbed.com/2018/8/24/17775290/new-york-city-automated-decision-systems; Mary Madden et al., "Privacy, Poverty, and Big Data: A Matrix of Vulnerabilities for Poor Americans," *Washington University Law Review* 95, no. 1 (2017): 53–125.

5. Eubanks, *Automating Inequality.*

6. Mary Madden, "The Devastating Consequences of Being Poor in the Digital Age," *New York Times*, April 25, 2019, sec. Opinion, https://www.nytimes.com/2019/04/25/opinion/privacy-poverty.html.

7. There are, of course, many exceptions to this. For instance, Georgetown Law's Center on Privacy and Technology holds a "Color of Surveillance" yearly conference that highlights the differential impacts of privacy along lines of race, class, employment, and immigration status.

8. Barbara Ehrenreich, *Nickel and Dimed: On (Not) Getting By in America* (New York: Macmillan, 2010).

9. Michele E. Gilman, "The Class Differential in Privacy Law," *Brooklyn Law Review* 77, no. 4 (2012), http://papers.ssrn.com/sol3/papers.cfm?abstract_id=2182773; Khiara M. Bridges, *The Poverty of Privacy Rights* (Stanford, CA: Stanford University Press, 2017).

10. Madison Van Oort, "The Emotional Labor of Surveillance: Digital Control in Fast Fashion Retail," *Critical Sociology* 45, no. 7–8 (2019): 1167–79, https://doi.org/10.1177/0896920518778087; Karen Levy and Solon Barocas, "Privacy at the Margins | Refractive Surveillance: Monitoring Customers to Manage Workers," *International Journal of Communication* 12 (2018): 1166–88.

11. For example, see EPIC's Freedom of Information Act request for the FBI's documents relating to the Stingray technology, which states, "As the Government's own documents make clear, the use of cell site simulator technology implicates not only the privacy of the targets in federal investigations, it also affects other innocent users in the vicinity of the technology." See also Jeffrey Lane, *The Digital Street* (New York: Oxford University Press, 2018), on police surveillance of urban youth and street gangs on social media.

12. Torin Monahan and Rodolfo D. Torres, *Schools under Surveillance: Cultures of Control in Public Education* (New Brunswick, NJ: Rutgers University Press, 2009).

13. Bridges, *Poverty of Privacy Rights*.

14. Gilman, "Class Differential in Privacy Law"; Virginia Eubanks, "Technologies of Citizenship: Surveillance and Political Learning in the Welfare System," in *Surveillance and Security: Technological Politics and Power in Everyday Life*, edited by Torin Monahan (New York: Routledge, 2006), 89–107.

15. Delia Paunescu, "The Faulty Technology behind Ankle Monitors," *Vox*, December 1, 2019, https://www.vox.com/recode/2019/12/1/20986262/ankle-monitor-technology-reset-podcast.

16. Lauren Kilgour, "The Ethics of Aesthetics: Stigma, Information, and the Politics of Electronic Ankle Monitor Design," *The Information Society* 36, no. 3 (2020): 131–46, https://doi.org/10.1080/01972243.2020.1737606.

17. Eubanks, *Automating Inequality*; Bridges, *Poverty of Privacy Rights*; Gilman, "Class Differential in Privacy Law."

18. Eubanks, *Automating Inequality*.

19. Eubanks, 24; Howard Markel and Alexandra Minna Stern, "The Foreignness of Germs: The Persistent Association of Immigrants and Disease in American Society," *Milbank Quarterly* 80, no. 4 (2002): 757–88, https://doi.org/10.1111/1468-0009.00030.

20. Sarah E. Igo, *The Known Citizen: A History of Privacy in Modern America* (Cambridge, MA: Harvard University Press, 2018), 53.

21. Jade Boyd et al., "Supportive Housing and Surveillance," *International Journal on Drug Policy* 34 (August 2016): 72–79, https://doi.org/10.1016/j.drugpo.2016.05.012.

22. Premilla Nadasen, *Welfare Warriors: The Welfare Rights Movement in the United States* (New York: Routledge, 2004).

23. Nadasen, 4; David Zucchino, *Myth of the Welfare Queen: A Pulitzer Prize–Winning Journalist's Portrait of Women on the Line* (New York: Scribner, 1997).

24. Nadasen, *Welfare Warriors*.

25. Eubanks, *Automating Inequality*, 29; Gwendolyn Mink, *The Wages of Motherhood: Inequality in the Welfare State, 1917–1942* (Ithaca, NY: Cornell University Press, 1996).

26. Eubanks, *Automating Inequality*, 29.

27. Nadasen, *Welfare Warriors*.

28. Julilly Kohler-Hausmann, "'The Crime of Survival': Fraud Prosecutions, Community Surveillance, and the Original 'Welfare Queen,'" *Journal of Social History* 41, no. 2 (Winter 2007): 332.

29. Dorothy E. Roberts, "Digitizing the Carceral State," *Harvard Law Review* 132, no. 6 (2019): 1695–1728.

30. Bridges, *Poverty of Privacy Rights*, 7.

31. Gilman, "Class Differential in Privacy Law"; John Gilliom, *Overseers of the Poor: Surveillance, Resistance, and the Limits of Privacy* (Chicago: University of Chicago Press, 2001).

32. Barton Gellman and Sam Adler-Bell, *The Disparate Impact of Surveillance* (New York: Century Foundation, December 21, 2017), https://tcf.org/content/report/disparate-impact -surveillance/.

33. Mimi Abramovitz, *Regulating the Lives of Women: Social Welfare Policy from Colonial Times to the Present* (Boston: South End, 1996).

34. Martin Gilens, *Why Americans Hate Welfare: Race, Media, and the Politics of Antipoverty Policy* (Chicago: University of Chicago Press, 2009); Rachel Wetts and Robb Willer, "Privilege on the Precipice: Perceived Racial Status Threats Lead White Americans to Oppose Welfare Programs," *Social Forces* 97, no. 2 (2018): 793–822, https://doi.org/10.1093/sf/soy046.

35. Kohler-Hausmann, "Crime of Survival," 333.

36. Josh Levin, "The Real Story of Linda Taylor, America's Original Welfare Queen," *Slate*, December 19, 2013, http://www.slate.com/articles/news_and_politics/history/2013/

12/linda_taylor_welfare_queen_ronald_reagan_made_her_a_notorious_american_villain
.html.

37. Levin; Kohler-Hausmann, "Crime of Survival."

38. Levin, "Real Story of Linda Taylor."

39. Kohler-Hausmann, "Crime of Survival," 329.

40. Kohler-Hausmann, 337.

41. Sean Illing, "How Big Data Is Helping States Kick Poor People off Welfare," *Vox*,
February 6, 2018, https://www.vox.com/2018/2/6/16874782/welfare-big-data-technology
-poverty.

42. Richelle S. Swan et al., "The Untold Story of Welfare Fraud," *Journal of Sociology &
Social Welfare* 35 (2008): 133–51; Dorothy E. Chunn and Shelley A. M. Gavigan, "Welfare
Law, Welfare Fraud, and the Moral Regulation of the 'Never Deserving' Poor," *Social & Legal
Studies* 13, no. 2 (2004): 219–43, https://doi.org/10.1177/0964663904042552.

43. Janet Mosher and Joe Hermer, "Welfare Fraud: The Construction of Social Assistance as Crime," in *Constructing Crime: Contemporary Processes of Criminalization*, ed. Janet
Mosher and Joan Brockman (Toronto: UBC Press, 2010), 17–52.

44. Natasha Singer, "Bringing Big Data to the Fight against Benefits Fraud," *New York
Times*, February 20, 2015, sec. Technology, https://www.nytimes.com/2015/02/22/technology/
bringing-big-data-to-the-fight-against-benefits-fraud.html.

45. LexisNexis, "Health and Human Services," LexisNexis Risk Solutions, 2019, https://
risk.lexisnexis.com/government/health-and-human-services.

46. Andrea Ucini, "Access Denied: Faulty Automated Background Checks Freeze Out
Renters," The Markup, May 28, 2020, https://themarkup.org/locked-out/2020/05/28/access
-denied-faulty-automated-background-checks-freeze-out-renters.

47. Michele Gilman and Mary Madden, *Digital Barriers to Economic Justice in the Wake
of COVID-19* (New York: Data & Society Research Institute, 2021), https://datasociety.net/
wp-content/uploads/2021/04/Digital-Barriers-to-Economic-Justice-in-the-Wake-of-COVID
-19.pdf.

48. Gilman and Madden, 15; Dave Gershgorn, "21 States Are Now Vetting Unemployment Claims with a 'Risky' Facial Recognition System," *OneZero*, February 4, 2021, https://
onezero.medium.com/21-states-are-now-vetting-unemployment-claims-with-a-risky-facial
-recognition-system-85c9ad882b60.

49. Eubanks, *Automating Inequality*, chap. 4; Dan Hurley, "Can an Algorithm Tell When
Kids Are in Danger?," *New York Times Magazine*, January 2, 2018, https://www.nytimes.com/
2018/01/02/magazine/can-an-algorithm-tell-when-kids-are-in-danger.html.

50. Eubanks, *Automating Inequality*, chap. 4.

51. Eubanks, 182.

52. Spencer Headworth, "Getting to Know You: Welfare Fraud Investigation and the Appropriation of Social Ties," *American Sociological Review* 84, no. 1 (2019): 171–96; Eubanks, *Automating Inequality*.

53. Alice Goffman, "On the Run: Wanted Men in a Philadelphia Ghetto," *American Sociological Review* 74, no. 3 (2009): 339–57.

54. Headworth, "Getting to Know You," 188.

55. Wendy A. Bach, "The Hyperregulatory State: Women, Race, Poverty and Support," *Yale Journal of Law & Feminism* 25, no. 2 (2014): 2, http://papers.ssrn.com/sol3/Papers.cfm?abstract_id=2383908.

56. Sarah Brayne, "Surveillance and System Avoidance: Criminal Justice Contact and Institutional Attachment," *American Sociological Review* 79, no. 3 (2014): 367–91.

57. Sarah Anderson et al., *The Souls of Poor Folk: Auditing America 50 Years after the Poor People's Campaign Challenged Racism, Poverty, the War Economy/Militarism and Our National Morality* (Washington, DC: Institute for Policy Studies, April 2018), https://ips-dc.org/wp-content/uploads/2018/04/PPC-Audit-Full-410835a.pdf; Robert Paul Hartley, "Unleashing the Power of Poor and Low-Income Americans," Poor People's Campaign, August 11, 2020, https://www.poorpeoplescampaign.org/resource/power-of-poor-voters/.

58. William J. Stuntz, "The Distribution of Fourth Amendment Privacy," *George Washington Law Review* 67 (1999): 1266.

59. Stuntz.

60. Marisa Antos-Fallon, "The Fourth Amendment and Immigration Enforcement in the Home: Can ICE Target the Utmost Sphere of Privacy?," *Fordham Urban Law Journal* 35 (2008): 999–1032; White and Fradella, *Stop and Frisk*.

61. Brian Dolan, "To Knock or Not to Knock: No-Knock Warrants and Confrontational Policing," *St. John's Law Review* 93 (2019): 201–31; *PBS NewsHour*, "The War on Drugs Gave Rise to 'No-Knock' Warrants. Breonna Taylor's Death Could End Them," June 12, 2020, https://www.pbs.org/newshour/politics/the-war-on-drugs-gave-rise-to-no-knock-warrants-breonna-taylors-death-could-end-them.

62. Terry Skolnik, "Homelessness and the Impossibility to Obey the Law," *Fordham Urban Law Journal* 43, no. 3 (2016): 741–87.

63. The most controversial portions of the law were struck down by the Supreme Court, but the law has had long consequences. Nigel Duara, "Arizona's Once-Feared Immigration Law, SB 1070, Loses Most of Its Power in Settlement," *Los Angeles Times*, September 15, 2016, sec. World & Nation, https://www.latimes.com/nation/la-na-arizona-law-20160915-snap-story.html; Kristina M. Campbell, "The Road to SB 1070: How Arizona Became Ground

Zero for the Immigrants' Rights Movement and the Continuing Struggle for Latino Civil Rights in America," *Harvard Latino Law Review* 14 (2011): 1–21.

64. Reginald Dwayne Betts, "How the Surveillance State Destroys the Lives of Poor Whites and People of Color," *American Prospect*, June 22, 2018, https://prospect.org/api/content/934d013a-7d3f-52e7-a998-e76e3e090db2/.

65. Thank you to my research assistant Ben Clancy (Department of Communication, UNC–Chapel Hill) for his work on this section.

66. Alexa Van Brunt and Locke E. Bowman, "Toward a Just Model of Pretrial Release," *Journal of Criminal Law and Criminology* 108, no. 4 (2018): 701–74; Gabrielle Costa, "The Future of Pretrial Detention in a Criminal System Looking for Justice," *Journal of Race, Gender, and Ethnicity* 9, no. 1 (2020): 78–100; Alec Karakatsanis, "The Punishment Bureaucracy: How to Think About 'Criminal Justice Reform,'" *Yale Law Journal Forum* 128 (March 28, 2019): 848–935.

67. Denise Lavoie, "Drivers Challenge License Suspensions for Unpaid Court Debt," *AP News*, July 4, 2018, https://apnews.com/article/nc-state-wire-lawsuits-us-news-ap-top-news-courts-3f83b360a1f141f4a794f4203c7eab2f.

68. Thomas B. Edsall, "The Expanding World of Poverty Capitalism," *New York Times*, August 26, 2014, sec. Opinion, https://www.nytimes.com/2014/08/27/opinion/thomas-edsall-the-expanding-world-of-poverty-capitalism.html.

69. Simone Browne, *Dark Matters: On the Surveillance of Blackness* (Durham, NC: Duke University Press, 2015).

70. Alexandra Mateescu et al., "Social Media Surveillance and Law Enforcement," *Data and Civil Rights* 27 (2015): 2015–27.

71. Fanny Anne Ramirez, "The Digital Turn in Public Criminal Defense" (PhD diss., Rutgers University–School of Graduate Studies, 2019).

72. Jeffrey Lane, Fanny A. Ramirez, and Katy E. Pearce, "Guilty by Visible Association: Socially Mediated Visibility in Gang Prosecutions," *Journal of Computer-Mediated Communication* 23, no. 6 (2018): 354–69.

73. McKenzie Funk, "How ICE Picks Its Targets in the Surveillance Age," *New York Times Magazine*, October 2, 2019, https://www.nytimes.com/2019/10/02/magazine/ice-surveillance-deportation.html; George Joseph, "Where ICE Already Has Direct Lines to Law-Enforcement Databases with Immigrant Data," *NPR.org*, May 12, 2017, https://www.npr.org/sections/codeswitch/2017/05/12/479070535/where-ice-already-has-direct-lines-to-law-enforcement-databases-with-immigrant-d; Antos-Fallon, "Fourth Amendment and Immigration Enforcement in the Home"; Raquel Aldana, "Of *Katz* and 'Aliens': Privacy Expectations and the Immigration Raids," *UC Davis Law Review* 41 (2007): 1081–1136; Anil

Kalhan, "Immigration Policing and Federalism through the Lens of Technology, Surveillance, and Privacy," *Ohio State Law Journal* 74 (2013): 1105–65; Kalhan, "The Fourth Amendment and Privacy Implications of Interior Immigration Enforcement," *UC Davis Law Review* 41 (2007): 1137–1218.

74. Aldana, "Of *Katz* and 'Aliens.'"

75. Lane, *Digital Street*; Ramirez, "Digital Turn in Public Criminal Defense"; James P. Walsh and Christopher O'Connor, "Social Media and Policing: A Review of Recent Research," *Sociology Compass* 13, no. 1 (2019): e12648; Andrew Guthrie Ferguson, *The Rise of Big Data Policing: Surveillance, Race, and the Future of Law Enforcement* (New York: New York University Press, 2017); Sarah Brayne, *Predict and Surveil: Data, Discretion, and the Future of Policing* (New York: Oxford University Press, 2020).

76. Rashida Richardson, Jason Schultz, and Kate Crawford, "Dirty Data, Bad Predictions: How Civil Rights Violations Impact Police Data, Predictive Policing Systems, and Justice," *New York University Law Review Online* 94 (2019): 15–55; Matthew Hutson, "The Trouble with Crime Statistics," *New Yorker*, January 9, 2020, https://www.newyorker.com/culture/annals-of-inquiry/the-trouble-with-crime-statistics; Clayton J. Mosher, Terance D. Miethe, and Timothy C. Hart, "Introduction: The Pervasiveness (and Limitations) of Measurement," in *The Mismeasure of Crime*, 2nd ed., ed. Clayton J. Mosher, Terance D. Miethe, and Timothy C. Hart (Thousand Oaks, CA: Sage, 2011), 1–29, https://doi.org/10.4135/9781483349497.

77. Ferguson, *Rise of Big Data Policing*; Brian Jordan Jefferson, "Predictable Policing: Predictive Crime Mapping and Geographies of Policing and Race," *Annals of the American Association of Geographers* 108, no. 1 (2018): 1–16.

78. Kristian Lum, "Predictive Policing Reinforces Police Bias," HRDAG—Human Rights Data Analysis Group, October 10, 2016, http://hrdag.org/2016/10/10/predictive-policing-reinforces-police-bias/.

79. Ferguson, *Rise of Big Data Policing*, 68–69.

80. Ferguson, 82.

81. Torin Monahan, "Regulating Belonging: Surveillance, Inequality, and the Cultural Production of Abjection," *Journal of Cultural Economy* 10, no. 2 (2017): 191–206.

82. Justin Jouvenal, "The New Way Police Are Surveilling You: Calculating Your Threat 'Score,'" *Washington Post*, January 10, 2016, sec. Local, https://www.washingtonpost.com/local/public-safety/the-new-way-police-are-surveilling-you-calculating-your-threat-score/2016/01/10/e42bccac-8e15-11e5-baf4-bdf37355da0c_story.html.

83. Brayne, *Predict and Surveil*.

84. Karen Levy, "The Contexts of Control: Information, Power, and Truck-Driving Work," *Information Society* 31, no. 2 (2015): 160–74, https://doi.org/10.1080/01972243.2015

.998105; Tamara Mose Brown, *Raising Brooklyn: Nannies, Childcare, and Caribbeans Creating Community* (New York: New York University Press, 2011); Julia Ticona and Alexandra Mateescu, "Trusted Strangers: Carework Platforms' Cultural Entrepreneurship in the On-Demand Economy," *New Media & Society* 20, no. 11 (2018): 4384–4404, https://doi.org/10.1177/1461444818773727; Alex Rosenblat, *Uberland: How Algorithms Are Rewriting the Rules of Work* (Oakland: University of California Press, 2018); Winifred R. Poster, "Emotion Detectors, Answering Machines, and e-Unions: Multi-surveillances in the Global Interactive Service Industry," *American Behavioral Scientist* 55, no. 7 (2011): 868–901; Christopher Shane Elliott and Gary Long, "Manufacturing Rate Busters: Computer Control and Social Relations in the Labour Process," *Work, Employment and Society* 30, no. 1 (2016): 135–51; Mary L. Gray and Siddharth Suri, *Ghost Work: How to Stop Silicon Valley from Building a New Global Underclass* (Boston: Houghton Mifflin Harcourt, 2019).

85. Van Oort, "Emotional Labor of Surveillance."

86. Van Oort.

87. Van Oort.

88. Adam Reich and Peter Bearman, *Working for Respect: Community and Conflict at Walmart* (New York: Columbia University Press, 2018); Elizabeth Anderson, *Private Government: How Employers Rule Our Lives (and Why We Don't Talk about It)*, University Center for Human Values Series (Princeton, NJ: Princeton University Press, 2017).

89. Gabriel Mac, "I Was a Warehouse Wage Slave," *Mother Jones*, February 2012, https://www.motherjones.com/politics/2012/02/mac-mcclelland-free-online-shipping-warehouses-labor/.

90. Ceylan Yeğinsu, "If Workers Slack Off, the Wristband Will Know. (And Amazon Has a Patent for It.)," *New York Times*, February 1, 2018, sec. Technology, https://www.nytimes.com/2018/02/01/technology/amazon-wristband-tracking-privacy.html.

91. Jessica Bruder, *Nomadland: Surviving America in the Twenty-First Century* (New York: Norton, 2017); David Streitfeld, "How Amazon Crushes Unions," *New York Times*, March 16, 2021, sec. Technology, https://www.nytimes.com/2021/03/16/technology/amazon-unions-virginia.html.

92. McClelland, "I Was a Warehouse Wage Slave"; James Bloodworth, *Hired: Six Months Undercover in Low-Wage Britain* (New York: Atlantic Books, 2018).

93. Jenna Jacobson and Anatoliy Gruzd, "Cybervetting Job Applicants on Social Media: The New Normal?," *Ethics and Information Technology*, March 2020, 1–21; Kelsey McKeon, "5 Personal Branding Tips for Your Job Search," *The Manifest*, April 28, 2020, https://themanifest.com/digital-marketing/5-personal-branding-tips-job-search.

94. Marianne Bertrand and Esther Duflo, "Field Experiments on Discrimination," in *Handbook of Economic Field Experiments*, edited by Esther Duflo and Abhijit Banerjee, vol. 1 (Amsterdam: Elsevier, 2017), 309–93.

95. Note that the authors did not use "Muslim" names for their subjects and instead assigned all the false profiles generic American names such as "Adam." Alessandro Acquisti and Christina Fong, "An Experiment in Hiring Discrimination via Online Social Networks," *Management Science* 66, no. 3 (2020): 1005–24.

96. Matthieu Manant, Serge Pajak, and Nicolas Soulié, "Can Social Media Lead to Labor Market Discrimination? Evidence from a Field Experiment," *Journal of Economics & Management Strategy* 28, no. 2 (2019): 225–46.

97. Karen Gift and Thomas Gift, "Does Politics Influence Hiring? Evidence from a Randomized Experiment," *Political Behavior* 37, no. 3 (2015): 653–75; Acquisti and Fong, "Experiment in Hiring Discrimination."

98. Jacobson and Gruzd, "Cybervetting Job Applicants on Social Media."

99. Michele Silverstein, "What Percentage of Companies Use an ATS or HRIS?," *Criteria Corp Blog*, October 23, 2019, https://blog.criteriacorp.com/what-percentage-of-companies -use-an-ats-or-hris/.

100. Anders Persson, "Implicit Bias in Predictive Data Profiling within Recruitments," in *Privacy and Identity Management: Facing Up to Next Steps*, ed. Anja Lehmann et al. (Cham, Switzerland: Springer, 2016), 212–30.

101. Madden et al., "Privacy, Poverty, and Big Data."

102. Manish Raghavan et al., "Mitigating Bias in Algorithmic Hiring: Evaluating Claims and Practices," in *Proceedings of the 2020 Conference on Fairness, Accountability, and Transparency* (New York: ACM, 2020), 469–81.

103. Merve Emre, *The Personality Brokers: The Strange History of Myers-Briggs and the Birth of Personality Testing* (Toronto: Random House Canada, 2018); Julie Furr Youngman, "The Use and Abuse of Pre-employment Personality Tests," *Business Horizons* 60, no. 3 (2017): 261–69, https://doi.org/10.1016/j.bushor.2016.11.010.

104. Natasha Duarte, Emma Llanso, and Anna Loup, *Mixed Messages? The Limits of Automated Social Media Content Analysis* (Washington, DC: Center for Democracy & Technology, 2018), https://cdt.org/wp-content/uploads/2017/11/Mixed-Messages-Paper.pdf.

105. Miranda Bogen and Aaron Rieke, *Help Wanted: An Examination of Hiring Algorithms, Equity, and Bias* (Washington, DC: Upturn, December 2018), https://www.upturn .org/reports/2018/hiring-algorithms.

106. Social Intelligence, "How It Works," accessed May 27, 2020, https://www.socialintel .com/solutions/how-it-works/.

107. danah boyd, Karen Levy, and Alice E. Marwick, "The Networked Nature of Algorithmic Discrimination," in *Data and Discrimination: Collected Essays*, ed. Seeta Peña Gangadharan, Virginia Eubanks, and Solon Barocas (Washington, DC: New America, 2014), 43–57, http://www.newamerica.org/downloads/OTI-Data-an-Discrimination-FINAL-small.pdf; Alex Rosenblat, Tamara Kneese, and danah boyd, "Networked Employment Discrimination"

(Open Society Foundations' Future of Work Commissioned Research Papers, 2014), SSRN, December 31, 2014, http://papers.ssrn.com/sol3/papers.cfm?abstract_id=2543507.

108. Xiaoqian Li, Wenhong Chen, and Joseph D. Straubhaar, "Privacy at the Margins | Concerns, Skills, and Activities: Multilayered Privacy Issues in Disadvantaged Urban Communities," *International Journal of Communication* 12 (2018): 1269–90.

109. Reich and Bearman, *Working for Respect.*

110. Monahan and Torres, *Schools under Surveillance*; Emmeline Taylor, Jo Deakin, and Aaron Kupchik, "The Changing Landscape of School Discipline, Surveillance, and Social Control," in *The Palgrave International Handbook of School Discipline, Surveillance, and Social Control,* edited by Jo Deakin, Emmeline Taylor, and Aaron Kupchik (Cham, Switzerland: Springer, 2018), 1–13.

111. Catherine Y. Kim, Daniel J. Losen, and Damon T. Hewitt, *The School-to-Prison Pipeline: Structuring Legal Reform* (New York: New York University Press, 2010).

112. Johanna Wald and Daniel J. Losen, "Defining and Redirecting a School-to-Prison Pipeline," *New Directions for Youth Development*, no. 99 (Fall 2003): 9–15.

113. Sara Morrison, "How Teachers Are Sacrificing Student Privacy to Stop Cheating," *Vox,* December 18, 2020, https://www.vox.com/recode/22175021/school-cheating-student -privacy-remote-learning.

114. Jodi S. Cohen, "A Teenager Didn't Do Her Online Schoolwork. So a Judge Sent Her to Juvenile Detention," ProPublica, July 14, 2020, https://www.propublica.org/article/a -teenager-didnt-do-her-online-schoolwork-so-a-judge-sent-her-to-juvenile-detention; Elizabeth Hornsby, "#FreeGrace and the Racialized Surveillance State of COVID-19 Learning," *Journal of Underrepresented & Minority Progress* 5, no. SI (2021): 13–26.

115. Jodi S. Cohen, "'Grace,' the Oakland Co. Teen Detained for Skipping Homework Is Released." *Detroit Free Press*, July 31, 2020, https://www.freep.com/story/news/local/ michigan/oakland/2020/07/31/free-grace-oakland-county-probation-homework-appeal -release/5560282002/.

116. David Rosen and Aaron Santesso, "School Surveillance and Privacy," in Deakin, Taylor, and Kupchik, *Palgrave International Handbook of School Discipline, Surveillance, and Social Control,* 491–507; Priscilla M. Regan and Jolene Jesse, "Ethical Challenges of Edtech, Big Data and Personalized Learning: Twenty-First Century Student Sorting and Tracking," *Ethics and Information Technology* 21, no. 3 (2019): 167–79.

117. This is of course further accelerated by COVID-19 and the implementation of distance learning at scale.

118. Regan and Jesse, "Ethical Challenges."

119. Ryan J. Watson and John L. Christensen, "Big Data and Student Engagement among Vulnerable Youth: A Review," *Current Opinion in Behavioral Sciences* 18 (2017): 23–27.

120. Scott Jaschik, "More Admissions Officers than Last Year Check Social Media," *Inside Higher Ed*, January 13, 2020, https://www.insidehighered.com/admissions/article/2020/01/13/more-admissions-officers-last-year-check-social-media.

121. Jill Barshay and Sasha Aslanian, "Predictive Analytics Are Boosting College Graduation Rates, but Do They Also Invade Privacy and Reinforce Racial Inequities?," Hechinger Report, August 6, 2019, https://hechingerreport.org/predictive-analytics-boosting-college-graduation-rates-also-invade-privacy-and-reinforce-racial-inequities/.

122. Alan Rubel and Kyle M. L. Jones, "Student Privacy in Learning Analytics: An Information Ethics Perspective," *Information Society* 32, no. 2 (2016): 143–59, https://doi.org/10.1080/01972243.2016.1130502.

123. Madden et al., "Privacy, Poverty, and Big Data," 97–98.

124. Rubel and Jones, "Student Privacy in Learning Analytics."

125. Rubel and Jones.

126. Vanessa Scholes, "The Ethics of Using Learning Analytics to Categorize Students on Risk," *Educational Technology Research and Development* 64, no. 5 (2016): 939–55.

127. Barshay and Aslanian, "Predictive Analytics Are Boosting College Graduation Rates."

128. Lane, *Digital Street*.

129. Gilliom, *Overseers of the Poor*; Marwick, Fontaine, and boyd, "'Nobody Sees It, Nobody Gets Mad'"; Goffman, "On the Run."

130. Lisa Dodson and Leah Schmalzbauer, "Poor Mothers and Habits of Hiding: Participatory Methods in Poverty Research," *Journal of Marriage and Family* 67, no. 4 (2005): 949–59.

131. Eubanks, *Automating Inequality*; Michele Gilman and Rebecca Green, "The Surveillance Gap: The Harms of Extreme Privacy and Data Marginalization," *NYU Review of Law & Social Change* 42 (2018): 253–307.

132. Dodson and Schmalzbauer, "Poor Mothers and Habits of Hiding."

133. Evelyn Brooks Higginbotham, *Righteous Discontent: The Women's Movement in the Black Baptist Church, 1880–1920* (Cambridge, MA: Harvard University Press, 1993); Paisley Jane Harris, "Gatekeeping and Remaking: The Politics of Respectability in African American Women's History and Black Feminism," *Journal of Women's History* 15, no. 1 (2003): 212–20; Pitcan, Marwick, and boyd, "Performing a Vanilla Self."

134. Michel Foucault calls this "panopticism." See Foucault, *Discipline and Punish* (New York: Knopf Doubleday, 1977).

135. Brayne, "Surveillance and System Avoidance."

136. Daniel J. Solove, "'I've Got Nothing to Hide' and Other Misunderstandings of Privacy," *San Diego Law Review* 44 (2007): 745–72.

6. Beyond the Binary

1. Tumblr banned pornography on the platform in December 2018. Shannon Liao, "Tumblr Will Ban All Adult Content on December 17th," *The Verge*, December 3, 2018, https://www.theverge.com/2018/12/3/18123752/tumblr-adult-content-porn-ban-date-explicit-changes-why-safe-mode.

2. DACA (Deferred Action for Childhood Arrivals) is an Obama-era program in which adults brought to the United States as children could receive a two-year deferral from deportation and a work permit. The program has been heavily opposed by Republicans and has been challenged in state and federal courts. DACA recipients are known colloquially as "DREAMers" after Obama's proposed DREAM (Development, Relief, and Education for Alien Minors) Act, which provided a path to citizenship for immigrants who entered the United States as minors.

3. Avtar Brah and Ann Phoenix, "Ain't I A Woman? Revisiting Intersectionality," *Journal of International Women's Studies* 5, no. 3 (2004): 75–86.

4. Colombia is actually a leader in LGBTQ+ rights in Latin America, and gay marriage was legalized there in 2016.

5. Lauren Berlant and Michael Warner, "Sex in Public," *Critical Inquiry* 24, no. 2 (1998): 547–66.

6. Michael Warner, *Publics and Counterpublics* (New York: Zone Books, 2002).

7. While some college conservatives are fond of claiming that they must stay closeted at traditionally liberal universities for fear of retaliation, the power structure of US society privileges both Christianity and conservativism.

8. Gayle Rubin, "Thinking Sex: Notes for a Radical Theory of the Politics of Sexuality," in *Pleasure and Danger*, ed. Carole Vance (Boston: Routledge and Kegan Paul, 1984), 267–319.

9. Erving Goffman, *Stigma: Notes on the Management of Spoiled Identity* (New York: J. Aronson, 1974).

10. Warner, *Publics and Counterpublics*, 25.

11. Lisa Duggan, "The New Homonormativity: The Sexual Politics of Neoliberalism," in *Materializing Democracy: Toward a Revitalized Cultural Politics*, ed. Russ Castronovo and Dana D. Nelson, vol. 10 (Durham, NC: Duke University Press, 2002), 175–94.

12. Lain A. B. Mathers, J. E. Sumerau, and Ryan T. Cragun, "The Limits of Homonormativity: Constructions of Bisexual and Transgender People in the Post-Gay Era," *Sociological Perspectives* 61, no. 6 (2018): 934–52, https://doi.org/10.1177/0731121417753370.

13. David Gudelunas, "There's an App for That: The Uses and Gratifications of Online Social Networks for Gay Men," *Sexuality & Culture* 16, no. 4 (2012): 347–65, https://doi.org/10.1007/s12119-012-9127-4.

14. Allyson Hobbs, *A Chosen Exile: A History of Racial Passing in American Life* (Cambridge, MA: Harvard University Press, 2014).

15. Kenji Yoshino, *Covering: The Hidden Assault on Our Civil Rights* (New York: Random House, 2007).

16. This example appears in the HBO show *Insecure*, season 1, episode 3, "Code-Switch." In the episode, the upper-middle-class, Black lawyer Molly tells her Black intern Rasheeda to "switch it up a bit" to fit the white norms of the law firm.

17. Warner, *Publics and Counterpublics*, 23.

18. Rokhaya Diallo, "France's Latest Vote to Ban Hijabs Shows How Far It Will Go to Exclude Muslim Women," *Washington Post*, April 21, 2021, sec. Global Opinions, https://www.washingtonpost.com/opinions/2021/04/21/france-hijab-ban-vote-exclusion/.

19. Toby Beauchamp, *Going Stealth: Transgender Politics and US Surveillance Practices* (Durham, NC: Duke University Press, 2019).

20. Goffman, *Stigma*.

21. Beauchamp, *Going Stealth*; Thomas J. Billard, "'Passing' and the Politics of Deception: Transgender Bodies, Cisgender Aesthetics, and the Policing of Inconspicuous Marginal Identities," in *The Palgrave Handbook of Deceptive Communication*, edited by Tony Docan-Morgan (Cham, Switzerland: Springer, 2019), 463–77.

22. Of course, other trans people do not want to "pass" or do not feel that they need to conform to cisgender presentation. As always, what people consider "private" is individual and contextual.

23. Beauchamp, *Going Stealth*, 9.

24. Billard, "'Passing' and the Politics of Deception."

25. Moya Lloyd, "Heteronormativity and/as Violence: The 'Sexing' of Gwen Araujo," *Hypatia* 28, no. 4 (2013): 818–34; Talia Mae Bettcher, "Evil Deceivers and Make-Believers: On Transphobic Violence and the Politics of Illusion," *Hypatia* 22, no. 3 (2007): 43–65.

26. Seth Hemmelgarn and Cynthia Laird, "Ten Years Later, Araujo's Murder Resonates," *Bay Area Reporter*, October 3, 2012, sec. News, https://www.ebar.com/news///242932.

27. Patrick Hoge, "Defense Calls Transgender Victim Guilty of 'Deception and Betrayal,'" *SFGATE*, April 16, 2004, sec. News, https://www.sfgate.com/bayarea/article/HAYWARD-Defense-calls-transgender-victim-guilty-2792421.php.

28. C. Riley Snorton, "'A New Hope': The Psychic Life of Passing," *Hypatia* 24, no. 3 (2009): 77–92.

29. Bettcher, "Evil Deceivers and Make-Believers," 47.

30. Lloyd, "Heteronormativity and/as Violence," 818.

31. Berlant and Warner, "Sex in Public."

32. Eve Kosofsky Sedgwick, *Epistemology of the Closet* (Berkeley: University of California Press, 1990), 68.

33. D. Travers Scott, "'Coming out of the Closet'—Examining a Metaphor," *Annals of the International Communication Association* 43, no. 3 (2018): 145–54.

34. Patricia Boling, *Privacy and the Politics of Intimate Life* (Ithaca, NY: Cornell University Press, 1996).

35. "Two-spirit" is a modern umbrella term in Native American / First Nations communities. Its use is meant to "communicate numerous tribal traditions and social categories of gender outside dominant European binaries," as a practice of decolonizing. As such, its use by non-Native people is considered cultural appropriation. Qwo-Li Driskill, "Doubleweaving Two-Spirit Critiques: Building Alliances between Native and Queer Studies," *GLQ: A Journal of Lesbian and Gay Studies* 16, nos. 1–2 (2010): 69–92; White Noise Collective, "A Letter to White People Using the Term 'Two Spirit,'" *The White Noise Blog*, May 18, 2015, https://www.conspireforchange.org/a-letter-to-white-people-using-the-term-two-spirit/.

36. Like many young queer women, I shaved my head at nineteen and immediately experienced both being read as queer all the time and taken out of the dance of heterosexuality, which was very freeing at the time.

37. "Stan" is modern slang for "big fan," taken from the Eminem song "Stan," in which an obsessive fan commits suicide and kills his girlfriend after being ignored by his idol.

38. danah boyd, "Social Network Sites as Networked Publics: Affordances, Dynamics, and Implications," in *A Networked Self: Identity, Community, and Culture on Social Network Sites*, ed. Zizi Papacharissi (New York: Routledge, 2010), 39–58.

39. Starbucks, for instance, famously calls itself a "third place," using the sociologist Ray Oldenburg's phrasing for spaces between home and work where people can meet neighbors, relax, and converse. However, it is an explicitly commercial space with the goal to sell coffee. After Starbucks came under fire for a viral video of two Black men arrested in a Philadelphia store for using the restroom, the company established "Principles for Upholding the Third Place," which include, "Everyone should feel welcomed at Starbucks" and "Discrimination is inconsistent with our mission and our values." See Ray Oldenburg, *The Great Good Place: Cafés, Coffee Shops, Community Centers, Beauty Parlors, General Stores, Bars, Hangouts, and How They Get You through the Day* (New York: Paragon House, 1989); Ann-Derrick Gaillot, "A Short Timeline of Starbucks' Fraught History with Race," *The Outline*, April 19, 2018, https://theoutline.com/post/4192/starbucks-racism-timeline; Starbucks, "Starbucks Principles for Upholding the Third Place: For Our Partners, Our Customers and Our Communities," *Starbucks Stories*, January 24, 2019, https://stories.starbucks.com/stories/2019/starbucks-principles-for-upholding-the-third-place-for-our-partners-our-customers-and-our-communities/.

40. Sedgwick, *Epistemology of the Closet.*

41. George Chauncey, "A Gay World, Vibrant and Forgotten," *New York Times*, June 26, 1994, sec. Opinion, https://www.nytimes.com/1994/06/26/opinion/a-gay-world-vibrant-and-forgotten.html; Eric Garber, "A Spectacle in Color: The Lesbian and Gay Subculture of Jazz Age Harlem," in *Hidden from History: Reclaiming the Gay and Lesbian Past*, edited by George Chauncey, Martha Vicinus, and Martin Bauml Duberman (New York: Penguin, 1989), 318–31; Lillian Faderman, *Odd Girls and Twilight Lovers: A History of Lesbian Life in Twentieth-Century America* (New York: Columbia University Press, 1991).

42. George Chauncey, *Gay New York: Gender, Urban Culture, and the Making of the Gay Male World, 1890–1940* (New York: Basic Books, 1994).

43. Lillian Faderman, *The Gay Revolution: The Story of the Struggle* (New York: Simon and Schuster, 2015); David K. Johnson, *The Lavender Scare: The Cold War Persecution of Gays and Lesbians in the Federal Government* (Chicago: University of Chicago Press, 2009).

44. Chauncey, *Gay New York*, 273.

45. Laud Humphreys, *Tearoom Trade: Impersonal Sex in Public Places* (Chicago: Aldine, 1970).

46. Even those men who did live in "gay spaces" typically had to perform as straight during the day. The pioneering lesbian anthropologist Esther Newton conducted fieldwork on drag queens in the late 1960s. One of her informants told her, "When the queen is coming home, she wants to come home to a campy apartment that's hers—it's very queer—because all day long she's often very straight." Newton, *Mother Camp: Female Impersonators in America* (Chicago: University of Chicago Press, 1972).

47. Johnson, *Lavender Scare.*

48. Humphreys, *Tearoom Trade*, 25.

49. Wendy Hui Kyong Chun, *Updating to Remain the Same: Habitual New Media* (Cambridge, MA: MIT Press, 2016), chap. 4.

50. Chun, *Updating to Remain the Same*; Benjamin Haber, "The Digital Ephemeral Turn: Queer Theory, Privacy, and the Temporality of Risk," *Media, Culture & Society* 41, no. 8 (2019): 1069–87, https://doi.org/10.1177/0163443719831600.

51. Chun, *Updating to Remain the Same*, 158.

52. Tarleton Gillespie, *Custodians of the Internet: Platforms, Content Moderation, and the Hidden Decisions That Shape Social Media* (New Haven, CT: Yale University Press, 2018).

53. I have described this as clearly as I could, but it is still hard to follow. Just presume that the information flowed through a small-town gay-adjacent social network.

54. At the time of our interview, Tumblr had a binary model of privacy that allowed for either public or private Tumblr accounts. Private Tumblr accounts could not be accessed from

the "dashboard" (similar to the Twitter Feed or the Facebook News Feed), de facto erasing them from people's awareness and decreasing community engagement.

55. Mark S. Granovetter, "The Strength of Weak Ties," *American Journal of Sociology* 78, no. 6 (1973): 1360–80.

56. GLAAD, "LGBT Life in the South," GLAAD, May 3, 2018, https://www.glaad.org/southernstories/life.

57. Christy Mallory, Andrew Flores, and Brad Sears, "LGBT in the South," Williams Institute, UCLA School of Law, March 15, 2016, https://williamsinstitute.law.ucla.edu/research/census-lgbt-demographics-studies/lgbt-in-the-south/; Christy Mallory, Andrew Flores, and Brad Sears, "LGBT People in North Carolina," fact sheet, Williams Institute, UCLA School of Law, 2017, https://williamsinstitute.law.ucla.edu/wp-content/uploads/North-Carolina-fact-sheet.pdf.

58. Jaime Harker, *The Lesbian South: Southern Feminists, the Women in Print Movement, and the Queer Literary Canon* (Chapel Hill: University of North Carolina Press, 2018); John Howard, *Men Like That: A Southern Queer History*, new ed. (Chicago: University of Chicago Press, 2001); Frank Bruni, "The Worst (and Best) Places to Be Gay in America," *New York Times*, August 25, 2017, sec. Opinion, https://www.nytimes.com/interactive/2017/08/25/opinion/sunday/worst-and-best-places-to-be-gay.html.

59. Mary L. Gray, *Out in the Country: Youth, Media, and Queer Visibility in Rural America* (New York: New York University Press, 2009); Tom Boellstorff, *The Gay Archipelago: Sexuality and Nation in Indonesia* (Princeton, NJ: Princeton University Press, 2005); Elisabeth L. Engebretsen, *Queer Women in Urban China: An Ethnography* (New York: Routledge, 2015).

7. Public Myths, Private Networks

1. For extensive critiques of self-branding rhetoric, see my first book, *Status Update: Celebrity, Publicity, and Branding in the Social Media Age* (New Haven, CT: Yale University Press, 2013).

2. Danielle Keats Citron, "Sexual Privacy," *Yale Law Journal* 128, no. 7 (2018): 1870–1960; Cynthia Southworth et al., "Intimate Partner Violence, Technology, and Stalking," *Violence against Women* 13, no. 8 (2007): 842–56; Diana Freed et al., "'A Stalker's Paradise': How Intimate Partner Abusers Exploit Technology," in *Proceedings of the 2018 CHI Conference on Human Factors in Computing Systems* (New York: ACM, 2018), 1–13.

3. Freed et al., "'Stalker's Paradise.'"

4. Academics have conducted many experimental studies attempting to demonstrate, disprove, or understand the disconnect between attitudes and practices. Most such studies show that people will reveal personal information for trivially small amounts of money

(a coupon, for example). Other studies have shown that people are unwilling to pay more for increased privacy protection. Still more research finds that even people who claim to care about privacy do not widely engage in certain forms of privacy work, including reading privacy policies, deleting cookies, or encrypting email correspondence. And quite a few studies focus on social media use, as if using social media is prima facie evidence of a lack of concern about privacy. However, privacy researchers continually wring their hands over the privacy paradox, as these studies are highly contradictory, often measure wildly disparate behaviors, and come to a wide variety of conclusions about whether the privacy paradox exists and, if it does exist, what causes it. This calls into question whether the concept is useful at all. See Sarah Spiekermann, Jens Grossklags, and Bettina Berendt, "E-Privacy in 2nd Generation E-Commerce: Privacy Preferences versus Actual Behavior," in *Proceedings of the 3rd ACM Conference on Electronic Commerce* (New York: ACM, 2001), 38–47, http:// dl.acm.org/citation.cfm?id=501163; Alessandro Acquisti and Jens Grossklags, "Privacy and Rationality in Individual Decision Making," *IEEE Security & Privacy* 3, no. 1 (2005): 26–33; Alastair R. Beresford, Dorothea Kübler, and Sören Preibusch, "Unwillingness to Pay for Privacy: A Field Experiment," *Economics Letters* 117, no. 1 (2012): 25–27, https://doi.org/10.1016/ j.econlet.2012.04.077; Susan Barnes, "A Privacy Paradox: Social Networking in the United States," *First Monday* 11, no. 9 (2006), http://firstmonday.org/htbin/cgiwrap/bin/ojs/index .php/fm/article/view/1394; Zeynep Tufekci, "Can You See Me Now? Audience and Disclosure Regulation in Online Social Network Sites," *Bulletin of Science, Technology & Society* 28, no. 1 (2008): 20–36; Spyros Kokolakis, "Privacy Attitudes and Privacy Behaviour: A Review of Current Research on the Privacy Paradox Phenomenon," *Computers & Security* 64 (January 1, 2017): 122–34, https://doi.org/10.1016/j.cose.2015.07.002; Lemi Baruh, Ekin Secinti, and Zeynep Cemalcilar, "Online Privacy Concerns and Privacy Management: A Meta-analytic Review," *Journal of Communication* 67, no. 1 (2017): 26–53, https://doi.org/10.111/jcom .12276; Susanne Barth and Menno D. T. De Jong, "The Privacy Paradox: Investigating Discrepancies between Expressed Privacy Concerns and Actual Online Behavior—A Systematic Literature Review," *Telematics and Informatics* 34, no. 7 (2017): 1038–58.

5. "Millennials" refers generally to the generation born between 1981 and 1996. This means that most Millennials are in their twenties and thirties, and the oldest Millennials are in their early forties. However, the term still seems to have currency when used to refer to "young people" as a whole. See Michael Dimock, "Defining Generations: Where Millennials End and Generation Z Begins," *Fact Tank* (blog), Pew Research Center, January 17, 2019, https:// www.pewresearch.org/fact-tank/2019/01/17/where-millennials-end-and-generation-z-begins/.

6. A. W. Geiger, "How Americans Have Viewed Surveillance and Privacy since Snowden Leaks," *Fact Tank* (blog), Pew Research Center, June 4, 2018, https://www.pewresearch.org/

fact-tank/2018/06/04/how-americans-have-viewed-government-surveillance-and-privacy
-since-snowden-leaks/.

7. Brooke Auxier et al., "Americans and Privacy: Concerned, Confused and Feeling Lack of Control over Their Personal Information," *Internet, Science & Tech* (blog), Pew Research Center, November 15, 2019, https://www.pewresearch.org/internet/2019/11/15/americans-and -privacy-concerned-confused-and-feeling-lack-of-control-over-their-personal-information/.

8. Ari Ezra Waldman, "Cognitive Biases, Dark Patterns, and the 'Privacy Paradox,'" *Current Opinion in Psychology* 31 (2020): 108.

9. Woodrow Hartzog, *Privacy's Blueprint: The Battle to Control the Design of New Technologies* (Cambridge, MA: Harvard University Press, 2018).

10. All non-PII information is affected by context and framework. Recall that Helen Nissenbaum's theory of contextual integrity emphasizes that what is considered appropriate and safe to disclose changes depending on context and audience and that Foucault's theory of discursive frameworks defines information not as a packet that is transferred from one person to another, per cybernetic theory, but as intrinsically social. But context and framework are the first to go when this information leaks, and my study participants were very aware of this. When privacy is fully networked, context collapse due to leaks is nearly inevitable. People thus struggle to determine the risk of sharing particular information, often because they cannot ascertain the context in which the information will be shared and the audience (or that audience's discursive framework) that they will reach.

11. Eszter Hargittai and Alice E. Marwick, "'What Can I Really Do?': Explaining the Privacy Paradox with Online Apathy," *International Journal of Communication* 10 (2016): 3737–57; Alice E. Marwick and Eszter Hargittai, "Nothing to Hide, Nothing to Lose? Incentives and Disincentives to Sharing Information with Institutions Online," *Information, Communication & Society* 22, no. 12 (2019): 1697–1713.

12. Michal Kosinski, David Stillwell, and Thore Graepel, "Private Traits and Attributes Are Predictable from Digital Records of Human Behavior," *Proceedings of the National Academy of Sciences* 110, no. 15 (2013): 5802–5, https://doi.org/10.1073/pnas.1218772110.

13. Matthew Crain, "The Limits of Transparency: Data Brokers and Commodification," *New Media & Society* 20, no. 1 (2018): 88–104, https://doi.org/10.1177/1461444816657096.

14. Bruce Schneier, *Data and Goliath: The Hidden Battles to Collect Your Data and Control Your World* (New York: Norton, 2015).

15. Nina Gerber, Paul Gerber, and Melanie Volkamer, "Explaining the Privacy Paradox: A Systematic Review of Literature Investigating Privacy Attitude and Behavior," *Computers & Security* 77 (August 1, 2018): 226–61, https://doi.org/10.1016/j.cose.2018.04.002.

16. Jinyoung Min and Byoungsoo Kim's discussion of the privacy calculus explains that people share information on social network sites because it benefits them, a decision that

the researchers refer to as "behavior enticements." Min and Kim, "How Are People Enticed to Disclose Personal Information despite Privacy Concerns in Social Network Sites? The Calculus between Benefit and Cost," *Journal of the Association for Information Science and Technology* 66, no. 4 (2015): 839–57, https://doi.org/10.1002/asi.23206; Jo Bryce and James Fraser, "The Role of Disclosure of Personal Information in the Evaluation of Risk and Trust in Young Peoples' Online Interactions," *Computers in Human Behavior* 30 (January 2014): 299–306, https://doi.org/10.1016/j.chb.2013.09.012.

17. Carl Shapiro and Hal R. Varian, *Information Rules: A Strategic Guide to the Network Economy* (Boston: Harvard Business School Press, 1998).

18. Nathaniel Meyersohn, "There Are Still 100,000 Pay Phones in America," *CNNMoney*, March 19, 2018, https://money.cnn.com/2018/03/19/news/companies/pay-phones/index .html.

19. I have two Alexas and use them multiple times a day. Just saying. See Martin Porcheron et al., "Voice Interfaces in Everyday Life," in *Proceedings of the 2018 CHI Conference on Human Factors in Computing Systems* (New York: ACM, 2018), 1–12, https://doi.org/10.1145/ 3173574.3174214; Josephine Lau, Benjamin Zimmerman, and Florian Schaub, "Alexa, Are You Listening? Privacy Perceptions, Concerns and Privacy-Seeking Behaviors with Smart Speakers," *Proceedings of the ACM on Human-Computer Interaction* 2, no. CSCW (November 1, 2018): article 102, https://doi.org/10.1145/3274371.

20. David Garcia, "Leaking Privacy and Shadow Profiles in Online Social Networks," *Science Advances* 3, no. 8 (2017): e1701172, https://doi.org/10.1126/sciadv.1701172.

21. Garcia.

22. Kurt Wagner, "This Is How Facebook Collects Data on You Even If You Don't Have an Account," *Vox*, April 20, 2018, https://www.vox.com/2018/4/20/17254312/facebook -shadow-profiles-data-collection-non-users-mark-zuckerberg.

23. Russell Brandom, "Shadow Profiles Are the Biggest Flaw in Facebook's Privacy Defense," *The Verge*, April 11, 2018, https://www.theverge.com/2018/4/11/17225482/facebook -shadow-profiles-zuckerberg-congress-data-privacy.

24. Kashmir Hill, "What Happens When Our Faces Are Tracked Everywhere We Go?," *New York Times Magazine*, March 18, 2021, https://www.nytimes.com/interactive/2021/03/ 18/magazine/facial-recognition-clearview-ai.html.

25. Jocelyn Kaiser, "We Will Find You: DNA Search Used to Nab Golden State Killer Can Home in on about 60% of White Americans," *Science*, October 11, 2018, https://www .sciencemag.org/news/2018/10/we-will-find-you-dna-search-used-nab-golden-state-killer -can-home-about-60-white.

26. Justin Rohrlich, "In Just Two Years, 9,000 of These Cameras Were Installed to Spy on Your Car," *Quartz*, February 5, 2019, https://qz.com/1540488/in-just-two-years-9000-of

-these-cameras-were-installed-to-spy-on-your-car/; Sarah Kessler, "Think You Can Live Of-fline without Being Tracked? Here's What It Takes," *Fast Company*, October 15, 2013, http://www.fastcompany.com/3019847/think-you-can-live-offline-without-being-tracked-heres-what-it-takes.

27. Nora A. Draper and Joseph Turow, "The Corporate Cultivation of Digital Resignation," *New Media & Society* 21, no. 8 (2019): 1824–39; Joseph Turow et al., *Divided We Feel: Partisan Politics Drive Americans' Emotions Regarding Surveillance of Low-Income Populations* (Philadelphia: Annenberg School of Communication, University of Pennsylvania, 2018); Auxier et al., "Americans and Privacy."

28. Draper and Turow, "Corporate Cultivation of Digital Resignation," 1824.

29. Hargittai and Marwick, "'What Can I Really Do?'"; Marwick and Hargittai, "Nothing to Hide, Nothing to Lose?"

30. Draper and Turow, "Corporate Cultivation of Digital Resignation," 1825.

31. Daniel J. Solove, "The Myth of the Privacy Paradox," *George Washington Law Review* 89 (2021), https://papers.ssrn.com/sol3/papers.cfm?abstract_id=3536265.

32. Virginia Eubanks, *Automating Inequality: How High-Tech Tools Profile, Police, and Punish the Poor* (New York: St. Martin's, 2018), 212.

33. Matt Goerzen, Elizabeth Anne Watkins, and Gabrielle Lim, "Entanglements and Exploits: Sociotechnical Security as an Analytic Framework," in *9th USENIX Workshop on Free and Open Communications on the Internet (FOCI 19)* (Santa Clara, CA: USENIX Association, 2019), https://www.usenix.org/conference/foci19/presentation/goerzen.

34. Kelly Anguiano, Eno Darkwa, and Desmond U. Patton, "Recommendations to End Virtual Stop and Frisk Policing on Social Media," *Tech Policy Press*, April 13, 2021, https://techpolicy.press/recommendations-to-end-virtual-stop-and-frisk-policing-on-social-media/.

Appendix

1. Robert M. Emerson, Rachel I. Fretz, and Linda L. Shaw, *Writing Ethnographic Fieldnotes* (Chicago: University of Chicago Press, 1995).

2. María Elena Torre et al., "Critical Participatory Action Research as Public Science," in *APA Handbook of Research Methods in Psychology*, vol. 2, *Research Designs: Quantitative, Qualitative, Neuropsychological, and Biological*, ed. Harris Cooper (Washington, DC: American Psychological Association, 2012), 171–84, http://psycnet.apa.org/books/13620/011; María Elena Torre, Caitlin Cahill, and Madeline Fox, "Participatory Action Research in Social Research," in *International Encyclopedia of the Social and Behavioral Sciences*, 2nd ed., ed. James D. Wright (Amsterdam: Elsevier, 2015), 540–44; Patricia Krueger, "It's Not Just a Method! The Epistemic and Political Work of Young People's Lifeworlds at the School-Prison Nexus," *Race Ethnicity and Education* 13, no. 3 (2010): 383–408.

3. Carol Gilligan and Lyn Mikel Brown, *Meeting at the Crossroads: Women's Psychology and Girls' Development* (Cambridge, MA: Harvard University Press, 1992).

4. Yvonna S. Lincoln and Egon G. Guba, *Naturalistic Inquiry*, vol. 75 (Beverly Hills, CA: Sage, 1985).

5. Jacquelin W. Scarbrough, "Welfare Mothers' Reflections on Personal Responsibility," *Journal of Social Issues* 57, no. 2 (2001): 261–76.

6. Carmen DeNavas-Walt and Bernadette D. Proctor, *Income and Poverty in the United States: 2014*, Current Population Reports, US Census Bureau (Washington, DC: US Government Printing Office, September 2015), https://www.census.gov/content/dam/Census/library/publications/2015/demo/p60-252.pdf.

7. Patricia Hill Collins, "Toward a New Vision: Race, Class, and Gender as Categories of Analysis and Connection," *Race, Sex & Class* 1, no. 1 (1993): 25–45.

8. Juliet Corbin and Anselm Strauss, *Basics of Qualitative Research: Techniques and Procedures for Developing Grounded Theory*, 3rd ed. (Thousand Oaks, CA: Sage, 2007).

9. Johnny Saldana, *The Coding Manual for Qualitative Researchers* (Thousand Oaks, CA: Sage, 2009).

10. Gilligan and Brown, *Meeting at the Crossroads*.

11. Kathy Charmaz, *Constructing Grounded Theory: A Practical Guide through Qualitative Analysis* (Thousand Oaks, CA: Sage, 2006).

Bibliography

Abidin, Crystal. "Visibility Labour: Engaging with Influencers' Fashion Brands and #OOTD Advertorial Campaigns on Instagram." *Media International Australia* 161, no. 1 (2016): 86–100.

Abramovitz, Mimi. *Regulating the Lives of Women: Social Welfare Policy from Colonial Times to the Present.* Boston: South End, 1996.

Abramson, Kate. "Turning Up the Lights on Gaslighting." *Philosophical Perspectives* 28, no. 1 (2014): 1–30.

Acquisti, Alessandro, and Christina Fong. "An Experiment in Hiring Discrimination via Online Social Networks." *Management Science* 66, no. 3 (2020): 1005–24.

Acquisti, Alessandro, and Jens Grossklags. "Privacy and Rationality in Individual Decision Making." *IEEE Security & Privacy* 3, no. 1 (2005): 26–33.

AI Now. *Algorithmic Accountability Policy Toolkit.* New York: AI Now Institute at New York University, October 2018. https://ainowinstitute.org/aap-toolkit.pdf.

Albertson, Bethany L. "Dog-Whistle Politics: Multivocal Communication and Religious Appeals." *Political Behavior* 37, no. 1 (2015): 3–26.

Albury, Kath, Kate Crawford, Paul Byron, and Benjamin P. Mathews. *Young People and Sexting in Australia: Ethics, Representation and the Law.* Sydney: ARC Centre for Creative Industries and Innovation / Journalism and Media Research Centre, the University of New South Wales, Australia, 2013.

Aldana, Raquel. "Of *Katz* and 'Aliens': Privacy Expectations and the Immigration Raids." *UC Davis Law Review* 41 (2007): 1081–1136.

Alhabash, Saleem, and Mengyan Ma. "A Tale of Four Platforms: Motivations and Uses of Facebook, Twitter, Instagram, and Snapchat among College Students?" *Social Media + Society* 3, no. 1 (2017). https://doi.org/10.1177/2056305117691544.

Allen, Anita L., and Erin Mack. "How Privacy Got Its Gender." *Northern Illinois University Law Review* 10 (1989): 441–78.

Altman, Irwin. *The Environment and Social Behavior: Privacy, Personal Space, Territory, and Crowding*. Monterey, CA: Brooks/Cole, 1975.

———. "Privacy Regulation: Culturally Universal or Culturally Specific?" *Journal of Social Issues* 33, no. 3 (1977): 66–84.

Anderson, Elizabeth. *Private Government: How Employers Rule Our Lives (and Why We Don't Talk about It)*. University Center for Human Values Series. Princeton, NJ: Princeton University Press, 2017.

Anderson, Sarah, Marc Bayard, Phyllis Bennis, John Cavanagh, Karen Dolan, Lindsay Koshgarian, Aaron Noffke, et al. *The Souls of Poor Folk: Auditing America 50 Years after the Poor People's Campaign Challenged Racism, Poverty, the War Economy/Militarism and Our National Morality*. Washington, DC: Institute for Policy Studies, April 2018. https://ips-dc.org/wp-content/uploads/2018/04/PPC-Audit-Full-410835a.pdf.

Andrejevic, Mark. *ISpy: Surveillance and Power in the Interactive Era*. Lawrence: University Press of Kansas, 2007.

Anguiano, Kelly, Eno Darkwa, and Desmond U. Patton. "Recommendations to End Virtual Stop and Frisk Policing on Social Media." *Tech Policy Press*, April 13, 2021. https://techpolicy.press/recommendations-to-end-virtual-stop-and-frisk-policing-on-social-media/.

Anthes, Gary. "Data Brokers Are Watching You." *Communications of the ACM* 58, no. 1 (2014): 28–30. https://doi.org/10.1145/2686740.

Antos-Fallon, Marisa. "The Fourth Amendment and Immigration Enforcement in the Home: Can ICE Target the Utmost Sphere of Privacy?" *Fordham Urban Law Journal* 35 (2008): 999–1032.

Armatta, Judith. "Ending Sexual Violence through Transformative Justice." *Interdisciplinary Journal of Partnership Studies* 5, no. 1 (2018): article 4.

Auxier, Brooke, Lee Rainie, Monica Anderson, Andrew Perrin, Madhu Kumar, and Erica Turner. "Americans and Privacy: Concerned, Confused and Feeling Lack of Control over Their Personal Information." *Internet, Science & Tech* (blog), Pew Research Center, November 15, 2019. https://www.pewresearch.org/internet/2019/11/15/americans-and-privacy-concerned-confused-and-feeling-lack-of-control-over-their-personal-information/.

Bach, Wendy A. "The Hyperregulatory State: Women, Race, Poverty and Support." *Yale Journal of Law & Feminism* 25, no. 2 (2014). http://papers.ssrn.com/sol3/ Papers.cfm?abstract_id=2383908.

Baird, Addy. "Nancy Pelosi Said Katie Hill's Resignation after Details of Her Sex Life Were Published without Her Consent Shows That Young People Need to 'Be Careful.'" *BuzzFeed News*, October 31, 2019. https://www.buzzfeednews .com/article/addybaird/nancy-pelosi-katie-hill-resignation-pictures.

Banet-Weiser, Sarah, and Kate M. Miltner. "#MasculinitySoFragile: Culture, Structure, and Networked Misogyny." *Feminist Media Studies* 16, no. 1 (2016): 171–74.

Barnes, Susan. "A Privacy Paradox: Social Networking in the United States." *First Monday* 11, no. 9 (2006). http://firstmonday.org/htbin/cgiwrap/bin/ojs/index .php/fm/article/view/1394.

Barocas, Solon, and Karen Levy. "Privacy Dependencies." SSRN, September 3, 2019. https://papers.ssrn.com/abstract=3447384.

Baron, Jessica. "Vulnerable Moms Engage in 'Sharenting' Even When They Know the Dangers." *Forbes*, June 29, 2019. https://www.forbes.com/sites/jessicabaron/ 2019/07/29/vulnerable-moms-engage-in-sharenting-even-when-they-know -the-dangers/.

Barrett, Lindsey. "Our Collective Privacy Problem Is Not Your Fault." *Fast Company*, January 2, 2020. https://www.fastcompany.com/90447583/our-collective -privacy-problem-is-not-your-fault.

Barshay, Jill, and Sasha Aslanian. "Predictive Analytics Are Boosting College Graduation Rates, but Do They Also Invade Privacy and Reinforce Racial Inequities?" Hechinger Report, August 6, 2019. https://hechingerreport.org/predictive -analytics-boosting-college-graduation-rates-also-invade-privacy-and-reinforce -racial-inequities/.

Barth, Susanne, and Menno D. T. De Jong. "The Privacy Paradox: Investigating Discrepancies between Expressed Privacy Concerns and Actual Online Behavior—A Systematic Literature Review." *Telematics and Informatics* 34, no. 7 (2017): 1038–58.

Barton, Alana, and Hannah Storm. *Violence and Harassment against Women in the News Media: A Global Picture*. Washington, DC: International Women's Media Foundation, 2014. http://www.iwmf.org/our-research/journalist-safety/violence -and-harassment-against-women-in-the-news-media-a-global-picture/.

Baruh, Lemi, Ekin Secinti, and Zeynep Cemalcilar. "Online Privacy Concerns and Privacy Management: A Meta-analytic Review." *Journal of Communication* 67, no. 1 (2017): 26–53. https://doi.org/10.111/jcom.12276.

Beauchamp, Toby. *Going Stealth: Transgender Politics and US Surveillance Practices.* Durham, NC: Duke University Press, 2019.

Bendor, Jonathan, and Piotr Swistak. "The Evolution of Norms." *American Journal of Sociology* 106, no. 6 (2001): 1493–1545.

Benjamin, Ruha. *Race after Technology: Abolitionist Tools for the New Jim Code.* New York: Wiley, 2019.

Benoliel, Uri, and Shmuel I. Becher. "The Duty to Read the Unreadable." SSRN, January 11, 2019. https://papers.ssrn.com/abstract=3313837.

Beresford, Alastair R., Dorothea Kübler, and Sören Preibusch. "Unwillingness to Pay for Privacy: A Field Experiment." *Economics Letters* 117, no. 1 (2012): 25–27. https://doi.org/10.1016/j.econlet.2012.04.077.

Berlant, Lauren, and Michael Warner. "Sex in Public." *Critical Inquiry* 24, no. 2 (1998): 547–66.

Bertrand, Marianne, and Esther Duflo. "Field Experiments on Discrimination." In *Handbook of Economic Field Experiments*, edited by Esther Duflo and Abhijit Banerjee, vol. 1, 309–93. Amsterdam: Elsevier, 2017.

Bettcher, Talia Mae. "Evil Deceivers and Make-Believers: On Transphobic Violence and the Politics of Illusion." *Hypatia* 22, no. 3 (2007): 43–65.

Betts, Reginald Dwayne. "How the Surveillance State Destroys the Lives of Poor Whites and People of Color." *American Prospect*, June 22, 2018. https://prospect .org/api/content/934d013a-7d3f-52e7-a998-e76e3e090db2/.

Billard, Thomas J. "'Passing' and the Politics of Deception: Transgender Bodies, Cisgender Aesthetics, and the Policing of Inconspicuous Marginal Identities." In *The Palgrave Handbook of Deceptive Communication*, edited by Tony Docan-Morgan, 463–77. Cham, Switzerland: Springer, 2019.

Binns, Amy. "Fair Game? Journalists' Experiences of Online Abuse." *Journal of Applied Journalism & Media Studies* 6, no. 2 (2017): 183–206. https://doi.org/10 .1386/ajms.6.2.183_1.

Blackwell, Lindsay, Tianying Chen, Sarita Schoenebeck, and Cliff Lampe. "When Online Harassment Is Perceived as Justified." In *Proceedings of the 12th International Conference on Web and Social Media*, 22–31. Stanford, CA: AAAI, 2018.

Bloodworth, James. *Hired: Six Months Undercover in Low-Wage Britain*. New York: Atlantic Books, 2018.

Boellstorff, Tom. *The Gay Archipelago: Sexuality and Nation in Indonesia*. Princeton, NJ: Princeton University Press, 2005.

Bogen, Miranda, and Aaron Rieke. *Help Wanted: An Examination of Hiring Algorithms, Equity, and Bias*. Washington, DC: Upturn, December 2018. https://www.upturn.org/reports/2018/hiring-algorithms.

Boling, Patricia. *Privacy and the Politics of Intimate Life*. Ithaca, NY: Cornell University Press, 1996.

boyd, danah. "Friendster and Publicly Articulated Social Networking." In *Conference on Human Factors in Computing Systems: CHI '04 Extended Abstracts on Human Factors in Computing Systems*, vol. 24, 1279–82. New York: ACM, 2004.

———. *It's Complicated: The Social Lives of Networked Teens*. New Haven, CT: Yale University Press, 2014.

———. "Networked Privacy." *Surveillance & Society* 10, nos. 3–4 (December 22, 2012): 348–50.

———. "Social Network Sites as Networked Publics: Affordances, Dynamics, and Implications." In *A Networked Self: Identity, Community, and Culture on Social Network Sites*, edited by Zizi Papacharissi, 39–58. New York: Routledge, 2010.

———. "Why Youth ♥ Social Network Sites: The Role of Networked Publics." In *Youth, Identity and Digital Media*, edited by David Buckingham, 119–42. Cambridge, MA: MIT Press, 2007.

boyd, danah, and Kate Crawford. "Critical Questions for Big Data." *Information, Communication & Society* 15, no. 5 (2012): 662–79. https://doi.org/10.1080/1369118X.2012.678878.

———. "Six Provocations for Big Data." In *A Decade in Internet Time: Symposium on the Dynamics of the Internet and Society*. SSRN, September 21, 2011. http://papers.ssrn.com/sol3/papers.cfm?abstract_id=1926431.

boyd, danah, Karen Levy, and Alice E. Marwick. "The Networked Nature of Algorithmic Discrimination." In *Data and Discrimination: Collected Essays*, edited by Seeta Peña Gangadharan, Virginia Eubanks, and Solon Barocas, 43–57. Washington, DC: New America, 2014. http://www.newamerica.org/downloads/OTI-Data-an-Discrimination-FINAL-small.pdf.

boyd, danah, and Alice E. Marwick. "Social Privacy in Networked Publics: Teens' Attitudes, Practices, and Strategies." Paper presented at "A Decade in Internet Time: Symposium on the Dynamics of the Internet and Society," Oxford, UK, September 2011. SSRN, September 22, 2011. http://papers.ssrn.com/sol3/papers.cfm?abstract_id=1925128.

Boyd, Jade, David Cunningham, Solanna Anderson, and Thomas Kerr. "Supportive Housing and Surveillance." *International Journal on Drug Policy* 34 (August 2016): 72–79. https://doi.org/10.1016/j.drugpo.2016.05.012.

Brady, William J., Molly Crockett, and Jay Joseph Van Bavel. "The MAD Model of Moral Contagion: The Role of Motivation, Attention and Design in the Spread of Moralized Content Online." *Perspectives on Psychological Science* 15, no. 4 (2020): 978–1010. https://doi.org/10.1177/1745691620917336.

Brah, Avtar, and Ann Phoenix. "Ain't I a Woman? Revisiting Intersectionality." *Journal of International Women's Studies* 5, no. 3 (2004): 75–86.

Braithwaite, Andrea. "It's about Ethics in Games Journalism? Gamergaters and Geek Masculinity." *Social Media + Society* 2, no. 4 (2016). https://doi.org/10.1177/2056305116672484.

Branch, Kathryn, Carly M. Hilinski-Rosick, Emily Johnson, and Gabriela Solano. "Revenge Porn Victimization of College Students in the United States: An Exploratory Analysis." *International Journal of Cyber Criminology* 11, no. 1 (2017): 128–42.

Brandom, Russell. "Shadow Profiles Are the Biggest Flaw in Facebook's Privacy Defense." *The Verge*, April 11, 2018. https://www.theverge.com/2018/4/11/17225482/facebook-shadow-profiles-zuckerberg-congress-data-privacy.

Brayne, Sarah. *Predict and Surveil: Data, Discretion, and the Future of Policing*. New York: Oxford University Press, 2020.

———. "Surveillance and System Avoidance: Criminal Justice Contact and Institutional Attachment." *American Sociological Review* 79, no. 3 (2014): 367–91.

Bridges, Khiara M. *The Poverty of Privacy Rights*. Stanford, CA: Stanford University Press, 2017.

Brown, Tamara Mose. *Raising Brooklyn: Nannies, Childcare, and Caribbeans Creating Community*. New York: New York University Press, 2011.

Browne, Simone. *Dark Matters: On the Surveillance of Blackness*. Durham, NC: Duke University Press, 2015.

Bruder, Jessica. *Nomadland: Surviving America in the Twenty-First Century*. New York: Norton, 2017.

Bruni, Frank. "The Worst (and Best) Places to Be Gay in America." *New York Times*, August 25, 2017, sec. Opinion. https://www.nytimes.com/interactive/2017/08/25/opinion/sunday/worst-and-best-places-to-be-gay.html.

Bryce, Jo, and James Fraser. "The Role of Disclosure of Personal Information in the Evaluation of Risk and Trust in Young Peoples' Online Interactions." *Computers in Human Behavior* 30 (January 2014): 299–306. https://doi.org/10.1016/j.chb.2013.09.012.

Budds, Diana. "One of New York City's Most Urgent Design Challenges Is Invisible." *Curbed NY*, August 24, 2018. https://ny.curbed.com/2018/8/24/17775290/new-york-city-automated-decision-systems.

Bumiller, Kristin. *In an Abusive State: How Neoliberalism Appropriated the Feminist Movement against Sexual Violence*. Durham, NC: Duke University Press, 2008.

Buolamwini, Joy, and Timnit Gebru. "Gender Shades: Intersectional Accuracy Disparities in Commercial Gender Classification." *PLMR: Conference on Fairness, Accountability and Transparency* 81 (2018): 77–91.

Burgess, Jean, and Ariadna Matamoros-Fernández. "Mapping Sociocultural Controversies across Digital Media Platforms: One Week of #Gamergate on Twitter, YouTube, and Tumblr." *Communication Research and Practice* 2, no. 1 (2016): 79–96.

Burgess, Melinda C. R., Felicia Byars, Leila Sadeghi-Azar, and Karen E. Dill-Shackleford. "Online Misogyny Targeting Feminist Activism: Anita Sarkeesian and Gamergate." In *The Wiley Handbook of Violence and Aggression*, edited by Peter Sturmey, 1–13. Hoboken, NJ: Wiley, 2017.

Cainkar, Louis A. *Homeland Insecurity: The Arab American and Muslim American Experience after 9/11*. New York: Russell Sage Foundation, 2009.

Campbell, Kristina M. "The Road to SB 1070: How Arizona Became Ground Zero for the Immigrants' Rights Movement and the Continuing Struggle for Latino Civil Rights in America." *Harvard Latino Law Review* 14 (2011): 1–21.

Canella, Gino. "Racialized Surveillance: Activist Media and the Policing of Black Bodies." *Communication, Culture and Critique* 11, no. 3 (2018): 378–98. https://doi.org/10.1093/ccc/tcy013.

Casilli, Antonio. "Four Theses on Digital Mass Surveillance and the Negotiation of Privacy." Paper presented at the eighth annual Privacy Law Scholar Conference, Berkeley Center for Law & Technology, Berkeley, CA, June 4–5, 2015. https://halshs.archives-ouvertes.fr/halshs-01147832.

CBS Boston. "Women Fired after Facebook Photo at Tomb of Unknowns Goes Viral." November 21, 2012. https://boston.cbslocal.com/2012/11/21/women-fired-after-facebook-photo-at-tomb-of-unknowns-goes-viral/.

Chan, Stephanie. "Hidden but Deadly: Stalkerware Usage in Intimate Partner Stalking." In *Introduction to Cyber Forensic Psychology: Understanding the Mind of the Cyber Deviant Perpetrators*, edited by Majeed Khader, Loo Seng Neo, and Whistine Xiau Ting Chai, 45–65. Singapore: World Scientific, 2021.

Charmaz, Kathy. *Constructing Grounded Theory: A Practical Guide through Qualitative Analysis*. Thousand Oaks, CA: Sage, 2006.

Chauncey, George. *Gay New York: Gender, Urban Culture, and the Making of the Gay Male World, 1890–1940*. New York: Basic Books, 1994.

———. "A Gay World, Vibrant and Forgotten." *New York Times*, June 26, 1994, sec. Opinion. https://www.nytimes.com/1994/06/26/opinion/a-gay-world-vibrant-and-forgotten.html.

Chen, Gina Masullo, Paromita Pain, Victoria Y. Chen, Madlin Mekelburg, Nina Springer, and Franziska Troger. "'You Really Have to Have a Thick Skin': A Cross-Cultural Perspective on How Online Harassment Influences Female Journalists." *Journalism* 21, no. 7 (2020): 877–95. https://doi.org/1177/1464884918768500.

Chou, Wen-ying Sylvia, Abby Prestin, and Stephen Kunath. "Obesity in Social Media: A Mixed Methods Analysis." *Translational Behavioral Medicine* 4, no. 3 (2014): 314–23. https://doi.org/10.1007/s13142-014-0256-1.

Chun, Wendy Hui Kyong. *Updating to Remain the Same: Habitual New Media*. Cambridge, MA: MIT Press, 2016.

Chunn, Dorothy E., and Shelley A. M. Gavigan. "Welfare Law, Welfare Fraud, and the Moral Regulation of the 'Never Deserving' Poor." *Social & Legal Studies* 13, no. 2 (2004): 219–43. https://doi.org/10.1177/0964663904042552.

Churchill, Ward, and Jim Vander Wall. *Agents of Repression: The FBI's Secret Wars against the Black Panther Party and the American Indian Movement*. Boston: South End, 2002.

Cillizza, Chris. "Why Mitt Romney's '47 Percent' Comment Was So Bad." *Washington Post*, March 4, 2013. https://www.washingtonpost.com/news/the-fix/wp/2013/03/04/why-mitt-romneys-47-percent-comment-was-so-bad/.

Citron, Danielle. *Hate Crimes in Cyberspace*. Cambridge, MA: Harvard University Press, 2014.

———. "Sexual Privacy." *Yale Law Journal* 128, no. 7 (2018): 1870–1960.

Citron, Danielle, and Mary Anne Franks. "Criminalizing Revenge Porn." *Wake Forest Law Review* 49 (2014): 345–91.

Clark, Meredith D. "Drag Them: A Brief Etymology of So-Called 'Cancel Culture.'" *Communication and the Public* 5, nos. 3–4 (September 1, 2020): 88–92. https://doi.org/10.1177/2057047320961562.

Clifford, Stephanie, and Quentin Hardy. "Attention, Shoppers: Store Is Tracking Your Cell." *New York Times*, July 14, 2013. http://www.nytimes.com/2013/07/15/business/attention-shopper-stores-are-tracking-your-cell.html.

Cloud, Morgan. "Property Is Privacy: Locke and Brandeis in the Twenty-First Century." *Georgetown Law Review* 55, no. 1 (Winter 2018): 37–75.

Cohen, Jodi S. "'Grace,' the Oakland Co. Teen Detained for Skipping Homework Is Released." *Detroit Free Press*, July 31, 2020. https://www.freep.com/story/news/local/michigan/oakland/2020/07/31/free-grace-oakland-county-probation-homework-appeal-release/5560282002/.

———. "A Teenager Didn't Do Her Online Schoolwork. So a Judge Sent Her to Juvenile Detention." ProPublica, July 14, 2020. https://www.propublica.org/article/a-teenager-didnt-do-her-online-schoolwork-so-a-judge-sent-her-to-juvenile-detention?token=3z8OgwQv1k2eDd34GVY7YTGsk3jdqslM.

Cohen, Julie E. *Configuring the Networked Self: Law, Code, and the Play of Everyday Practice*. New Haven, CT: Yale University Press, 2012.

Cole, Simon A. *Suspect Identities: A History of Fingerprinting and Criminal Identification*. Cambridge, MA: Harvard University Press, 2002.

Collins, Patricia Hill. "Toward a New Vision: Race, Class, and Gender as Categories of Analysis and Connection." *Race, Sex & Class* 1, no. 1 (1993): 25–45.

Combahee River Collective. "A Black Feminist Statement." In *Capitalist Patriarchy and the Case for Socialist Feminism*, edited by Zillah Eisenstein, 264. New York: Monthly Review Press, 1979.

Condis, Megan. *Gaming Masculinity: Trolls, Fake Geeks, and the Gendered Battle for Online Culture.* Iowa City: University of Iowa Press, 2018.

Conroy, Nicole E. "Rethinking Adolescent Peer Sexual Harassment: Contributions of Feminist Theory." *Journal of School Violence* 12, no. 4 (2013): 340–56. https://doi.org/10.1080/15388220.2013.813391.

Corbin, Juliet, and Anselm Strauss. *Basics of Qualitative Research: Techniques and Procedures for Developing Grounded Theory.* 3rd ed. Thousand Oaks, CA: Sage, 2007.

Costa, Gabrielle. "The Future of Pretrial Detention in a Criminal System Looking for Justice." *Journal of Race, Gender, and Ethnicity* 9, no. 1 (2020): 78–100.

Cox, Joseph. "How the U.S. Military Buys Location Data from Ordinary Apps." *Vice*, November 16, 2020. https://www.vice.com/en/article/jgqm5x/us-military-location-data-xmode-locate-x.

Crain, Matthew. "The Limits of Transparency: Data Brokers and Commodification." *New Media & Society* 20, no. 1 (2018): 88–104. https://doi.org/10.1177/1461444816657096.

Crawford, Kate, and Jason Schultz. "Big Data and Due Process: Toward a Framework to Redress Predictive Privacy Harms." *Boston College Law Review* 55 (2014): 93–128.

Crenshaw, Kimberlé. "Demarginalizing the Intersection of Race and Sex: A Black Feminist Critique of Antidiscrimination Doctrine, Feminist Theory and Antiracist Politics." *University of Chicago Legal Forum* 1989, no. 1 (1989): 139–67.

———. "Mapping the Margins: Intersectionality, Identity Politics, and Violence against Women of Color." *Stanford Law Review* 43, no. 6 (1991): 1241–99.

Crunchbase. "Acxiom." Accessed October 27, 2013. http://www.crunchbase.com/company/acxiom#ixzz2iy4tNOK7.

Cutler, Kim-Mai. "Early Instagram Folks Had Very Deliberate Discussions *not* to Have a Re-Share Feature *because* Images Could Become so Easily Decontextualized." Twitter post, September 20, 2018. https://twitter.com/kimmaicutler/status/1042920045146337280.

Dalton, Craig M., and Jim Thatcher. "Inflated Granularity: Spatial 'Big Data' and Geodemographics." *Big Data & Society* 2, no. 2 (2015). https://doi.org/10.1177/2053951715601144.

D'Amato, Pete. "Woman Fired over Offensive Photo Says She Can Finally Google Herself." *Daily Mail*, February 23, 2015. https://www.dailymail.co.uk/news/

article-2964489/I-really-obsessed-reading-Woman-fired-photo-giving-middle
-finger-Arlington-National-Cemetery-says-finally-Google-without-fear.html.

Daniels, Arlene Kaplan. "Invisible Work." *Social Problems* 34, no. 5 (1987): 403–15.

Das, Sauvik, and Adam Kramer. "Self-Censorship on Facebook." In *Proceedings of the Seventh International AAAI Conference on Weblogs and Social Media*, 120–27. Cambridge, MA: AAAI Press, 2013. http://www.aaai.org/ocs/index.php/ICWSM/ICWSM13/paper/viewFile/6093/6350Davies.

Debus-Sherrill, Sara, and Michael B. Field. "Familial DNA Searching: An Emerging Forensic Investigative Tool." *Science & Justice* 59, no. 1 (2019): 20–28. https://doi.org/10.1016/j.scijus.2018.07.006.

DeNavas-Walt, Carmen, and Bernadette D. Proctor. *Income and Poverty in the United States: 2014*. Current Population Reports. US Census Bureau. Washington, DC: US Government Printing Office, September 2015. https://www.census.gov/content/dam/Census/library/publications/2015/demo/p60-252.pdf.

DeVault, Marjorie L. "Mapping Invisible Work: Conceptual Tools for Social Justice Projects." *Sociological Forum* 29, no. 4 (2014): 775–90. https://doi.org/10.1111/socf.12119.

Dewar, Sofia, Schinria Islam, Elizabeth Resor, and Niloufar Salehi. "Finsta: Creating 'Fake' Spaces for Authentic Performance." In *Extended Abstracts of the 2019 CHI Conference on Human Factors in Computing Systems*, LBW1214. New York: ACM, 2019.

Diallo, Rokhaya. "France's Latest Vote to Ban Hijabs Shows How Far It Will Go to Exclude Muslim Women." *Washington Post*, April 21, 2021, sec. Global Opinions. https://www.washingtonpost.com/opinions/2021/04/21/france-hijab-ban-vote-exclusion/.

Dimock, Michael. "Defining Generations: Where Millennials End and Generation Z Begins." *Fact Tank* (blog), Pew Research Center, January 17, 2019. https://www.pewresearch.org/fact-tank/2019/01/17/where-millennials-end-and-generation-z-begins/.

Doctorow, Cory. "Why Is It so Hard to Convince People to Care about Privacy?" *Guardian*, October 2, 2015, sec. Technology. https://www.theguardian.com/technology/2015/oct/02/why-is-it-so-hard-to-convince-people-to-care-about-privacy.

Dodson, Lisa, and Leah Schmalzbauer. "Poor Mothers and Habits of Hiding: Participatory Methods in Poverty Research." *Journal of Marriage and Family* 67, no. 4 (2005): 949–59.

Dolan, Brian. "To Knock or Not to Knock: No-Knock Warrants and Confrontational Policing." *St. John's Law Review* 93 (2019): 201–31.

Draper, Nora A. "From Privacy Pragmatist to Privacy Resigned: Challenging Narratives of Rational Choice in Digital Privacy Debates." *Policy & Internet*, June 1, 2017. https://doi.org/10.1002/poi3.142.

Draper, Nora A., and Joseph Turow. "The Corporate Cultivation of Digital Resignation." *New Media & Society* 21, no. 8 (2019): 1824–39.

Driskill, Qwo-Li. "Doubleweaving Two-Spirit Critiques: Building Alliances between Native and Queer Studies." *GLQ: A Journal of Lesbian and Gay Studies* 16, nos. 1–2 (2010): 69–92.

Duara, Nigel. "Arizona's Once-Feared Immigration Law, SB 1070, Loses Most of Its Power in Settlement." *Los Angeles Times*, September 15, 2016, sec. World & Nation. https://www.latimes.com/nation/la-na-arizona-law-20160915-snap-story.html.

Duarte, Natasha, Emma Llanso, and Anna Loup. *Mixed Messages? The Limits of Automated Social Media Content Analysis.* Washington, DC: Center for Democracy & Technology, 2018. https://cdt.org/wp-content/uploads/2017/11/Mixed-Messages-Paper.pdf.

Dubrofsky, Rachel E., and Shoshana Amielle Magnet. *Feminist Surveillance Studies.* Durham, NC: Duke University Press, 2015.

Duggan, Lisa. "The New Homonormativity: The Sexual Politics of Neoliberalism." In *Materializing Democracy: Toward a Revitalized Cultural Politics*, edited by Russ Castronovo and Dana D. Nelson, vol. 10, 175–94. Durham, NC: Duke University Press, 2002.

Duguay, Stefanie. "'He Has a Way Gayer Facebook than I Do': Investigating Sexual Identity Disclosure and Context Collapse on a Social Networking Site." *New Media & Society* 18, no. 6 (2016): 891–907. https://doi.org/10.1177/1461444814549930.

Duguay, Stefanie, Jean Burgess, and Nicolas Suzor. "Queer Women's Experiences of Patchwork Platform Governance on Tinder, Instagram, and Vine." *Convergence* 26, no. 2 (2020): 237–52. https://doi.org/10.1177/1354856518781530.

Duhigg, Charles. "Bilking the Elderly, with a Corporate Assist." *New York Times*, May 20, 2007, sec. Business. https://www.nytimes.com/2007/05/20/business/20tele.html.

Edsall, Thomas B. "The Expanding World of Poverty Capitalism." *New York Times*, August 26, 2014, sec. Opinion. https://www.nytimes.com/2014/08/27/opinion/thomas-edsall-the-expanding-world-of-poverty-capitalism.html.

Ehrenreich, Barbara. *Nickel and Dimed: On (Not) Getting By in America*. New York: Macmillan, 2010.

Eikren, Emilee, and Mary Ingram-Waters. "Dismantling 'You Get What You Deserve': Toward a Feminist Sociology of Revenge Porn." *Ada: A Journal of Gender, New Media, and Technology*, no. 10 (2016). http://adanewmedia.org/2016/10/issue10-eikren-ingramwaters/.

Elliott, Christopher Shane, and Gary Long. "Manufacturing Rate Busters: Computer Control and Social Relations in the Labour Process." *Work, Employment and Society* 30, no. 1 (2016): 135–51.

Ellison, Nicole B., and danah boyd. "Sociality through Social Network Sites." In *The Oxford Handbook of Internet Studies*, edited by William Dutton, 151–72. Oxford: Oxford University Press, 2013.

Emerson, Robert M., Rachel I. Fretz, and Linda L. Shaw. *Writing Ethnographic Fieldnotes*. Chicago: University of Chicago Press, 1995.

Emirbayer, Mustafa, and Jeff Goodwin. "Network Analysis, Culture, and the Problem of Agency." *American Journal of Sociology* 99, no. 6 (1994): 1411–54. https://doi.org/10.1086/230450.

Emre, Merve. *The Personality Brokers: The Strange History of Myers-Briggs and the Birth of Personality Testing*. Toronto: Random House Canada, 2018.

Engebretsen, Elisabeth L. *Queer Women in Urban China: An Ethnography*. New York: Routledge, 2015.

Englander, Elizabeth. "Coerced Sexting and Revenge Porn among Teens." *Bullying, Teen Aggression & Social Media* 1, no. 2 (2015): 19–21.

Erlich, Yaniv, Tal Shor, Itsik Pe'er, and Shai Carmi. "Identity Inference of Genomic Data Using Long-Range Familial Searches." *Science* 362, no. 6415 (November 9, 2018): 690–94. https://doi.org/10.1126/science.aau4832.

Ervin-Tripp, Susan. "Context in Language." In *Social Interaction, Social Context, and Language: Essays in Honor of Susan Ervin-Tripp*, edited by Dan Isaac Slobin,

Julie Gerhardt, Amy Kyratzis, and Jiansheng Guo, 39–54. New York: Psychology Press, 2014.

Eubanks, Virginia. *Automating Inequality: How High-Tech Tools Profile, Police, and Punish the Poor*. New York: St. Martin's, 2018.

———. "Technologies of Citizenship: Surveillance and Political Learning in the Welfare System." *Surveillance and Security: Technological Politics and Power in Everyday Life*, edited by Torin Monahan, 89–107. New York: Routledge, 2006.

European Union. Regulation (EU) 2016/679 of the European Parliament and of the Council of 27 April 2016 on the Protection of Natural Persons with Regard to the Processing of Personal Data and on the Free Movement of Such Data, and Repealing Directive 95/46/EC (General Data Protection Regulation), OJ 2016 L 119/1 § (2016).

Facebook. "What Types of ID Does Facebook Accept?" Facebook Help Center, 2021. https://www.facebook.com/help/159096464162185?helpref=faq_content.

Faderman, Lillian. *The Gay Revolution: The Story of the Struggle*. New York: Simon and Schuster, 2015.

———. *Odd Girls and Twilight Lovers: A History of Lesbian Life in Twentieth-Century America*. New York: Columbia University Press, 1991.

Fairchild, Amy L., Ronald Bayer, James Colgrove, and Daniel Wolfe. *Searching Eyes: Privacy, the State, and Disease Surveillance in America*. Berkeley: University of California Press, 2007.

Fairclough, Norman. *Analysing Discourse: Textual Analysis for Social Research*. New York: Routledge, 2003.

———. "'Political Correctness': The Politics of Culture and Language." *Discourse & Society* 14, no. 1 (2003): 17–28. https://doi.org/10.1177/0957926503014001927.

Fairclough, Norman, and Ruth Wodak. "Critical Discourse Analysis." In *Discourse as Social Interaction*, edited by Teun A. Van Dijk, 258–84. London: Sage, 1997.

Fang, Lee. "IRS, Department of Homeland Security Contracted Firm That Sells Location Data Harvested from Dating Apps." *The Intercept* (blog), February 18, 2022. https://theintercept.com/2022/02/18/location-data-tracking-irs-dhs-digital-envoy/.

Federal Trade Commission. *Data Brokers: A Call for Transparency and Accountability: A Report of the Federal Trade Commission*. Washington, DC: Federal

Trade Commission, May 2014. http://www.ftc.gov/reports/data-brokers-call
-transparency-accountability-report-federal-trade-commission-may-2014.

Ferguson, Andrew Guthrie. *The Rise of Big Data Policing: Surveillance, Race, and the
Future of Law Enforcement*. New York: New York University Press, 2017.

Fono, David, and Kate Raynes-Goldie. "Hyperfriendship and Beyond: Friendship
and Social Norms on LiveJournal." In *Internet Research Annual: Selected Papers
from the Association of Internet Researchers Conference*, vol. 4, edited by Mia
Consalvo and Caroline Haythornthwaite, 91–104. New York: Peter Lang, 2005.

Foucault, Michel. *The Archaeology of Knowledge and the Discourse on Language*. New
York: Vintage Books, 1970.

———. *Discipline and Punish*. New York: Knopf Doubleday, 1977.

———. *Power/Knowledge: Selected Interviews and Other Writings, 1972–1977*. New
York: Vintage, 1980.

Foulger, Davis. "Models of the Communication Process." Unpublished paper, 2004.

Franks, Mary Anne. "Drafting an Effective 'Revenge Porn' Law: A Guide for Legislators." SSRN, August 17, 2015. https://papers.ssrn.com/sol3/papers.cfm
?abstract_id=2468823.

Freed, Diana, Jackeline Palmer, Diana Minchala, Karen Levy, Thomas Ristenpart,
and Nicola Dell. "'A Stalker's Paradise': How Intimate Partner Abusers Exploit
Technology." In *Proceedings of the 2018 CHI Conference on Human Factors in
Computing Systems*, 1–13. New York: ACM, 2018.

Freiwald, Susan. "First Principles of Communications Privacy." *Stanford Technology
Law Review* 2007 (2007): 3–20.

Fritz, Niki, and Amy Gonzales. "Not the Normal Trans Story: Negotiating Trans
Narratives While Crowdfunding at the Margins." *International Journal of Communication* 12 (2018): 1189–1208.

Funk, McKenzie. "How ICE Picks Its Targets in the Surveillance Age." *New York
Times Magazine*, October 2, 2019. https://www.nytimes.com/2019/10/02/
magazine/ice-surveillance-deportation.html.

Gaillot, Ann-Derrick. "A Short Timeline of Starbucks' Fraught History with Race."
The Outline, April 19, 2018. https://theoutline.com/post/4192/starbucks-racism
-timeline.

Gal, Susan. "A Semiotics of the Public/Private Distinction." *Differences: A Journal of
Feminist Cultural Studies* 13, no. 1 (2002): 77–95.

Garber, Eric. "A Spectacle in Color: The Lesbian and Gay Subculture of Jazz Age Harlem." In *Hidden from History: Reclaiming the Gay and Lesbian Past*, edited by George Chauncey, Martha Vicinus, and Martin Bauml Duberman, 318–31. New York: Penguin, 1989.

Garcia, David. "Leaking Privacy and Shadow Profiles in Online Social Networks." *Science Advances* 3, no. 8 (2017): e1701172. https://doi.org/10.1126/sciadv .1701172.

Garcia, Sandra E. "U.S. Requiring Social Media Information from Visa Applicants." *New York Times*, June 2, 2019, sec. U.S. https://www.nytimes.com/2019/ 06/02/us/us-visa-application-social-media.html.

Gates, Anita, and Katharine Q. Seelye. "Linda Tripp, Key Figure in Clinton Impeachment, Dies at 70." *New York Times*, April 8, 2020, sec. U.S. https://www .nytimes.com/2020/04/08/us/politics/linda-tripp-dead.html.

Gavison, Ruth. "Privacy and the Limits of Law." *Yale Law Journal* 89 (1979): 421–71.

Geiger, A. W. "How Americans Have Viewed Surveillance and Privacy since Snowden Leaks." *Fact Tank* (blog), Pew Research Center, June 4, 2018. https:// www.pewresearch.org/fact-tank/2018/06/04/how-americans-have-viewed -government-surveillance-and-privacy-since-snowden-leaks/.

Gellman, Barton, and Sam Adler-Bell. *The Disparate Impact of Surveillance*. New York: Century Foundation, December 21, 2017. https://tcf.org/content/report/ disparate-impact-surveillance/.

Gerber, Nina, Paul Gerber, and Melanie Volkamer. "Explaining the Privacy Paradox: A Systematic Review of Literature Investigating Privacy Attitude and Behavior." *Computers & Security* 77 (August 1, 2018): 226–61. https://doi.org/10 .1016/j.cose.2018.04.002.

Gershgorn, Dave. "21 States Are Now Vetting Unemployment Claims with a 'Risky' Facial Recognition System." *OneZero*, February 4, 2021. https://onezero .medium.com/21-states-are-now-vetting-unemployment-claims-with-a-risky -facial-recognition-system-85c9ad882b60.

Gershon, Ilana. *The Breakup 2.0: Disconnecting over New Media*. Ithaca, NY: Cornell University Press, 2010.

Gift, Karen, and Thomas Gift. "Does Politics Influence Hiring? Evidence from a Randomized Experiment." *Political Behavior* 37, no. 3 (2015): 653–75.

Gilbert, David. "Facebook Says It's Your Fault That Hackers Got Half a Billion User Phone Numbers." *Vice*, April 7, 2021. https://www.vice.com/en/article/88awzp/facebook-says-its-your-fault-that-hackers-got-half-a-billion-user-phone-numbers.

Gilens, Martin. *Why Americans Hate Welfare: Race, Media, and the Politics of Antipoverty Policy*. Chicago: University of Chicago Press, 2009.

Gillespie, Tarleton. *Custodians of the Internet: Platforms, Content Moderation, and the Hidden Decisions That Shape Social Media*. New Haven, CT: Yale University Press, 2018.

Gilligan, Carol, and Lyn Mikel Brown. *Meeting at the Crossroads: Women's Psychology and Girls' Development*. Cambridge, MA: Harvard University Press, 1992.

Gilliom, John. *Overseers of the Poor: Surveillance, Resistance, and the Limits of Privacy*. Chicago: University of Chicago Press, 2001.

Gilman, Michele E. "The Class Differential in Privacy Law." *Brooklyn Law Review* 77, no. 4 (2012). http://papers.ssrn.com/sol3/papers.cfm?abstract_id=2182773.

Gilman, Michele E., and Rebecca Green. "The Surveillance Gap: The Harms of Extreme Privacy and Data Marginalization." *NYU Review of Law & Social Change* 42 (2018): 253–307.

Gilman, Michele E., and Mary Madden. *Digital Barriers to Economic Justice in the Wake of COVID-19*. New York: Data & Society Research Institute, 2021. https://datasociety.net/wp-content/uploads/2021/04/Digital-Barriers-to-Economic-Justice-in-the-Wake-of-COVID-19.pdf.

GLAAD. "LGBT Life in the South." May 3, 2018. https://www.glaad.org/southernstories/life.

Glancy, Dorothy J. "Privacy and the Other Miss M." *Northern Illinois University Law Review* 10 (1989): 401–40.

Gleick, James. *The Information: A History, a Theory, a Flood*. New York: Knopf Doubleday, 2011.

Goerzen, Matt, Elizabeth Anne Watkins, and Gabrielle Lim. "Entanglements and Exploits: Sociotechnical Security as an Analytic Framework." In *9th USENIX Workshop on Free and Open Communications on the Internet (FOCI 19)*. Santa Clara, CA: USENIX Association, 2019. https://www.usenix.org/conference/foci19/presentation/goerzen.

Goffman, Alice. "On the Run: Wanted Men in a Philadelphia Ghetto." *American Sociological Review* 74, no. 3 (2009): 339–57.

Goffman, Erving. *The Presentation of Self in Everyday Life*. New York: Doubleday, 1959.

———. *Stigma: Notes on the Management of Spoiled Identity*. New York: J. Aronson, 1974.

Goldmacher, Shane, and Nicholas Fandos. "Ted Cruz's Cancún Trip: Family Texts Detail His Political Blunder." *New York Times*, February 18, 2021, sec. U.S. https://www.nytimes.com/2021/02/18/us/politics/ted-cruz-storm-cancun.html.

Goldman, Adam, Katie Benner, and Zolan Kanno-Youngs. "How Trump's Focus on Antifa Distracted Attention from the Far-Right Threat." *New York Times*, January 30, 2021, sec. U.S. https://www.nytimes.com/2021/01/30/us/politics/trump-right-wing-domestic-terrorism.html.

Goodman, J. David. "Travelers Say They Were Denied Entry to U.S. for Twitter Jokes." *The Lede* (blog), *New York Times*, January 30, 2012. https://thelede.blogs.nytimes.com/2012/01/30/travelers-say-they-were-denied-entry-to-u-s-for-twitter-jokes/.

Granovetter, Mark S. "The Strength of Weak Ties." *American Journal of Sociology* 78, no. 6 (1973): 1360–80.

Grauer, Yael. "What Are 'Data Brokers,' and Why Are They Scooping Up Information about You?" *Motherboard* (blog), *Vice*, March 27, 2018. https://www.vice.com/en/article/bjpx3w/what-are-data-brokers-and-how-to-stop-my-private-data-collection.

Gray, Mary L. *Out in the Country: Youth, Media, and Queer Visibility in Rural America*. New York: New York University Press, 2009.

Gray, Mary L., and Siddharth Suri. *Ghost Work: How to Stop Silicon Valley from Building a New Global Underclass*. Boston: Houghton Mifflin Harcourt, 2019.

Greenberg, Andy. "Hacker Eva Galperin Has a Plan to Eradicate Stalkerware." *Wired*, March 4, 2019. https://www.wired.com/story/eva-galperin-stalkerware-kaspersky-antivirus/.

Gudelunas, David. "There's an App for That: The Uses and Gratifications of Online Social Networks for Gay Men." *Sexuality & Culture* 16, no. 4 (2012): 347–65. https://doi.org/10.1007/s12119-012-9127-4.

Haber, Benjamin. "The Digital Ephemeral Turn: Queer Theory, Privacy, and the Temporality of Risk." *Media, Culture & Society* 41, no. 8 (2019): 1069–87. https://doi.org/10.1177/0163443719831600.

Hackworth, Lucy. "Limitations of 'Just Gender': The Need for an Intersectional Reframing of Online Harassment Discourse and Research." In *Mediating Misogyny: Gender, Technology, and Harassment*, edited by Jacqueline Ryan Vickery and Tracy Everbach, 51–70. Cham, Switzerland: Springer, 2018.

Haimson, Oliver L., Jed R. Brubaker, Lynn Dombrowski, and Gillian R. Hayes. "Digital Footprints and Changing Networks during Online Identity Transitions." In *Proceedings of the 2016 CHI Conference on Human Factors in Computing Systems*, 2895–2907. New York: ACM, 2016. https://doi.org/10.1145/2858036.2858136.

Haimson, Oliver L., and Anna Lauren Hoffmann. "Constructing and Enforcing 'Authentic' Identity Online: Facebook, Real Names, and Non-normative Identities." *First Monday*, June 10, 2016. https://doi.org/10.5210/fm.v21i6.6791.

Hall, Rachel. *The Transparent Traveler: The Performance and Culture of Airport Security*. Durham, NC: Duke University Press, 2015.

Hanisch, Carol. "The Personal Is Political." In *Notes from the Second Year: Women's Liberation*, edited by Shulamith Firestone and Anne Koedt, 76–78. New York: New York Radical Women, 1970.

Harcourt, Bernard. *Against Prediction*. Chicago: University of Chicago Press, 2007.

Hargittai, Eszter. "Digital Na(t)ives? Variation in Internet Skills and Uses among Members of the 'Net Generation.'" *Sociological Inquiry* 80, no. 1 (2010): 92–113.

Hargittai, Eszter, and Alice E. Marwick. "'What Can I Really Do?': Explaining the Privacy Paradox with Online Apathy." *International Journal of Communication* 10 (2016): 3737–57.

Hargittai, Eszter, Anne Marie Piper, and Meredith Ringel Morris. "From Internet Access to Internet Skills: Digital Inequality among Older Adults." *Universal Access in the Information Society* 18 (2019): 881–90. https://doi.org/10.1007/s10209-018-0617-5.

Harker, Jaime. *The Lesbian South: Southern Feminists, the Women in Print Movement, and the Queer Literary Canon*. Chapel Hill: University of North Carolina Press, 2018.

Harris, Paisley Jane. "Gatekeeping and Remaking: The Politics of Respectability in African American Women's History and Black Feminism." *Journal of Women's History* 15, no. 1 (2003): 212–20.

Hartley, Peter. *Interpersonal Communication.* New York: Routledge, 2002.

Hartley, Robert Paul. "Unleashing the Power of Poor and Low-Income Americans." Poor People's Campaign, August 11, 2020. https://www.poorpeoplescampaign .org/resource/power-of-poor-voters/.

Hartley-Parkinson, Richard. "'I'm Going to Destroy America and Dig Up Marilyn Monroe': British Pair Arrested in U.S. on Terror Charges over Twitter Jokes." *Mail Online,* January 30, 2012. https://www.dailymail.co.uk/news/article -2093796/Emily-Bunting-Leigh-Van-Bryan-UK-tourists-arrested-destroy -America-Twitter-jokes.html.

Hartzog, Woodrow. *Privacy's Blueprint: The Battle to Control the Design of New Technologies.* Cambridge, MA: Harvard University Press, 2018.

Hartzog, Woodrow, and Frederic D. Stutzman. "The Case for Online Obscurity." SSRN, February 23, 2012. https://papers.ssrn.com/abstract=1597745.

———. "Obscurity by Design." *Washington Law Review* 88 (2013): 385–418.

Hasinoff, Amy Adele. *Sexting Panic: Rethinking Criminalization, Privacy, and Consent.* Urbana: University of Illinois Press, 2015.

Hasinoff, Amy Adele, Anna D. Gibson, and Niloufar Salehi. "The Promise of Restorative Justice in Addressing Online Harm." *Tech Stream* (blog), Brookings, July 27, 2020. https://www.brookings.edu/techstream/the-promise-of -restorative-justice-in-addressing-online-harm/.

Hasinoff, Amy Adele, and Tamara Shepherd. "Sexting in Context: Privacy Norms and Expectations." *International Journal of Communication* 8 (2014): 2932–55.

Haythornthwaite, Caroline. "Exploring Multiplexity: Social Network Structures in a Computer-Supported Distance Learning Class." *Information Society* 17, no. 3 (2001): 211–26.

Headworth, Spencer. "Getting to Know You: Welfare Fraud Investigation and the Appropriation of Social Ties." *American Sociological Review* 84, no. 1 (2019): 171–96.

Heitner, Keri L., Eric E. Muenks, and Kenneth C. Sherman. "The Rhetoric of Gaydar Research: A Critical Discourse Analysis." *Journal of Psychological Issues in Organizational Culture* 6, no. 3 (2015): 60–69.

Hemmelgarn, Seth, and Cynthia Laird. "Ten Years Later, Araujo's Murder Resonates." *Bay Area Reporter*, October 3, 2012, sec. News. https://www.ebar.com/news///242932.

Henig, Samantha. "The Tale of Dog Poop Girl Is Not So Funny After All." *Columbia Journalism Review*, July 7, 2005. https://www.cjr.org/behind_the_news/the_tale_of_dog_poop_girl_is_n.php.

Hennessey, Matthew. "Why Millennials Will Learn Nothing from Facebook's Privacy Crisis." *New York Post*, April 7, 2018. https://nypost.com/2018/04/07/why-millennials-will-learn-nothing-from-facebooks-privacy-crisis/.

Henry, Nicola, and Anastasia Powell. "Embodied Harms: Gender, Shame, and Technology-Facilitated Sexual Violence." *Violence against Women* 21, no. 6 (2015): 758–79. https://doi.org/10.1177/1077801215576581.

Hern, Alex. "'Anonymous' Browsing Data Can Be Easily Exposed, Researchers Reveal." *Guardian*, August 1, 2017, sec. Technology. https://www.theguardian.com/technology/2017/aug/01/data-browsing-habits-brokers.

Higginbotham, Evelyn Brooks. *Righteous Discontent: The Women's Movement in the Black Baptist Church, 1880–1920*. Cambridge, MA: Harvard University Press, 1993.

Hill, Kashmir. "How Facebook Figures Out Everyone You've Ever Met." *Gizmodo Australia* (blog), November 11, 2017. https://www.gizmodo.com.au/2017/11/how-facebook-figures-out-everyone-youve-ever-met/.

———. "'People You May Know': A Controversial Facebook Feature's 10-Year History." *Gizmodo*, August 8, 2018. https://gizmodo.com/people-you-may-know-a-controversial-facebook-features-1827981959.

———. "What Happens When Our Faces Are Tracked Everywhere We Go?" *New York Times Magazine*, March 18, 2021. https://www.nytimes.com/interactive/2021/03/18/magazine/facial-recognition-clearview-ai.html.

Hill, Kashmir, and Aaron Krolik. "How Photos of Your Kids Are Powering Surveillance Technology." *New York Times*, October 11, 2019, sec. Technology. https://www.nytimes.com/interactive/2019/10/11/technology/flickr-facial-recognition.html.

Hobbs, Allyson. *A Chosen Exile: A History of Racial Passing in American Life*. Cambridge, MA: Harvard University Press, 2014.

Hochschild, Arlie Russell. "Emotion Work, Feeling Rules, and Social Structure." *American Journal of Sociology* 85, no. 3 (1979): 551–75.

———. *The Managed Heart*. Berkeley: University of California Press, 1983.

Hoffmann, Anna Lauren. "Reckoning with a Decade of Breaking Things." *Model View Culture*, July 30, 2014. https://modelviewculture.com/pieces/reckoning -with-a-decade-of-breaking-things.

Hogan, Bernie. "The Presentation of Self in the Age of Social Media: Distinguishing Performances and Exhibitions Online." *Bulletin of Science, Technology & Society* 30, no. 6 (2010): 377–86.

Hoge, Patrick. "Defense Calls Transgender Victim Guilty of 'Deception and Betrayal.'" *SFGATE*. April 16, 2004, sec. News. https://www.sfgate.com/bayarea/ article/HAYWARD-Defense-calls-transgender-victim-guilty-2792421.php.

Holpuch, Amanda. "Facebook Still Suspending Native Americans over 'Real Name' Policy." *Guardian*, February 16, 2015. http://www.theguardian.com/technology/ 2015/feb/16/facebook-real-name-policy-suspends-native-americans.

Hommels, Anique, Jessica Mesman, and Wiebe E. Bijker. "Studying Vulnerability in Technological Cultures." In *Vulnerability in Technological Cultures: New Directions in Research and Governance*, edited by Anique Hommels, Jessica Mesman, and Wiebe E. Bijker, 1–25. Cambridge, MA: MIT Press, 2014.

Hornsby, Elizabeth. "#FreeGrace and the Racialized Surveillance State of COVID-19 Learning." *Journal of Underrepresented & Minority Progress* 5, no. SI (2021): 13–26.

Howard, John. *Men Like That: A Southern Queer History*. New ed. Chicago: University of Chicago Press, 2001.

Humphreys, Laud. *Tearoom Trade: Impersonal Sex in Public Places*. Chicago: Aldine, 1970.

Hurley, Dan. "Can an Algorithm Tell When Kids Are in Danger?" *New York Times Magazine*, January 2, 2018. https://www.nytimes.com/2018/01/02/magazine/ can-an-algorithm-tell-when-kids-are-in-danger.html.

Hutson, Matthew. "The Trouble with Crime Statistics." *New Yorker*, January 9, 2020. https://www.newyorker.com/culture/annals-of-inquiry/the-trouble-with -crime-statistics.

Igo, Sarah E. *The Known Citizen: A History of Privacy in Modern America*. Cambridge, MA: Harvard University Press, 2018.

Illing, Sean. "How Big Data Is Helping States Kick Poor People off Welfare." *Vox*, February 6, 2018. https://www.vox.com/2018/2/6/16874782/welfare-big-data -technology-poverty.

Jacobson, Jenna, and Anatoliy Gruzd. "Cybervetting Job Applicants on Social Media: The New Normal?" *Ethics and Information Technology*, March 2020, 1–21.

Jane, Emma A. "'Your a Ugly, Whorish, Slut' Understanding E-Bile." *Feminist Media Studies* 14, no. 4 (2014): 531–46.

Janik, Rachel, and Keegan Hankes. "The Year in Hate and Extremism 2020." Southern Poverty Law Center, February 1, 2021. https://www.splcenter.org/ news/2021/02/01/year-hate-2020.

Jaschik, Scott. "More Admissions Officers than Last Year Check Social Media." *Inside Higher Ed*, January 13, 2020. https://www.insidehighered.com/admissions/ article/2020/01/13/more-admissions-officers-last-year-check-social-media.

———. "New Data on How College Admissions Officers View Social Media of Applicants." *Inside Higher Ed*, April 23, 2018. https://www.insidehighered.com/ admissions/article/2018/04/23/new-data-how-college-admissions-officers-view -social-media-applicants.

Jefferson, Brian Jordan. "Predictable Policing: Predictive Crime Mapping and Geographies of Policing and Race." *Annals of the American Association of Geographers* 108, no. 1 (2018): 1–16.

Jenkins, Henry, Sam Ford, and Joshua Green. *Spreadable Media: Creating Value and Meaning in a Networked Culture*. New York: New York University Press, 2013.

Jernigan, Carter, and Behram F. T. Mistree. "Gaydar: Facebook Friendships Expose Sexual Orientation." *First Monday* 14, no. 10 (2009).

Johnson, David K. *The Lavender Scare: The Cold War Persecution of Gays and Lesbians in the Federal Government*. Chicago: University of Chicago Press, 2009.

Joseph, George. "Where ICE Already Has Direct Lines to Law-Enforcement Databases with Immigrant Data." *NPR.org*, May 12, 2017. https://www.npr.org/ sections/codeswitch/2017/05/12/479070535/where-ice-already-has-direct-lines -to-law-enforcement-databases-with-immigrant-d.

Jouvenal, Justin. "The New Way Police Are Surveilling You: Calculating Your Threat 'Score.'" *Washington Post*, January 10, 2016, sec. Local. https://www .washingtonpost.com/local/public-safety/the-new-way-police-are-surveilling

-you-calculating-your-threat-score/2016/01/10/e42bccac-8e15-11e5-baf4
-bdf37355da0c_story.html.

Kaiser, Jocelyn. "We Will Find You: DNA Search Used to Nab Golden State Killer Can Home In On about 60% of White Americans." *Science*, October 11, 2018. https://www.sciencemag.org/news/2018/10/we-will-find-you-dna-search-used -nab-golden-state-killer-can-home-about-60-white.

Kaiser, Laurie. "The Black Madonna: Notions of True Womanhood from Jacobs to Hurston." *South Atlantic Review* 60, no. 1 (1995): 97–109. https://doi.org/10 .2307/3200715.

Kalhan, Anil. "The Fourth Amendment and Privacy Implications of Interior Immigration Enforcement." *UC Davis Law Review* 41 (2007): 1137–1218.

———. "Immigration Policing and Federalism through the Lens of Technology, Surveillance, and Privacy." *Ohio State Law Journal* 74 (2013): 1105–65.

Karakatsanis, Alec. "The Punishment Bureaucracy: How to Think about 'Criminal Justice Reform.'" *Yale Law Journal Forum* 128 (March 28, 2019): 848–935.

Kasunic, Anna, and Geoff Kaufman. "'At Least the Pizzas You Make Are Hot': Norms, Values, and Abrasive Humor on the Subreddit r/RoastMe." In *Twelfth International AAAI Conference on Web and Social Media*, 161–70. Palo Alto, CA: AAAI Press, 2018.

Kelley, Noah. "DIY Feminist Cybersecurity." Hack*Blossom, 2016. https:// hackblossom.org/cybersecurity/.

Kelly, Kristin Anne. *Domestic Violence and the Politics of Privacy*. Ithaca, NY: Cornell University Press, 2003.

Kelly, Liz. "The Continuum of Sexual Violence." In *Women, Violence and Social Control*, edited by Jalna Hamner and Mary Maynard, 46–60. Cham, Switzerland: Springer, 1987.

———. Foreword to *Men's Intrusion, Women's Embodiment: A Critical Analysis of Street Harassment*, by Fiona Vera-Gray, x–xi. London: Routledge, 2016.

———. *Surviving Sexual Violence*. Cambridge, UK: Polity, 1988.

Kessler, Sarah. "Think You Can Live Offline without Being Tracked? Here's What It Takes." *Fast Company*, October 15, 2013. http://www.fastcompany.com/ 3019847/think-you-can-live-offline-without-being-tracked-heres-what-it-takes.

Khoo, Cynthia, Kate Robertson, and Ronald Deibert. *Installing Fear: A Canadian Legal and Policy Analysis of Using, Developing, and Selling Smartphone Spy-*

ware and Stalkerware Applications. Toronto: Citizen Lab, 2019. https://www
.citizenlab.ca/docs/stalkerware-legal.pdf.

Kilgour, Lauren. "The Ethics of Aesthetics: Stigma, Information, and the Politics of
Electronic Ankle Monitor Design." *Information Society* 36, no. 3 (2020): 131–46.
https://doi.org/10.1080/01972243.2020.1737606.

Kim, Catherine Y., Daniel J. Losen, and Damon T. Hewitt. *The School-to-Prison
Pipeline: Structuring Legal Reform.* New York: New York University Press, 2010.

Knibbs, Kate. "Data Brokers Accidentally Gave an Identity Thief Access to 200
Million Consumer Records." *Daily Dot*, March 11, 2014. http://www.dailydot
.com/technology/experian-data-brokers-give-thief-data/.

Koerner, Brendan. "Your Relative's DNA Could Turn You into a Suspect." *Wired*,
October 13, 2015. https://www.wired.com/2015/10/familial-dna-evidence-turns
-innocent-people-into-crime-suspects/.

Kohler-Hausmann, Julilly. "'The Crime of Survival': Fraud Prosecutions, Community Surveillance, and the Original 'Welfare Queen.'" *Journal of Social History*
41, no. 2 (Winter 2007): 329–54.

Kohnen, Melanie. "'The Power of Geek': Fandom as Gendered Commodity at
Comic-Con." *Creative Industries Journal* 7, no. 1 (2014): 75–78. https://doi.org/
10.1080/17510694.2014.892295.

Kokolakis, Spyros. "Privacy Attitudes and Privacy Behaviour: A Review of Current Research on the Privacy Paradox Phenomenon." *Computers & Security* 64
(January 1, 2017): 122–34. https://doi.org/10.1016/j.cose.2015.07.002.

Kosinski, Michal, David Stillwell, and Thore Graepel. "Private Traits and Attributes
Are Predictable from Digital Records of Human Behavior." *Proceedings of the
National Academy of Sciences* 110, no. 15 (2013): 5802–5. https://doi.org/10.1073/
pnas.1218772110.

Krook, Mona Lena. "Violence against Women in Politics." *Journal of Democracy* 28,
no. 1 (2017): 74–88.

Krueger, Patricia. "It's Not Just a Method! The Epistemic and Political Work of
Young People's Lifeworlds at the School-Prison Nexus." *Race Ethnicity and
Education* 13, no. 3 (2010): 383–408.

Laestadius, Linnea. "Instagram." In *The Sage Handbook of Social Media Research
Methods*, edited by Luke Sloan and Anabel Quan-Haase, 573–92. Thousand
Oaks, CA: Sage, 2017.

Lake, Jessica. *The Face That Launched a Thousand Lawsuits: The American Women Who Forged a Right to Privacy*. New Haven, CT: Yale University Press, 2016.

Lampinen, Airi, Vilma Lehtinen, Asko Lehmuskallio, and Sakari Tamminen. "We're in It Together: Interpersonal Management of Disclosure in Social Network Services." In *Proceedings of the SIGCHI Conference on Human Factors in Computing Systems*, 3217–26. New York: ACM, 2011. http://dl.acm.org/citation.cfm?id=1979420.

Lane, Jeffrey. *The Digital Street*. New York: Oxford University Press, 2018.

Lane, Jeffrey, Fanny A. Ramirez, and Katy E. Pearce. "Guilty by Visible Association: Socially Mediated Visibility in Gang Prosecutions." *Journal of Computer-Mediated Communication* 23, no. 6 (2018): 354–69.

Larkin, June. "Walking through Walls: The Sexual Harassment of High School Girls." *Gender and Education* 6, no. 3 (1994): 263–80.

Larkin, Leah. "Frequently Asked Questions (FAQ)." *The DNA Geek* (blog), November 11, 2016. https://thednageek.com/faq/.

Lau, Josephine, Benjamin Zimmerman, and Florian Schaub. "Alexa, Are You Listening? Privacy Perceptions, Concerns and Privacy-Seeking Behaviors with Smart Speakers." *Proceedings of the ACM on Human-Computer Interaction* 2, no. CSCW (November 1, 2018): article 102. https://doi.org/10.1145/3274371.

Lavoie, Denise. "Drivers Challenge License Suspensions for Unpaid Court Debt." *AP News*, July 4, 2018. https://apnews.com/article/nc-state-wire-lawsuits-us-news-ap-top-news-courts-3f83b360a1f141f4a794f4203c7eab2f.

Lawson, Caitlin E. "Platform Vulnerabilities: Harassment and Misogynoir in the Digital Attack on Leslie Jones." *Information, Communication & Society* 21, no. 6 (2018): 818–33.

Lenhart, Amanda, Michele L. Ybarra, Kathryn Zickuhr, and Myeshia Price-Feeney. *Online Harassment, Digital Abuse, and Cyberstalking in America*. New York: Data & Society Research Institute, November 21, 2016.

Levin, Josh. "The Real Story of Linda Taylor, America's Original Welfare Queen." *Slate*, December 19, 2013. http://www.slate.com/articles/news_and_politics/history/2013/12/linda_taylor_welfare_queen_ronald_reagan_made_her_a_notorious_american_villain.html.

Levinson-Waldman, Rachel. "How ICE and Other DHS Agencies Mine Social Media in the Name of National Security." *Brennan Center for Justice Blog*,

June 3, 2019. https://www.brennancenter.org/blog/how-ice-and-other-dhs
-agencies-mine-social-media-name-national-security.

Levy, Karen. "The Contexts of Control: Information, Power, and Truck-Driving
Work." *Information Society* 31, no. 2 (2015): 160–74. https://doi.org/10.1080/
01972243.2015.998105.

Levy, Karen, and Solon Barocas. "Privacy at the Margins | Refractive Surveillance:
Monitoring Customers to Manage Workers." *International Journal of Communication* 12 (2018): 1166–88.

Levy, Karen, and danah boyd. "Networked Rights and Networked Harms." Paper
presented at the Privacy Law Scholars Conference, Washington, DC, June 5–6,
2014.

Lewis, Rebecca, Alice Marwick, and William Partin. "'We Dissect Stupidity and
Respond to It': Response Videos and Networked Harassment on YouTube."
American Behavioral Scientist 65, no. 5 (2021): 735–56.

LexisNexis. "Health and Human Services." LexisNexis Risk Solutions, 2019. https://
risk.lexisnexis.com/government/health-and-human-services.

Li, Xiaoqian, Wenhong Chen, and Joseph D. Straubhaar. "Privacy at the Margins |
Concerns, Skills, and Activities: Multilayered Privacy Issues in Disadvantaged
Urban Communities." *International Journal of Communication* 12 (2018):
1269–90.

Liao, Shannon. "Tumblr Will Ban All Adult Content on December 17th." *The Verge*,
December 3, 2018. https://www.theverge.com/2018/12/3/18123752/tumblr-adult
-content-porn-ban-date-explicit-changes-why-safe-mode.

Light, Ben, Peta Mitchell, and Patrik Wikström. "Big Data, Method and the Ethics of Location: A Case Study of a Hookup App for Men Who Have Sex
with Men." *Social Media + Society* 4, no. 2 (2018). https://doi.org/10.1177/
2056305118768299.

Lincoln, Yvonna S., and Egon G. Guba. *Naturalistic Inquiry*. Newbury Park,
CA: Sage, 1985.

Lindley, Susan Hill. *"You Have Stept Out of Your Place": A History of Women and
Religion in America*. Louisville, KY: Westminster John Knox Press, 1996.

Lingel, Jessa, and Adam Golub. "In Face on Facebook: Brooklyn's Drag Community and Sociotechnical Practices of Online Communication." *Journal of
Computer-Mediated Communication* 20, no. 5 (2015): 536–53.

Liptak, Adam. "In Ruling on Cellphone Location Data, Supreme Court Makes Statement on Digital Privacy." *New York Times*, June 22, 2018, sec. U.S. https://www.nytimes.com/2018/06/22/us/politics/supreme-court-warrants-cell-phone-privacy.html.

Litt, Eden. "Knock, Knock. Who's There? The Imagined Audience." *Journal of Broadcasting & Electronic Media* 56, no. 3 (2012): 330–45.

Lloyd, Moya. "Heteronormativity and/as Violence: The 'Sexing' of Gwen Araujo." *Hypatia* 28, no. 4 (2013): 818–34.

Lomas, Natasha. "Researchers Spotlight the Lie of 'Anonymous' Data." *TechCrunch* (blog), July 24, 2019. http://social.techcrunch.com/2019/07/24/researchers-spotlight-the-lie-of-anonymous-data/.

Lum, Kristian. "Predictive Policing Reinforces Police Bias." HRDAG—Human Rights Data Analysis Group, October 10, 2016. http://hrdag.org/2016/10/10/predictive-policing-reinforces-police-bias/.

Lyles, Taylor. "Facebook Will Start Verifying the Identities of Accounts That Keep Going Viral." *The Verge*, May 28, 2020. https://www.theverge.com/2020/5/28/21273784/facebook-id-verification-suspicious-accounts-viral-misinformation.

Lyon, David. *Surveillance Studies: An Overview*. Cambridge, UK: Polity, 2007.

Mac, Gabriel. "I Was a Warehouse Wage Slave." *Mother Jones*, February 2012. https://www.motherjones.com/politics/2012/02/mac-mcclelland-free-online-shipping-warehouses-labor/.

MacKinnon, Catharine A. *Toward a Feminist Theory of the State*. Cambridge, MA: Harvard University Press, 1989.

Madden, Mary. "The Devastating Consequences of Being Poor in the Digital Age." *New York Times*, April 25, 2019, sec. Opinion. https://www.nytimes.com/2019/04/25/opinion/privacy-poverty.html.

Madden, Mary, Michele Gilman, Karen Levy, and Alice Marwick. "Privacy, Poverty, and Big Data: A Matrix of Vulnerabilities for Poor Americans." *Washington University Law Review* 95, no. 1 (2017): 53–125.

Madden, Stephanie, Melissa Janoske, Rowena Briones Winkler, and Amanda Nell Edgar. "Mediated Misogynoir: Intersecting Race and Gender in Online Harassment." In *Mediating Misogyny: Gender, Technology, and Harassment*, edited by Jacqueline Ryan Vickery and Tracy Everbach, 71–90. London: Palgrave Macmillan, 2018.

Madejski, Michelle, Maritza Johnson, and Steven M. Bellovin. "A Study of Privacy Settings Errors in an Online Social Network." In *2012 IEEE International Conference on Pervasive Computing and Communications Workshops*, 340–45. New York: IEEE, 2012.

Mallonee, Laura. "How Photos Fuel the Spread of Fake News." *Wired*, December 21, 2016. https://www.wired.com/2016/12/photos-fuel-spread-fake-news/.

Mallory, Christy, Andrew Flores, and Brad Sears. "LGBT in the South." Williams Institute, UCLA School of Law, March 15, 2016. https://williamsinstitute.law.ucla.edu/research/census-lgbt-demographics-studies/lgbt-in-the-south/.

———. "LGBT People in North Carolina." Fact sheet. Williams Institute, UCLA School of Law, 2017. https://williamsinstitute.law.ucla.edu/wp-content/uploads/North-Carolina-fact-sheet.pdf.

Manant, Matthieu, Serge Pajak, and Nicolas Soulié. "Can Social Media Lead to Labor Market Discrimination? Evidence from a Field Experiment." *Journal of Economics & Management Strategy* 28, no. 2 (2019): 225–46.

Manderson, Lenore, Mark Davis, Chip Colwell, and Tanja Ahlin. "On Secrecy, Disclosure, the Public, and the Private in Anthropology." *Current Anthropology* 56, no. S12 (December 1, 2015): S183–90. https://doi.org/10.1086/683302.

Manne, Kate. *Down Girl: The Logic of Misogyny*. Oxford: Oxford University Press, 2017.

Mantilla, Karla. "Gendertrolling: Misogyny Adapts to New Media." *Feminist Studies* 39, no. 2 (2013): 563–70. https://doi.org/10.2307/23719068.

"Man Wins Facebook Battle over 'Fake' Gaelic Name." *Scotsman*, February 15, 2015. https://www.scotsman.com/news/man-wins-facebook-battle-over-fake-gaelic-name-1511563.

March, James G., and Zur Shapira. "Managerial Perspectives on Risk and Risk Taking." *Management Science* 33, no. 11 (1987): 1404–18.

Marcus, Amy Dockser. "Customers Handed Over Their DNA. The Company Let the FBI Take a Look." *Wall Street Journal*, August 22, 2019, sec. US. https://www.wsj.com/articles/customers-handed-over-their-dna-the-company-let-the-fbi-take-a-look-11566491162.

Markel, Howard, and Alexandra Minna Stern. "The Foreignness of Germs: The Persistent Association of Immigrants and Disease in American Society." *Milbank Quarterly* 80, no. 4 (2002): 757–88. https://doi.org/10.1111/1468-0009.00030.

Martin, D. D. "Identity Management of the Dead: Contests in the Construction of Murdered Children." *Symbolic Interaction* 33, no. 1 (2010): 18–40.

Marwick, Alice E. "Morally Motivated Networked Harassment as Normative Reinforcement." *Social Media + Society* 7, no. 2 (2021). https://doi.org/10.1177/20563051211021378.

———. "The Public Domain: Social Surveillance in Everyday Life." *Surveillance & Society* 9, no. 4 (2012). http://library.queensu.ca/ojs/index.php/surveillance-and-society/article/view/pub_dom.

———. "Scandal or Sex Crime? Gendered Privacy and the Celebrity Nude Photo Leaks." *Ethics and Information Technology* 19, no. 3 (2017): 177–91. https://doi.org/10.1007/s10676-017-9431-7.

———. *Status Update: Celebrity, Publicity, and Branding in the Social Media Age.* New Haven, CT: Yale University Press, 2013.

Marwick, Alice E, and danah boyd. "'It's Just Drama': Teen Perspectives on Conflict and Aggression in a Networked Era." *Journal of Youth Studies* 17, no. 9 (2014): 1187–1204. https://doi.org/10.1080/13676261.2014.901493.

———. "I Tweet Honestly, I Tweet Passionately: Twitter Users, Context Collapse, and the Imagined Audience." *New Media & Society* 13, no. 1 (2011): 114–33.

———. "Networked Privacy: How Teenagers Negotiate Context in Social Media." *New Media & Society* 16, no. 7 (2014): 1051–67.

Marwick, Alice E., and Robyn Caplan. "Drinking Male Tears: Language, the Manosphere, and Networked Harassment." *Feminist Media Studies* 18, no. 4 (2018): 543–59.

Marwick, Alice E., and Nicole B. Ellison. "'There Isn't Wifi in Heaven!': Negotiating Visibility on Facebook Memorial Pages." *Journal of Broadcasting & Electronic Media* 56, no. 3 (2012): 378–400. https://doi.org/10.1080/08838151.2012.705197.

Marwick, Alice E., Claire Fontaine, and danah boyd. "'Nobody Sees It, Nobody Gets Mad': Social Media, Privacy, and Personal Responsibility among Low-SES Youth." *Social Media & Society* 3, no. 2 (2017). http://journals.sagepub.com/doi/abs/10.1177/2056305117710455.

Marwick, Alice E., and Eszter Hargittai. "Nothing to Hide, Nothing to Lose? Incentives and Disincentives to Sharing Information with Institutions Online." *Information, Communication & Society* 22, no. 12 (2019): 1697–1713.

Massanari, Adrienne. "#Gamergate and The Fappening: How Reddit's Algorithm, Governance, and Culture Support Toxic Technocultures." *New Media & Society* 19, no. 3 (2015): 329–46. https://doi.org/10.1177/1461444815608807.

Mateescu, Alexandra, Douglas Brunton, Alex Rosenblat, Desmond Patton, Zachary Gold, and danah boyd. "Social Media Surveillance and Law Enforcement." *Data and Civil Rights* 27 (2015): 2015–27.

Mathers, Lain A. B., J. E. Sumerau, and Ryan T. Cragun. "The Limits of Homonormativity: Constructions of Bisexual and Transgender People in the Post-Gay Era." *Sociological Perspectives* 61, no. 6 (2018): 934–52. https://doi.org/10.1177/0731121417753370.

Matias, J. Nathan. "Preventing Harassment and Increasing Group Participation through Social Norms in 2,190 Online Science Discussions." *Proceedings of the National Academy of Sciences* 116, no. 20 (2019): 9785–89. https://doi.org/10.1073/pnas.1813486116.

Maus, Gregory. "How Data Brokers Sell Your Life, and Why It Matters." *The Stack* (blog), August 24, 2015. https://thestack.com/security/2015/08/24/how-corporate-data-brokers-sell-your-life-and-why-you-should-be-concerned/.

McCallister, Erika, Timothy Grance, and Karen A. Scarfone. *Guide to Protecting the Confidentiality of Personally Identifiable Information (PII)*. Special publication, Computer Security. Washington, DC: National Institute of Standards and Technology, April 2010. http://csrc.nist.gov/publications/nistpubs/800-122/sp800-122.pdf.

McCarroll, Estefania. "Weapons of Mass Deportation: Big Data and Automated Decision-Making Systems in Immigration Law." *Georgetown Immigration Law Journal* 34 (2019): 705–31.

McCluney, Courtney L., and Verónica Caridad Rabelo. "Conditions of Visibility: An Intersectional Examination of Black Women's Belongingness and Distinctiveness at Work." In "Managing Visibility and Invisibility in the Workplace." Special issue. *Journal of Vocational Behavior* 113 (August 1, 2019): 143–52. https://doi.org/10.1016/j.jvb.2018.09.008.

McDonald, Aleecia M., and Lorrie Faith Cranor. "The Cost of Reading Privacy Policies." *I/S: A Journal of Law and Policy for the Information Society* 4, no. 3 (2008): 540–65.

McFall, Liz. "Personalizing Solidarity? The Role of Self-Tracking in Health Insurance Pricing." *Economy and Society* 48, no. 1 (2019): 52–76.

McGlynn, Clare, Erika Rackley, and Ruth Houghton. "Beyond 'Revenge Porn': The Continuum of Image-Based Sexual Abuse." *Feminist Legal Studies* 25, no. 1 (2017): 25–46. https://doi.org/10.1007/s10691-017-9343-2.

McKeon, Kelsey. "5 Personal Branding Tips for Your Job Search." *The Manifest*, April 28, 2020. https://themanifest.com/digital-marketing/5-personal-branding-tips -job-search.

McLean, Lavinia, and Mark D. Griffiths. "Female Gamers' Experience of Online Harassment and Social Support in Online Gaming: A Qualitative Study." *International Journal of Mental Health and Addiction* 17 (2019): 970–94.

Merton, Robert K. *Social Theory and Social Structure.* Enlarged ed. New York: Free Press, 1968.

Meyersohn, Nathaniel. "There Are Still 100,000 Pay Phones in America." *CNNMoney,* March 19, 2018. https://money.cnn.com/2018/03/19/news/companies/pay -phones/index.html.

Michener, Jamila, Mallory SoRelle, and Chloe Thurston. "From the Margins to the Center: A Bottom-Up Approach to Welfare State Scholarship." *Perspectives on Politics* 20, no. 1 (2022): 154–69. https://doi.org/10.1017/S15375927200 0359X.

Miller, Claire Cain. "Americans Say They Want Privacy, but Act as If They Don't." *The Upshot* (blog), *New York Times*, November 12, 2014. https://www.nytimes .com/2014/11/13/upshot/americans-say-they-want-privacy-but-act-as-if-they -dont.html.

Min, Jinyoung, and Byoungsoo Kim. "How Are People Enticed to Disclose Personal Information despite Privacy Concerns in Social Network Sites? The Calculus between Benefit and Cost." *Journal of the Association for Information Science and Technology* 66, no. 4 (2015): 839–57. https://doi.org/10.1002/asi .23206.

Min, Sarah. "Social Security May Use Your Facebook and Instagram Photos to Nix Disability Claims." *CBS News*, March 21, 2019. https://www.cbsnews.com/

news/social-security-disability-benefits-your-facebook-instagram-posts-could
-affect-your-social-security-disability-claim/.

Mingus, Mia. "The Practice in the Service of Longing: Everyday Transformative Justice." Keynote, Social Justice Summit, Humboldt State University, Arcata, CA, March 6, 2020. https://scholarworks.calstate.edu/concern/publications/ 7s75df87v?locale=en.

Mink, Gwendolyn. *The Wages of Motherhood: Inequality in the Welfare State, 1917–1942*. Ithaca, NY: Cornell University Press, 1996.

Mishna, Faye, Kaitlin J. Schwan, Arija Birze, Melissa Van Wert, Ashley Lacombe-Duncan, Lauren McInroy, and Shalhevet Attar-Schwartz. "Gendered and Sexualized Bullying and Cyber Bullying: Spotlighting Girls and Making Boys Invisible." *Youth & Society* 52, no. 3 (2020): 403–26. https://doi.org/10.1177/ 0044118X18757150.

Molla, Rani. "People Say They Care about Privacy but They Continue to Buy Devices That Can Spy on Them." *Vox*, May 13, 2019. https://www.vox.com/ recode/2019/5/13/18547235/trust-smart-devices-privacy-security.

Monahan, Torin. "Regulating Belonging: Surveillance, Inequality, and the Cultural Production of Abjection." *Journal of Cultural Economy* 10, no. 2 (2017): 191–206.

Monahan, Torin, and Rodolfo D. Torres. *Schools under Surveillance: Cultures of Control in Public Education*. New Brunswick, NJ: Rutgers University Press, 2009.

Monroe, Rachel. "From Pickup Artist to Pariah." *The Cut*, January 20, 2016. http:// www.thecut.com/2016/01/jared-rutledge-pickup-artist-c-v-r.html.

Montjoye, Yves-Alexandre de, Laura Radaelli, Vivek Kumar Singh, and Alex "Sandy" Pentland. "Unique in the Shopping Mall: On the Reidentifiability of Credit Card Metadata." *Science* 347, no. 6221 (January 30, 2015): 536–39. https://doi.org/10.1126/science.1256297.

Moore, Barrington, Jr. *Privacy: Studies in Social and Cultural History*. New York: Routledge, 1984.

Morales, Mark, and Laura Ly. "Released NYPD Emails Show Extensive Surveillance of Black Lives Matter Protesters." CNN, January 18, 2019. https://www .cnn.com/2019/01/18/us/nypd-black-lives-matter-surveillance/index.html.

Morrison, Sara. "How Teachers Are Sacrificing Student Privacy to Stop Cheating." *Vox*, December 18, 2020. https://www.vox.com/recode/22175021/school -cheating-student-privacy-remote-learning.

Mosher, Clayton J., Terance D. Miethe, and Timothy C. Hart. "Introduction: The Pervasiveness (and Limitations) of Measurement." In *The Mismeasure of Crime*, 2nd ed., edited by Clayton J. Mosher, Terance D. Miethe, and Timothy C. Hart, 1–29. Thousand Oaks, CA: Sage, 2011. https://doi.org/10.4135/9781483349497.

Mosher, Janet, and Joe Hermer. "Welfare Fraud: The Constitution of Social Assistance as Crime." In *Constructing Crime: Contemporary Processes of Criminalization*, edited by Janet Mosher and Joan Brockman, 17–52. Toronto: UBC Press, 2010.

Muhammad, Khalil Gibran. *The Condemnation of Blackness*. Cambridge, MA: Harvard University Press, 2011.

Mullis, Steve. "Leaked Video Shows Romney Discussing 'Dependent' Voters." *NPR.org*, September 17, 2012. https://www.npr.org/sections/itsallpolitics/2012/09/17/161313644/leaked-video-purports-to-show-romney-discuss-dependent-voters.

Murphy, Heather. "Most White Americans' DNA Can Be Identified through Genealogy Databases." *New York Times*, October 11, 2018, sec. Science. https://www.nytimes.com/2018/10/11/science/science-genetic-genealogy-study.html.

Nadasen, Premilla. *Welfare Warriors: The Welfare Rights Movement in the United States*. New York: Routledge, 2004.

Nash, Jennifer C. "From Lavender to Purple: Privacy, Black Women, and Feminist Legal Theory." *Cardozo Women's Law Journal* 11 (2004): 303–30.

Nelson, Julie A. "The Study of Choice or the Study of Provisioning? Gender and the Definition of Economics." In *Beyond Economic Man: Feminist Theory and Economics*, edited by Marianne A. Ferber and Julie A. Nelson, 23–36. Chicago: University of Chicago Press, 1993.

Newman, Lily Hay. "Internal Docs Show How ICE Gets Surveillance Help from Local Cops." *Wired*, March 13, 2019. https://www.wired.com/story/ice-license-plate-surveillance-vigilant-solutions/.

Newton, Esther. *Mother Camp: Female Impersonators in America*. Chicago: University of Chicago Press, 1972.

Nichols, Sam. "Your Phone Is Listening and It's Not Paranoia." *Vice*, June 4, 2018. https://www.vice.com/en_uk/article/wjbzzy/your-phone-is-listening-and-its-not-paranoia.

Nippert-Eng, Christena E. *Islands of Privacy*. Chicago: University of Chicago Press, 2010.

Nissenbaum, Helen. *Privacy in Context: Technology, Policy, and the Integrity of Social Life*. Stanford, CA: Stanford University Press, 2010.

Nixon, Ron. "U.S. to Collect Social Media Data on All Immigrants Entering Country." *New York Times*, September 28, 2017, sec. U.S. https://www.nytimes.com/2017/09/28/us/politics/immigrants-social-media-trump.html.

Nocella, Anthony J., III. "An Overview of the History and Theory of Transformative Justice." *Peace & Conflict Review* 6, no. 1 (2011): 1–10.

Oldenburg, Ray. *The Great Good Place: Cafés, Coffee Shops, Community Centers, Beauty Parlors, General Stores, Bars, Hangouts, and How They Get You through the Day*. New York: Paragon House, 1989.

Olsen, Frances. "Constitutional Law: Feminist Critiques of the Public/Private Distinction." *Constitutional Commentary* 10 (1993): 319–27.

Olson, Candi Carter, and Victoria LaPoe. "Combating the Digital Spiral of Silence: Academic Activists versus Social Media Trolls." In *Mediating Misogyny: Gender, Technology, and Harassment*, edited by Jacqueline Ryan Vickery and Tracy Everbach, 271–91. Cham, Switzerland: Springer, 2018. https://doi.org/10.1007/978-3-319-72917-6_14.

O'Neil, Cathy. "How Algorithms Rule Our Working Lives." *Guardian*, September 1, 2016, sec. Science. https://www.theguardian.com/science/2016/sep/01/how-algorithms-rule-our-working-lives.

Oolo, Egle, and Andraa Siibak. "Performing for One's Imagined Audience: Social Steganography and Other Privacy Strategies of Estonian Teens on Networked Publics." *Cyberpsychology: Journal of Psychosocial Research on Cyberspace* 7, no. 1 (2013): article 7.

O'Reilly, Michelle, and Nicola Parker. "'Unsatisfactory Saturation': A Critical Exploration of the Notion of Saturated Sample Sizes in Qualitative Research." *Qualitative Research* 13, no. 2 (2013): 190–97.

Osucha, Eden Koren. "The Subject of Privacy: Race, Rights, and Intimate Personhood in Modern American Literature and Law." PhD diss., Duke University, 2007. https://search.proquest.com/docview/304863177/abstract/245E6F169324FB5PQ/1.

———. "The Whiteness of Privacy: Race, Media, Law." *Camera Obscura: Feminism, Culture, and Media Studies* 24, no. 1 (70) (May 1, 2009): 67–107. https://doi.org/10.1215/02705346-2008-015.

Parenti, Christian. *The Soft Cage: Surveillance in America from Slavery to the War on Terror*. New York: Basic Books, 2003.

Patel, Faiza, Rachel Levinson-Waldman, Sophia DenUyl, and Raya Koreh. *Social Media Monitoring: How the Department of Homeland Security Uses Digital Data in the Name of National Security*. New York: Brennan Center for Justice at New York University School of Law, May 22, 2019. https://www.brennancenter.org/sites/default/files/publications/2019_DHS-SocialMediaMonitoring_FINAL.pdf.

Pateman, Carole. "Feminist Critiques of the Public/Private Dichotomy." In *Public and Private in Social Life*, edited by Stanley I. Benn and G. F. Gaus, 118–40. London: St. Martin's and Croom Helm, 1983.

Paunescu, Delia. "The Faulty Technology behind Ankle Monitors." *Vox*, December 1, 2019. https://www.vox.com/recode/2019/12/1/20986262/ankle-monitor-technology-reset-podcast.

PBS NewsHour. "The War on Drugs Gave Rise to 'No-Knock' Warrants. Breonna Taylor's Death Could End Them." PBS, June 12, 2020. https://www.pbs.org/newshour/politics/the-war-on-drugs-gave-rise-to-no-knock-warrants-breonna-taylors-death-could-end-them.

Perkins, Linda M. "The Impact of the 'Cult of True Womanhood' on the Education of Black Women." *Journal of Social Issues* 39, no. 3 (1983): 17–28.

Persson, Anders. "Implicit Bias in Predictive Data Profiling within Recruitments." In *Privacy and Identity Management: Facing Up to Next Steps*, edited by Anja Lehmann, Diane Whitehouse, Simone Fischer-Hübner, Lothar Fritsch, and Charles Raab, 212–30. Cham, Switzerland: Springer, 2016.

Petronio, Sandra. *Boundaries of Privacy: Dialectics of Disclosure*. Albany: SUNY Press, 2002.

Phillips, Whitney. *This Is Why We Can't Have Nice Things: Mapping the Relationship between Online Trolling and Mainstream Culture*. Cambridge, MA: MIT Press, 2015.

Pitcan, Mikaela, Alice E. Marwick, and danah boyd. "Performing a Vanilla Self: Respectability Politics, Social Class, and the Digital World." *Journal of Computer-Mediated Communication* 23, no. 3 (2018): 163–79.

Piwek, Lukasz, and Adam Joinson. "'What Do They Snapchat About?': Patterns of Use in Time-Limited Instant Messaging Service." *Computers in Hu-*

man Behavior 54 (January 1, 2016): 358–67. https://doi.org/10.1016/j.chb.2015 .08.026.

Porcheron, Martin, Joel E. Fischer, Stuart Reeves, and Sarah Sharples. "Voice Interfaces in Everyday Life." In *Proceedings of the 2018 CHI Conference on Human Factors in Computing Systems*, 1–12. New York: ACM, 2018. https://doi.org/10 .1145/3173574.3174214.

Poster, Winifred R. "Emotion Detectors, Answering Machines, and e-Unions: Multi-surveillances in the Global Interactive Service Industry." *American Behavioral Scientist* 55, no. 7 (2011): 868–901.

Poussaint, Alvin F. "A Negro Psychiatrist Explains the Negro Psyche." *New York Times*, August 20, 1967. https://www.nytimes.com/1967/08/20/archives/a-negro -psychiatrist-explains-the-negro-psyche-the-negro-psyche.html.

Raghavan, Manish, Solon Barocas, Jon Kleinberg, and Karen Levy. "Mitigating Bias in Algorithmic Hiring: Evaluating Claims and Practices." In *Proceedings of the 2020 Conference on Fairness, Accountability, and Transparency*, 469–81. New York: ACM, 2020.

Raji, Inioluwa Deborah, and Genevieve Fried. "About Face: A Survey of Facial Recognition Evaluation." Paper presented at AAAI 2020 Workshop on AI Evaluation, February 1, 2021. http://arxiv.org/abs/2102.00813.

Rakow, Lana F. *Gender on the Line: Women, the Telephone, and Community Life.* Urbana: University of Illinois Press, 1992.

Ramirez, Fanny Anne. "The Digital Turn in Public Criminal Defense." PhD diss., Rutgers University–School of Graduate Studies, 2019.

Reaves, Brian A. *Police Response to Domestic Violence, 2006–2015.* Washington, DC: US Department of Justice, Office of Justice Programs, Bureau of Justice Statistics, 2017.

Redmiles, Elissa M., and Eszter Hargittai. "New Phone, Who Dis? Modeling Millennials' Backup Behavior." *ACM Transactions on the Web* 13, no. 1 (2018): article 4. https://doi.org/10.1145/3208105.

Regalado, Antonio. "More than 26 Million People Have Taken an At-Home Ancestry Test." *MIT Technology Review*, February 11, 2019. https://www .technologyreview.com/s/612880/more-than-26-million-people-have-taken-an -at-home-ancestry-test/.

Regan, Priscilla M. *Legislating Privacy: Technology, Social Values, and Public Policy.* Chapel Hill: University of North Carolina Press, 1995.

Regan, Priscilla M., and Jolene Jesse. "Ethical Challenges of Edtech, Big Data and Personalized Learning: Twenty-First Century Student Sorting and Tracking." *Ethics and Information Technology* 21, no. 3 (2019): 167–79.

Reich, Adam, and Peter Bearman. *Working for Respect: Community and Conflict at Walmart.* New York: Columbia University Press, 2018.

Reinarman, Craig, and Harry G. Levine. "Crack in the Rearview Mirror: Deconstructing Drug War Mythology." *Social Justice* 31, nos. 1–2 (95–96) (2004): 182–99.

Renaud, Karen, Stephen Flowerday, Merrill Warkentin, Paul Cockshott, and Craig Orgeron. "Is the Responsibilization of the Cyber Security Risk Reasonable and Judicious?" *Computers & Security* 78 (September 1, 2018): 198–211. https://doi.org/10.1016/j.cose.2018.06.006.

Renner, Nausicaa. "As Immigrants Become More Aware of Their Rights, ICE Steps Up Ruses and Surveillance." *The Intercept* (blog), July 25, 2019. https://theintercept.com/2019/07/25/ice-surveillance-ruse-arrests-raids/.

Reuters. "Data Brokers Sold Payday Loan Applicants' Information to Scammers: FTC." *NBC News*, August 12, 2015. http://www.nbcnews.com/business/business-news/data-brokers-sold-payday-loan-applicants-information-scammers-ftc-n408606.

Richards, Neil M., and Woodrow Hartzog. "Taking Trust Seriously in Privacy Law." SSRN, September 3, 2015. https://papers.ssrn.com/abstract=2655719.

Richardson, Rashida, Jason Schultz, and Kate Crawford. "Dirty Data, Bad Predictions: How Civil Rights Violations Impact Police Data, Predictive Policing Systems, and Justice." *New York University Law Review Online* 94 (2019): 15–55.

Ringrose, Jessica, Rosalind Gill, Sonia Livingstone, and Laura Harvey. *A Qualitative Study of Children, Young People and "Sexting": A Report Prepared for the NSPCC.* London: National Society for the Prevention of Cruelty to Children, 2012. http://eprints.lse.ac.uk/44216.

Roberts, Dorothy E. "Digitizing the Carceral State." *Harvard Law Review* 132, no. 6 (2019): 1695–1728.

Roberts, Mary Louise. "True Womanhood Revisited." *Journal of Women's History* 14, no. 1 (2002): 150–55.

Roberts, Roxanne. "Linda Tripp Wanted to Make History. Instead, It Nearly Destroyed Her." *Washington Post*, April 9, 2020. https://www.washingtonpost

.com/lifestyle/linda-tripp-clinton-lewinsky-scandal/2020/04/09/0c3b7d68
-7a7b-11ea-a130-df573469f094_story.html.

Rocher, Luc, Julien M. Hendrickx, and Yves-Alexandre de Montjoye. "Estimating the Success of Re-identifications in Incomplete Datasets Using Generative Models." *Nature Communications* 10, no. 1 (2019): 1–9. https://doi.org/10.1038/s41467-019-10933-3.

Rohrlich, Justin. "In Just Two Years, 9,000 of These Cameras Were Installed to Spy on Your Car." *Quartz*, February 5, 2019. https://qz.com/1540488/in-just-two-years-9000-of-these-cameras-were-installed-to-spy-on-your-car/.

Roland, Denise. "How Drug Companies Are Using Your DNA to Make New Medicine." *Wall Street Journal*, July 22, 2019, sec. Business. https://www.wsj.com/articles/23andme-glaxo-mine-dna-data-in-hunt-for-new-drugs-11563879881.

Rollins, Judith. *Between Women: Domestics and Their Employers*. Philadelphia: Temple University Press, 1985.

Ronson, Jon. "'Overnight, Everything I Loved Was Gone': The Internet Shaming of Lindsey Stone." *Guardian*, February 21, 2015, sec. Technology. https://www.theguardian.com/technology/2015/feb/21/internet-shaming-lindsey-stone-jon-ronson.

Rosen, David, and Aaron Santesso. "School Surveillance and Privacy." In *The Palgrave International Handbook of School Discipline, Surveillance, and Social Control*, edited by Jo Deakin, Emmeline Taylor, and Aaron Kupchik, 491–507. Cham, Switzerland: Springer, 2018.

Rosenblat, Alex. *Uberland: How Algorithms Are Rewriting the Rules of Work*. Oakland: University of California Press, 2018.

Rosenblat, Alex, Tamara Kneese, and danah boyd. "Networked Employment Discrimination." Open Society Foundations' Future of Work Commissioned Research Papers, 2014. SSRN, December 31, 2014. http://papers.ssrn.com/sol3/papers.cfm?abstract_id=2543507.

Rothschild, Zachary K., and Lucas A. Keefer. "A Cleansing Fire: Moral Outrage Alleviates Guilt and Buffers Threats to One's Moral Identity." *Motivation and Emotion* 41, no. 2 (2017): 209–29. https://doi.org/10.1007/s11031-017-9601-2.

Rubel, Alan, and Kyle M. L. Jones. "Student Privacy in Learning Analytics: An Information Ethics Perspective." *Information Society* 32, no. 2 (2016): 143–59. https://doi.org/10.1080/01972243.2016.1130502.

Rubin, Gayle. "Thinking Sex: Notes for a Radical Theory of the Politics of Sexuality." In *Pleasure and Danger*, edited by Carole Vance, 267–319. Boston: Routledge and Kegan Paul, 1984.

Russell, N. Cameron, Joel R. Reidenberg, Elizabeth Martin, and Thomas B. Norton. "Transparency and the Marketplace for Student Data." *Virginia Journal of Law & Technology* 22, no. 3 (2019): 107–57.

Saldana, Johnny. *The Coding Manual for Qualitative Researchers*. Thousand Oaks, CA: Sage, 2009.

Salter, Anastasia, and Bridget Blodgett. "Hypermasculinity & Dickwolves: The Contentious Role of Women in the New Gaming Public." *Journal of Broadcasting & Electronic Media* 56, no. 3 (2012): 401–16. https://doi.org/10.1080/08838151.2012.705199.

———. *Toxic Geek Masculinity in Media: Sexism, Trolling, and Identity Policing.* Cham, Switzerland: Springer, 2017.

Samaha, Albert, Jason Leopold, and Rosalind Adams. "Newly Released Documents Reveal How the Feds Were Monitoring BLM Protests." *BuzzFeed News*, August 13, 2020. https://www.buzzfeednews.com/article/albertsamaha/newly-released-documents-reveal-how-the-feds-were.

Satell, Greg. "Let's Face It, We Don't Really Care about Privacy." *Forbes*, December 1, 2014. https://www.forbes.com/sites/gregsatell/2014/12/01/lets-face-it-we-dont-really-care-about-privacy/.

Scarbrough, Jacquelin W. "Welfare Mothers' Reflections on Personal Responsibility." *Journal of Social Issues* 57, no. 2 (2001): 261–76.

Schneier, Bruce. *Data and Goliath: The Hidden Battles to Collect Your Data and Control Your World.* New York: Norton, 2015.

Schoenebeck, Sarita, Oliver L. Haimson, and Lisa Nakamura. "Drawing from Justice Theories to Support Targets of Online Harassment." *New Media & Society* 23, no. 5 (2021): 1278–1300. https://doi.org/10.1177/1461444820913122.

Scholes, Vanessa. "The Ethics of Using Learning Analytics to Categorize Students on Risk." *Educational Technology Research and Development* 64, no. 5 (2016): 939–55.

Scott, D. Travers. "'Coming Out of the Closet'—Examining a Metaphor." *Annals of the International Communication Association* 43, no. 3 (2018): 145–54.

Sedgwick, Eve Kosofsky. *Epistemology of the Closet*. Berkeley: University of California Press, 1990.

Selk, Avi. "The Ingenious and 'Dystopian' DNA Technique Police Used to Hunt the 'Golden State Killer' Suspect." *Washington Post*, April 28, 2018, sec. True Crime. https://www.washingtonpost.com/news/true-crime/wp/2018/04/27/golden -state-killer-dna-website-gedmatch-was-used-to-identify-joseph-deangelo-as -suspect-police-say/.

Sethi, Arjun Singh. "The FBI Needs to Stop Spying on Muslim-Americans." *Politico Magazine*, March 29, 2016. https://www.politico.com/magazine/story/2016/ 03/muslim-american-surveillance-fbi-spying-213773.

Shamir, Ronen. "The Age of Responsibilization: On Market-Embedded Morality." *Economy and Society* 37, no. 1 (2008): 1–19. https://doi.org/10.1080/ 03085140701760833.

Shapiro, Ari. "Police Use DNA to Track Suspects through Family." *All Things Considered*, NPR, December 12, 2007. https://www.npr.org/templates/story/story .php?storyId=17130501.

Shapiro, Carl, and Hal R. Varian. *Information Rules: A Strategic Guide to the Network Economy*. Boston: Harvard Business School Press, 1998.

Shepherd, Tamara, Alison Harvey, Tim Jordan, Sam Srauy, and Kate Miltner. "Histories of Hating." *Social Media + Society* 1, no. 2 (2015). https://doi.org/10.1177/ 2056305115603997.

Shere, Anjuli R. K., and Jason Nurse. "Police Surveillance of Black Lives Matter Shows the Danger Technology Poses to Democracy." *The Conversation*, July 24, 2020. http://theconversation.com/police-surveillance-of-black-lives-matter -shows-the-danger-technology-poses-to-democracy-142194.

Shore, Jennifer, and Jill Steinman. "Did You Really Agree to That? The Evolution of Facebook's Privacy Policy." *Journal of Technology Science*, August 11, 2015.

Shute, Rosalyn, Larry Owens, and Phillip Slee. "High School Girls' Experience of Victimization by Boys: Where Sexual Harassment Meets Aggression." *Journal of Aggression, Maltreatment & Trauma* 25, no. 3 (2016): 269–85.

Silva, Jennifer M. *Coming Up Short: Working-Class Adulthood in an Age of Uncertainty*. New York: Oxford University Press, 2013.

Silverstein, Michele. "What Percentage of Companies Use an ATS or HRIS?" *Criteria Corp Blog*, October 23, 2019. https://blog.criteriacorp.com/what-percentage-of-companies-use-an-ats-or-hris/.

Simmel, Georg. "The Sociology of Secrecy and of Secret Societies." *American Journal of Sociology* 11, no. 4 (1906): 441–98.

Singer, Natasha. "Bringing Big Data to the Fight against Benefits Fraud." *New York Times*, February 20, 2015, sec. Technology. https://www.nytimes.com/2015/02/22/technology/bringing-big-data-to-the-fight-against-benefits-fraud.html.

Singh, Sourabh. "How Should We Study Relational Structure? Critically Comparing the Epistemological Positions of Social Network Analysis and Field Theory." *Sociology* 53, no. 4 (2019): 762–78. https://doi.org/10.1177/0038038518821307.

Skolnik, Terry. "Homelessness and the Impossibility to Obey the Law." *Fordham Urban Law Journal* 43, no. 3 (2016): 741–87.

Sleeper, Manya, Rebecca Balebako, Sauvik Das, Amber Lynn McConahy, Jason Wiese, and Lorrie Faith Cranor. "The Post That Wasn't: Exploring Self-Censorship on Facebook." In *Proceedings of the 2013 Conference on Computer Supported Cooperative Work*, 793–802. New York: ACM, 2013.

Slupska, Julia. "Safe at Home: Towards a Feminist Critique of Cybersecurity." SSRN, May 1, 2019. https://papers.ssrn.com/abstract=3429851.

Small, Mario Luis. "'How Many Cases Do I Need?': On Science and the Logic of Case Selection in Field-Based Research." *Ethnography* 10, no. 1 (2009): 5–38.

Smith, Christen A. "Impossible Privacy: Black Women and Police Terror." *Black Scholar* 51, no. 1 (2021): 20–29.

Snell, Robert. "Feds Use Anti-Terror Tool to Hunt the Undocumented." *Detroit News*, May 18, 2017. https://www.detroitnews.com/story/news/local/detroit-city/2017/05/18/cell-snooping-fbi-immigrant/101859616/.

Snorton, C. Riley. "'A New Hope': The Psychic Life of Passing." *Hypatia* 24, no. 3 (2009): 77–92.

Sobieraj, Sarah. "Bitch, Slut, Skank, Cunt: Patterned Resistance to Women's Visibility in Digital Publics." *Information, Communication & Society* 21, no. 11 (2018): 1700–1714.

———. *Credible Threat: Attacks against Women Online and the Future of Democracy.* New York: Oxford University Press, 2020.

Sobieraj, Sarah, Gina M. Masullo, Philip N. Cohen, Tarleton Gillespie, and Sarah J. Jackson. "Politicians, Social Media, and Digital Publics: Old Rights, New Terrain." *American Behavioral Scientist* 64, no. 11 (2020): 1646–69. https://doi.org/ 10.1177/0002764220945357.

Social Intelligence. "How It Works." Accessed May 27, 2020. https://www.socialintel .com/solutions/how-it-works/.

Solove, Daniel J. "Access and Aggregation: Privacy, Public Records, and the Constitution." SSRN, September 24, 2001. https://papers.ssrn.com/abstract =Steganography283924.

———. "'I've Got Nothing to Hide' and Other Misunderstandings of Privacy." *San Diego Law Review* 44 (2007): 745–72.

———. "The Meaning and Value of Privacy." In *Social Dimensions of Privacy: Interdisciplinary Perspectives*, edited by Beate Roessler and Dorota Mokrosinska, 71–82. Cambridge: Cambridge University Press, 2015.

———. "The Myth of the Privacy Paradox." *George Washington Law Review* 89 (2021). https://papers.ssrn.com/sol3/papers.cfm?abstract_id=3536265.

———. *Understanding Privacy*. Cambridge, MA: Harvard University Press, 2008.

Soni-Sinha, Urvashi, and Charlotte A. B. Yates. "'Dirty Work?': Gender, Race and the Union in Industrial Cleaning." *Gender, Work & Organization* 20, no. 6 (2013): 737–51. https://doi.org/10.1111/gwao.12006.

Southworth, Cynthia, Jerry Finn, Shawndell Dawson, Cynthia Fraser, and Sarah Tucker. "Intimate Partner Violence, Technology, and Stalking." *Violence against Women* 13, no. 8 (2007): 842–56.

Spiekermann, Sarah, Jens Grossklags, and Bettina Berendt. "E-Privacy in 2nd Generation E-Commerce: Privacy Preferences versus Actual Behavior." In *Proceedings of the 3rd ACM Conference on Electronic Commerce*, 38–47. New York: ACM, 2001. http://dl.acm.org/citation.cfm?id=501163.

Srinivasan, Janaki, Savita Bailur, Emrys Schoemaker, and Sarita Seshagiri. "Privacy at the Margins | The Poverty of Privacy: Understanding Privacy Trade-Offs from Identity Infrastructure Users in India." *International Journal of Communication* 12 (2018): 1228–47.

Star, Susan Leigh, and Anselm Strauss. "Layers of Silence, Arenas of Voice: The Ecology of Visible and Invisible Work." *Computer Supported Cooperative Work (CSCW)* 8, no. 1 (1999): 9–30. https://doi.org/10.1023/A:1008651105359.

Starbucks. "Starbucks Principles for Upholding the Third Place: For Our Partners, Our Customers and Our Communities." *Starbucks Stories*, January 24, 2019. https://stories.starbucks.com/stories/2019/starbucks-principles-for-upholding -the-third-place-for-our-partners-our-customers-and-our-communities/.

Stoycheff, Elizabeth, Juan Liu, Kai Xu, and Kunto Wibowo. "Privacy and the Panopticon: Online Mass Surveillance's Deterrence and Chilling Effects." *New Media & Society* 21, no. 3 (2019): 602–19. https://doi.org/10.1177/14614448188 01317.

Streitfeld, David. "How Amazon Crushes Unions." *New York Times*, March 16, 2021, sec. Technology. https://www.nytimes.com/2021/03/16/technology/ amazon-unions-virginia.html.

Stryker, Susan. "Transgender Studies: Queer Theory's Evil Twin." *GLQ: A Journal of Lesbian and Gay Studies* 10, no. 2 (2004): 212–15.

Stuntz, William J. "The Distribution of Fourth Amendment Privacy." *George Washington Law Review* 67 (1999): 1265–89.

Sue, Derald Wing, Christina M. Capodilupo, Gina C. Torino, Jennifer M. Bucceri, Aisha Holder, Kevin L. Nadal, and Marta Esquilin. "Racial Microaggressions in Everyday Life: Implications for Clinical Practice." *American Psychologist* 62, no. 4 (2007): 271–86.

Suk, Jeannie. *At Home in the Law: How the Domestic Violence Revolution Is Transforming Privacy*. New Haven, CT: Yale University Press, 2009.

Swan, Richelle S., Linda L. Shaw, Sharon Cullity, and Mary Roche. "The Untold Story of Welfare Fraud." *Journal of Sociology & Social Welfare* 35 (2008): 133–51.

Swanson, Ana, Mike Isaac, and Paul Mozur. "Trump Targets WeChat and TikTok, in Sharp Escalation with China." *New York Times*, August 7, 2020, sec. Technology. https://www.nytimes.com/2020/08/06/technology/trump-wechat -tiktok-china.html.

Szameitat, André J., Yasmin Hamaida, Rebecca S. Tulley, Rahmi Saylik, and Pauldy C. J. Otermans. "'Women Are Better than Men'—Public Beliefs on Gender Differences and Other Aspects in Multitasking." *PloS One* 10, no. 10 (2015): e0140371.

Tanner, Adam. *Our Bodies, Our Data: How Companies Make Billions Selling Our Medical Records*. Boston: Beacon, 2017.

Taylor, Emmeline, Jo Deakin, and Aaron Kupchik. "The Changing Landscape of School Discipline, Surveillance, and Social Control." In *The Palgrave International Handbook of School Discipline, Surveillance, and Social Control*, edited by Jo Deakin, Emmeline Taylor, and Aaron Kupchik, 1–13. Cham, Switzerland: Springer, 2018.

Taylor, Linnet, Luciano Floridi, and Bart van der Sloot. "Introduction: A New Perspective on Privacy." In *Group Privacy: New Challenges of Data Technologies*, edited by Linnet Taylor, Luciano Floridi, and Bart van der Sloot, 1–12. Philosophical Studies Series. Cham, Switzerland: Springer, 2017. https://doi.org/10.1007/978-3-319-46608-8_1.

Tene, Omer, and Jules Polonetsky. "A Theory of Creepy: Technology, Privacy and Shifting Social Norms." *Yale Journal of Law & Technology* 16 (2013): 59–102.

Thorson, Kjerstin. "Facing an Uncertain Reception: Young Citizens and Political Interaction on Facebook." *Information, Communication & Society* 17, no. 2 (2014): 203–16.

Ticona, Julia, and Alexandra Mateescu. "Trusted Strangers: Carework Platforms' Cultural Entrepreneurship in the On-Demand Economy." *New Media & Society* 20, no. 11 (2018): 4384–4404. https://doi.org/10.1177/1461444818773727.

Tiffany, Kaitlyn. "The Perennial Debate about Whether Your Phone Is Secretly Listening to You, Explained." *Vox*, December 28, 2018. https://www.vox.com/the-goods/2018/12/28/18158968/facebook-microphone-tapping-recording-instagram-ads.

Torre, María Elena, Caitlin Cahill, and Madeline Fox. "Participatory Action Research in Social Research." In *International Encyclopedia of the Social and Behavioral Sciences*, 2nd ed., edited by James D. Wright, 540–44. Amsterdam: Elsevier, 2015.

Torre, María Elena, Michelle Fine, Brett G. Stoudt, and Madeline Fox. "Critical Participatory Action Research as Public Science." In *APA Handbook of Research Methods in Psychology*, vol. 2, *Research Designs: Quantitative, Qualitative, Neuropsychological, and Biological*, edited by Harris Cooper, 171–84. Washington, DC: American Psychological Association, 2012. http://psycnet.apa.org/books/13620/011.

Trottier, Daniel. "Scandal Mining: Political Nobodies and Remediated Visibility." *Media, Culture & Society* 40, no. 6 (2018): 893–908. https://doi.org/10.1177/0163443717734408.

———. *Social Media as Surveillance: Rethinking Visibility in a Converging World.* Burlington, VT: Ashgate, 2012.

Tufekci, Zeynep. "Can You See Me Now? Audience and Disclosure Regulation in Online Social Network Sites." *Bulletin of Science, Technology & Society* 28, no. 1 (2008): 20–36.

Turow, Joseph, Michael Hennessy, and Nora Draper. *The Tradeoff Fallacy: How Marketers Are Misrepresenting American Consumers and Opening Them Up to Exploitation.* Philadelphia: Annenberg School for Communication, University of Pennsylvania, 2015. https://www.asc.upenn.edu/sites/default/files/TradeoffFallacy_1.pdf.

Turow, Joseph, Michael Hennessy, Nora Draper, Ope Akanbi, and Diami Virgilio. *Divided We Feel: Partisan Politics Drive Americans' Emotions Regarding Surveillance of Low-Income Populations.* Philadelphia: Annenberg School of Communication, University of Pennsylvania, 2018.

Ucini, Andrea. "Access Denied: Faulty Automated Background Checks Freeze Out Renters." The Markup, May 28, 2020. https://themarkup.org/locked-out/2020/05/28/access-denied-faulty-automated-background-checks-freeze-out-renters.

Vaidhyanathan, Siva. *Antisocial Media: How Facebook Disconnects Us and Undermines Democracy.* New York: Oxford University Press, 2018.

Van Brunt, Alexa, and Locke E. Bowman. "Toward a Just Model of Pretrial Release." *Journal of Criminal Law and Criminology* 108, no. 4 (2018): 701–74.

Van den Broeck, Evert, Karolien Poels, and Michel Walrave. "Older and Wiser? Facebook Use, Privacy Concern, and Privacy Protection in the Life Stages of Emerging, Young, and Middle Adulthood." *Social Media + Society* 1, no. 2 (2015). https://doi.org/10.1177/2056305115616149.

Van Noorden, Richard. "The Ethical Questions That Haunt Facial-Recognition Research." *Nature* 587, no. 7834 (November 18, 2020): 354–58. https://doi.org/10.1038/d41586-020-03187-3.

Van Oort, Madison. "The Emotional Labor of Surveillance: Digital Control in Fast Fashion Retail." *Critical Sociology* 45, no. 7–8 (2019): 1167–79. https://doi.org/10.1177/0896920518778087.

Veletsianos, George, Shandell Houlden, Jaigris Hodson, and Chandell Gosse. "Women Scholars' Experiences with Online Harassment and Abuse: Self-Protection, Resistance, Acceptance, and Self-Blame." *New Media & Society*, June 22, 2018. https://doi.org/10.1177/1461444818781324.

Vera-Gray, Fiona. *Men's Intrusion, Women's Embodiment: A Critical Analysis of Street Harassment*. London: Routledge, 2016.

———. *The Right Amount of Panic: How Women Trade Freedom for Safety*. Bristol, UK: Policy, 2018.

Vera-Gray, Fiona, and Bianca Fileborn. "Recognition and the Harms of 'Cheer Up.'" *Philosophical Journal of Conflict and Violence* 2, no. 1 (2018). https://trivent-publishing.eu/triventvechi/journals/pjcv2-1/06.%20Fiona%20Vera-Gray,%20Bianca%20Fileborn.pdf.

Vickery, Jacqueline Ryan. *Worried about the Wrong Things: Youth, Risk, and Opportunity in the Digital World*. John D. and Catherine T. MacArthur Foundation Series on Digital Media and Learning. Cambridge, MA: MIT Press, 2018.

Vitak, Jessica. "The Impact of Context Collapse and Privacy on Social Network Site Disclosures." *Journal of Broadcasting & Electronic Media* 56, no. 4 (2012): 451–70.

Vitak, Jessica, Kalyani Chadha, Linda Steiner, and Zahra Ashktorab. "Identifying Women's Experiences with and Strategies for Mitigating Negative Effects of Online Harassment." In *Proceedings of the 20th ACM Conference on Computer Supported Cooperative Work and Social Computing*, 1231–45. New York: ACM, 2017. https://vitak.files.wordpress.com/2009/02/vitak_etal-2017-cscw-online-harassment.pdf.

Vitak, Jessica, and Jinyoung Kim. "'You Can't Block People Offline': Examining How Facebook's Affordances Shape the Disclosure Process." In *Proceedings of the 17th ACM Conference on Computer Supported Cooperative Work & Social Computing*, 461–74. New York: ACM, 2014. https://doi.org/10.1145/2531602.2531672.

Wagner, Kurt. "This Is How Facebook Collects Data on You Even If You Don't Have an Account." *Vox*, April 20, 2018. https://www.vox.com/2018/4/20/17254312/facebook-shadow-profiles-data-collection-non-users-mark-zuckerberg.

Wakefield, Alison, and Jenny Fleming. "Responsibilization." In *The Sage Dictionary of Policing*, edited by Alison Wakefield and Jenny Fleming, 277–78. London: Sage, 2009. https://doi.org/10.4135/9781446269053.

Wald, Johanna, and Daniel J. Losen. "Defining and Redirecting a School-to-Prison Pipeline." *New Directions for Youth Development*, no. 99 (Fall 2003): 9–15.

Waldman, Ari Ezra. "Cognitive Biases, Dark Patterns, and the 'Privacy Paradox.'" *Current Opinion in Psychology* 31 (2020): 105–9.

———. *Privacy as Trust: Information Privacy for an Information Age*. New York: Cambridge University Press, 2018.

———. "Privacy as Trust: Sharing Personal Information in a Networked World." *University of Miami Law Review* 69 (2014): 559–630.

Walkowski, Debbie. "What Is the CIA Triad?" F5 Labs, July 9, 2019. https://www.f5 .com/labs/articles/education/what-is-the-cia-triad.

Walsh, James P., and Christopher O'Connor. "Social Media and Policing: A Review of Recent Research." *Sociology Compass* 13, no. 1 (2019): e12648.

Warner, Michael. *Publics and Counterpublics*. New York: Zone Books, 2002.

Warren, Samuel D., and Louis D. Brandeis. "Right to Privacy." *Harvard Law Review* 4 (1890): 193–220.

Wasserman, Stanley, and Katherine Faust. *Social Network Analysis: Methods and Applications*. New York: Cambridge University Press, 1994.

Watson, Ryan J., and John L. Christensen. "Big Data and Student Engagement among Vulnerable Youth: A Review." *Current Opinion in Behavioral Sciences* 18 (2017): 23–27.

Weiss, Robert S. *Learning from Strangers: The Art and Method of Qualitative Interview Studies*. New York: Simon and Schuster, 1995.

Welter, Barbara. "The Cult of True Womanhood: 1820–1860." *American Quarterly* 18, no. 2 (1966): 151–74.

Westin, Alan F. *Privacy and Freedom*. New York: Atheneum, 1967.

Wetts, Rachel, and Robb Willer. "Privilege on the Precipice: Perceived Racial Status Threats Lead White Americans to Oppose Welfare Programs." *Social Forces* 97, no. 2 (2018): 793–822. https://doi.org/10.1093/sf/soy046.

White, Michael D., and Henry F. Fradella. *Stop and Frisk: The Use and Abuse of a Controversial Policing Tactic*. New York: New York University Press, 2019.

White Noise Collective. "A Letter to White People Using the Term 'Two Spirit.'" *The White Noise Blog*, May 18, 2015. https://www.conspireforchange.org/a-letter -to-white-people-using-the-term-two-spirit/.

Wilkins, Richard G. "Defining the Reasonable Expectation of Privacy: An Emerging Tripartite Analysis." *Vanderbilt Law Review* 40 (1987): 1077–1129.

Wilson, John K. *The Myth of Political Correctness: The Conservative Attack on Higher Education*. Durham, NC: Duke University Press, 1995.

XOXO Festival. "Anita Sarkeesian, Feminist Frequency—XOXO Festival (2014)." YouTube, October 7, 2014. https://www.youtube.com/watch?v=ah8mh Steganography DW6Shs&t=35s.

Yee, Shirley J. *Black Women Abolitionists: A Study in Activism, 1828–1860*. Knoxville: University of Tennessee Press, 1992.

Yeğinsu, Ceylan. "If Workers Slack Off, the Wristband Will Know. (And Amazon Has a Patent for It.)" *New York Times*, February 1, 2018, sec. Technology. https://www.nytimes.com/2018/02/01/technology/amazon-wristband-tracking-privacy.html.

Yoshino, Kenji. *Covering: The Hidden Assault on Our Civil Rights*. New York: Random House, 2007.

Young, Alyson Leigh, and Anabel Quan-Haase. "Privacy Protection Strategies on Facebook." *Information, Communication & Society* 16, no. 4 (2013): 479–500. https://doi.org/10.1080/1369118X.2013.777757.

Youngman, Julie Furr. "The Use and Abuse of Pre-employment Personality Tests." *Business Horizons* 60, no. 3 (2017): 261–69. https://doi.org/10.1016/j.bushor.2016.11.010.

Zandwijk, Jan Peter van, and Abdul Boztas. "The iPhone Health App from a Forensic Perspective: Can Steps and Distances Registered during Walking and Running Be Used as Digital Evidence?" *Digital Investigation* 28 (April 1, 2019): S126–33. https://doi.org/10.1016/j.diin.2019.01.021.

Zekany, Eva. "The Gendered Geek: Performing Masculinities in Cyberspace." Master's thesis, Central European University, Budapest, 2011. http://www.etd.ceu.hu/2011/zekany_eva.pdf.

Zhang, Sarah. "When a DNA Test Shatters Your Identity." *Atlantic*, July 17, 2018. https://www.theatlantic.com/science/archive/2018/07/dna-test-misattributed-paternity/562928/.

Zheng Xiao, Cheng Wang, Weili Han, and Changjun Jiang. "Unique on the Road: Re-identification of Vehicular Location-Based Metadata." In *Security and Privacy in Communication Networks: 12th International Conference, SecureComm*

2016, Guangzhou, China, October 10–12, 2016, Proceedings, edited by Robert Deng, Jian Weng, Kui Ren, and Vinod Yegneswaran, 496–513. Lecture Notes of the Institute for Computer Sciences, Social Informatics and Telecommunications Engineering. Cham, Switzerland: Springer, 2017.

Zimmer, Michael. "Addressing Conceptual Gaps in Big Data Research Ethics: An Application of Contextual Integrity." *Social Media + Society* 4, no. 2 (2018). https://doi.org/10.1177/2056305118768300.

Zimmerman, Neetzan. "Happy Now? 'Good Employee' Lindsey Stone Fired over Facebook Photo." *Gawker*, November 22, 2012. http://gawker.com/5962796/happy-now-good-employee-lindsey-stone-fired-over-facebook-photo.

Zucchino, David. *Myth of the Welfare Queen: A Pulitzer Prize–Winning Journalist's Portrait of Women on the Line.* New York: Scribner, 1997.

Index